Russia's Women

Russia's Women

Accommodation, Resistance, Transformation

EDITED BY

Barbara Evans Clements
Barbara Alpern Engel
Christine D. Worobec

UNIVERSITY OF CALIFORNIA PRESS
Berkeley   Los Angeles   Oxford

University of California Press
Berkeley and Los Angeles, California

University of California Press, Ltd.
Oxford, England

Library of Congress Cataloging-in-Publication Data

Russia's women : accommodation, resistance, transformation / edited by
    Barbara Evans Clements, Barbara Alpern Engel, Christine D. Worobec.
        p.   cm.
    Includes bibliographical references and index.
    ISBN 0-520-07023-2 (alk. paper).—ISBN 0-520-07024-0 (pbk : alk.
paper)
        1. Women—Soviet Union—History.   2. Women—Soviet Union—
Social conditions.   I. Clements, Barbara Evans, 1945–   .   II. Engel,
Barbara Alpern.   III. Worobec, Christine.
    HQ1662.R88   1990
    305.4'0947—dc20   90-37203
                                                                   CIP

Printed in the United States of America
2   3   4   5   6   7   8   9

CONTENTS

PART II • TRANSFORMING TRADITION

ILLUSTRATIONS

ACKNOWLEDGMENTS

The articles in this collection were written originally for a conference held August 11–14, 1988, at the University of Akron and Kent State University. Neither the conference nor the collection would have been possible without the support of several institutions and the hard work of many people. Financial assistance came principally from the Division of Research Programs of the National Endowment for the Humanities (an independent federal agency), with the generous support of the University of Akron and Kent State University as well as the history departments of both universities. Dean Claibourne E. Griffin of the University of Akron encouraged us from the beginning, and his backing ensured that the conference would be held. Dean Rudolph Buttlar and Assistant Dean Linda Rinker of Kent State University were also very supportive. Thanks also are due Charmaine Streharsky and John Mulhauser of the University of Akron and Charlee Heimlich of Kent State University for leading us through the maze of applications and helping us understand complicated accounting procedures. Brenda Meehan-Waters and Rochelle Ruthchild served on the Program Committee for the conference, helping to sort through all of the paper proposals and put together conference panels. Without Edie Richeson, Mia O'Connor, and especially Susan Hill, who spent many long hours at the photocopier, the conference would not have run smoothly. Edie Richeson and Mia O'Connor also typed the manuscript, learned different software programs to accommodate our authors, and made numerous corrections, always cheerfully and efficiently. Special appreciation goes to Eve Levin, who provided us with invaluable suggestions concerning the translation of N. L. Pushkareva's article. We must also thank Eve, as well as Nancy Shields Kollmann, for keeping us from making blunders in our discussion of medieval Russian women's lives. Warm thanks go to Sheila Levine of the University of California Press, whose constant encouragement, enthusiasm, and efficiency made this volume possible.

We owe a great deal to those who chaired panels and to those who presented papers at the meeting but whose articles are not included in this volume. A list of their names follows. They and all the other scholars and students attending persevered through three days of intense discussions, only mildly daunted by the hottest summer on record in the United States. Their enthusiasm and stimulating ideas demonstrated that the history of Russian women is alive and well: Dorothy Atkinson, Laurie Bernstein, Moira Donald, Linda Edmondson, June Pachuta Farris, Beate Fieseler, Barbara Heldt, Patricia Herlihy, Daniel H. Kaiser, Ann Kleimola, Ann Hibner Koblitz, Brenda Meehan-Waters, Carol S. Nash, Barbara Norton, Maureen Perrie, Christine Ruane, Rochelle Ruthchild, Mary Grace Swift, G. A. Tishkin, and Mary Zirin.

NOTE ON TRANSLITERATION AND DATES

We have usually employed the Library of Congress system of transliterating the Cyrillic alphabet. Exceptions include the names of tsars, which we have anglicized (Peter, not Petr) and the names of other persons well known in the West by a particular spelling (Trotsky, not Trotskii).

Russia followed the Julian calendar until February 1918. Dates from the years before 1918 will be given according to that calendar, which was twelve days behind the Western (Gregorian) calendar in the nineteenth century and thirteen days behind it in the twentieth.

Introduction: Accommodation, Resistance, Transformation

Barbara Evans Clements

What has been the history of women in Russia? How have they lived their lives during the centuries since their people first appeared on the eastern frontier of Europe? In what ways have they changed as their society grew from an insignificant principality within the Mongol Empire into the superpower of today? The essays in this book address these questions by examining the history of Russian women from the eleventh to the twentieth centuries.

Questions such as these have only begun to be asked in the last two decades. Earlier Russian historians, like historians of Western Europe or the United States, worked within a long-established tradition that defined history as the actions of great men and of governments. In the study of Russia this tradition endured well into the second half of the twentieth century, even after historians of other nations had developed social history, a subdiscipline that includes the study of previously ignored groups such as workers and women. Russian historians continued to concentrate on political elites, partly because Soviet authorities denied access to many of the documentary sources necessary to social history and partly because these same historians remained fascinated by the considerable power of Russia's long-lived autocratic state.

The preoccupation with political history, and even more narrowly with the history of the central government, began to fade in the 1970s. A new generation of scholars, inspired by the rise of social history, searched through the documents for material on the lives of peasants, factory workers, and women. They quickly found that even in Russia, a country where politics, fire, and flood have taken their toll on the historical record, there remains a wealth of published and archival sources in which the history of ordinary people is preserved. Historians of women began to publish the results of their work in these sources in the mid-1970s. First came studies of prominent

1

feminists and revolutionaries; examination of less-exceptional women followed. Peasant women and factory workers in the late nineteenth and early twentieth centuries, the masses of Soviet women in the 1920s, even elite women in the medieval period—all these found their historians.[1] This scholarship laid the foundations for the present volume.

This book, in surveying the history of women in Russia, makes a contribution to the study of Russian history in general. It reinforces the current tendency to look out to the provinces, away from the court circles of St. Petersburg and Moscow. By so doing, it enriches our knowledge of Russian social history, particularly the history of the family, and, perhaps more surprisingly, helps bring into being a more panoramic yet also more finely detailed picture of political history. Exploring the roles women have taken in Russian politics forces us to analyze not only the decisions of the male leadership but also the ways in which those decisions were shaped by the will of the people, whether expressed directly through petition and protest or indirectly through pressures rising from the bottom of Russian society to the top, from the ostensibly powerless to the ostensibly all-powerful. Thus the study of women's lives brings us to reconsider some of the oldest questions in the historian's trade even as it provokes new ones.

Several of the newer questions must be asked at the outset of this survey. Does Russian women's history divide into definable periods, and if so, what are they? It is well known that Russian culture, like culture throughout Europe, was patriarchal. How did this patriarchal system shape women's lives? And how did women respond to the demands the patriarchy made on them? In what ways did women, living within the constraints of a society that wished them to be powerless, affect the history of that society by responding creatively to its attempts to control them? The essays published here address all of these issues and taken together suggest a number of conclusions.

It is apparent that there have been two great periods in the history of Russian women. There was the period of traditional society from the eleventh to the nineteenth centuries, when values, folkways, and political and economic structures changed slowly. In the late seventeenth century influences from Western Europe began to flood into Russia, but for more than a century they primarily affected elite women at court. Provincial noblewomen lived much as their medieval ancestors had until the mid-nineteenth century; for peasant women and the women of the urban poor the patterns of traditional society continued little altered until at least the 1880s. These facts must stand as a reminder that the chronological boundaries of "traditional society," as a tool of analysis, will necessarily remain somewhat fluid.

The second great period of Russian women's history is the last hundred years, when rapid change resulted from westernization, industrialization,

---

1. For references to this scholarship see the bibliography at the end of this volume.

urbanization, war, and revolution. Even here, however, change came to women unevenly, altering life in the cities first and making inroads into the countryside more slowly. For throughout these two periods Russian patriarchal institutions remained strong, influencing women's lives in a myriad of ways, defended more than once when under siege by women themselves. Women supported patriarchy in part because it was not so oppressive as a simple reading of its didactic literature might at first suggest.

These essays show that in both periods patriarchy provided rewards and some limited opportunities to women who obeyed its dictates, making it possible for Russian women to be more active members of their society than has been previously thought. Russian patriarchal values, in their essentials, differed little from those of Central and Western Europe. At their core was the injunction that women subordinate themselves to men, an imperative justified by a definition of woman's nature that was applied to all women regardless of social rank. Russian folk sayings and the teachings of the Russian Orthodox church agreed that women were physically and morally weaker than men and therefore more prone to sin. Men had a responsibility to govern them for their own good and for the good of society. Women were obliged to submit to male authority, follow male guidance, and serve their families. But as in most patriarchal societies, the power men held over women was not absolute; it was subject to dilution by other traditional claims such as those of social status and age. Elite women could command lower-ranking men, and older women could exercise authority over the younger men in their families, at least in concert with their husbands. Older women also governed younger women, particularly their daughters-in-law, whom they were permitted to control with an absolutism rivaling the patriarch's. And widows could sometimes wield considerable independent authority.

Thus the injunction that women obey men was not unqualified. Nor were patriarchal institutions immutable. Across the centuries since Kievan times Russian patriarchy has changed in ways that sometimes benefited women and at other times increased their burdens. The transformation of patriarchy, particularly over the last hundred years, attracted the attention of women's historians from the first, but there have been few attempts to generalize across the various social classes about the impact of all this change. Earlier scholarship and the essays here permit us now to venture a certain distance down this path.

As we proceed, however, the reader should keep in mind that our focus is on Russian women, not the women of other nationalities that have lived within the steadily expanding borders of the Russian Empire. Although it is highly likely that much of what is presented here is true of other European women within Russia as well, we make no claims for the universality of our generalizations.

TRADITIONAL SOCIETY

Institutional Arrangements

From the eleventh to the fifteenth centuries there was no centralized political authority among the Russians. There had been a grand prince to whom all the lesser princes answered in the Kievan Rus' era (the tenth to the thirteenth centuries), but Kievan unity, always minimal, had disintegrated as Rus' princes spread out across their vast land and as ties within the princely dynasty became attenuated. Mongol rule from the thirteenth to the fifteenth centuries exacerbated the internecine violence inherited from the Kievan period. Princes fought princes for hegemony, backed up by alliances among elite families, particularly the families of the boyars, the richest and most powerful members of the elite. Within this world of clan-based politics princely and boyar women sometimes were important power brokers, but they were barred from holding political authority in their own right.

Centralized power began to emerge in the fifteenth century as the princes of Moscow built significant support within the other principalities. Rulers from Ivan III to Ivan IV (1462–1581) succeeded in creating an autocratic state, but it differed significantly from the nation-states then emerging in Western Europe. Russia had no prosperous, ambitious middle class to support its kings' bids for power, nor could its sovereigns base their claims on feudal prerogatives. Instead the Muscovite monarchy grew by harnessing the entire elite—the old boyar clans, the lower-ranking military officers, and the expanding civilian bureaucracy—to the service of the crown. The tsars rested their claims to legitimacy on a patriarchal conception of the monarch as the divinely ordained father of all his people, the great lords included. The Orthodox church often seconded this claim of divine right. Never did the church form an effective alternative locus of power in Russia, as the Roman Catholic church did in Western Europe.

The tsar was assisted in his power building by the fact that, for a variety of reasons too complex to elucidate here, the boyars and lower-ranking military officers did not develop the corporate unity and the class prerogatives possessed by the nobles of the Germanic states, Poland, or England. Those who supported the tsar were rewarded with power, land, and other riches. Those who rebelled were isolated and destroyed. And the entire elite was offered a lucrative payoff for its submission to royal power—the enserfment of the peasantry. Gradually, over the centuries, the peasants were bound for life to the estates where they worked.

It has often been argued that in Western Europe the position of aristocratic women declined as the kings increased their authority. This was so because the kings drained power away from elite families (where women had been accorded influence derived from their importance as wives and mothers) and channeled it instead into public institutions, chiefly the bureaucracy and the army, from which women were excluded. The latter aspect of this process did not occur in Russia as centralized monarchy emerged, for public institutions were weakly developed there until the reign of Peter the Great (1682–1725). Thus the palaces of boyar families remained stages on which the political drama was played out, and women remained important actors, deriving influence from their position as liaisons between their natal families and the families into which they had married as well as from their power to oversee the arranging of the marriages through which alliances within the ruling clans were solidified.

Peasant women also arranged the marriages of their children; but unlike elite women, peasant women's primary occupation was grueling physical labor. They grew vegetables, made and washed clothes, cooked the family's food, worked in the fields, cared for small livestock, manufactured and sold handicrafts, tended the sick, and bore and nursed babies. As yet we know far less about the workings of the village in the medieval period than we do about the politics of the elite, so it is difficult to say what part women took in community governance or in decision making within the peasant family. We can make inferences from the nineteenth century, however, when traditional practices were still strong in the countryside. What we find then is that across most of Russia women were excluded from membership in the *skhod*, the village assembly of heads-of-household that made decisions about land distribution among families and about the growing and harvesting of crops. The *skhod* also elected male village elders, who negotiated with the serf owner and his agents (until the emancipation of serfs in 1861), mediated conflicts among peasants, and performed a variety of administrative duties. Women were generally not permitted to vote or even speak at assembly meetings, though as widows they might head households. Within the family, peasant custom formally relegated women to a position of almost complete subordination to their fathers, husbands, and mothers-in-law.

Women's Responses: Accommodation and Resistance

Russian women, elite and peasant, dealt with the institutions of their world in ways that may be understood broadly as accommodation. That is, they generally accepted the dictates of society and conformed to its demands. Women seem to have accepted the truth of what they were taught by their parents, the elites, and the priests, that men had a God-given right to rule over them because of their sex's natural moral frailty. But the authorities' messages to women were not wholly negative. They also taught that women, despite their weaknesses, were loved by God and could achieve virtuous lives on earth and eternal bliss in heaven. In other words, the authorities promised rewards to those who accommodated themselves to the social order. The most virtuous path a woman could take was the path to the convent, and over the centuries thousands of Russian women, many of them widows with grown children, became nuns. Many more women, however, remained in the secular world, pursuing the rewards that Russian society offered to those who lived respectable married lives. If a peasant woman performed her household tasks efficiently, if she had the strength to toil long hours in the fields, if she survived the hazardous years of childbearing, and if she was dutiful toward the men in her family, then in middle age she could rise to a position of honor and some power as matriarch within a large household. For elite women and women of the tiny merchant population in the towns the demands and rewards of life were much the same as those for peasants, save that such women did not perform heavy manual labor. Instead merchant women worked in their family businesses and elite women managed their households. That Russians recognized the importance of women's contributions to the survival and prosperity of the family, especially of peasant and serf families, is attested to by a wealth of proverbs that sang the praises of the hardworking wife: "A good housekeeper's house is like a brimming cup"; "A good housekeeper will save the house, a poor housekeeper ruin it." David Ransel argues in his analysis of infant-care practices that Russian peasants valued women's productive work in the family economy even more highly than their reproductive work of rearing healthy babies.

Accommodation and the rewards a woman could earn from it are discussed at length in several of the essays in this collection. N. L. Pushkareva demonstrates that marriage law in the medieval period provided fairly remarkable protection to women, even extending to the right to divorce or legal separation in the event that a husband forced his wife to have sexual relations. Another example of the benefits of accommodation comes from Nancy Shields Kollmann's analysis of seventeenth-century court cases in which women won judgments against men who had insulted them. Under certain circumstances peasant women could also derive power from their importance to the family, as Rodney Bohac demonstrates in his analysis of serf widows in the early nineteenth century.

But women occasionally fought societal constraints; sometimes, rather than accommodate themselves to men, they resisted them. Usually this resistance was more sidelong than direct, thanks to the power of male authority and control. Perhaps the most frequent manifestation of resistance came in women's refusal to obey unquestioningly, a refusal reflected in folk sayings enjoining men to maintain control over their wives: "Sad is the house in which the cow instructs the bull"; "Giving in to foolish women makes the chickens laugh." Women responded to such barnyard criticisms with their own proverbs. One acknowledged that "if there's no husband, there's no head," but continued, "If there's no woman, there's no brain." Women's questioning of male governance may also be inferred from certain ecclesiastical court cases from the sixteenth and seventeenth centuries. Here the records recount occasions on which women thwarted the authority of their natal and marital families by leaving home to make their own way in the world.[2]

2. I would like to thank Eve Levin for bringing these court cases to my attention.

Several other types of female resistance are discussed in the essays in this volume. Resistance could take gentle, unobjectionable forms when women drew on the prevailing sexual stereotypes to justify the establishment of spheres of activity from which men were excluded. Eve Levin discusses one such sphere, that of childbirth, and Rose Glickman shows how throughout Russian history women have made a niche for themselves in folk medicine. Such female-dominated activities may be considered forms of resistance rather than forms of accommodation because they enabled women to achieve independence from male control. Accommodation, as we have defined it, entailed submission to male control.

From time to time women also joined men in resistance movements against Russia's rulers. These movements loosened the grip of custom, permitting women to participate far more actively than usual in the public world beyond the family. Although such participation became much more common during the nineteenth and twentieth centuries, when resistance to tsarist rule was endemic, there were instances of it in earlier centuries as well. Valerie Kivelson analyzes a rare but in some ways archetypal example—witch hunts. Women also played prominent parts in far larger, more important resistance movements, such as the Great Schism that rent the Orthodox church in the seventeenth century and the peasant revolts led by Sten'ka Razin (1667–71) and Emel'ian Pugachev (1773–74).

Resistance was never a course favored by many Russian women, however, because it was too costly. Until the revolution, and indeed afterward, women who rebelled risked imprisonment and death. For individual women who resisted the patriarchs closer to home—their husbands or neighbors—punishment could be severe as well. Tongue-lashings, gossip, shaming, and ostracism were all employed to keep the disobedient in line. Men encouraged one another to beat their wives, perhaps sensing the shared value of the exercise. "The more you beat the old woman," ran the proverb, "the tastier the soup will be." It thus becomes easy to understand why throughout Russian history the difficulty and futility of most forms of resistance have made it the last resort of the desperate. It was far safer for a woman to choose accommodation, maximizing the opportunities available to her without challenging the status quo.

TRADITION VERSUS TRANSFORMATION

Peter the Great's decision to reform Russia by adapting Western institutions and ideas ushered in three centuries of turbulent, sometimes violent change. First affected was the aristocracy, which eagerly took up the clothes, manners, and amusements of the French. Soon the nobles were reading German philosophy, French drama and poetry, and even the political tracts of the English and Americans. This new, imported culture was accessible also to noblewomen, a minority of whom was becoming literate by the middle of the eighteenth century. Their cultural opportunities were further extended by the Empress Catherine (1762–96). A devoted student of the Enlightenment, Catherine encouraged the development of education for women by setting a fairly cultivated tone at court and establishing the Smolnyi Institute, Russia's first boarding school for women.

The tsars who followed Catherine to the throne viewed women's education with suspicion. But the nineteenth-century rulers of Russia did agree on the need to strengthen the country's economy, and by the nineteenth century this task required industrialization. Until 1855 change proceeded slowly, as two cautious brothers, Alexander I (1801–25) and Nicholas I (1825–55), shrank from genuine reform for fear of upsetting the status quo. Alexander II (1855–81) had such fears too, but he embraced reform, most notably the emancipation of the serfs in 1861, out of the conviction that further stagnation threatened the power of the monarchy and nobility even more than change did. In addition to encouraging reforms in local government, the courts, the military, and the educational system, Alexander also promoted the development of the economy. He initiated the building of a railroad network in Russia; his successors, Alexander III (1881–94) and Nicholas II (1894–1917), presided over the rapid expansion of the railroads and the construction of huge, modern factories.

By 1914 many of the tsars' hopes and fears had been realized. The nation had its industrial base: steel and textile mills employed thousands of workers; railroads and telegraph lines linked the urban centers to one another. In the cities Russian culture shone brightly, illuminated by the accomplishments of brilliant writers, composers, and artists. But despite Russia's progress in modernizing, it was seething with discontent in the early twentieth century— discontent with the continuing poverty of the peasants, with the misery of life in the urban slums to which the peasants migrated looking for work, and with government incompetence and repression, which had seemed to grow worse over the course of the nineteenth century. The anger boiled over in 1905, when people from all sectors of the population—peasants, factory workers, businessmen, white-collar workers, professionals, soldiers, and sailors—rose up to demand political reform. Grudgingly Nicholas allowed the establishment of a legislature and granted limited civil rights, but these concessions were not enough to solve the accumulating social problems of his country. When he blundered into World War I in 1914, Nicholas heaped on his unwilling people and his inept government a burden too great for them to bear. The result was revolution in 1917.

Women of all ranks of Russian society were actively involved in the social and political turmoil caused by Russia's entry into the modern world. Merely surviving often required all their powers of accommodation, as Alfred Meyer demonstrates in his essay on women in World War I. The war increased the difficulties of women's lives, intensifying the struggle of working-class women in the cities to support themselves and their children and forcing women in the countryside to take on more and more of the work once done by sons or husbands. But the instability caused by rapid social change also made resistance more possible than ever before. In the nineteenth century upper-class women joined reform movements, working in charity projects among the urban poor, in peasant schools, and in the *zemstva* (provincial councils established in 1864 to promote the local development of education, medicine, and the economy). Gentry women and the women of the growing middle class were active in illegal revolutionary organizations, making up one-third of the leadership of the People's Will, the group that plotted the assassination of Alexander II in 1881, and some 10 to 15 percent of the Social Democratic party on the eve of World War I.[3] In fact, it was a protest march of working-class women on February 23, 1917, that is credited with setting off that greatest of all acts of resistance—the Russian revolution.

Yet despite their participation in the efforts to reform Russia, despite their work in the factories, shops, offices, and schools that was integral to Russia's industrialization, women did not reap all the benefits that men did. Throughout the transformation men gained first and more substantially than women. In the eighteenth century young men of the aristocracy traveled abroad to study in German universities, whereas young women learned needlepoint at the Smolnyi Institute. In the nineteenth century peasant boys went to work in the factories and discovered there the heady world of political protest, whereas peasant girls remained in the villages, under the control of their fathers and mothers-in-law. Even when new manufacturing enterprises opened up in the countryside in the second half of the nineteenth century, men quickly monopolized the better-paying jobs, as Judith Pallot shows in her essay on rural manufacturing. After the revolution male metalworkers joined the Communist party, studied engineering, and moved into important managerial positions, whereas female textile workers earned high-school diplomas, found jobs as clerks in Soviet offices, and married the engineers. At every stage of these developments women had to fight for the benefits they did gain, for education and access to the professions in the nineteenth century, higher wages and better working conditions in the early twentieth century, and job-training programs and contraception after the revolution.

Women lagged behind men because the sweeping social changes of the nineteenth and twentieth centuries, despite their ability to transform the political and economic systems of Russia, did not substantially alter those

---

3. These figures come from Barbara Alpern Engel, *Mothers and Daughters: Women of the Intelligentsia in Nineteenth-Century Russia* (New York, 1983), 107; Barbara Evans Clements, "The Enduring Kinship of the *Baba* and the Bolshevik Woman," *Soviet Union* 12, pt. 2 (1985): 165; and Barbara Evans Clements, "Working-Class and Peasant Women in the Russian Revolution," *Signs* 8 (1982): 233n.

most fundamental of patriarchal values, the allocation of power to men and the requirement of service from women. To be sure, Russia was hardly unusual in this. Patriarchalism survived the industrial revolution across the European continent—albeit in weakened form, for the contemporary era is hostile in many ways to older practices of hierarchy and submission. In the twentieth century parents no longer have the rights they once did to control adult children, and the authority of husbands over wives has diminished. But contemporary patriarchalism still contains the injunction that a woman should subordinate herself to the men in her family. In Russia the survival of patriarchalism has meant that although certain opportunities and rights available to women—for education, employment, recreation, divorce, and abortion—have expanded significantly since 1900, the opportunities for men, particularly their access to political and economic power, have expanded far more.

There were also significant differences in the ways industrialization, urbanization, and Western influences affected privileged and poor women. Elite women had long lived more comfortably than had the masses of Russian women, but in the second half of the nineteenth century the gap between the two groups grew steadily. Improved diet and better medical care meant longer, healthier lives for upper-class women. Educational opportunities expanded, so that by the end of the nineteenth century most noblewomen and many middle-class women were completing secondary school, and a few were even enjoying university educations. Some of these women joined the intelligentsia, becoming members of that bright community of writers, artists, professionals, and social reformers that flourished in the late nineteenth century. As elite women seized their new opportunities, they widened the cultural distance between themselves and the peasants. These growing differences in values and in standards of living made it difficult for reform-minded women of the intelligentsia to win the trust of the uneducated, and they therefore inhibited the formation in Russia of a broadly based feminist movement. Nor was there a consensus even among elite women about how women's lives should be improved. Like the peasants, many conservative upper-class women felt deep allegiance to their religion, their traditional customs, and even those patriarchal institutions that encumbered them but from which they derived what security they had. Thus the transformation of Russia increased the possibilities for resistance but also accentuated the divisions among women.

In the twentieth century the revolution reversed this trend toward greater class differentiation by bringing to power the Communist party, which was pledged to ending gender inequality. The party never accomplished this high objective; patriarchalism proved to be too strong an enemy, with a fifth column even in the camp of the Marxists. But the party did preside over, and to some extent direct, the establishment of a new social definition of womanhood. The "new Soviet woman," an ideal promoted by the government from the 1930s onward, was to be man's equal, working with him in building bridges, flying airplanes, and managing factories. At the same time she was to continue to minister to the emotional needs of her husband and children. In practice this meant she was responsible for most of the housework and child care and was expected to defer to her husband. Communist party leaders were too wedded to Marxist feminism to endorse openly the survival of patriarchy's core idea—woman's subordination to man in marriage—but neither did they take strong action to eradicate it. And so traditional ideas insinuated themselves into the emerging Soviet value system. This complex process is analyzed in some detail by Elizabeth Waters in her discussion of the images of women employed by Soviet graphic designers and by Wendy Goldman in her study of abortion in the 1920s and 1930s.

The revolution and the Communist party that rode it to power did more than break down class differences in the conceptions of womankind that had grown during the nineteenth century. They also abolished the privileged position of the upper classes, ushering in a time when virtually all women were subject to the same set of economic demands. Primary among these was the fact that, beginning in the 1920s, women were required to find paying jobs. Communist ideology demanded that women join the paid labor force, but the government was also motivated by dire necessity to push women into work outside the village. All hands were needed to build the Soviet economy. Driven by poverty and in many instances inspired by calls to enlist in the great campaign to build a new, socialist world, women flocked to work in the factories, in government offices, and in the fields of the collective farms. No longer did privileged origins guarantee an easy life or promote values different from those that governed the lives of the masses of women. Therefore by 1940 the revolutionary process begun in 1917 had minimized the role of social origins in structuring women's lives and had made gender once again the primary determinant, as it had been earlier in Russian history.

The transformation of Russia from medieval monarchy to modern superpower has had mixed results for women. On the one hand, women have benefited. Their standard of living has improved. However inadequate the Soviet economy—and its shortcomings are now publicly proclaimed even by its leaders—it does provide better food, housing, consumer goods, and health care for women today than was experienced by their great-grandmothers in the villages at the turn of the century. Furthermore, the Communist government did establish legal penalties for the worst excesses of patriarchy, such as wife beating, and during most of the Soviet period it has guaranteed women the right to divorce and abortion. The government has also provided considerable educational and employment opportunities for women. These improvements have been accompanied by a flood of propaganda proclaiming the equality of women and men.

The accomplishments of the Soviet Union attest to the capacity of a powerful centralized government to change women's position in society, even over opposition from the population. But they also suggest how great was the age-old capacity of the Russian autocracy to thwart impulses for change originating among women themselves. Only when convinced that programs beneficial to women would also serve the interests of men has the Russian government, whether in its tsarist or Communist phase, proven willing to give priority to those reforms. When not so persuaded, the government has turned down requests for reform. Laura Engelstein provides a graphic example of this intransigence in her analysis of the long, ultimately futile lobbying of physicians and lawyers to rewrite the abortion laws in the first decades of the twentieth century.

Thus the emancipating potential of revolution for women has been limited by the continuing hold of patriarchy on Russian and Soviet values and institutions. It bears noting, however, that this is true throughout the Western world. Government remains the preserve of men in Paris and Washington just as in Moscow. Nor have the majority of European or North American women managed to redraw the division of labor and power within marriage and society to create true equality for themselves.

Nineteenth-century reformers who decried the often dreary lives of peasant women were wont to quote the poet Nikolai Nekrasov. In his 1863 poem "Red-Nosed Frost" he wrote:

> Three hideous portions to woman Fate gave:
> The one: to a slave to be mated;
> The second: the mother to be to a slave;
> The third: to a slave subjugated.
> And each of these burdens has heavily lain
> On the women of Russia's domain.[4]

Our findings bear the poet out. Russian women, particularly peasant women, were overburdened by a society that asked much of them. Soviet women continue to be so burdened today. But the history of Russian women is more than a dirge keened across the centuries. It contains accomplishments, victories large and small, refusals to submit, joy, love, self-sacrifice, and conflict. Closely studied, it reveals itself as a complex story not easily told but well worth every effort to understand.

More than eighty years ago American historian Henry Adams wrote in his autobiography, "The study of history is useful to the historian by teaching

---

4. N. A. Nekrasov, *Poems*, trans. Juliet M. Soskice, reprint of the 1929 Oxford University Press edition (Wilmington, Del., 1974), 143.

him his ignorance of woman; and the mass of this ignorance crushes one who is familiar enough with what are called historical sources to realize how few women have ever been known. The woman who is known only through a man is known wrong."[5] We would add that the past that is known only through men is also known wrong but that historians are well on the way to finally getting it right. We offer this history of the women of Russia to the growing story.

5. Henry Adams, *The Education of Henry Adams*, in *Novels* (New York, 1983), 1042.

PART ONE

Traditional Society

Accommodation and Resistance

Christine D. Worobec

Traditional histories of Kievan Rus' (tenth to thirteenth centuries) and Muscovy (fourteenth to seventeenth centuries) are generally silent about women's roles except in those rare cases when a woman assumed a male position by acquiring political power or defying the law. For example, the earliest native history of Rus', the *Primary Chronicle* (completed in 1116), portrays a vigorous and politically active Princess Ol'ga of tenth-century Kievan Rus'. As regent from 945 to 964 she went to war and became the first known member of a princely clan to adopt Christianity. Accordingly she was fondly remembered in medieval church records as "the wisest among human beings" and earned canonization.[1]

After Ol'ga the political historical record, with a few minor exceptions, relegates medieval Russian women to obscurity until the mid-fifteenth century, when the defiant Marfa Boretskaia, widow of a former mayor of Novgorod, led an unsuccessful struggle against Muscovite control over the city of Novgorod. Ivan III, the same grand prince who vanquished the Boretskaia faction in 1470–71, earned international prestige through his marriage to Sofiia Palaeologa, niece of the last Byzantine emperor. The marriage confirmed his claim as rightful heir to Byzantium. Several decades later, from 1533 to 1538, Grand Princess Elena Glinskaia, Vasilii III's widow, rose to prominence as regent of Muscovy. Near the end of the century Irina Godunova, the wife of Tsar Fedor, last heir to the royal Daniilovich branch of the Riurikid dynasty, was a power broker for her ambitious brother, Boris Godunov. Even though aristocratic factions fearful of her power forced her

---

1. Translation from *Povest' vremennykh let* provided by Eve Levin. The same passage is translated by Serge A. Zenkovsky as "wiser than all other men." See *Medieval Russia's Epics, Chronicles, and Tales*, ed. and trans. Serge A. Zenkovsky, rev. ed. (New York, 1974), 68.

into a convent after her husband's death, she was not inhibited from advising and prodding her brother into claiming rights to the Russian throne. Boris legitimized his successful bid to become tsar less on the election by the *Zemskii sobor* (Assembly of the Land) than on his inheritance from his sister. In the mid-seventeenth century Boyarina Feodosiia Morozova, immortalized by the nineteenth-century painter Vasilii Surikov, openly challenged church and state by adhering to traditional Orthodoxy in the religious schism that irreparably divided the Russian Orthodox church into a conservative faction and a secularizing and westernizing wing. She suffered and died for her supposedly heretical beliefs.[2] Later in that century (1682–89) Tsarevna Sofiia Alekseevna was the first woman to assert an independent role in Muscovite politics by seizing the initiative from Nataliia Naryshkina, Peter I's mother, and becoming regent. Despite the prominence of these Muscovite women none of them had the opportunity to govern Russia in her own right.

The hierarchical and patriarchal structures of both Kievan and Muscovite societies may explain in part the relative obscurity of Russian women. Though it is possible that a matriarchy ruled various East Slavic tribes before the Kievan period, over the centuries men, through their military prowess, established hegemony over the body politic. Succession to the grand-princely Kievan and later Muscovite thrones was a male prerogative. With the increasing militarization, centralization, and bureaucratization of Muscovy's government, beginning in the late fifteenth century and culminating in the seventeenth century, the hierarchy of social relations became rigidly defined. All subjects were the autocrat's slaves and as such owed him complete and unwavering obedience and allegiance, at least within Christian limits. Obedience did not extend to following the autocrat into heresy and sin. Women and children had similar obligations to husbands, fathers, and other male superiors. In this hierarchy of relations men, in return for vital military service to the tsar, received the major economic, social, and political rewards.

In the sixteenth and seventeenth centuries centralization and concern for the maintenance of autocratic power in the hands of the Muscovite tsar's family and close circle of boyars relegated elite women to separate living quarters called a *terem*.[3] Women's sequestration was linked to a political system based on kinship ties and served as a marker of social class status. Russian elite women could receive visitors in the *terem*, leave their rooms to man-

2. For a discussion of Morozova, see H. W. Dewey and A. M. Kleimola, "Muted Eulogy: Women Who Inspired Men in Medieval Rus'," *Russian History* 10, pt. 2 (1983): 196–97.

3. Historians had previously thought that the sequestration of elite women in the *terem* was borrowed from Mongol practice. That belief has proved to be erroneous. See Charles J. Halperin, *Russia and the Golden Horde: The Mongol Impact on Medieval Russian History* (Bloomington, Ind., 1985), 116.

age the household, and interact daily with men but were barred from socializing with men, even of their own families, and from participating directly in politics. When they ventured outside their homes to churches and convents, largely for ceremonial reasons, their closed or curtained carriages made them invisible to the public eye.[4]

After men had begun to dominate political power, Christianity placed its own patriarchal and misogynistic stamp on the developing Rus' culture. With the Christianization of Kievan Rus' in 988, the Orthodox church began a lengthy campaign to make converts to the new faith, instill in converts a God-fearing respect for male authority, and wipe out all vestiges of pagan practices. Other aspects of proselytization were far more successful than the campaign against paganism. In the end the church was forced to accommodate and assimilate various pagan beliefs into its own belief structure.[5] The Kievan Rus' elite was influenced by Christianity earlier than the lower urban classes, peasantry, and indentured population. But by the fourteenth and fifteenth centuries, in the midst of Mongol domination over much of Russia, Christianity had permeated all levels of society. And with Christianization came the denigration of woman and the justification of her subordination to man as churchmen linked her to Eve, the "temptress," and to the Fall. In didactic literature misogynistic Orthodox authors contrasted the good woman with the evil woman, suggesting that only a woman who accommodated herself entirely to Christian mores, subordinated herself to males, and devoted her life to domesticity and the bearing and nurturing of children was worthy of the epithet *good*. Only when piety and chastity conflicted with submission to men were women justified in defying their male superiors. The "evil" woman, by contrast, was an adulteress, a bad housekeeper, and a pagan. Such an independent-minded woman had the effrontery to overstep the bounds of decency by entering the public domain.[6] On the basis of these sources historians have assumed that Russian women were entirely subordinate to their husbands and relegated to the obscurity of the household. The absence of a literature of courtly love so prevalent in medieval Western Europe merely confirmed historians' impression that women were held in low esteem.

An entirely negative portrayal of traditional Russian patriarchalism, however, masks the complexity of the system to which Russian women

4. See Nancy Shields Kollmann, "The Seclusion of Elite Muscovite Women," *Russian History* 10, pt. 2 (1983): 239–46.

5. For a discussion of the durability of certain pagan practices, see the essays by N. L. Pushkareva and Eve Levin in this volume.

6. N. L. Pushkareva and Eve Levin, "Women in Medieval Novgorod from the Eleventh to the Fifteenth Century," *Soviet Studies in History* 23, no. 4 (Spring 1985): 72–73; Dewey and Kleimola, "Muted Eulogy," 189; Eve Levin, *Sex and Society in the World of the Orthodox Slavs, 900–1700* (Ithaca, 1989), 52–59, 61.

accommodated themselves. Archaeological discoveries and the advent of social histories that shift emphasis from the political sphere to the lives of the
masses and the so-called silent members of society have radically altered the
traditional view of medieval Russian women. Penitential church records,
church manuals, private testaments, court records, marriage contracts, and
birchbark documents, relating to state as well as private affairs, reveal that
medieval Russian women were able to reconcile themselves to the patriarchy
by maximizing their power within the roles assigned to them. In consequence
they were not utterly dependent on men. Nor was the delineation between
the public (male) and private (female) spheres inflexible. Patriarchal subordination often victimized women, perpetuating the belief in their inferior-
ity. And women certainly had little choice but to accept male power in the
state, church, and economy since their families' survival was intertwined
with that power. Nevertheless, they were not simply puppets. By continually
drawing on cultural and socioeconomic traditions that empowered them and
sometimes permitted them to cross the artificial boundary between the private and public domains, women mitigated the worst features of male
domination. Control over the bearing and nurturing of children, influence
over their offsprings' marriage alliances, economic responsibilities, and the
honor accorded women in the patriarchal system gave women informal
power. As actors with a stake in the survival of their families and society,
women accommodated themselves to the patriarchy, rarely resisting sub-
jugation overtly. Women's contributions and sacrifices must finally be recognized as enabling their society to operate effectively.

Women of all classes in medieval Russia drew their power within society
in part from their role in reproduction. Even the most misogynistic society
cannot deny the importance of women's childbearing to the survival of the
group. Despite the abysmally low success rate in keeping children alive, even
in the modern period,[7] reproduction in itself defined women's worth both in
spiritual and economic ways. Canon law, which frowned on sexual intercourse in general, applauded the conception and delivery of a child as proof
that a woman "did not have sex in vain."[8] From an economic standpoint
children, especially in the lower ranks of society, guaranteed the household
both a ready supply of labor and security for elderly parents.[9] In all social
classes they perpetuated the family line and kept patrimonial property within
the family's possession.[10]

7. See the essay by David Ransel in this volume.
8. See the essay by Eve Levin in this volume.
9. Levin, *Sex and Society*, 132. For practices among nineteenth-century Russian peasants, see
Christine D. Worobec, "Customary Law and Property Devolution among Russian Peasants in
the 1870s," *Canadian Slavonic Papers* 26 (1984): 222–23.
10. Medieval Russian inheritance practices generally favored males but permitted daughters, in the absence of sons, to inherit the patrimony. In fifteenth-century Muscovy and Novgor-

Married women of medieval Russia were able to turn to their advantage the misogynistic apprehensions about their sexuality and rituals of impurity relating to their bodies and menstrual blood. Interpreting original sin as a sexual act initiated by the serpent on a weak Eve, who then led Adam into sexual sin, Orthodox church fathers viewed women as temptresses. They reinforced ancient and Old Testament taboos concerning menstruating women, suggesting that they were polluted and in danger of fornicating with the devil.[11] Russian women accepted the belief in their bodies' pollution, obeying church strictures against their entering the church sanctuary and approaching the high altar. At the same time this belief permitted women to achieve autonomy over childbirth practices.[12] In so doing, women reinforced the fear and awe their reproductive capacities inspired in men and thus resisted total subordination to men. Many childbirth practices had strong pagan roots. Women gave birth in isolation or with the aid of a midwife in the bathhouse, an outbuilding associated in Russian folklore with "prophecy, sorcery, and magical cures."[13] They also maintained church taboos by not entering the public domain for forty days until the performance of ritual purification through the ceremony of churching. Such activities not only reinforced beliefs in the magical powers of the female body but also gave women absolute control over newborn life.[14]

The patriarchal system empowered women in yet another way by setting limits on their abuse and protecting their honor. Though the Orthodox church and the patriarchal culture viewed women as temptresses, they also placed great emphasis on the abilities of a woman and her family to maintain her chastity. The moral code, intent on safeguarding male authority and the

---

od daughters might receive as much as equal shares with their brothers. For more information about women's property rights, see Eve Levin, "Women and Property in Medieval Novgorod: Dependence and Independence," *Russian History* 10, pt. 2 (1983): 154–69; and Sandra Levy, "Women and the Control of Property in Sixteenth-Century Muscovy," *Russian History* 10, pt. 2 (1983): 201–12.

11. Levin, *Sex and Society*, 45–57, 169–72, 274–75. For further information about taboos relating to women, see V. Iu. Leshchenko, "The Position of Women in the Light of Religious-Domestic Taboos among the East Slavic Peoples in the Nineteenth and Early Twentieth Centuries," *Soviet Anthropology and Archeology* 17, no. 3 (Winter 1978–79): 22–40; Dorothy Atkinson, "Society and the Sexes in the Russian Past," in *Women in Russia,* ed. Dorothy Atkinson, Alexander Dallin, and Gail Warshofsky Lapidus (Stanford, 1977), 14; and Christine D. Worobec, "Temptress or Virgin? The Precarious Sexual Position of Women in Post-Emancipation Ukrainian Peasant Society," *Slavic Review* 49, no. 2 (1990): 227–38.

12. See the essay by Eve Levin in this volume.

13. Joanna Hubbs, *Mother Russia: The Feminine Myth in Russian Culture* (Bloomington, Ind., 1988), 15. For a discussion of the importance of the midwife from the Kievan through the Soviet periods, see the essays by N. L. Pushkareva, Eve Levin, Rose Glickman, and Wendy Goldman in this volume.

14. See the essay by Eve Levin in this volume.

purity of the bloodline, demanded that women retain their virginity until marriage and subsequently become virtuous wives and mothers. Casting false aspersions on a woman's reputation had to be swiftly punished because a woman's loss of honor extended to her entire family.

Kievan and Muscovite civil and ecclesiastical laws accordingly provided judicial support for verbally dishonored women and rape victims. These abused women were allowed to act as their own litigants or seek the aid of male kin in representing their interests in court.[15] In both theory and practice the burden of proof lay with the accused and not the victim. Judges levied fines on the basis of the victim's social status, passing the money directly to the dishonored woman. According to a trade treaty between Smolensk and Riga even slave women and prostitutes were entitled to monetary compensation for rape. Canon law went so far as to protect a woman from unwanted sex in her marriage, giving her the right to seek a divorce if her husband attempted to rape her. The protection afforded women did not, however, originate out of a solicitude for a woman's physical well-being. After all, Orthodox teachings actively countenanced wife beating that did not seriously injure a woman. The laws protecting women derived instead from the ecclesiastical belief that all sexual intercourse, even in marriage, was evil, originating with the devil. The Catholic concept of conjugal debt, whereby sexual intercourse was viewed as an obligation to one's spouse, was totally absent from Orthodox teachings.[16] Furthermore, rape outside of marriage was considered a grave offense because of the shame that a woman and her family suffered. This patriarchal society significantly reduced the marital prospects for a woman who had lost her virginity. Rape also reflected badly on the victim's male kin, who had been unable to protect their ward from the predation of other men.[17]

Women also gained public power indirectly through their children. Mothers of all social ranks were key players in arranging their children's marriages, a responsibility that, as one went up the social ladder, acquired increasing social and political importance. At the village level mothers were on the lookout for conscientious, hardworking, and sober husbands for their daughters and obedient, strong, healthy, and diligent wives for their sons. They were also interested in increasing, if possible, the family's social position within the community by marrying their children into prosperous families. Among the richest families even women secluded in the *terem* had immense influence over their children's choice of marriage partners,

15. See the essay by Nancy Shields Kollmann in this volume.

16. Eve Levin, "Rape and Violence against Women in Pre-Petrine Russia" (Paper presented at the Midwest Slavic Conference, South Bend, Ind., April 19–21, 1985); Eve Levin, "Canon Law and Sexual Practice in Medieval Russia" (Paper presented at the Midwest Slavic Conference, Columbus, Ohio, May 4, 1984); Levin, *Sex and Society*, 212–46.

17. See the essay by Nancy Shields Kollmann in this volume.

interviewing prospective candidates and passing their evaluations on to male kin.[18] According to the revisionist studies by Robert Crummey and Nancy Shields Kollmann elite Muscovite families looked at the political rather than economic importance of prospective marital alliances. Marriages with members of the tsar's family and boyar families had immense political ramifications. Marriages solidified and in some cases created vital political ties in an autocratic system manipulated and controlled by the leading families of the realm. Even after the expansion of the tsarist bureaucracy in the seventeenth century, autocratic politics remained highly personal. They depended on the tsar's and his advisors' skillful manipulation of court factions, a feature Russia shared with medieval and absolutist Europe.[19] The Romanovs' bid for the Russian throne in 1613 owed its success to the clan's manipulation of marriage politics in the previous century, resulting in one of their members, Anastasiia Romanovna, marrying Ivan IV in 1547. When Fedor I, Ivan IV's only surviving heir, died a premature death, several male contenders to the Muscovite throne legitimized their claims either on direct genealogical links to the Riurikid princes or Chingisid dynasty of Kazan or on indirect links to royal lines through wives or sisters. In the end the Muscovites elected a Romanov, a linkage to the Daniilovich dynasty, to the throne. The importance of women in the tsarina's court in forging such important marriage alliances cannot be underestimated.

Women's power in traditional Russian society derived not only from their role in reproduction but also from their vital participation in the economic activities of their society. Russian women bore various economic responsibilities in their households according to their social status. At the bottom of society a sexual division of labor prevailed in the serf, state-peasant, and (after emancipation in 1861) free-peasant household. Detailed source material for this division of responsibilities dates from the late eighteenth and the nineteenth centuries. A similar pattern seems to have prevailed in pre-Petrine Russia.[20] A household head's wife oversaw the management of household and garden, while her husband had responsibility for farming the household's land allotments. However, the line between household labor and field labor could not be strictly maintained. During planting and harvesting,

18. Kollmann, "Seclusion," 184.

19. Robert O. Crummey, *Aristocrats and Servitors: The Boyar Elite in Russia, 1613–1689* (Princeton, 1983); Nancy Shields Kollmann, *Kinship and Politics: The Making of the Muscovite Political System, 1345–1547* (Stanford, 1987). This is not to suggest that elite marriages in medieval Russia did not have an economic basis. Indeed, dowries of upper-class Russian brides often included estates. However, given the scattered nature of noble estates and the fact that dowry lands were the wife's inalienable property and located far from her husband's holdings, these lands did not have the primary importance they had in Western Europe. Crummey, *Aristocrats and Servitors*, 76–77.

20. Levin notes that in the pre-Petrine period a sexual division of labor existed among all classes and that male peasants did heavy field work. Levin, *Sex and Society*, 132.

when there was much work to be done in the fields, women joined men in heavy labor there. They still divided tasks according to gender, relegating those jobs requiring less muscular strength to women. Women harvested rye, winter wheat, and oats with the sickle, tied grain into sheaves, loaded hay, and gleaned harvested fields for precious leftover grain. The heavier tasks of plowing, harrowing, cutting hay, and harvesting with the scythe were left to men.[21] In the winter months, when peasants engaged in nonagricultural work, the demarcation between home and fields largely disappeared as men were forced to spend a good deal of time indoors. Husband and wife might pursue separate endeavors, with men repairing agricultural implements and mending fishnets and women spinning and weaving. Or they might complement each others' work in such auxiliary trades as making spoons, gloves, fishnets, and bast mats for market. The profits from these trades supplemented the agricultural income of the household. Women's work was thus an integral part of the household economy, a fact recognized under serfdom, a system finally established by law in 1649 after a lengthy development. According to modern data serf owners divided their laborers into work units, or *tiagla*, each comprising a husband-and-wife team. Indeed, the economic function of peasant women was so important for their households' survival that their role as mother had to take second place; this priority contributed to Russia's extraordinarily high infant mortality rate well into the late imperial period.[22]

Women of the Russian elite also had important and active economic functions, although not on the same scale as men. Like their Western European counterparts, they managed the family estates while their husbands were serving in the tsar's army.[23] At least in commercial Novgorod they could also, if they wished, participate in their husbands' businesses and even run their own businesses. It is not clear whether elite women controlled the household budget. The property might have legally been their husbands', but women certainly seem to have been the operational managers. No ambiguity in the sources exists with regard to elite women's dowried land and movable property, which affirmed their independent economic status. When such property was substantial, these women acted as moneylenders, contributed to the building of churches and dowering of convents and monasteries, owned, bought, and sold slaves, and doled out charity to the poor.[24] Further-

21. Steven L. Hoch, *Serfdom and Social Control in Nineteenth-Century Russia: Petrovskoe, A Village in Tambov* (Chicago, 1986), 92.

22. See the essay by David Ransel in this volume.

23. Levy, "Women and the Control of Property," 211; Levin, *Sex and Society*, 132. For a discussion of noblewomen's important managerial role in the eighteenth century, see Marc Raeff, *Origins of the Russian Intelligentsia: The Eighteenth-Century Nobility* (New York, 1966), 122.

24. Pushkareva and Levin, "Women in Medieval Novgorod," 80–82; Daniel H. Kaiser, "Women's Property in Muscovite Families, 1500–1725" (Paper presented at the conference

more, it was not unusual for them to maintain active economic links with their natal families, exchanging goods and property with kinsmen.[25] They had the right to sell or bequeath recently purchased lands but had to seek family permission for the alienation of any patrimonial property, which rightfully devolved to clan members only. A married woman's rights over her immovable property were even protected from her husband's encroachment. For a husband to gain control of his wife's property, "a formal purchase document was deemed necessary to transfer land from the private holdings of a woman to her husband."[26] By contrast, any property that a woman acquired together with her spouse remained in the possession of her husband's clan.[27]

As was often the case in Western Europe, elderly women, particularly widows, at all levels of medieval Russian society and among the enserfed and free peasants of the imperial period, sometimes exercised greater authority and independence than younger women. Like the mature Mother of God, an elderly woman had fulfilled her social responsibilities by bearing and nurturing children. Society in turn accorded the postmenopausal and therefore no longer sexually dangerous woman honor and prestige. As manager of domestic tasks, the *bol'shukha*, the household head's wife, enjoyed full powers over her daughters-in-law, sisters-in-law, and children. Widows of all classes could under the right circumstances assume full control over household management by stepping into the male role of household head or could divest themselves of worldly concerns and enter a convent.[28]

The medieval civil and criminal code, *Russkaia Pravda*,[29] made provision for widows among the upper classes, noting that they were entitled to use their husbands' estate until their children became adults. But a widow who remarried immediately forfeited that right.[30] The same law code stipulated that a widow did not have any rights to her husband's patrimonial or ancestral land (*votchina*) except for that portion he had bequeathed her. Practice,

---

"Women in the History of the Russian Empire," Kent State University and the University of Akron, Kent and Akron, Ohio, August 11–14, 1988).

25. Levy, "Women and the Control of Property," 211.

26. Levin, "Women and Property," 156–57, 164.

27. See the essay by Nancy Shields Kollmann in this volume.

28. Levin, *Sex and Society*, 109, 112–13; Levin, "Women and Property," 157–61; Marie A. Thomas, "Muscovite Convents in the Seventeenth Century," *Russian History* 10, pt. 2 (1983): 230. See also the essay by Rodney D. Bohac in this volume for a discussion of serf widows in the early nineteenth century.

29. The earlier version of the *Russkaia Pravda* dates from the late eleventh or early twelfth century, the expanded redaction from the thirteenth century. For a discussion of medieval Russian law codes, see Daniel H. Kaiser, *The Growth of the Law in Medieval Russia* (Princeton, 1980).

30. Pushkareva and Levin, "Women in Medieval Novgorod," 79–80.

however, often departed from these legal strictures, providing widows more advantageous property and authority rights. It was not unusual for women to remain undisputed household heads when their children reached maturity. Furthermore, numerous wills from Novgorod in the fourteenth and fifteenth centuries demonstrate that husbands made provisions for their wives to inherit use of the patrimonial property in addition to the widow's portion.[31] Law codes after the *Russkaia Pravda*, including the Pskov Charter, the *Sudebnik* of 1550, and the *Ulozhenie* of 1649, all confirmed women's inheritance rights, guaranteeing a widow's possession of her dowry and purchased lands inherited from her family as well as one-quarter of her deceased husband's movable property from his patrimonial estate, some or all of his purchased property, and a fixed portion of his service estate as a maintenance allotment. In consequence many Muscovite and Novgorodian elite widows were quite wealthy. Several of the wealthiest persons in Novgorod in the last years of its independence were women, with Marfa Boretskaia taking the lead.[32]

Widows could forsake the secular world, become nuns, and pursue a life of holiness. Living in a community of women in and of itself was an improvement over living directly under male control in the outer world. Convents derived their wealth from the endowments paid by women entering as novices (endowments were mandatory by the mid-sixteenth century) and from donations by the laity, who sought the nuns' advice, prayers, memorial services, and offering of thanks to God.[33] But women did not always take the veil voluntarily. Husbands could force wives into convents as a pretext for divorce (an action tsars and members of the elite often took), and families sometimes used convents, as in Western Europe, to house unmarriageable young daughters.[34]

Women religious in Russia sometimes achieved power as abbesses and spiritual advisors. However, they did not achieve the sort of status and independence that nuns and abbesses did in Western Europe. In the seventeenth century Russian nuns found their activities somewhat circumscribed. They were not managers of their convents' estates, and they did not represent their institutions before secular authorities.[35] Only those women who rejected all worldly comforts and concerns achieved political importance in the outside

---

31. Levin, "Women and Property," 157–61.

32. In Moscow after the 1654 plague Prince I. A. Vorotynskii's widow had an immense household that included more than one hundred servants and several pious poor women whom she supported as an act of charity. One would assume that she also possessed several estates to help maintain such a large domestic operation. Crummey, *Aristocrats and Servitors*, 116–117, 145–46. The information about Novgorod was supplied by Eve Levin.

33. Thomas, "Muscovite Convents," 232.

34. Ibid., 234, 237; Levin, *Sex and Society*, 121–22.

35. Thomas, "Muscovite Convents," 241–42.

world. In the seventeenth century Marfa of Moscow and in the eighteenth century Evdokiia of Suzdal and Kseniia of St. Petersburg, for example, attained the venerated title of holy fool, or fool for Christ, because of their abilities to predict the future and utter religious truths under divine inspiration. Because of their presumed powers both male and female holy fools were permitted to indulge in antisocial behavior, neglecting bodily needs, abandoning clothes and all creature comforts, and dispensing with conventional moral norms. More important, the fools for Christ became symbols of resistance to the established order, often expressing contempt for political and spiritual authorities.[36]

Altogether, women's lives in traditional Russian society were not as bleak as historians have assumed. On the one hand, women were subject to a misogynistic patriarchal system that justified their subordination by alleging they were evil, lustful temptresses. On the other hand, they were integral members of a system whose survival depended on their accommodation and active participation. Acknowledging male spiritual, political, and social domination in a highly militarized society whose rigid command structure seemed necessary for survival, Russian women were willing to make sacrifices and contribute to the system. In so doing, they took advantage of those patriarchal traditions that empowered them. Their success depended to some extent on social status. Elite women, even in their isolation, had more economic and social advantages than their urban, peasant, serf, and slave counterparts. Nonetheless, women of all ranks shared cultural traditions that empowered them as bearers and nurturers of children. After all, the patriarchal system could not perpetuate itself without their reproductive capacities. The male obsession with a bride's virginity so as to ensure the purity of the bloodline endowed women with honor. Women and their families were responsible for upholding that honor, even if it meant striking out at dishonorable men in a court of law. Women could also influence political developments indirectly through their children. Women of all ranks affected their family's social position by arranging marriages for their children. Through their economic activities they were actors within and outside the family. It is little wonder that women collectively accommodated themselves to a system that gave them some authority and protection and ultimately guaranteed the survival of their families.

Women's active resistance to patriarchy came only when men's collective powers were weakened by outside forces, as they were during periods of crisis—particularly in the turmoil of the seventeenth century, with the succession crisis and foreign invasion of the Time of Troubles, religious revival-

36. Natalia Challis, "Glorification of Saints in the Orthodox Church," *Russian History* 7, pt. 1–2 (1980): 239–46; Ewa M. Thompson, *Understanding Russia: The Holy Fool in Russian Culture* (Lanham, N.Y., 1987).

ism, the church schism, and formal imposition of serfdom. In such times some women emerged as public resisters to their subordination by claiming to be hexed. Those who accused men of bewitching them could momentarily step into the public arena and manipulate public commendation of their accusations to their advantage.[37] Other women opposed the ecclesiastical hierarchy and the state's challenge to traditional Orthodox beliefs. As defenders of the Old Belief (after the Great Schism) they risked state persecution. Boyarina Morozova and her sister Evdokiia, protectors of Archpriest Avvakum, a leader of the Old Belief, died in prison after suffering torture. Their martyrdom inspired those courageous women who later chose self-immolation rather than submission to what they believed to be the Antichrist. Still others, including Matrena Razin and a widow from Arzamas, risked their lives commanding rebel detachments and disseminating propaganda in 1670–71 in support of Sten'ka Razin against the forces of a centralizing state.[38]

In the political realm in normal times only regents and powerful women religious were visible, and in community affairs only widows who, because of favorable economic circumstances and previous success in childbearing, could assume total control over their households. Other women, content to remain out of the public domain, nevertheless influenced it indirectly by using the powers that patriarchy gave them.

37. See the essay by Valerie Kivelson in this volume.

38. The widow from Arzamas led a detachment of seven thousand men. The government later burned her as a rebel and witch. Razin's mother was also executed for her role in the rebellion. See Paul Avrich, *Russian Rebels, 1600–1800* (New York, 1972), 67, 91–92.

Women in the
Medieval Russian Family of the
Tenth through Fifteenth Centuries

N. L. Pushkareva

Ethnographers have long studied the historical forms of family, marriage, and marriage ceremonies. Scholars have paid insufficient attention, however, to the earlier period of medieval Rus'. The paucity of materials and the disparate nature of existing sources help explain this lacuna.[1] The property rights of various classes of medieval Russian women and women's place in criminal law have been examined to a certain degree in both prerevolutionary and Soviet historiography.[2] Nevertheless, there are serious gaps in the study of medieval Russian women's status within the family, their place in wedding traditions and practices, and the rights of women from various social classes to divorce, among other questions. Piecing together the details of medieval wedding rituals and family customs from chronicles, canonical literature, archaeological materials, and other sources provides a much fuller characterization of some of the traditions that existed from the tenth through

Translated by Christine D. Worobec, Barbara Evans Clements, and Barbara Alpern Engel, with much-appreciated help from Eve Levin.

1. A. I. Kozachenko, a scholar of wedding traditions, maintained that it is impossible to describe Russian family and wedding traditions before the end of the fifteenth and early sixteenth centuries. A. I. Kozachenko, "K istorii velikorusskogo svadebnogo obriada," *Sovetskaia etnografiia*, 1957, no. 1: 61.

2. K. Alekseev, "Ob otnosheniiakh suprugov po imushchestvu v Drevnei Rossii i Pol'she," *Chteniia obshchestva istorii i drevnostei rossisskikh pri Moskovskom Universitete* (henceforth *ChOIDR*), bk. 2 (1868): 1–108; O. Pergament, "K voprosu ob imushchestvennykh otnosheniiakh suprugov po drevneishemu russkomu pravu," *Zhurnal ministerstva narodnago prosveshcheniia*, 1894, no. 11: 1–21; N. L. Pushkareva, "Imushchestvennye prava zhenshchin v russkom gosudarstve X–XV v.v.," *Istoricheskie zapiski* 114 (1986): 180–224; N. L. Pushkareva, "Pravovoe polozhenie zhenshchiny v Drevnei Rusi X–XV vv.: Voprosy prestupleniia i nakazaniia," *Sovetskoe gosudarstvo i pravo*, 1985, no. 4: 121–26; N. L. Pushkareva and E. Levin, "Zhenshchina v srednevekovom Novgorode XI–XV vv.," *Vestnik Moskovskogo universiteta*, 8th ser. (History), 3 (1983): 78–89 (translated as "Women in Medieval Novgorod from the Eleventh to the Fifteenth Century," *Soviet Studies in History* 23, no. 4 [Spring 1985]: 71–90).

fifteenth centuries. These "mechanisms of social inheritance"[3] stabilized existing relationships and reproduced them in the generations that followed not only in the period under study but even later, from the seventeenth through the nineteenth centuries.

In Rus' the oldest form of marriage was bride capture, which dates to pre-Christian times. The performance of the abduction "from water" was typical of the Indo-European variant of such weddings.[4] The ritual took place on holidays honoring the god of marriage, Lado. According to the *Gustynskaia Chronicle*, "Lado is a god who is worshiped as the god of marriage, happiness, comfort, and all types of prosperity, like the Greek Bacchus, by whose help marriage was good and loving."[5] The holidays began in early spring on Krasnaia Gorka (Red/Beautiful Mountain) and ended in the summer on the day of Ivan Kupalo, the Nativity of John the Baptist (June 24).[6] The way ancient Russian chronicles describe the abduction ritual demonstrates that both the suitor's and bride's families agreed to the marriage and that the bride exercised free choice in the matter: "And each abducted a wife for himself, having agreed with her beforehand."[7] The "simple folk" (i.e., the dependent population) preserved this ritual, like the dances in Lado's honor, right up until the sixteenth century.[8] Traces of it can also be found in various epic poems (*byliny*) and songs dating from that time.

In addition to an abduction ritual in early medieval Russia there was also a formal marriage contract called *brakprivedenie*: "The bridegroom did not go for the bride, but rather she was brought in the evening, and the next day what she owned was brought for her."[9] But as opposed to the abduction ritual, in which the bride's will prevailed, the bride's relatives or parents rather than the bride herself played the primary role in concluding this agreement. Chroniclers used the term *brakprivedenie* to describe the marriages of princes and when emphasizing the bride's lack of autonomy in matrimonial affairs.[10]

3. I. V. Sukhanov, *Obychai, traditsii i preemstvennost' pokolenii* (Moscow, 1976), 24.

4. N. I. Sumtsov, *O svadebnykh obriadakh, preimushchestvenno russkikh* (Kharkov, 1881), 100–105.

5. *Polnoe sobranie russkikh letopisei* (henceforth *PSRL*), vol. 2, *Gustynskaia letopis'* (St. Petersburg, 1843), 257.

6. N. Khlebnikov, *Obshchestvo i gosudarstvo v domongol'skii period russkoi istorii* (St. Petersburg, 1872), 147. For a description of Krasnaia Gorka, a festival honoring spring and the dead, see Janet Hubbs, *Mother Russia: The Feminine Myth in Russian Culture* (Bloomington, Ind., 1988), 70–71.

7. *PSRL*, vol. 1, *Lavrent'evskaia letopis'* (St. Petersburg, 1846), 6.

8. "Poslanie vladimirskago episkopa k mestnomu kniaziu XIII v.," *Russkaia istoricheskaia biblioteka* (henceforth *RIB*), vol. 6, *Pamiatniki drevnerusskago kanonicheskago prava XI–XV vv.* (St. Petersburg, 1880), 137; "Poslanie mitropolita Fotiia v Novgorod 1410 g.," in *RIB*, 6: 272ff.

9. *PSRL*, 1: 6.

10. *PSRL*, 1: 12 (under the year 823), 32 (under the year 897), 118 (under the year 1102); vol. 2, *Ipat'evskaia letopis'*, 286 (under the year 1102), 290 (under the year 1104).

When the Rus' became Christian, the church claimed the exclusive right to solemnize marriages. Marriage law developed, together with marriage rituals conforming to that law. This led to a number of changes in women's rights and in the status of the family. The process was twofold. First, ancient marriage rituals performed by the family were transformed into customs sanctified by law. Second, the church authorities created new marriage customs on the basis of the Byzantine marital canons. The oldest texts, from the tenth and eleventh centuries, testify to the influence of pre-Christian Russian rituals in premarital and marriage ceremonies from the tenth through the fifteenth centuries. They discuss the preliminary marriage contract that sealed the betrothal. The ancient Russian custom of betrothal was accompanied by a feast of pies, kasha, and cheese at the home of the bride's parents. The slicing of the cheese formalized the betrothal. A groom who rejected his fiancée after performing this ritual was perceived to have done her a great dishonor. The Statute of Iaroslav prescribed, "If the cheese has been cut for a maiden, then a grivna must be paid for the cheese, three grivnas for her shame, and she must be repaid for whatever else has been lost."[11]

The betrothal eventually became merely one part of the marriage agreement, the primary purpose of which was to secure a written contract (*riad*). This contract not only confirmed the parents' approval of the marriage and stipulated the property settlement and timing of the wedding but also indicated that the future bride and groom had consented to the marriage. Articles of the Statute of Iaroslav imposed a special monetary fine (to be paid to the metropolitan of the church) on parents when "a maiden wishes to marry someone, and her father and mother do not permit it."[12] The *Primary Chronicle* tells the half-legendary story of Princess Rogneda of Polotsk, who refused to marry the suitor whom her father had selected.[13] The use of written marriage contracts may be definitively confirmed no earlier than the thirteenth century. The example of the famous Novgorodian birchbark document (no. 377) dates from this period: "From Mikita to Ul'ianitsa. Marry me. I want you, and you want me. Ignato is witness to this." There are other examples as well.[14]

In medieval Rus' the handfast (*rukobit'e*) and then the betrothal (*obruchenie*) in church constituted the final acts of the marriage agreement. Some ethnographers have proposed that the term *obruchenie* may have arisen much earlier than the church ritual (in which rings called *obruchei* were exchanged)

11. *PSRL*, vol. 3, *Novgorodskie i Pskovskie letopisi* (St. Petersburg, 1841), 52; "Ustav kniazia Iaroslava Vladimirovicha," in *Pamiatniki russkogo prava* (henceforth *PRP*), vol. 1 (Moscow, 1952), 269, art. 33.

12. "Ustav kniazia Iaroslava Vladimirovicha," 268–69, arts. 20, 26.

13. *PSRL*, 1: 32 (under the year 1128).

14. A. V. Artsikhovskii, *Novgorodskie gramoty na bereste: Iz raskopok 1958–1961* (henceforth *NGB*) (Moscow, 1963), 76–77; "Riadnaia Teshaty i Iakima XIII v.," in *PRP*, vol. 2 (Moscow, 1953), 278.

since this term refers to the passing of the marriage contract from hand to hand.[15] The *rukobit'e* before giving the bride in marriage and the betrothal in church confirmed before the community the boy's obligation to marry the girl: "And he may marry no other; but shall take this one as his wife." In conformity with popular custom, church law enjoined the boy to marry his betrothed even if someone else had "seduced and defiled her."[16] Various church anthologies describe the betrothal ritual: the priest completed it by placing a gold ring on the future husband's right hand and an iron ring on the betrothed woman's.[17]

After the handfast and betrothal the period known as the Great Week began. Its purpose was purely practical—to get ready for the wedding, assemble the dowry, and so on. It could last for two or three months or even longer. Not one medieval Russian document notes a time limitation for this period. Indeed, the betrothal, marriage contract, and handfast were often completed even before the young couple had reached marriageable age. Girls in medieval Rus' became marriageable at age thirteen or fourteen; a church law forbidding "the marriage of maidens less than twelve years old" appeared only in the fifteenth century. Before that time royal children far from the minimum marriageable age were allowed to marry. Princess Verkhuslava Vsevolodovna was "very young, eight years old," on her wedding day, and the son of Vasilii Vasil'evich the Dark, the minor Ivan, was "smitten by a beautiful maiden," the five-year-old daughter of Prince Boris Aleksandrovich of Tver.[18]

A variety of socioeconomic and religious factors, as well as common-law traditions, helped shape other traditional prohibitions regarding whom a person could marry in medieval Russian society. The Russian Orthodox church produced specific canons limiting the circle of eligible spouses. Whatever her social class, a woman was prohibited from marrying close blood relatives (up to the sixth degree), relatives by marriage, or even someone who might become a relative in the future. Likewise, a man was forbidden to marry a son's former fiancée.[19] The medieval Russian church also introduced a law forbidding young women to marry foreigners, particularly the non-Orthodox, to restrict the ethnic integration of medieval Russian and

15. D. D. Khanykov, *Russkie byliny* (Moscow, 1860), 122.

16. *Materialy dlia istorii drevnerusskoi pokaiannoi distsipliny*, ed. S. I. Smirnov (Moscow, 1913), 50, 146.

17. "Chin obruchen'e devitse i muzhiu, tsarem i prochim (XIII v.)," in M. Gorchakov, *O taine supruzhestva: Proiskhozhdenie, istoriko-iuridicheskoe znachenie i kanonicheskoe dostoinstvo 50 glavy pechatnoi kormchei knigi* (St. Petersburg, 1880), Appendix, 6.

18. "Poslanie mitropolita Fotiia novgorodtsam 1410 g.," *RIB*, 6: 275; *PSRL*, 2: 136 (under the year 1187); N. P. Likhachev, *Inoka Fomy slovo pokhval'noe o blagorodnom i velikom kniaze Borise Aleksandroviche* (St. Petersburg, 1908), 37–38.

19. "Ustav kniazia Iaroslava Vladimirovicha," 268–69, arts. 20–26; "Rospisanie stepenei rodstva i svoistva, prepiatstvuiushchikh braku (XIV v.)," in *RIB*, 6: 143–44, arts. 1–4.

neighboring peoples. For "unworthy and improper ties" with a nonbeliever, a Russian woman was punished by forcible banishment to a convent. Subsequently, under the influence of political circumstances, representatives of the Russian Orthodox clergy abandoned their attempts to restrict ethnic integration. They substituted a monetary fine for the sentence of banishment and freed grand princesses, many of whom were already married to foreign kings, from the prohibition against marriage to the non-Orthodox.[20]

Medieval Russian churchmen developed an additional set of rules limiting the choice of whom a person could marry. These rules involved social or class differences, which it was forbidden to mix in marriage. In the best of circumstances peasant or slave women who married men of the privileged classes were considered concubines, or secondary wives. In the worst case a freeman who married a slave woman lost his freedom and became a slave. It is interesting that there was no statute to cover the reverse situation, making a freewoman who married a male slave a slave; neither was this done in reality. Among Novgorodian families, for example, there were cases in which the father was a slave but "his wife and daughters are free."[21] The man who considered marrying a woman of the lowest social status must have been frightened by such didactic literature as *Pchela*, which noted that "it is known a wife from among slaves is evil and brutish."[22]

Whereas medieval Russian tradition and common law imposed no restrictions on the number of marriages a woman could have during her lifetime, Christian morals permitted no more than two. Permission for a third marriage was given only in exceptional cases, and then only in Novgorod and Pskov, "if someone is young and has no children from the first or second marriages."[23] Church authorities demanded immediate dissolution of a woman's fourth marriage. They declared, "The first marriage is law, the second is dispensation, the third is transgression, the fourth is dishonor, for it is a swinish life."[24]

Traditionally the preservation of virginity had not been a precondition for marriage. With the spread of Christian morality, however, it became a norm for future priests' wives and wives of other churchmen. For everyone else the

20. "Ustav kniazia Iaroslava Vladimirovicha," 268, art. 17; "Kanonicheskie otvety mitropolita Ioanna II (XI v.)," in *RIB*, 6: 7, art. 13; "Belozerskaia ustavnaia gramota 1488 g.," in *PRP*, vol. 3 (Moscow, 1955), 173.

21. *Russkaia Pravda*, in *PRP*, 1: 11, art. 10; *Gramoty Velikogo Novgoroda i Pskova*, ed. S. N. Valk (Moscow-Leningrad, 1949), 168, no. 110.

22. *Russkaia Pravda*, in *PRP*, 1: 110, art. 119; *Pchela* (XV v.), Otdel rukopisei Gosudarstvennoi publichnoi biblioteki im. Saltykova-Shchedrina (henceforth OR GPB) F. p. 1, no. 44, f. 184. *Pchela* is a collection of aphorisms drawn primarily from Greek sources.

23. "Poslanie mitropolita Fotiia v Novgorod 1410 g.," 273.

24. Ibid., 273–74; "Poslanie mitropolita Fotiia vo Pskov o sobliudenii zakonopolozhenii tserkovnykh 1410 g.," in *RIB*, 6: 281.

law ordered a penance for a woman who "married impure."[25] The ultimate goal of the medieval Russian clergy in introducing new prohibitions was not to restrict but, on the contrary, to increase the number of persons marrying in the church. Church literature is filled with exhortations such as "Compel them to marry and live according to the law" and "Mary off those girls who are mature, so that they will do no evil."[26]

Guided by pre-Christian traditions holding parents responsible for their children's future, the medieval Russian church imposed fines on parents who failed to marry off their daughters (*zasevshie devki*) promptly.[27] The church had the overriding goal of making a Christian wedding the norm. However, church wedding rites were slow to displace pre-Christian practices. Pre-Christian wedding rituals continued to exist, and old rituals and traditions were intermixed with the new ways. Nonetheless, Christianization continued. This process is well documented in wedding rites dating from the tenth through the fifteenth centuries. Russian didactic and normative sources for this period contain only occasional references, but foreign travelers to Russia compiled detailed descriptions of Russian weddings, albeit only at the end of the fifteenth century and later, in the sixteenth and seventeenth centuries. It is therefore necessary, on the one hand, to systematize and generalize from separate references in medieval chronicles and acts; but it is permissible, on the other, to utilize some of the travel accounts from the fifteenth and sixteenth centuries because rituals often remained unaltered for several centuries. It is no accident that the author who described the wedding of Vasilii III and Elena Glinskaia in the sixteenth century emphasized that everything was done "as in the olden days of Prince Semen Ivanovich,"[28] that is, in the fourteenth century.

Shortly before the wedding a ritual bath and maiden's party (*devichnik*) were held. The bride's attempt to win her future husband's love through magical means may explain the persistence of pre-Christian traditions connected with the bathwater in marriage rites dating from the tenth through the fifteenth centuries. Brides carefully collected the bathwater after the ritual bath and gave it to their grooms to drink after the wedding ceremony. Even

25. "Voprosy Kirika, Savvy i Il'i s otvetami Nifonta, episkopa novgorodskogo," in *RIB*, 6: 46, art. 81; "Tri sviatitel'skie poucheniia dukhovenstvu i mirianam o raznykh predmetakh tserkovnoi distsipliny," in *RIB*, 6: 924.

26. *Materialy dlia istorii drevnerusskoi pokaiannoi distsipliny*, 92.

27. "Ustav kniazia Iaroslava Vladimirovicha," 267, art. 5. In the historical literature there are also other interpretations of the term *zasevshaia devka*: a sinful young girl who has entered a church institution or convent, a malefactor, etc. See A. A. Zimin, "Istoriko-pravovoi obzor Ustava kniazia Iaroslava Vladimirovicha," in *PRP*, 1: 281. Slaveholders were placed under penance for not marrying off their slaves. "Tri sviatitel'skie poucheniia," 918–19, 925.

28. I. Sakharov, *Skazaniia russkago naroda o semeinoi zhizni svoikh predkov*, pt. 3, bk. 2 (St. Petersburg, 1837), appendix, "Russkie svadebnye zapisi," 20.

in the twelfth century the monk Kirik asked the Novgorod bishop Nifont for permission to impose a weeklong penance on brides who practiced this rite. Despite such censure the ritual continued to exist and was documented in descriptions of fifteenth- and sixteenth-century weddings.[29]

At the maiden's party a wreath or *kokoshnik* (a headdress for unmarried women that left the crown of the head exposed) was removed from the bride's head, and her single braid, the symbol of maidenhood, was unplaited. These rituals took place in the outer chambers of the bride's home, out of the groom's sight, in symbolic representation of the fact that the bride and groom did not yet know one another. It is possible that the very word for bride, *nevesta*, is related to the adjective *neizvestnaia*, the unknown one.[30] The proverb "In muddied waters one cannot see the bottom, and in a bride one cannot see the truth" is listed among the aphorisms in the Old Russian *Pchela*.[31]

The main rites of the wedding day included the giving away of the bride, the rebraiding of the bride's hair, the church ceremony, the reception of the bride in the groom's home, and the ceremony round the marriage bed. From the tenth through the fifteenth centuries the ritual of giving away the bride began with preparing the middle room of the house (*srednaia palata*) for the arrival of the young couple. The bride entered the room before the groom, preceded by women carrying the wedding bread decorated with money, which portended a prosperous and satisfying life for the future family.[32] Significantly, such good wishes were directed to the bride, in recognition of her future role as manager of the domestic budget. The bride was then handed over to the groom, who seated her beside him. Next the matchmakers rebraided the bride's hair into two braids (symbolic of marriage) and placed a married woman's headdress (*kika* or *pokoinik*) on her head. Married women's headdresses covered all the hair, unlike those of unmarried women. It is worth noting that by the twelfth century anyone who intentionally removed a married woman's headdress became subject to a monetary fine for insulting female honor.[33] Since ancient times a woman who wore a comb instead of the

29. "Voproshanie Kirika," in *RIB*, 6: 41; *Sbornik russkago istoricheskago obshchestva*, vol. 35 (St. Petersburg, 1882), 187.

30. Sakharov, *Skazaniia russkago naroda*, 120.

31. *Pchela* (XV v.), OR GPB, F. p. 1, no. 44, f. 184. In Novgorod and surrounding territories prenuptial rites did not necessarily follow these rules, which provided the nineteenth-century Russian historian N. I. Kostomarov a basis on which to note the peculiarities of Novgorodian weddings. In describing fifteenth-century Novgorodian weddings, Kostomarov mentioned the following ritual: "Before the arrival the best man shouted, 'We did not come to see the bridal veil, but the bride.' The groom then saw his betrothed." N. I. Kostomarov, *Istoricheskie monografii i issledovaniia*, vol. 1 (St. Petersburg, 1872), 158–59.

32. Sakharov, *Skazaniia russkago naroda*, 26.

33. Ibid.; "Dogovor 1189–1199 g.g.," in *PRP*, 2: 126, art. 8.

headdress appropriate for her family status had been reproachingly called a comb wearer (*grebenshchitsa*), a term laden with contempt.[34]

Before the wedding party left for the church, rites of sympathetic magic were enacted to ensure the future family's prosperity. For example, guests threw hops at the bride for happiness and lined her path with fur coats for a rich life, a straw rug to bring her easy childbirth, sheaves of grain for fertility, and the like.[35] In the church the groom stood to the right of the priest, the bride to the left, and each received a candle in accordance with the sacrament of marriage described in numerous medieval Russian prayer books. After exchanging rings, the newlyweds joined right hands. The priest then placed crowns over their heads, blessed them with incense, and prayed aloud as he turned to the east. Next he blessed the marriage, wishing the newlyweds "a peaceful and long life" and "children and grandchildren, to fill your house with abundance and beauty."[36]

Church wedding rituals were followed by the traditional rituals of receiving the bride in the groom's home and ceremonies around the marriage bed. For example, the ritual episode of the wife taking off her husband's boots after the wedding is widely described in the ethnographic literature. Nestor referred to it in the oldest Russian chronicle when he wrote that Princess Rogneda of Polotsk refused to "remove the boots of a slave's son."[37] This ritual was not mentioned in descriptions of the weddings of grand princes and tsars in the fifteenth and sixteenth centuries. It appears again in the accounts of foreigners who visited Russia in the sixteenth and seventeenth centuries, but now as a ritual game to determine the wife's future place and rights in the family.[38] The ritual of breaking a goblet, recorded in many wedding descriptions of the fifteenth century and accounts by foreign travelers of a later period, has a similar meaning. If in ancient times a cup was broken (a rite of sympathetic magic) to ensure the young couple's happiness, by the sixteenth century that ritual had acquired a different meaning, becoming a playful action in the struggle for authority within the family.[39] As marriage became more patriarchal and the husband's authority increased, that act disappeared entirely from the wedding ritual. Seventeenth-century docu-

---

34. V. I. Dal', *Tolkovyi slovar' zhivogo velikorusskogo iazyka*, vol. 1 (Moscow, 1955), 393.

35. *Sbornik russkago istoricheskago obshchestva*, 35: 186; Sakharov, *Skazaniia russkago naroda*, 34.

36. *Trebniki* (XV v.), in OR GPB, Mikh. O. p. 1, no. 9, ff. 23–24v; Gil'f. 21, ff. 15v–17; O. p. 1, no. 473, f. 243.

37. *Povest' vremennykh let*, ed. V. P. Adrianova-Peretts, vol. 1 (Moscow-Leningrad, 1950), 54.

38. "The groom puts gold and silver coins into one of his boots. . . . The bride is supposed to remove whichever boot she chooses. If she succeeds in taking off the boot containing money, she not only receives the money but will not have to remove her husband's boots ever again." "Opisanie Rossii neizvestnago anglichanina, sluzhivshego zimu 1557–1558 gg. pri tsarskom dvore," in *ChOIDR* (October 1884), 26–27.

39. "Whoever of the two [the groom or bride] makes the first move is victorious and will always be the master." Ibid., 26.

ments do not mention it. The ritual of welcoming the bride into the husband's home invariably involved the groom's family giving gifts to the bride's family as well as the groom giving gifts to the bride. Some of these gifts, such as needles and a whip, were symbolic. From the tenth through the fifteenth centuries these objects were still endowed with the ancient magical meanings they had long had in pre-Christian rituals, and they did not abase and subordinate women. According to popular belief the needles warded off the evil eye, and the lashes of the whip led to the conception of children. After the fifteenth century these same gifts merely underlined the husband's authority in the home and symbolized the wife's responsibility for domestic tasks.[40]

After the gift exchange and the wedding feast, which customarily included pies and a chicken, the young couple was led to the storeroom.[41] The custom of examining the bride to ensure her virginity, often described by gossiping foreigners, was never part of popular custom, as it lowered a woman's worth. It appeared with the spread of church marriages and the demand that a bride maintain her virginity until marriage.[42]

The medieval Russian wedding rituals described above make it clear that not only customary law and popular traditions but also growing Christianization influenced women's status in the evolution of marriage and the family from the tenth through the fifteenth centuries. To a great extent Christian morality came to govern relations within the family in later years. In theory Orthodox sermonizers did not consider marriage and the family obstacles to salvation, but theologians nevertheless thought them less virtuous than asceticism and celibacy. "Virginity is much more virtuous than marriage. . . . Those who can should remain virgins," enjoined Metropolitan Ioann in the eleventh century.[43] Theologians unfavorably compared the meaning of earthly things, including woman's procreative function in the family, with transcendent values, such as love of God and self-abnegation. "Marriage is usually evil for a person," declared *Pchela*.[44]

Teachings about the relationship of the soul and the body played an important role in determining the church's view of women's destiny and their place in the family. Churchmen taught that "the law does not allow a woman to be an elder. . . . As the prince answers to God, so a man answers to his prince, and a woman to her husband."[45] The ideal wife was supposed to be

40. Sumtsov, *O svadebnykh obriadakh*, 94.

41. F. I. Buslaev, *Istoricheskie ocherki russkoi narodnoi slovesnosti i iskusstva*, vol. 1, *Epicheskaia poeziia* (St. Petersburg, 1861), 46–47.

42. "Opisanie svad'by Eleny Ivanovny, docheri v. kn. Ivana III," *Sbornik russkago istoricheskago obshchestva*, 35: 187.

43. "Kanonicheskie otvety mitropolita Ioanna (XI v.)," *RIB*, 6: 70.

44. *Pchela* (XIV v.), Tsentral'nyi gosudarstvennyi arkhiv drevnikh aktov (hereafter TsGADA), F. 180, no. 658/1170, f. 212.

45. *Prolog* (XIV v.), TsGADA, F. 381, no. 171, f. 195; *Pchela* (XV v.), OR GPB, F. p. 1, no. 44, f. 10 v.

"good," that is, "submissive," "quiet," "humble," and "silent."[46] According to one didactic collection, "There is no worse foolishness than to be ruled by a woman. Such men are spineless, shameless, foolish, dependent, servile, and simpletons."[47] In practice, however, the question of who ruled the family could be decided differently. The chronicles describe princely families in which the wife "rules her husband."[48] Confessional miscellanies provide a collective portrait of a woman "confined to the home," who nevertheless "barked at," "fought with," and even "spit at the face" of her own husband.[49] Frequently in their daily practice clerics wrote that they met "husbands who ruled towns but slaved for their wives."[50]

In the final analysis the atmosphere of the family depended directly on the women, according to the didactic literature produced by the church. The sources of the fourteenth and fifteenth centuries contain many appeals to husbands: "Do not deprive yourself of your wives' advice"; "It befits a wife to revere her husband as the head on her shoulders, and a husband to revere his wife as the soul in his body."[51] A chronicler cited as examples of "harmony and caring" in medieval Russian families Ian and his wife Mariia (eleventh century), Prince Mstislav Vladimirovich and his wife Kristina (twelfth century), the Volynian prince Vladimir Vasil'kovich and "his dear Princess Ol'ga" (thirteenth century), Prince Mikhail Iaroslavich of Tver and his wife Anna Dmitrievna (fourteenth century), and many others.[52] And though all of these people were representatives of princely families—"born with virtue," in the words of the chronicler—the descriptions of them doubtless reflect the attitudes of their contemporaries and their demand for highly moral familial relations. Nevertheless, a fourteenth-century love letter dis-

---

46. *Pamiatnik drevnerusskoi tserkovno-uchitel'noi literatury*, pt. 4, ed. A. I. Ponomarev (St. Petersburg, 1898), nos. 60, 120.

47. OR GPB, F. p. 1, no. 44, ff. 10, 134.

48. *PSRL*, 2: 265 (under the year 6533), 2: 296 (under the year 6648).

49. "Ustav kniazia Iaroslava Vladimirovicha," 269–70, arts. 39–40; *Sluzhebnik s trebnikom* (XV v.), OR GPB, F. p. 1, no. 875, f. 133; *Trebnik* (XV v.), Rukopisnyi Otdel Biblioteki Akademii Nauk (henceforth RO BAN) (Leningrad), Arkhan. D-73, f. 44; *Sbornaia rukopis'* (XV v.), OR GPB, F. p. 1, no. 729, f. 174 v.

50. "Otryvok iz poucheniia Efrema Sirina XI v.," RO BAN (Leningrad) 24.4.20. (Sreznevsk. 67), f. 3 v.

51. *Trebnik* (XV v.), OR GPB. Sof. 875, f. 134 v.; *Pamiatniki drevnerusskoi tserkovno-uchitel'noi literatury*, 118–20; *Izmaragd* (XV v.), RO BAN. IZ. 2.7. f. 81 v.

52. "They lived according to God's commandments and there was love between them." *PSRL*, 1: 91. "The princess Kristina loved me greatly, and we lived in true love, and although I frequently visited other women, she . . . did not get angry. Now the princess wants to enjoy herself as a young person and may do something unseemly; but it is awkward for me to do anything; it is enough that no one learns about it."*PSRL*, 2: 76–79. V. N. Tatishchev, *Istoriia Rossiiskaia*, vol. 2, (Moscow-Leningrad, 1963), 242. *PSRL*, 2: 111 (under the year 6682), 5:210–13; 7:191–95; 8:197.

covered in Novgorod confirms that many townspeople of the time did not accept the church's ascetic ideal: "As my heart and my body and my soul burn for your body and the sight of you, so your heart and your body and your soul burn for me."[53] Clerics resolutely condemned such "bodily love," not only because it contradicted the prescribed model of conjugal relations. The medieval Russian church fought long and hard against pagan ways of using magic "to entice a spouse" and arouse feelings that were hardly platonic. Magical ways of winning the love of a spouse included, for example, preparing a mixture of "love root" from woman's milk, perspiration, and honey.[54]

Having declared all carnal pleasures sinful, the Orthodox clerics still encouraged couples to have many children, pointing out that "it is a great evil if children are not born—a double outrage."[55] There were severe punishments for infanticide, abortion, and contraception in the thirteenth through the fifteenth centuries. The Statute of Iaroslav demanded that those married women who "destroy children" must take the veil as punishment.[56] Church regulations safeguarded a pregnant woman's health, forbidding on penalty of a penance that she do heavy work in the fields, prostrate herself, and so on. [57] "Women idolaters" who taught women how to avoid pregnancies with the aid of herbal potions and how to induce abortions faced severe penalties: "If the child has quickened, it is fifteen years' penance; if it has visible form, seven years; if an embryo, five years."[58] The church's struggle with sorcerers and healers was also an attempt to wipe out the remnants of the cult of the Rozhanitsy (pagan deities associated with fertility, birth, and clan) and the rituals connected with childbirth. Echoes of archaic rituals linked to sorcery are found in apocryphal prayers, such as "When a woman is ill with child" and "When a woman begins to give birth to a child slowly," which describe a feast for the Rozhanitsy of breads, cheese, honey, and kasha.[59]

Female sorcerers in medieval Russian villages not only were midwives; they also preserved and passed on the techniques of popular healing. In the

53. V. L. Ianin, "Kompleks gramot no. 519–521 iz Novgoroda," in *Obshchestvo i gosudarstvo feodal'noi Rossii* (Moscow, 1975), 36–37, no. 521.

54. *Trebnik* (XV v.), RO BAN, Arkh. D-71, f. 164 v.; "Voproshanie Kirika," *RIB*, 6: 60; *Trebnik* (XV v.), OR GPB, Q. p. 1, no. 6/1083, f. 97.

55. *Prolog* (XV v.), TsGADA, F. 381, no. 355, f. 256.

56. "Ustav kniazia Iaroslava Vladimirovicha," 266, art. 4. For a more thorough discussion of infanticide, see Eve Levin, "Infanticide in Pre-Petrine Russia," *Jahrbücher für Geschichte Osteuropas* 34 (1986): 215–24.

57. *Trebnik* (XIV–XV vv.), OR GPB, F. p. 1, no. 582, f. 254 v.; *Materialy dlia istorii drevnerusskoi pokaiannoi distsipliny*, 59.

58. *Trebniki* (XV v.), OR GPB, F. p. 1, no. 1088, f. 360 v.; Q. p. 1, no. 473, f. 119; "Pouchenie dukhovnika ispovedaiushchimsia," *RIB*, 6: 862, art. 28.

59. *Materialy dlia istorii drevnerusskoi pokaiannoi distsipliny*, 46.

twelfth century Kirik of Novgorod complained that "if a child is sick," he or she is brought to the healers and not to "the priest for a prayer."[60] Female healers (*znakharki*) even tried to cure barrenness, but they did so in conformity with the contemporary state of medical knowledge, advising women to eat a child's umbilical cord or the placenta.[61]

Medieval Russians viewed the birth of children as "a blessing," "a joy," and "an honor for the home."[62] Child rearing traditionally belonged within the woman's domain. It was up to the mother to "correct her children's morals" and "watch over her offspring."[63] The church demanded that women teach their children obedience, patience, and respect for the elders in the home. "A youngster should be silent in the presence of elders," *Pchela* prescribed.[64] Parents were expected to be reasonable as well as strict with their children and to treat them kindly and affectionately: "Don't lose your temper when you punish your children!"[65] Parents' love for their children is reflected in the affectionate nicknames given them. For example, the *Laurentian Chronicle* records the nickname Izmaragd, or Emerald, for Efrosin'ia.[66] Children who were "insubordinate" to their mother were condemned; churchmen promised that children who "sinned by hard-heartedness" toward her would be damned.[67] "Did you curse your mother, or strike her, or abuse her?" and "Did you annoy your mother?" were listed among questions priests asked during confession. The church had a variety of penalties, from prostrations and fasts to monetary fines, for misdemeanors of that type.[68] Nevertheless, conflicts between a mother and her children occurred frequently in medieval Russian families. In the fifteenth century a Novgorodian woman complained to a court official, "Greetings from Fevroniia to Felix with a complaint. My stepson beat me and drove me out of the house." Apparently the stepson had to answer for his actions before both civil and ecclesiastical courts. The civil court demanded compensation for the physical injury the woman had suffered, while the ecclesiastical court imposed a penance "in this lifetime and in the next until he comes to his senses."[69]

60. "Voproshanie Kirika," 60, arts. 16–18.

61. *Trebnik* (XV v.), OR GPB, Q. p. 2, no.6/1083, f. 97 v.; Sof. 875, f. 133. Magical properties had been ascribed to the placenta since ancient times.

62. *Pchela* (XV v.), OR GPB, F. p. 1, no. 44, f. 188 v.; TsGADA, F. 181, no. 658/1170, f. 223.

63. *Pchela* (XV v.), OR GPB, F. p. 1, no. 44, f. 71v.

64. S. A. Shcheglova, *"Pchela" po rukopisiam kievskikh bibliotek* (St. Petersburg, 1910), 67, art. 7.

65. *Pamiatniki drevnerusskoi tserkovno-uchitelnoi literatury*, pt. 4, 125.

66. *PSRL*, 2: 152 (under the year 6706).

67. *Pamiatniki drevnerusskoi tserkovno-uchitel'noi literatury*, pt. 4, 126, no. 64.

68. *Materialy dlia istorii drevnerusskoi pokaiannoi distsipliny*, 141; *Sbornaia rukopis'* (XV v.), OR GPB, Q. p. 1, no. 6/1083, ff. 98v–99.

69. *Dopolneniia k aktam istoricheskim, sobrannym i izdannym Arkheograficheskoi komissiei*, vol. 1 (St. Petersburg, 1846), 10 (from 1455).

A widowed mother had the right to head her family even if she had adult sons. In their wills princes charged their children "to honor and obey their mother . . . in their father's place."[70] Church teachings demanded that children "not reproach their mother," even if in her old age she "becomes senile."[71]

The law also obliged spouses to care for and support one another. "An evil ailment, blindness, or a long illness" under no circumstances gave a spouse the right to abandon or divorce his or her lifelong companion. Yet several grounds for divorce did exist in Rus' during the period under discussion. Adultery was the main one, and the only one officially recognized. However, it was defined differently for husband and wife. Keeping a concubine was not enough for a husband to be considered an adulterer; he had to have children by her as well. Bigamous marriages and concubinage are vividly described in manuscripts and birchbark documents.[72] One of the latter contains a wife's complaint that her husband, having beaten her, "expelled" her and "married another."[73] It was especially common for such bigamous unions to involve a second wife of much lower social status, usually a slave.[74] The social standing of its parishioners complicated the church's struggle against polygamy and concubinage because polygamists almost always belonged to the ruling class.

The law treated married women more strictly than their husbands. Women who entered into a relationship with another man were considered adulteresses. A husband who learned of his wife's infidelity was supposed to divorce her; to forgive and not punish her ("do as she wished") were themselves punishable acts.[75] For a long time a woman did not have the right to seek divorce on the grounds of her husband's infidelity; a priest simply fined her unfaithful husband. Only in the middle of the fifteenth century did a wife gain the right to divorce her husband for adultery.[76]

Until the fourteenth century only the husband could obtain a divorce on grounds other than adultery. A man could divorce his wife if she attempted to murder him, if she ate, drank, or slept away from home, if she visited public

70. *PSRL*, 4: 107; *Dukhovnye i dogovornye gramoty velikikh i udel'nykh kniazei XIV–XVI vv.* (Moscow-Leningrad, 1950), nos. 12, 17, 20, 21, 22, 61, 71.

71. OR GPB, F. pt. 1, no. 44, f. 72 v.; *Pamiatniki drevnerusskoi tserkovno-uchitel'noi literatury*, pt. 4, 127, no. 64.

72. *PSRL*, 1: 29 (under the year 6478), 2: 563–64 (under the year 6488).

73. A. V. Artsikhovskii, *Iz raskopok 1952 g.* (Moscow, 1954), 41, no. 9 (eleventh century).

74. "Voproshanie Kirika," 41–42; *Materialy dlia istorii drevnerusskoi pokaiannoi distsipliny*, 5, 68.

75. "Knigi zakonnye, imi zhe goditsia vsiakoe delo ispravliati (XIIIv.)," in *Vestnik Imperatorskago obshchestva russkago iazyka i slovesnosti* 38, otdeleniia 3 (St. Petersburg, 1858), pt. 2, "Zakon o kaznekh," 73, art. 49.

76. Ibid., 83, art . 16; "Zapis' 'o razluchenii' XV v.," in Ia. N. Shchapov, "Novyi pamiatnik russkogo prava XV v.," in *Slaviane i Rus'* (Moscow, 1968), 207.

entertainments, or if she tried to steal his property.[77] In the fourteenth and fifteenth centuries these acts became punishable only by fine.[78] Both spouses had a right to divorce for material and physiological reasons, such as impotence and barrenness.[79] There were also grounds for divorce that pertained exclusively to the wife. She could petition for divorce if her husband had hidden his identity as a bondsman or indentured himself without her knowledge, if he unjustly accused her of committing an "evil deed" (including "a husband's casting aspersions on his wife's chastity"), if he forced her to have intercourse with him, and in other circumstances.[80]

Aside from divorce with the knowledge of a priest, unauthorized separation also existed in Rus' at least until the fifteenth century. Both men and women practiced it. The Statute of Iaroslav defended "old" or legal wives by opposing separations and demanding that men's infidelity be punished.[81] In the thirteenth and fourteenth centuries the clergy fought against a woman's leaving her husband.[82] The bishop of Novgorod, Feodosii, ordered the priests of Ustiug-Zhelezopolsk not to marry those divorced women who "lawlessly and rebelliously join with other men, stirring up trouble."[83] The punishments described in ecclesiastical documents for separations without the church's knowledge demonstrate again that the clergy paid attention to the moral aspect of marital relations. If a husband voluntarily left his wife, he had to pay not only a fine to the church but also a compensatory sum to his spouse "for dishonor." The amount of the fine depended on the couple's status and material circumstances.[84] Even if both spouses agreed to a separation, a monetary fine was levied on the husband.[85]

Both the clergy and society viewed incompatibility, personal hostility, and other moral or psychological reasons as insufficient grounds for divorce. From the thirteenth through the fifteenth centuries the tendency to limit the grounds for divorce grew stronger. For example, at the end of the fifteenth century Metropolitan Daniil demanded that the law permit only one ground

77. Despite those prohibitions—against talking, eating, and drinking with "strangers"—women apparently often acted contrary to church sermons. "I'm hung over," complained a scribe of a fourteenth-century *prolog*. "I ought to go to the market, but I have no money. And my wife went visiting." TsGADA, F. 381, no. 174, ff. 31–34; "Ustav kniazia Iaroslava Vladimirovicha," 271, art. 53.

78. "Knigi zakonnye," 58, art. 26.

79. "Voproshanie Kirika," 48; "Ustav kniazia Iaroslava Vladimirovicha," 271.

80. "O razluchenii," 207; "Knigi zakonnye," 82; *Materialy dlia istorii drevnerusskoi pokaiannoi distsipliny*, 9.

81. "Ustav kniazia Iaroslava Vladimirovicha," 267, art. 8.

82. *Materialy dlia istorii drevnerusskoi pokaiannoi distsipliny*, 92; *Akty istoricheskie, sobrannye i izdannye Arkheograficheskoi komissiei*, vol. 1 (St. Petersburg, 1846), no. 109 (from 1499).

83. *Akty istoricheskie*, 545, no. 298.

84. "Ustav kniazia Iaroslava Vladimirovicha," 266, art. 3.

85. Ibid., 268, art. 16.

for divorce: "It does not befit a husband to divorce his wife except for reason of fornication."[86] On the whole the law was more lenient toward men and emphasized a woman's responsibility for maintaining a marriage.

Several conclusions about the rights of medieval Russian women in forging and dissolving marital unions and their place and role in marriage can be drawn from narrative literature, canonical materials, and historical-ethnographic sources. The traditional ritual of cementing family ties was transformed over several centuries into the prenuptial and wedding rites typical of a church wedding. Having legalized marriage, the church became a kind of regulator of matrimonial affairs. Accordingly, it drew up laws establishing specific punishments for parents who forced their daughters into irregular marriages, for the moral offense caused by a suitor's breaking off an engagement, and for failure to observe other conditions when contracting a marriage. At the same time elements of pre-Christian traditions emphasizing the important role of women in the family continued to exist and develop in the prenuptial and wedding rituals. The retention of those family traditions in which women had control over the domestic budget, organized the domestic economy, and had charge of the children hindered the affirmation of an ethic of submissiveness, "social control" of women, and their subordination to the will of their husbands as heads of the family. The right of women to divorce, despite numerous legal limitations, reflected the relatively high familial and social status of medieval Russian women.

86. "Poslanie mitropolita Fotiia XV v.," 523.

Childbirth in Pre-Petrine Russia:
Canon Law and Popular Traditions

Eve Levin

Childbirth was a critical event in the life of a woman, her family, and the community in medieval Russia.[1] The woman took on a new role, that of mother. In practical terms a child would assure a woman economic support and care in her old age. Furthermore, in a system of exogamy and arranged marriages women usually formed their closest emotional bonds with their children. The family secured its continuity into the next generation: the child would eventually assume the parents' place and responsibilities. A child represented an opportunity to extend the web of mutual support and obligation that underlay Kievan and Muscovite political structures. The community was enriched by a new member. Accompanying these benefits were risks of childbirth: the woman underwent a physical ordeal, and the newborn infant was completely dependent on others for its survival.

The significance of childbirth to the mother, the family, and the community crossed socioeconomic lines. Consequently, most of the practices associated with childbirth were common to all social classes. The major sources for the study of childbirth—parish service books, penitential literature, and codes of canon law—reveal consistency throughout the pre-Petrine period.

The author would like to acknowledge the assistance of the International Research and Exchanges Board (IREX) and the Fulbright-Hays Commission for providing research opportunities in the Soviet Union; the Summer Research Laboratory at the University of Illinois; and the Hilandar Research Library at Ohio State University.

1. The historiography of childbirth in medieval Russia is extremely sparse. B. A. Romanov in *Liudi i nravy drevnei Rusi* (Leningrad, 1966) and S. I. Smirnov in *Drevnerusskii dukhovnik* (Moscow, 1913) each devoted two pages to this question, drawing exclusively on three texts of episcopal questions (Nifont, Il'ia, and Ioann). For comparison with the West in the early modern period, see Jacques Gélis, *L'Arbre et le Fruit: La naissance dans l'Occident moderne (XVIe–XIXe siècle)* (Fayard, 1984).

Church teachings did not change. Ecclesiastical authorities remained unable to stamp out noncanonical practices; indeed, parish priests often participated in them. There was no improvement in medical knowledge or technology. The changes in women's status in the sixteenth and seventeenth centuries— most notably the seclusion of elite women in the *terem*—only reinforced their autonomy at the time of childbirth.

Given the importance of childbirth in medieval Russian society, it is not surprising that it was viewed as an occasion of spiritual significance. In childbirth the cosmic issues of life and death were played out. The vulnerability of the woman and child at the time of birth—and the consequent uncertainty in the fate of the family—promoted a sense of need for supernatural intervention. In an age when the scientific mind-set had not yet emerged, efforts to ensure the physical well-being of the mother and child—what we moderns call medicine—were indistinguishable from rituals to protect them from evil—what we call religion.

Dvoeverie (dual-faith), the combination of pagan and Christian practices, describes childbirth rituals of pre-Petrine Russia well. Christianity had no traditional rituals to surround the birth itself because membership in the community of believers was based on faith and confirmed by baptism rather than by birthright (as in the case of Judaism). Infant baptism partially filled this gap, even in the early church, but it traditionally took place some time after the birth and was theologically unconnected to it. The only other Christian ritual for childbirth was the purification of the mother after the birth— a rite based on ancient Semitic ideas of ritual impurity.

Thus most of the rituals surrounding childbirth came from pagan practices, either from the ancient Mediterranean or from the Slavs and other indigenous peoples of Eastern Europe. Although the limited sources do not permit a full reconstruction of pre-Christian Russian birthing practices, herbal potions, amulets, bathhouses, and cradles clearly emerged from pagan antecedents. However, the pagan rituals were reinterpreted in the light of Christian teachings, their original meanings submerged and obscured. The resultant rules and customs represent a fusion of Christian and pagan ideas. The church tended to accept popular practices, calling them Christian and incorporating them into ecclesiastical texts.

The survival of so many traditional rituals, albeit in Christianized form, might best be explained by the fact that childbirth was an exclusively female event. No men—not even the father—attended the birth. Except in the case of the imminent death of the woman or the child, even the priest kept his distance until well after the event. Thus the rituals surrounding childbirth reflect women's spirituality more than any other event in the life cycle. Women's control over childbirth should not suggest that they maintained an underground paganism as a form of resistance to the patriarchal order of church and society. On the contrary, women were convinced that they were

good Christians by virtue of their own baptism and adherence to the Orthodox faith. However, they would generally have an incomplete and inaccurate
understanding of the fine points of Christian theology and law, owing in part
to the tendency of the church to direct its religious instruction to men more
than to women. Far from being aware that they were preserving pagan
rituals, medieval Russian women thought that they were carrying out the
procedures required by the Orthodox church.

Russian Orthodox theology took an ambivalent view of childbirth. On the
one hand, the birth of children accorded with the divine commandment to be
fruitful and multiply (Gen. 1:28). On the other hand, conception resulted
from sexual activity, which was satanic in origin. There was no easy solution
to the logical dilemma. The Bogomil heretics in the Balkans resolved the
difficulty by declaring procreation to be evil and children to be demons in
human disguise. Orthodox clerics refused to accept this solution, asserting
that childbirth was indeed righteous, for "God did not condemn childbirth,
but fornication."[2] However, they stopped short of endorsing sexual intercourse even for married couples. The ideal marriage was never consum-
mated. Not even procreative intent sufficed to justify sexual relations between spouses; only the birth of a good and viable child could make the
sexual activity involved in conception licit. In short, the birth of a child was
deemed good, but the sexual intercourse essential to conception was bad.
Slavic Orthodox clerics preferred to maintain that the two were unrelated: a
woman conceived not through sexual activity but through God's will.[3]

The church also held an ambivalent view of the process of birth itself. The
most prominent ecclesiastical model for childbirth was that of Jesus Christ to
the Virgin Mary.[4] Mary never experienced sex, so the birth of her son could
be lauded with unadulterated approval. Indeed, in medieval prayers Mary
earns praise precisely because of miraculous fertility—that she managed to
bear a child without undergoing the defilement of sex. The birth of Jesus
was also remarkable because it was reputed to be clean and painless. Pain in
childbirth was a consequence of the Fall; it was the woman's equivalent of

2. Cf. M. G. Popruzhenko, "Sinodik tsaria Borila," *Bulgarski starini*, vol. 8 (Sofia, 1928),
45–46 art. 46, N. M. Petrovskii, "Pis'mo patriarkha Konstantinopol'skago Feofilakta tsariu
Bolgarii Petru," *Izvestiia otdeleniia russkago iazyka i slovesnosti imperatorskoi Akademii nauk* 18, no. 3
(1913): 370. See also Dimitur Angelov, *Bogomili* (N. p., 1961), 32–35. Historians who admire the
Bogomils often deny the existence of this tenet; e.g., "This statement cannot be true, because the
Bogomils called themselves Christians and strictly followed the law of Jeesus [sic]." Victor N.
Sharenoff, "A Study of Manichaeism in Bulgaria with Special Reference to the Bogomils"
(Ph.D. diss., Columbia University, 1927), 50.

3. On attitudes toward sexuality and the miraculous birth motif in Slavic ecclesiastical
literature, see Eve Levin, *Sex and Society in the World of the Orthodox Slavs, 900–1700* (Ithaca, 1989),
63–66.

4. Little research has been done on the Mary cult in Russia. See D. T. Strotmann, "Quelques aperçus historiques sur le culte marial en Russie," *Irénikon* 32 (1959): 178–202.

the man's need to work in order to eat. Mary was not subject to original sin and therefore did not suffer pain in labor. Furthermore, the Russians subscribed to the widespread medieval belief that Jesus was born not through Mary's vagina but through her ear. This peculiar idea actually makes sense given Christian theology. It explains how Mary's virginity could remain intact despite the birth of the child. In addition, because Jesus was the Word of God, like sound he became known through the ear.[5]

Of course, this model of childbirth represented an ideal unattainable for mortal women. Still, medieval Russian women found the symbol of the virgin birth to be an attractive one. Reverence for the Virgin subsumed many of the aspects of the pagan cult of the Moist Mother Earth, as in this seventeenth-century proverb:

> The first mother is the Most Holy Mother of God,
>
> The second mother is the Moist Earth,
>
> The third mother is the one who has the sorrow of childbirth.[6]

The Virgin was also associated with the Russian deities Rod and his multiplicity of Rozhanitsy, the protectors of the lineage and guarantors of the harvest. Mary and Rod are similar in that both celebrate miraculous fertility. Thus women celebrated the festivals of the church in honor of Mary, in particular the Nativity of the Virgin on September 8, by preparing a "second feast" of bread, honey, cheese, and kasha for Rod and the Rozhanitsy.[7] They brought the same foods to a new mother shortly after the birth.[8]

Christianity reinforced and justified the belief, common to many primitive societies, that menstrual and postpartum blood flow made women ritually impure. There was ample scriptural precedent, and both Eastern Orthodox and Roman Catholic law incorporated it into their canons. However, the Slavic Orthodox and the Roman Catholic treatment of this issue sharply diverged. To most Catholic churchmen ritual impurity from the blood flow

5. See the references to the Fall and its consequences in the prayers for the purification of the new mother and the building on the eighth day, Potrebnik mirskoi, Kiev 136, ff. 98–98v; Potrebnik, Kiev 191, f. 88. The Kiev collection of microfilms of early Russian printed books is in the Hilandar Research Library at Ohio State University.

6. Strotmann, "Quelques aperçus historiques," 185.

7. "Voprosy Kirika," art. 33, in V. N. Beneshevich, *Pamiatniki drevnerusskago kanonicheskago prava*, Russkaia istoricheskaia biblioteka (henceforth RIB), vol. 6 (St. Petersburg, 1908); B. A. Rybakov, *Iazychestvo drevnykh slavian* (Moscow, 1981), 468–69; Rybakov, *Iazychestvo drevnei Rusi* (Moscow, 1987), 234–36, 245–47; N. M. Gal'kovskii, *Bor'ba khristianstva s ostatkami iazychestva v drevnei Rusi*, vol. 2, Zapiski Moskovskogo arkheologicheskogo instituta, vol. 18 (Moscow, 1913), 43, 86–89, 93–94, 296–97. Rybakov attempts to distinguish between observances to Rod and those to the Rozhanitsy. Although his argument of separate origins for these deities is convincing, Russian paganism almost always paired them.

8. N. K. Gavriliuk, *Kartografirovanie iavlenii dukhovnoi kul'tury (po materialam rodil'noi obriadnosti ukraintsev)* (Kiev, 1981), 77–81, 86.

was an extremely minor concern; attention was focused instead on a prohibition on sex during pregnancy.[9] Russian canons included no restriction whatsoever on conjugal relations during pregnancy but discouraged sex while the wife experienced vaginal bleeding.

Russian conceptions about the impurity of childbirth went far beyond Judeo-Christian prohibitions on the new mother entering the sanctuary or sleeping with her husband. The dominant tradition of Orthodox canon law decreed a forty-day period of sexual abstinence after childbirth, which happens to coincide with modern gynecological advice. Unlike in biblical and early Western law, there was no differentiation in the period of abstinence based on the sex of the child.[10] A few Russian hierarchs were more lenient on postpartum sex, if not entry into the church. One provision read "If any woman gives birth to a baby, her husband shall not join with her for forty days. If they are impatient, then twenty days; if they are very impatient, then twelve days."[11] Bishop Nifont of Novgorod in the twelfth century required only eight days; anything more was optional.[12] Only priests and their wives were actually required to observe the full forty days of abstinence. Couples who violated the shortest term of required abstinence were placed under penance, but the punishment was slight—six days of exclusion from the church and communion.[13] This treatment of postpartum sex suggests that the Russian perception of impurity related to birth was not based solely on Orthodox teachings or the primitive fear of female bleeding. A comparison with rules concerning sexual intercourse during menstruation is enlightening. Canon law forbade husband and wife to sleep together while she was menstruating, and the penalties for violation were stringent, because menstruation marked the woman's failure to conceive, indicating that God had deemed her unworthy to conceive a child. The birth of a child, by contrast, indicated the woman's worthiness; she did not have sex in vain. Therefore it was not a major offense for her and her husband to have conjugal relations before the designated period of purification had passed.[14]

Whereas Russians moderated Orthodox canons concerning sexual relations after birth, they expanded prohibitions on other sorts of contact with

9. For the biblical precept, see Leviticus 12:1–8. See also James A. Brundage, *Law, Sex, and Christian Society in Medieval Europe* (Chicago, 1987), 53, 91–92, 156–57, 199, 242, 283, 452–53, 508.

10. "Voprosy Savy," art. 23, RIB, 6: 57; "Voprosy Kirika," art. 42, RIB, 6: 33; Potrebnik, Kiev 191, f. 163.

11. Smirnov, *Materialy*, 59, 61, 64. Smirnov points out that similar provisions are common to other codes as well, 341–42.

12. "Voprosy Savy," art. 24, RIB, 6: 57. See Smirnov, *Materialy*, 7–8, for another version of this ruling.

13. "Izlozhenie pravilom apostol'skim i otecheskim," in Smirnov, *Materialy*, art. 51, 59.

14. For a discussion of prohibitions on marital sexual relations during menstruation, see Levin, *Sex and Society*, 169–72.

the new mother. They believed that childbirth defiled the woman, the child, the attendants, and the building in which it took place. All had to be purified before they could be returned to mundane use. Medieval Russian ecclesiastical texts included a series of elaborate rituals for this purpose. Orthodox canon law, copied into Russian manuscripts without any amelioration, forbade the new mother to enter the church and participate in ecclesiastical rites such as kissing the Gospels or receiving communion until the fortieth day. This prohibition was not lifted even for Easter, when persons under severe penance were permitted communion.[15] However, women who had recently given birth were also excused from the usual Lenten fasts.[16] In essence canon law placed them in the category of excommunicants. A woman criminal under a sentence of death could not be executed until forty days after giving birth, so that she could confess her sins and receive communion before she died. To preserve the life of the child, who was innocent of its mother's offense, the state paid for a wet nurse for a year.[17]

Russian canons introduced an additional prohibition: no one was permitted to eat in the woman's company until her purification.[18] This rule created a particular problem for the newborn child, who in theory could not nurse from his or her mother. There were a number of solutions to this problem. One was to delay the baptism of the child until the fortieth day—an infant not yet admitted to the Christian community could not be defiled by association with its impure mother.[19] The concern for protecting Christians from a woman's postpartum impurity was so great as to raise questions about what to do if the infant's frailty prompted an early baptism. Metropolitan Ioann in the eleventh century had to rule specifically that an infant be allowed to nurse, even from an impure mother, to preserve life.[20]

There was a second alternative for the problem of feeding the newborn—

15. "Pravilo o veruiushchikh v gady," in S. I. Smirnov, *Materialy dlia istorii drevnerusskoi pokaiannoi distsipliny*, Chteniia obshchestva istorii i drevnostei rossiiskikh pri Moskovskom universitete, 1912, bk. 3, 148, art. 46; Sbornik, Hil. 302, f. 20, Hilandar Research Library.

16. Kormchaia Efremovskaia, Gosudarstvennyi istoricheskii muzei, Moscow, Sinodal'noe sobranie, 227, f. 211; Potrebnik, Kiev 191, f. 686v.

17. *Zakonodatel'nye akty russkogo gosudarstva vtoroi poloviny XVI–pervoi poloviny XVII veka* (Leningrad, 1986), 179, no. 244 (dated 1637). The law also forbade the execution of a pregnant woman.

18. "Zapoved' ko ispovedaiushchimsia synom i dshcheram," in Smirnov, *Materialy*, 119, art. 62. Compare with the Serbian custom, reported in this century, prohibiting women from cooking for others for forty days after childbirth. See M. E. Durham, *Some Tribal Origins, Laws and Customs of the Balkans* (London, 1928), 188.

19. "Pouchenie arkhiepiskopa Ilii," art. 13, RIB, 6, appendix, 361. Gavriliuk reports the survival of this custom in the Ukraine in the nineteenth and twentieth centuries, but then the concern was with allowing an unbaptized child to nurse from a woman who was already susceptible to evil because of her impurity. Ibid., 82.

20. "Kanonicheskie otvety Ioanna II," art. 1–2, RIB, 6: 1–3.

finding a *baba*. The word *baba* in medieval Russian texts on childbirth had three meanings. First, it was a derogatory term for an old woman who engaged in witchcraft.[21] However, *baba* could also mean wet nurse. By passing the newborn to another woman to feed, the problem of the mother's impurity could be overcome. The church regarded wet nurses favorably, comparing them to their biblical forebears. Blessings lauded them for "receiving this infant in Thy name."[22] It appears to have been rare for a new mother to have permanently turned over nursing of an infant to another woman except when she had no milk. Otherwise the mother would take up feeding the child herself as soon as she had undergone initial purification. When a wet nurse took on the responsibility of feeding an infant, she also acquired a special role in the rituals surrounding birth. If the mother was not able to present the child for naming or baptism, the *baba* would take on this role.[23] Furthermore, whoever nursed the infant, either its mother or the wet nurse, would undertake the prebaptismal fasts on behalf of the child. This involved abstinence from meat and milk for eight days—obviously impossible for the infant.[24]

A third meaning of *baba* was midwife. In the medieval context this *baba* would be an older woman who would assist women giving birth. Medieval midwives had no formal training, although they had practical experience and knowledge of folk medicine.[25] By attending the delivery, the *baba* contracted the new mother's impurity. Consequently, she also had to be purified, usually on the eighth day following the birth. Until then she also was banned from the church.[26] The three definitions of the word *baba* indicate that the three roles were not entirely distinct. A midwife who was able might also nurse the newborn baby. Certainly the midwife would have experience with spells and potions, which made her an easy target for ecclesiastical complaints about her "evil" influence.

Persons who attended the birth, even if they did not assist in any way,

21. See, for example, the warnings about evil *baby* by Metropolitan Fotii, "Poslanie v Novgorod," RIB, 6: 274; and "Gramota v Pskov," RIB, 6: 283; *Domostroi* (Letchworth, Eng., 1971), 73–74, chap. 26.

22. Potrebnik mirskoi, Kiev 136, f. 100; cf. Potrebnik, Kiev 191, ff. 89–89v, 93v; Trebnik, Kiev 49, f. 2v.

23. Potrebnik, Kiev 191, f. 113.

24. "Voprosy Kirika," art. 60, RIB, 6: 39; "Pouchenie arkhiepiskopa Ilii," art. 11, RIB, 6, appendix, 360; "Zapoved' ko ispovedaiushchimsia synom i dshcheram," in Smirnov, *Materialy*, 118, art. 46.

25. For a brief consideration of traditional midwifery and its modernization, see Samuel C. Ramer, "Childbirth and Culture: Midwifery in the Nineteenth-Century Russian Countryside," in *The Family in Imperial Russia: New Lines of Historical Research*, ed. David L. Ransel (Urbana, Ill., 1978), 218–35. Ramer alludes to the religious rituals fulfilled by the traditional midwife.

26. "Voprosy Ilii," art. 26, RIB, 6: 62; "Poslanie mitropolita Fotii pskovskomu dukhovenstvu," RIB, 6: 416. Compare this rule with the corrupted version in Smirnov, *Materialy*, 10, which mistakenly declares midwifery to be a sin deserving of fifteen years' penance.

became impure as a result. According to one version of the law a woman who merely came to watch the birth was excluded from the church for twelve, fifteen, or even twenty days. "If a woman is not called for some sort of service," the text read, "she should not go." A reduction of the exclusion for midwives to eight days, according to this text, was a dispensation in recognition of their "necessary service."[27] In this way canon law discouraged spectators to a woman's labor.

The place where the birth occurred also shared the impurity. Under canon law no one was to enter the building until after it had been cleaned and blessed. A person who did so became defiled and was subsequently banned from the church for three days.[28] Even the priest who came to perform this ritual recited the prayers for purification at the door before entering to cleanse the house and sprinkle holy water.[29] There were special prayers to repurify a church if a woman or animal gave birth inside.[30] The purification ritual could be performed on the first day after birth or later, on the third or even the eighth day.

The usual location chosen for the delivery, at least in northern Russia, was the bathhouse. Archbishop Il'ia of Novgorod in the twelfth century formulated specific instructions on how to purify it, citing the precedent of Bishop Nifont.[31] There were practical reasons behind this choice. The bathhouse was warm, clean, and private. It could be placed off limits for the delivery and cleansing without disrupting village routines. Furthermore, the bathhouse had a religious significance in Finno-Ugric paganism. It served as a center for gathering, worship, religious dance, and personal repurification.[32] The custom of giving birth in a bathhouse was ingrained to the point that women in the seventeenth century who gave birth out of wedlock and killed the newborn still went to the bathhouse for the delivery.[33]

Rituals to protect the health of the new mother and child were part of repurification. In the popular conception both were particularly vulnerable

27. Sbornik, Hil. 302, ff. 20–20v; Trebnik, Kiev 49, f. 667v.

28. "Voprosy Kirika," art. 46, RIB, 6: 34. See also the version in Smirnov, *Materialy*, 8.

29. Potrebnik mirskoi, Kiev 136, ff. 97–97v; Potrebnik, Kiev 191, ff. 87–87v.

30. "Voprosy Kirika," art. 46, RIB, 6: 34; Potrebnik mirskoi, Kiev 136, f. 57; Potrebnik, Kiev 191, ff. 49–49v.

31. "Poucheniia arkhiepiskopa Ilii," art. 10, RIB, 6, appendix, 358–60. A version of Bishop Nifont's advice is contained in the "Voprosy Kirika," art. 46, RIB, 6: 34.

32. Otto J. Sadovszky remarked on the similar purposes of bathhouses in Finno-Ugric and North American Indian cultures and the linguistically related terminology surrounding them in his unpublished paper "The New Genetic Relationship and the Paleolinguistics of the Central California Indian Ceremonial Houses." I am grateful to Professor Sadovszky for providing me with a copy of his paper.

33. *Akty kholmogorskoi i ustiuzhskoi eparkhii*, RIB, vol. 12, (St. Petersburg, 1890), 626–30, no. 149. See Eve Levin, "Infanticide in Pre-Petrine Russia," *Jahrbücher für Geschichte Osteuropas* 34 (1986): 215–24, for a discussion of infanticide in general and this incident in particular.

at the time of birth—the child because it was not yet baptized and the
woman because she was impure and outside the community.[34] The spirit of
evil, Nezhit (literally Not Alive), could attack mother and infant.[35] This
belief reflected reality; childbirth was in truth a period of danger to mother
and child.

Among the prayers recited over the new mother, the infant, and the
household were invocations of divine protection. Initial rituals of purification, sometimes on the third day after birth, were one occasion.[36] Jesus
Christ was asked to recall his own birth and have mercy on the new life:

> Lord Jesus Christ, Word of God the Father, Only Begotten Son, who, for our
> salvation . . . came down in the end into the womb of the Holy Virgin. . . .
> With good will and great mercy, Most Holy Lord Jesus Christ, protect from all
> threats of the enemy this your handmaiden N., who has now given birth. By
> your generosity and holiness cleanse and sanctify her with the gift of the coming
> of your Holy Spirit . . . together with all assisting women N. N. who are here in
> this house. . . . Grant also that this newborn N. be preserved from the threats
> of the enemy.[37]

Another prayer, a noncanonical one especially for the protection of the newborn, invoked God, St. John, St. Joseph, the martyr Fedor, and the Virgin to
prevent the devil from entering the house.[38] For the woman survival of her
child had a particular spiritual importance. The production of a child ex-
onerated her from sin in the sexual intercourse that conceived it. If the child
died, it was evidence of her unworthiness. Thus in the Serbian tradition the
woman prayed that God preserve the infant, so that she would not "be like
a dissolute prostitute," that is, a woman who engaged in sex merely for
pleasure.[39]

In addition to prayers of purification, the *baba* used cleansing herbs.
Creeping thyme was especially recommended for postpartum pain and failure to expel the placenta. Iris, mashed with honey and rubbed over the
genitals, was supposed to end postpartum bleeding. Potions of rose and goat-

34. Antonia Martynova, "Life of the Pre-Revolutionary Village as Reflected in Popular Lul-
labies," in Ransel, *Family in Imperial Russia*, 179.

35. A. Almazov, "K istorii molitv na raznye sluchai," *Letopis' istoriko-filologicheskago obshchestva
pri imperatorskom Novorossiiskom Universitete*, vol. 6 (Odessa, 1896), 380–432, esp. 388; I. Ia. Porfir'ev, "Apokrificheskiia molitvy po rukopisiam Solovetskoi biblioteki," *Trudy chetvertago arkheolo-
gicheskago s"ezda v Rossii, byvshago v Kazani s 31 iiulia po 18 avgusta 1877 goda*, vol. 2, pt. 2, 1–24, esp.
4–5. See a spell against Nezhit mentioning birth in Vladimir Kachanovskii, "Apokrifne molitve,
gatanja i priče," *Starine*, vol. 13 (Zagreb, 1881), 153. Gavriliuk, *Kartografirovanie*, 89–90, reports a
similar concern with evil spirits in the later Ukraine.

36. Trebnik, Kiev 49, ff. 2v–4v.

37. Potrebnik mirskoi, Kiev 136, ff. 99–99v; similarly, Potrebnik, Kiev 191, f. 88v.

38. A. I. Almazov, *Vracheval'nyia molitvy* (Odessa, 1900), 127.

39. Trebnik, Hil. 172, ff. 124–124v.

weed boiled with wine or honey could be drunk for cleansing the uterus. Dust from ebony wood, sprinkled on the genitals, was also considered an agent for purification.[40] Orthodox churchmen were always suspicious of herbal medicine because of its connection to paganism. However, there seem to have been no specific condemnations of the use of herbs in purification after childbirth, perhaps because the clerics themselves deemed it important.

Other rituals of pagan origin concerned disposal of the afterbirth. The placenta was considered to be a vestige of the child, and as such it could not simply be thrown out. Folk custom prescribed a number of methods. One was to bury it under the house, treating it in the same manner as the bones of ancestors in Slavic paganism. It would then still be present, protecting the newborn against evil spirits. A more Christianized method was to put the placenta in a casket and place it before the icons in the "beautiful corner" of the house. The same was done with the remnants of the umbilical cord when it fell from the infant's navel.[41] In this way the afterbirth was dedicated to God—or, more precisely, to the Virgin Mary, the patronness of fertility. The placenta might also be set on the altar in the church, either by the women or by the priest, despite official prohibitions. It was further believed that the placenta had the power to influence fertility in other women. Conflicting popular traditions taught that a woman who ate the afterbirth would either conceive or be able to prevent conception. The church equally condemned both uses of the placenta because both involved paganism.[42]

Other customs surrounded the caul, or water bag. When infants were born wearing it, custom dictated that it be kept because of its protective powers. The author of the *Primary Chronicle* recounted how Prince Voeslav was born with a caul; his pagan mother declared, "Anyone with a caul fastened on him will wear it all his life." According to the chronicler the

---

40. L. N. Pushkarev and A. A. Novosel'skii, *Redkie istochniki po istorii Rossii*, vol. 1 (Moscow, 1977), 44, 48, 51, 55, 62. I am gateful to Professor Ronald L. Stuckey of the Botany Department at Ohio State University for supplying me with the common English names of medicinal plants.

41. Gavriliuk, *Kartografirovanie*, 69. Similar customs were reported in early modern France. See Gélis, *L'Arbre et le Fruit*, 80, 285.

42. The penance for this offense was six weeks of fasting, the usual penance for pagan activity. See "Ot pravil sviatykh apostol," in Smirnov, *Materialy*, 65, art. 8; also A. Almazov, *Tainaia ispoved' v pravoslavnoi vostochnoi tserkvi* vol. 3, (Odessa, 1894), 159, 167, 168, 277; and Trebnik, Vatican Borgiano-Illirico 15, f. 477. However, Hil. 302, f. 63v, equates consumption of the placenta as a contraceptive with murder. Use of any sort of contraceptive agent violated canon law. See S. Smirnov, "Baby bogomerzskiia," in *Sbornik statei posviashchennykh Vasiliiu Osipovichu Kliuchevskomu* (Moscow, 1909), 232, quoting S. von Herberstein's report of an article in Kirik's Questions forbidding women to seek the advice of a wisewoman on how to conceive. Beliefs in the magical powers of the placenta were widespread. Early Byzantine canons forbade a woman to give the placenta from her body to another woman or accept it herself. See Apostles' Canons, art. 48, in V. N. Beneshevich, *Drevne-slavianskaia kormchaia XIV titulov bez tolkovanii* (St. Petersburg, 1906), 72. In early modern France women also believed that consuming the placenta would guarantee conception. See Gélis, *L'Arbre et le Fruit*, 286–89.

caul made Voeslav particularly bloodthirsty.[43] Another custom was for the
woman to ask her priest to lay the caul on the altar.[44] Or the priest might be
willing to baptize the caul along with the child. Apparently priests often
shared popular beliefs concerning the importance of these rituals, agreeing to
perform them despite the church's strong condemnation. A priest who performed such a ceremony over the caul was to be deposed from his office, and
a lay man or woman was to be banned from the church.[45]

The placing of the infant in the cradle for the first time was a momentous
occasion. It had to be prepared properly to assure the health of the child.[46]
Though this belief was pagan in origin, a service of the blessing of the cradle
found its way into the priestly service books of the seventeenth century,
indicating the Christianization of the custom.[47]

The ceremony of naming the newborn on the eighth day marked its entry
into the community. It could take place at home, as the fifteenth-century
metropolitan Fotii recommended, or at the doors of the church, according
to twelfth-century Novgorodian practices as well as seventeenth-century
rulings.[48] Although the baby was not supposed to be baptized at that time,
the priest blessed it, anointed it with myrrh, made the sign of the cross over
it, sprinkled it with holy water, prayed for its survival and growth, and
announced its name.[49] Full membership in the community came only with
baptism, usually on the fortieth day. There seems to have been a tendency to
combine the naming and the baptismal ceremonies into one, celebrated on
the eighth day, because Archbishop Il'ia of Novgorod condemned this
practice as a "double evil": it transgressed God's law, and the newly
baptized child would then be defiled by nursing from its impure mother.[50]

If all went well, the mother carried her baby to the church on the fortieth
day after its birth and presented it and herself to the Christian community for
acceptance. The woman first received the blessings of purification and then
addressed the icon of the Virgin outside the sanctuary. Then, after handing
the infant to the priest, she performed forty prostrations.[51] The priest carried

43. Novgorod fourth chronicle, *Polnoe sobranie russkikh letopisei*, vol. 4, pt. 1, no. 1 (Petrograd,
1915), 116.
44. *Stoglav* (St. Petersburg, 1863), 128–29, chap. 41, question 2.
45. Potrebnik, Kiev 191, f. 114.
46. For popular rituals involving the cradle, see Martynova, "Life of the Pre-Revolutionary
Village," 180–81.
47. Potrebnik, Kiev 191, ff. 90v–91.
48. "Pouchenie arkhiepiskopa Ilii," art. 10, RIB, 6: 416; "Poslanie metropolita Fotii pskovskomu dukhovenstvu," RIB, 6: 416.
49. For an example of this ritual, see Trebnik, Kiev 49, f. 1; or Trebnik of Peter Mogila, ff.
24–25.
50. "Pouchenie arkhiepiskopa Ilii," art. 13, RIB, 6, appendix, 361.
51. Potrebnik, Kiev 191, ff. 112–112v; Trebnik, Kiev 49, ff. 6v–8; Trebnik, Kiev 127, ff.
17–18. See also "Poslanie mitropolita Fotii pskovskomu dukhovenstvu," RIB, 6: 416. A priest

the baby inside and assisted it in kissing the icons of Christ and the Virgin on either side of the altar, afterward circling the church three times with the baby in his arms. If the baby was a boy, he would then be carried through the gates and around the altar itself. (Entry into the altar was forbidden to women.) The baptismal ceremony would follow.[52]

Complications in childbirth were common in medieval Russia. Insufficient medical knowledge and prenatal care contributed to the risks. Although it is not possible to reconstruct death rates for women in childbirth and among newborns, the presence of instructions to priests on how to alter ceremonies in case of the imminent death of mother and child attest to the frequency of these occurrences.

Potions and spells could be invoked in the case of a difficult labor. Popular traditions and herbal manuals recommended that pregnant women wear an acorn to assure an easy pregnancy, a painless delivery, and a healthy child.[53] Several herbal potions were supposed to be effective in hastening the birth of the baby. The midwife could lay wormwood, called the mother of all herbs, on the woman's navel or boil it with water or wine and give it to her to drink. Willow and figwort, boiled in water or wine, were also recommended for difficult deliveries. A paste of reindeer lichen, spread on the woman's navel, was supposed to make delivery fast and painless. Another cure was purple cockle, boiled with salt and water; it could also be burned, with the smoke directed into the woman's vagina. If the fetus died before birth, bryonia, false hellebore, and fermented goat's milk were thought to be useful in expelling it from the uterus.[54]

The spells reflected popular Russian Christianity; no Greek analogues are known.[55] Their passages were drawn from established Orthodox prayers, but phrases were juxtaposed without regard for the original context. The most popular spell read:

> This our Lord Jesus Christ said to John the Evangelist: "Find the woman who is giving birth with pain in her heart and cannot give birth." And our Lord said to John the Evangelist, "Go, John, and say to her: God was born from the right

---

was not permitted to perform this service for his own wife, although he might be allowed to purify his child. See "Voprosy i otvety pastyrskoi praktiki," art. 56, RIB, 6: 867.

52. Trebnik, Kiev 49, ff. 8v–9v.

53. N. A. Bogoiavlenskii, *Meditsina u pervoselov russkogo severa* (Leningrad, 1966), 143; Pushkarev and Novosel'skii, *Redkie istochniki*, 94.

54. Pushkarev and Novosel'skii, *Redkie istochniki*, 28, 32–33, 45, 55–56, 57, 58–59, 94, 108–9. For the use of smoke in cleansing a woman's vagina, see Bogoiavlenskii, *Meditsina*, 124. In medieval Serbia goat's milk with wine and honey was supposed to prevent the baby from dying inside the womb; see V. Jagić, "Opisi i izvodi iz nekoliko južnoslovinskih rukopisa," in *Starine*, vol. 10 (Zagreb, 1878), 99. Of these herbs the only one likely to be of any use at all was willow, which is a natural source of aspirin.

55. Almazov, *Vracheval'nyia molitvy*, 75–77.

ear. Go out, child of Christ. Christ calls you. Remember the sons of Edom in
the days of Jerusalem, saying flow out, flow out, until the founding of the
world." Now and forever.[56]

Certain authors suggested that the spell be recited into the woman's right
ear.[57] Another author called for the spell to be written down on paper and
then fastened around the woman's head.[58] Other variants have the prayer
written on a snakeskin, which was then made into a wreath and placed on the
woman's head, or written directly on her abdomen.[59]

If the situation became critical, an exception had to be made to the custom of excluding all men from the delivery, and the priest was called. Even
then, belief in the impurity of childbirth kept him out of the building. Instead, canon law directed that the dying woman be bathed and carried into
another house before she could receive communion and last rites.[60] It was
not necessary to wait until she had undergone purification for her to receive
communion in this case.[61] However, because it was considered improper to
give communion to someone impure, priests were advised to inquire whether
someone who had recently given birth had fallen sick. If she had, the priest
was to come to read the normal prayers for purification and then administer
the Eucharist.[62] If the woman died before the child was born, she was considered to be still undefiled, and the usual funeral service could be recited over
her. If she died after giving birth but before purification, her body could not
be brought into the church for the funeral. Instead, the funeral would be held
outside, in the entryway or refectory.[63] If it happened that the woman recovered after receiving emergency communion, she later had to undergo a
penitential fast of six weeks.[64] When the mother died in labor, the midwives were then instructed to try to rescue the unborn baby.[65]

56. Nikolai Tikhonravov, *Pamiatniki otrechennoi russkoi literatury*, vol. 2 (London, 1973), 356;
see a similar version at 355. The reference of John the Evangelist seems to derive from John
1:12–13; the reference to the sons of Edom is from Psalm 137. In context neither has anything to
do with childbirth. For a Serbian version, see V. Jagić, "Opisi i izvodi," 99.

57. Porfir'ev, "Apokrificheskiia molitvy," 22. The text of this spell reads a little differently.
Instead of "Go out, child of Christ. Christ calls you," this version says, "You are born of God
and nourished of God: go out, infant." See also Almazov, *Vracheval'nyia molitvy*, 124–25.

58. Almazov, *Vracheval'nyia molitvy*, 125; Pushkarev and Novosel'skii, *Redkie istochniki*, 101.

59. Almazov, *Vracheval'nyia molitvy*, 77.

60. "Voprosy Savy," art. 2, RIB, 6: 51–52. See also the version in Smirnov, *Materialy*, 8, as
well as similar rulings in the same text, 40, 91, 102.

61. Sbornik, Hil. 302, f. 20.

62. Potrebnik, Kiev 191, f. 92.

63. Potrebnik, Kiev 191, f. 92v. Gélis, *L'Arbre et le Fruit*, 295, discusses noncanonical ceremonies in early modern France to purify the body of a woman who died in childbirth to permit
burial in hallowed ground.

64. "Tri sviatitel'skiia poucheniia," RIB, 6: 920.

65. Trebnik of Peter Mogila, f. 9v.

Because the newborn infant shared its mother's impurity, the first priority in case of its imminent death was to arrange for baptism. Priests were reminded repeatedly not to delay a single day in baptizing a dying newborn; this admonition suggests that they often hesitated for fear of the impurity they might contract through contact, even indirect, with childbirth.[66] Although it was against canon law to perform baptisms outside of the church,[67] it could be done if an infant was about to die. A shortened baptismal service was included in the *trebnik* (parish service book) for such emergencies.[68] If the child was baptized before the mother had received purification, she was not permitted to witness her child's baptism. Instead, after presenting the infant to the priest, she yielded her place to the wet nurse and godparents and was sent home.[69] The baptism could not take place in the building in which the baby was born because it too was defiled.[70] Since the newborn was impure, one manual suggested that the baptism take place in the entryway of the church rather than inside the sanctuary. If the church did not have a baptismal font there, the priest could dig a hole in the earth, fill it with water, and then baptize the child. The hole had to be covered immediately afterward to prevent desecration of holy water.[71] It is tempting to see in this rite the survival of pagan beliefs in the power of Moist Mother Earth. In any case, use of an unorthodox baptismal procedure was deemed preferable to exposing the sanctuary to the impurity associated with childbirth.

Canon law forbade baptizing an infant in its mother's womb even as a precaution against stillbirth. A special set of rules in the *trebnik* of Peter Mogila from the seventeenth-century Ukraine concerned the proper procedure for baptizing a child not yet fully born. Of course, such action was acceptable only when the midwives and the priest expected the infant to be stillborn. If only the head or some other part of the body had emerged, that was sufficient for the baptism to be performed, provided the priest could ascertain that the baby was alive. If the child later fully emerged and died, it could then be buried with a full Orthodox ceremony.[72] An unbaptized or stillborn infant

---

66. "Zapoved' ko ispovedaiushchimsia synom i dshcheram," in Smirnov, *Materialy*, 119, art. 63; "Pravilo o tserkovnom ustroenii," In Smirnov, *Materialy*, 91, 102, art. 23; "Pouchenie Mitropolita Fotiia (1431)," RIB, 6: 517. The penance on the priest for this offense was three years. See "Tri sviatitel'skiia poucheniia," RIB, 6: 920; "Voprosy Savy," art. 3, RIB, 6: 52; Sbornik, Hil. 302, ff. 80v–81.

67. "Voprosy i otvety pastyrskoi praktiki," art. 54, RIB, 6: 867.

68. Kiev 127, ff. 102–104.

69. Potrebnik, Kiev 191, ff. 112v–113.

70. The foreign visitor John Struys noted this custom, although he did not entirely understand its significance. See *The Voyages and Travels of John Struys* (London, 1684), 153.

71. Potrebnik, Kiev 191, f. 92v.

72. Trebnik of Peter Mogila, ff. 9–9v.

could receive only brief prayers and could not be buried with Christians.[73] If the baby lived, a second baptism was prohibited, but the prayers omitted earlier might be included in the ceremony on the fortieth day.[74] Special instructions for multiple births were included in this section because of the likelihood that these children would die. The priest was permitted to recite the prayers for baptism over "two or three or more" children together in the interest of saving time. However, seventeenth-century texts reversed earlier Russian practice, ordering that each child be submerged in the baptismal water singly.[75] Further rules explained the procedure for baptizing Siamese twins and malformed infants.[76]

Rituals and beliefs usually serve a practical as well as a divine purpose. It is possible to speculate on what the customs of childbirth accomplished in medieval Russia. The emphasis on cleansing in purification rituals also must have had a practical value, even if the herbal potions were inefficacious. The belief in impurity, as insulting as it may seem to modern women, served medieval Russian women well. It kept the intervention of outsiders, especially men, to a minimum during the critical hours of delivery. The pregnant woman herself, together with her midwives, made the pertinent decisions without needing to defer to men, either lay or clergy. Recruiting a wet nurse for the period immediately after the delivery would permit the new mother to recover her strength more rapidly. Moreover, a woman who contaminated everything she touched could not be expected to work for her husband and family. As the belief in the impurity of birth declined, the expectations placed on women to return to their daily chores increased. The myth of female impurity worked in women's favor in this case; no wonder they seem to have accepted it easily.

The customs surrounding childbirth in medieval Russia combined pagan and Orthodox beliefs and rituals. Christian ideas about ritual impurity matched well with traditional notions. The church accepted the popular conception that supernatural intervention was necessary to protect the new mother and her child from evil and to shield the community from the dangers of their impurity. The church hierarchy officially endorsed Christianized versions of ceremonies for purification of the mother, dedication of the wet nurse, naming of the child, and blessing of the cradle. Parish priests went even further in their acceptance of popular custom, to the point of carrying

---

73. "Voprosy i otvety pastyrskoi praktiki," art. 35, RIB, 6: 864; Trebnik of Peter Mogila, f. 9v.

74. "Pouchenie arkhiepiskopa Ilii," art. 10, RIB, 6, appendix, 358. The author cited the authority of the Council of Nicaea, which established the doctrine of a single baptism.

75. Potrebnik, Kiev 191, f. 92v. Cf. "Voprosy i otvety pastyrskoi praktiki," art. 54, RIB, 6: 867.

76. Trebnik of Peter Mogila, ff. 10–11. Compare with early modern France, Gélis, L'Arbre et le Fruit, 368–69.

out noncanonical rituals concerning the afterbirth and the caul. Influence went in the other direction too. In popular rituals pagan deities were replaced by Christian venerables, in particular the Virgin Mary. Popular spells to ease delivery consisted of fragments of Orthodox liturgy and Orthodox ceremony. Where the scholar might see widespread evidence of *dvoeverie*, the medieval Russian laity and parish clergy saw only their own true faith, Russian Orthodoxy. The parish priest and the women of the community worked together to assure divine intervention on behalf of the pregnant woman and her child.

Women's Honor in Early Modern Russia

Nancy Shields Kollmann

If anyone dishonors with unseemly word anyone of any rank's wife or maiden daughter or underage son, then upon trial and investigation these wives, maiden daughters, and underage sons are to be compensated for their dishonor. Wives are to be awarded twice their husband's annual service allotment; maiden daughters four times their fathers' service allotment; underage sons half of their father's service allotment.

CONCILIAR LAW CODE OF 1649

What sense can we make of the fact that Muscovite society offered women protections far more generous than those offered men for insults to honor? As the clause from the Conciliar Law Code of 1649 quoted above details, women were compensated two and four times more than their husbands or fathers when insulted. We might conclude that such protections of honor effectively undermined women's secondary status in Muscovy and were therefore good for women. Alternatively, since women's honor was calculated in terms of men's status, we might condemn these protections as no great benefit for women because they perpetuated women's subordination to men. There is some sense in both these interpretations, particularly if we desire to see women enjoying equal status with men. But the awkward contradiction these conclusions pose might be resolved if we set aside modern expectations and examine the high value of women's honor as it fit into the Muscovite system of social values and relationships.

That the Muscovite system was patriarchal is universally recognized. As a rule, men held political power, enjoyed high social status as military servitors and members of elite patrilineal clans, took the lead in trade, controlled village councils, and constituted the Orthodox priesthood and hierarchy. Women, by contrast, were subordinated to their fathers and husbands. Elite women were physically secluded. Women in lesser social groups enjoyed greater physical mobility, but all Muscovite women shared in common un-

I would like to thank Eve Levin for her advice on church legal jurisdiction and for sharing her then-unpublished manuscript (now published as *Sex and Society in the World of the Orthodox Slavs, 900–1700* [Ithaca, 1989]), which gave me useful source citations. I want also to thank Valerie Kivelson for many helpful source references, published and archival. By early modern Russia, or Muscovy, I mean the grand principality and tsardom of Muscovy from the fourteenth through the seventeenth centuries; Novgorod has not been considered here.

prestigious, feminine tasks—childbirth and child rearing, domestic chores, household management, and the like. Women's subordinate role was affirmed in the misogyny preached by the Russian Orthodox church and in society's pervasive ethic of honor and shame. That set of values placed great stock in the patrilineal family's honor and accorded women respect only to the degree that their behavior reflected well on their fathers' or husbands' clans. Expectations of women's behavior were thereby severely constricted, as seen in artistic and literary imagery about women. Tales and hagiography pictured women mainly as pious and nurturing mothers or evil seducers, with a rare crafty and wise woman challenging the stereotypes.[1]

At the same time Muscovite society offered all the tsar's subjects, from the highest boyar to the lowliest slave, protection against insult to honor (*beschest'e*). Only verbal slander was considered an affront to honor, although assault often accompanied dishonor. Muscovites cried foul when their reputations for lawful conduct, loyalty to the tsar, appropriate service in their social rank, Christian piety, or sexual propriety had been insulted. Victims of insult to honor received compensation, generally in cash according to the annual cash allotment (*oklad*) for members of the privileged ecclesiastical, military, or merchant strata or according to a fixed scale for people subject to taxes. For insults to the highest secular or ecclesiastical ranks sanctions might also involve corporal punishment or symbolic disgrace. Litigation was initiated by complaint to the tsar or local judicial officers; trials were conducted in the same manner as other judicial proceedings. Women could initiate suits and act as witnesses, but generally men litigated on behalf of female kin and dependents. Most extant dishonor litigation is fragmentary, but those cases whose resolution is known show that the fines and punishments mandated by law codes were properly applied.[2]

1. On women in pre-Petrine Russia in general, see Ia. Orovich, *Zhenshchina v prave*, 2d ed. (St. Petersburg, 1896); *Entsiklopedicheskii slovar'*, ed. F. A. Brokgaus and I. A. Efron, s.v. "Zhenshchina"; S. S. Shashkov, *Istoriia russkoi zhenshchiny*, in *Sobranie sochinenii*, 2 vols. (St. Petersburg, 1898), 1: 697–894; V. Ikonnikov, "Russkaia zhenshchina nakanune reformy Petra I i posle neia: Sravnitel'no-istoricheskii ocherk," *Universitetskiia izvestiia Kievskago universiteta* 14, nos. 5, 6 (May, June 1874): 235–92, 411–55. On misogyny, see G. P. Fedotov, *The Russian Religious Mind*, vol. 2, *The Middle Ages: The Thirteenth to the Fifteenth Centuries* (Cambridge, Mass., 1966), 71–78; Joan Delaney Grossman, "Feminine Images in Old Russian Literature and Art," *California Slavic Studies* 11 (1980): 33–70; Susanne Janosik McNally, "From Public Person to Private Prisoner: The Changing Place of Women in Medieval Russia" (Ph.D. diss., State University of New York at Binghamton, 1976), chap. 4, 102–41; Nancy Shields Kollmann, "The Seclusion of Elite Muscovite Women," *Russian History* 10 (1983): 170–87. On the ethic of honor and shame in other societies, see note 57 below.

2. Muscovy knew two institutions to protect honor, precedence for the elite (*mestnichestvo*) and dishonor for all social groups (*beschest'e*); here I consider only the latter. For a bibliography on dishonor and an analysis of the full data base (a part of which is used here), see Nancy Shields Kollmann, "Honor and Dishonor in Early Modern Russia," *Forschungen zur osteuropäischen Geschichte*, forthcoming. On symbolic disgrace (*vydacha golovoiu*), see idem, "Ritual and Social Drama at the Muscovite Court," *Slavic Review* 45 (1986): 486–502.

Women's experience of institutions of honor in early modern Russia can be assessed by examining litigation. Of approximately 620 cases, about one-third concern insults to women. Analysis of those cases shows that throughout the period that they cover (late sixteenth to early eighteenth centuries) members of all social groups—from the highest Moscow military servitors and church hierarchs to taxed and enslaved people—took advantage of opportunities to protect their honor. Men sued against myriad allegations: criminal activity, treason, failure to serve or to pay taxes, sexual promiscuity, false accusation, and insults to their social rank, however lowly it might have been. Women, however, sued (or men sued on behalf of women) against a narrower range of complaints: allegations of criminal behavior were less frequent causes of women's litigations than were allegations of sexual impropriety. These cases abound in accusations of adultery, loose morals, premarital sex, and even incest.[3] Unlike for men, for women dishonor could also be certain kinds of physical assault, particularly assault on those appurtenances that protected and symbolized a woman's modesty. Women wore head coverings and braids and dressed in layers of full-length clothing; elite women were shrouded by veils or concealed in closed carriages when out in public. Disrupting a woman's headgear or hair, pulling her braids, or peeking into her closed carriage was considered dishonor even in the absence of verbal abuse.[4] Women's numerous complaints of unspecified verbal insult doubtless conceal some accusations of sexual impropriety.[5]

Among the more than two hundred cases that concern insults to women only about sixty contain resolutions. Some representative cases show that affronts to women's honor were taken seriously and that legal provisions for higher compensation to women were put into practice. In 1685, for example, a townsman (*posadskii chelovek*) sued because another townsman had insulted his wife and two sons with a mother-oath and had threatened them with a

3. Tsentral'nyi gosudarstvennyi arkhiv drevnikh aktov (TsGADA), f. 239, Sudnyi Prikaz, *opis'* (henceforth op.) 1, *chast* (henceforth ch.) 4, delo 5530, ll. 13, 18–19 (1713). TsGADA, f. 210, Prikaznyi stol, *stolbets* (henceforth stb.) 830, ll. 1–94 (1682); stb. 211, ll. 30–33 (1655); stb. 1998, ll. 337–71 and stb. 1534, ll. 105–8 (1691); stb. 139, ll. 473–94 (1635). *Russkaia istoricheskaia biblioteka* (henceforth *RIB*) 39 vols. (St. Petersburg, 1872–1927), 14 (1894), no. 359, cols. 766–67 (1653); no. 234, cols. 558–59 (1605). *RIB* 25 (1908), no. 63, cols. 72–73 (1628). *Moskovskaia delovaia i bytovaia pis'mennost' XVII veka* (Moscow, 1968), pt. 2, no. 14, 52 (1634).

4. *RIB* 25, no. 86, cols. 100–102 (1631). *RIB* 2 (1875), no. 206, cols. 946–49 (1642). *RIB* 14, no. 295, cols. 662–64 (1623); no. 336, cols. 729–30 (1641). TsGADA, f. 210, Prikaznyi stol, stb. 262, l. 45 (1680); stb. 15, ch. 2, ll. 708–10 (1625). TsGADA, f. 210, Sevskii stol, stb. 37, ll. 10–12 (1689). *Pamiatniki moskovskoi delovoi pis'mennosti XVII veka. Vladimirskii krai* (Moscow, 1984), no. 206, 220–21 (1618). *Moskovskaia delovaia*, pt. 2, no. 13, 51–52 (1634); no. 102, 97–98 (1676).

5. There are so many such cases that I will list only some published ones: *RIB* 14, nos. 242 (1606), 295 (1623), 371 (1675), 375 (1687). *RIB* 2, no. 164 (1) (1633). *Moskovskaia delovaia*, pt. 2, nos. 83 (1674), 57 (1659), 32 and 33 (1639), 18 (1635); pt. 5, no. 11 (1629). *Materialy dlia istorii prikaznogo sudoproizvodstva v Rossii*, ed. K. P. Pobedonostsev (Moscow, 1890), dela 2 and 3 (1703).

club.[6] According to the settlement the man was awarded the dishonor payment for townsmen of his category (seven rubles), his wife received fourteen rubles, and his two sons received seven between them, for a total of twenty-eight rubles.[7] In 1690 a provincial cavalryman of Elets won a case on behalf of his maiden daughter who had been beaten, insulted, and accused of stealing. He was awarded thirty-two rubles, four times his allotment of eight, but the judgment was overturned on procedural grounds.[8] In 1692 a minor sued on behalf of his widowed mother and himself for unspecified verbal abuse (*bran'*). He was awarded half his father's allotment of seventy-five rubles (his father had been a *zhilets*—a Moscow cavalry rank) and his mother received twice the allotment.[9] In 1709 a shipbuilder won a settlement for verbal insult to himself and his wife, including the accusation that she was a criminal (*vorovka*). They received 303 rubles (twice the shipbuilder's annual allotment of 101 rubles for his wife and 101 more for himself).[10] And in a complicated case of 1720 the litigants—all Armenians in Muscovite service—reached an out-of-court settlement that amounted to the plaintiff's annual allotment for himself (fifty rubles; he was a barber to Peter I's wife Catherine) and twice that for his wife. The charge was that the defendants had verbally insulted husband and wife and had beaten the man.[11] When a male litigant sued on behalf of women or other family members, it seems likely that they, not the insulted dependents, pocketed the award.

Thus the mandated fines for dishonor were consistently levied. Cases involving filial disobedience were punished even more harshly, with corporal sanctions instead of cash fines; here secular law affirmed the Judeo-Christian commandment to honor one's father and mother.[12] In 1701, accordingly, a son found guilty of dishonoring his parents (people of provincial cavalry rank) by beating them, ransacking their home, stealing their property, and verbally insulting them was ordered to be "whipped mercilessly with rods (*batogi*)."[13] In a similar case in 1667 a widow sued her son, a man in a European-style light-cavalry unit (*reitar*), for the dishonor of his verbally insulting her, beating her and her servants, and ransacking her home. He too was whipped with rods.[14]

6. Mother-oath: any of a wide range of insults derived from the word *mat'*, "mother."

7. TsGADA, f. 210, Prikaznyi stol, stb. 918, ll. 18–43.

8. TsGADA, f. 210, Prikaznyi stol, stb. 2608, ll. 1–58.

9. TsGADA, f. 210, Prikaznyi stol, stb. 1561, ll. 1–28.

10. TsGADA, f. 239, Sudnyi prikaz, op. 1, ch. 4, delo 5420, ll. 1–15v; published in part in Pobedonstsev, *Materialy*, 45–46.

11. TsGADA, f. 239, Sudnyi prikaz, op. 1, ch. 4, delo 5761, ll. 1–20v.

12. Conciliar Law Code of 1649, chap. 22, arts. 4–6, *Rossiiskoe zakonodatel' stvo X–XX vekov v deviati tomakh* (henceforth *RZ*), 5 vols. to date (Moscow, 1984–), 3 (1985): 248.

13. TsGADA, f. 210, Prikaznyi stol, stb. 2574, ll. 12–17.

14. TsGADA, f. 210, Prikaznyi stol, stb. 384, ll. 163–64. For a similar case in 1683 see *Dopolneniia k Aktam istoricheskim*, 12 vols. (St. Petersburg, 1846–72), 10 (1867), no. 107, 466–67.

Women could receive their cash awards directly. In 1693, for example, the widow of a highly placed Moscow servitor (a *stol'nik*), a woman who herself served as treasurer to the tsarevich, Aleksei Petrovich, won an award of twice her late husband's allotment, a total of 228 rubles, because another *stol'nik* had called her a criminal.[15] In 1717 a pregnant woman, apparently not a widow, sued on her own behalf for assault. She was awarded twice her husband's allotment (he was an urban dweller), but the sum was not specified.[16] And in 1713 the wife of a Moscow stonemason, not a widow, sued on her own behalf for assault, theft, and the insult of being called a criminal; she won the case and an unspecified cash fee "according to [her husband's] cash allotment."[17]

These successful cases, brought by husbands, sons, widows and wives and ranging socially from the Kremlin's elite to domestic servants, confirm that Muscovy's institutions of honor gave women high social esteem and real protections of their special regard. But most striking, perhaps, is the solicitude Muscovite legislators showed toward victims of the ultimate dishonor, rape.[18] The crime of rape directly transgressed fundamental values and relationships in Muscovite society. It is no wonder, then, that accusations of rape, like dishonor complaints in general, were taken seriously and dealt with expeditiously.

Jurisdiction over rape fell to the church and state jointly, but generally church courts heard the cases.[19] Even though rape was considered a dishonor—an interpretation unique in Slavic legal customs according to Eve Levin's comparative study of Slavic law on sexual crimes[20]—sanctions for rape were determined by ecclesiastical law. Law codes of native origin, such as the Church Statutes of Vladimir and Iaroslav (compiled in the fourteenth and fifteenth centuries and representing somewhat earlier norms) and the fifteenth-century Metropolitan's Justice (*Pravosudie mitropolichie*), adhere to an approach later taken for dishonor: they levy cash fines according to the social

15. TsGADA, f. 210, Prikaznyi stol, stb. 1657, ll. 1–31.

16. TsGADA, f. 239, Sudnyi prikaz, op. 1, ch. 4, delo 5638, ll. 1–7v; published in part in Pobedonostsev, *Materialy*, delo 28, 126.

17. TsGADA, f. 239, Sudnyi prikaz, op. 1, ch. 4, delo 5530, ll. 1–20v; published in part in Pobedonostsev, *Materialy*, delo 45, 98.

18. Rape, without mention of verbal abuse, is unambiguously called dishonor. In one case in 1632 the woman says, "He dishonored me with sexual assault [*bezchestil bludnym padeniem*]." *RIB* 25, no. 93, cols. 113–14. Another case of the same year uses similar language. *RIB* 25, no. 95, cols. 115–17. A case in 1686 settles an allegation of rape with payment of the women's dishonor. *RIB* 12 (1890), no. 166, cols. 724–30.

19. Civil jurisdiction was also occasionally used: of seventeen fairly complete trials on rape I have collected, four were heard by civil authorities.

20. Levin, *Sex and Society*, 219.

status of the victim.[21] Laws of Byzantine and South Slavic origin used in Muscovy suggest harsher punishment. The Court Law for the People (widespread in the Rus' lands from the appanage period), for example, decrees that a rapist should be sold into slavery and his property given to his victim if she is a betrothed maiden; if she is not betrothed, he should marry her or award her a significant portion of his property; even if a betrothed maiden consents to intercourse, the rapist should have his nose cut off.[22]

Of the twenty-eight full and partial cases involving rape that I have identified, only five record guilty verdicts and sanctions. Those verdicts followed all these various traditions in punishing perpetrators and compensating victims. In one case in 1594 an apparently secular sanction was levied: a civil court awarded a man a fine similar to a dishonor fine for his wife's rape. In 1657 a rapist whose victim died of the assault suffered a lesser punishment for the murder (a beating instead of execution)[23] because the victim was known as a drunkard and a loose woman who had previously been punished for sexual transgressions.[24] One case in 1698 left punishment up to the church authorities.[25] Two of the cases, in 1687 and 1689, levied sanctions according to Byzantine secular law codes contained in the Russian legal compendium the Rudder (*Kormchaia kniga*).[26] The sanctions included physical punishment and cash settlements calculated to take the place of the victim's dowry.[27]

Two aspects of extant litigation for rape are notable—the seriousness with which civil and ecclesiastical authorities treated the accusation of rape, and the social diversity of the litigants. A series of cases, the resolutions of which have not been preserved, testify to the credence courts gave to women's

21. Church Statute of Iaroslav, arts. 2–4, 7, *RZ* 1 (1984): 168. *Pravosudie metropolichie*, art. 7, *Pamiatniki russkoga prava* (henceforth *PRP*), 8 vols. (Moscow, 1952–63,), vol. 3 (1955): 427.

22. *Zakon sudnyi liudem kratkoi redaktsii*, ed. M. N. Tikhomirov (Moscow, 1961), chaps. 10–13, 37; *Zakon sudnyi liudem prostrannoi i svodnoi redaktsii*, ed. M. N. Tikhomirov (Moscow, 1961), 35.

23. The Conciliar Law Code of 1649 (chap. 22) in general mandated execution for murder. *RZ* 3 (1985): 248–51.

24. *Moskovskaia delovaia*, pt. 5, no. 19, 277–85.

25. On secular fines, see *Biblioteka i arkhiv moskovskikh gosudarei v XVI stoletii*, ed. N. P. Likhachev (St. Petersburg, 1894), app. 3, 49–52. On unspecified church sanctions, see *RIB* 14, pt. 2, no. 79, cols. 1280–84.

26. The two cases cite *gradskie zakony* (*Polnoe sobranie zakonov Rossiiskoi imperii, Pervoe sobranie* [henceforth *PSZ*], 44 vols. [St. Petersburg, 1830], 1, vol. 2, no. 1266, 905–6 [1687] or *zakon gradskii* (*RIB* 12, no. 199, cols. 948–54 [1689]). The latter case cites chapter and article of what is apparently the *Kormchaia kniga* published in two editions (1650, 1653); the cited chapter (49) contains excerpts from the *Ecloga* and *Procheiros nomos*, known as *zakon gradskii* in Russian. See *Entsiklopedicheskii slovar'*, ed. F. A. Brokgaus and I. A. Efron, s.v. "Kormchaia kniga," esp. 294.

27. Application of such foreign laws increased in Muscovite legal practice in the seventeenth century. Mikhail Benemanskii, *Zakon gradskii: Znachenie ego v russkom prave. Prilozheniia* (Moscow, 1917), 248–66.

charges. Fathers were so alarmed by threats of rape of their maiden daughters that they lodged formal protests with civil or church authorities;[28] they lodged similar complaints about attempted rape.[29] Several cases show the social breadth of litigants and their willingness to sue even highly placed personages. In 1632, for example, a peasant widow sued for rape and theft to the local metropolitan; another peasant in 1632 sued because she had been gang-raped while delirious with fever; numerous parties sued against corrupt officials, alleging rape; an urban maiden in 1691 sued for her rape by a townsman, who vigorously denied the charges; in 1686 a woman settled out of court in a case of forcible oral sex.[30]

A few convoluted cases testify to the court's willingness to investigate an accusation of rape even when the victim's credibility was impugned. In a case that began in an alleged incident in 1698 and lasted through charges and countercharges until at least 1701 (when the documentation ends), a soldier's wife accused a church deacon of assault, insult, and attempted rape. She persisted in her charges even though the deacon denied all and was supported by witnesses.[31] In 1683 officials of the metropolitan of Murom and Riazan entertained the case of Fekolka Kirilova. Sought out by church authorities since she was bearing an apparently illegitimate child, Fekolka initially accused a worker, Ivashko Bunda, of raping her and fathering the child. Then she accused the priest who had raised her as an orphan in his home of raping her and maintaining illicit sexual relations with her over several years. As the priest stood firm in his denials, Fekolka piece by piece recanted details of her testimony, eventually fully withdrawing the rape charge against the priest (although not the charge against Bunda). It is remarkable that the court so assiduously investigated the accusations of this increasingly compromised witness in a trial that lasted from May to August 1683.[32] In discussing a 1694 case in which a woman accused three different men of rape before recanting all charges, Eve Levin makes much the same observation of the court's willingness to investigate such accusations from

28. *RIB* 25, no. 54, cols. 60–61 (1628); no. 249, cols. 340–41 (1675). *Moskovskaia delovaia*, pt. 2, no. 128, 121–22 (1696).

29. *RIB* 2, no. 176 (6b), cols. 720–22 (1638). *RIB* 14, no. 328, cols. 719–21 (1634). *Pamiatniki moskovskoi delovoi*, no. 193, 212 (1691).

30. Peasant widow: *RIB* 25, no. 93, cols. 113–14. Gang rape: *RIB* 25, no. 95, cols. 115–17. Corrupt officials: *Akty Moskovskogo gosudarstva*, ed. N. A. Popov and D. Ia. Samokvasov, 3 vols. (St. Petersburg, 1890–1901), 1 (1890), no. 146, 172–73 (1622); *RIB* 2, no. 176 (9), cols. 724–47 (1639); *Pamiatniki moskovskoi delovoi*, no. 139, 171–73 (1639); TsGADA, f. 210, Moskovskii stol, stb. 349, 11. 478–79, 481–88 (1663); *DAI* 7 (1859), no. 75, 371–74 (1676). Urban girl: *Pamiatniki moskovskoi delovoi*, no. 194, 213–14. Oral sex: *Kungurskie akty XVII veka (1668–1699 g.)*, ed. A. A. Titov (St. Petersburg, 1888), no. 48, 112–14.

31. TsGADA, f. 210, Prikaznyi stol, stb. 2634, 11. 1–30.

32. *Pamiatniki moskovskoi delovoi*, no . 186, 205–9.

discredited plaintiffs. In the end the woman was beaten for her false accusations.[33]

Several cases show significant protection offered to women who sued priests, fathers-in-law, or their social superiors. In 1689, for example, a woman sued the son of a priest on behalf of her thirteen-year-old niece and won the suit; the specific cash award is not specified, but the defendant agreed to pay the girl's dowry (dogovor na veno), and the case includes excerpts of law codes mandating that a rapist pay one-third of his property to his victim.[34] In 1690 a woman settled out of court with the father of her illegitimate baby; she had accused him of raping her and then refusing to support her and the child; he agreed to pay child support, and she refused the opportunity to marry him.[35] In 1698 a woman sued her father-in-law, a widowed priest, for numerous attempts at rape; he admitted his guilt and was banished to a monastery to await further sanctions.[36]

A case of 1687 merits special attention since it shows the ability of a low-ranking woman to find compensation for rape at the hands of a highly placed Muscovite cavalryman. The incident unfolded when Stepan Korob'in ordered his servant, Serezhka Morev, to find him a woman for sexual dalliance; Serezhka, with the help of a female friend, Katerinka, lured a young girl, Mavrutka Ventsyleeva, to Korob'in's home under false pretenses. The court transcript records:

> They took that maiden Mavrutka from Katerinka's home, on Sereshka's horse, saying they were taking her [home] to her mother, the widow Dun'ka, but, not taking her to her mother, they took her to the home of Stepan Korob'in. . . . And he, Serezhka, dragging her, Mavrutka, to him, Stepan, to his home, gave her to him, Stepan, in his private rooms for sexual relations. And he, Stepan Korob'in, raped her, Mavrutka, in his home in the private rooms, and he, Stepan, having raped her, Mavrutka, cast her out of his home.

The case was heard by tsars Ioann and Peter and the tsarevna Sofiia, who ordered Serezhka beaten and exiled to Siberia with his family. Katerinka was put on stringent surety bond since her husband was away on military service and "for the criminal deeds of a wife, husbands are not also exiled. And so it is not appropriate to send her, Katerinka, alone without her husband." The tsars reserved their harshest punishment, appropriately, for the rapist:

> And for rape Stepan Korob'in is to be punished as well by beating with a knout, and the sum of 500 rubles is to be levied on him and, it having been

33. *RIB* 12, no. 245, cols. 1144–54. Levin, *Sex and Society*, chap. 5.
34. *RIB* 12, no. 199, cols. 948–54.
35. *RIB* 12, no. 212, cols. 988–90.
36. *RIB* 14, pt. 2, no. 79, cols. 1280–84.

collected, it is to be given over to the maiden Mavrutka for her dishonor and for her dowry, and he, Stepan, is to be sent under guard to Solovetskii monastery until [the tsar] orders. And as for the fact that he, Stepan, in his testimony and in face-to-face confrontation with her, Mavrutka, said that he, Stepan, engaged in sexual relations with her, Mavrutka, with her consent and [that he said that] he did not rape her, and [as for the fact that] he asked for a general investigation in the community [*poval'nyi obysk*] that he said would reveal previous deceit [*plutovstvo*] by her and her mother: there is no reason to carry out such a community questioning according to his request. Even without a community questioning his, Stepan's, guilt in this affair, is clear from the investigation and from his, Stepan's, own testimony, since he himself, Stepan, admitted in his testimony that he had told Serezhka Morev, before they brought the maiden to him, to bring him a woman or maiden for sexual relations, and in addition Serezhka Morev in testimony said about this also that he, Stepan, had spoken with him, Serezhka, about bringing [to him] a woman or maiden. And so the plan for this unlawful sexual attack was shown to be his, Stepan's. And those people mentioned above who brought this maiden to him, Stepan, also said in testimony, and others said after torture, that he, Stepan, raped her, Mavrutka, in a room in his home and she, Mavrutka, implored him, Stepan, not to rape her.

And according to secular laws [*gradskie zakony*] for such unlawful activity not only punishment but also penalty is ordered to be done, and it is ordered to give the maiden [a portion] from the property of him who raped her. And thus it is appropriate to punish him, Stepan, for his rape and for the dishonor of the maiden and for her dowry to collect from him that money, 500 rubles, so that other people in the future will not find it fitting to behave this way.

Soon thereafter the tsars pardoned Korob'in and rescinded his exile, but not the 500-ruble fine.[37]

Mavrutka Ventsyleeva's case is noteworthy in many respects. First of all, the crime was deemed so heinous that it merited the personal attention of the rulers themselves, or at least their direct judicial administration. Second, the defendant's social status did not carry weight in the face of the victim's and witnesses' testimony; his contemptible excuse that she participated willingly and that she was deceitful was dismissed out of hand. Third, the crime was perceived as crippling this woman's prospects for an honorable marriage, and thus the award specifically took the place of her dowry, providing her a lifetime source of support. The other cases cited above of rape and verbal dishonor affirm the message of this litigation, that Muscovite society offered women protections of their personal dignity and physical inviolability and followed through on those promises with judicious and responsible investigations and adequate compensation.

This evidence on women's honor in early modern Russia opens an in-

37. *PSZ* 1, vol. 2, nos. 1266 and 1267, 905–7.

teresting perspective on the patriarchal system of Muscovy. Women were given enhanced honor in this male-dominated society and were empowered by the tsar's judicial institutions to defend that honor in public. Women clearly had a higher stature than Muscovy's misogynistic social values would suggest. The degree to which women were active in litigation—over injured honor and other issues as well—confirms that they were not passive and oppressed beings. Granted, it was primarily as widows with property and children and as religious that women litigated on their own behalf. Nevertheless, in these situations they were respected and effective litigants.

This collection of cases includes instances of widows of provincial servitor rank suing for assault, theft, and verbal abuse to them and their maiden daughters[38] and of widows settling out of court in suits for assault and dishonor.[39] In 1682 a widowed dependent of a parish church sued the parish priest for dishonor and for failing to support her as promised; in 1685 a widow sued her son-in-law for assault; in 1680 a widow of a soldier sued for the dishonor of having her head covering pulled off.[40] These cases from a limited sample complement evidence on widows in Muscovy and other patriarchal societies.[41] Muscovite widows managed minor sons' property and by the seventeenth century de facto inherited service-tenure lands.[42] Similarly, women religious enjoyed a relatively autonomous social place; [43] the sample includes instances of abbesses and nuns suing on behalf of themselves or their

38. TsGADA, f. 210, Prikaznyi stol, stb. 558, 11. 492–98 (1645). TsGADA, f. 210, Belgorod stol, stb. 355, 11. 105–7 (1669).

39. TsGADA, f. 210, Prikaznyi stol, stb. 11, 11. 230–32 (1624), stb. 1104, 11. 1–7 (1688). TsGADA, f. 210, Belgorod stol, stb. 1360, 11. 184–85 (1691). *RIB* 12, no. 194, cols. 918–22 (1688).

40. Church support: *Pamiatniki moskovskoi delovoi*, no. 184, 202–3. Son-in-law: *Moskovskaia delovaia*, pt. 2, no. 126, 113–14. Soldier widow: TsGADA, f. 210, Prikaznyi stol, stb. 262, 1. 20.

41. The advantaged situation of Muscovite widows is comparable to that of widows in Renaissance Italy. See David Herlihy, "Vieillir à Florence au Quattrocento," *Annales: Economies, Sociétés, Civilisations* 24 (1969): 1338–52, and Stanley Chojnacki, "Dowries and Kinsmen in Early Renaissance Venice," *Journal of Interdisciplinary History* 5 (1975): 571–600.

42. On widows' rights in Muscovy, see M. F. Vladimirskii-Budanov, *Obzor istorii russkogo prava*, 6th ed. (St. Petersburg, 1909), 492–503; Alexandre Eck, "La situation juridique de la femme russe au moyen age," *Recueils de la société Jean Bodin pour l'histoire comparative des institutions* 12, pt. 2 (1962): 405–20; Stanislaw Roman, "Le statut de la femme dans l'Europe orientale (Pologne et Russie) au moyen age et aux temps modernes," *Recueils de la société de Jean Bodin . . .* 12, pt. 2 (1962): 389–403; Sandra Levy, "Women and the Control of Property in Sixteenth-Century Muscovy," *Russian History* 10 (1983): 201–12; and Carsten Goehrke, "Die Witwe im alten Russland," *Forschungen zur osteuropaischen Geschichte* 38 (1986): 64–96.

43. On women religious, see Claire Claus, *Die Stellung der russichen Frau von der Einführung des Christentums bei den Russen bis zu den Reformen Peter des Grossen* (Munich, 1959), chap. 8, 155–89; Eck, "La situation juridique"; Marie A. Thomas, "Muscovite Convents in the Seventeenth Century," *Russian History* 10 (1983): 230–42. On women religious in medieval Europe, see Suzanne Fonay Wemple, *Women in Frankish Society: Marriage and the Cloister, 500 to 900* (Philadelphia, 1981).

charges.[44] Even wives had more independence than might be expected; in rare dishonor cases they represented themselves in court (particularly when their husbands were away in service).[45] In 1713, for example, the wife of a cavalryman (*dragun*) sued a monastic servitor for calling her a slut (*kurva*); in 1626 a peasant wife sued for assault, aspersions on her sexual behavior, and theft; in 1631 the wife of a townsman twice sued on her own behalf for assault, theft, and dishonor.[46] This evidence complements scholars' observations that married women often shared control over conjugal property with their husbands and maintained personal control over dowry lands.[47]

Litigation not involving honor but featuring women as plaintiffs shows the same picture of women seeking legal protection of their interests. Widows and kinsmen sued and won reparations for a murdered husband in 1538 and 1650; in 1680 a wife sued about an assault on her family; a widow sued her husband's kin in 1603 for her dowry and widow's inheritance; a widow in 1634 requested upkeep from the tsar after she had returned with her family from exile in Poland-Lithuania; a widowed mother in 1627 sued her daughter's husband and his uncle for abuse of that daughter; another widowed mother in 1644 sued on behalf of her daughter, who was being physically abused by her husband and in-laws.[48]

As the latter cases suggest, women could seek defense against abusive husbands and other male kin. Although men were allowed to discipline their wives, Orthodox teaching urged them to inflict only just and moderate beatings.[49] Litigants declared that excessive beating invalidated a husband's conjugal authority over his wife: because of his beatings "he lives with her illegally," one irate stepfather declared of his abusive son-in-law in 1632.[50] Such complaints are abundant.[51] In one especially poignant case in 1687 a

44. TsGADA, f. 210, Prikaznyi stol, stb. 311, ll. 267–74 (1659). *RIB* 25, no. 82, cols. 96–97 (1630). *RIB* 14, pt. 2, no. 30, cols. 916–18 (1625).

45. TsGADA, f. 210, Belgorod stol, stb. 1102, ll. 153–55 (1678). TsGADA, f. 210, Prikaznyi stol, stb. 1090, ll. 99–127 (1686). Pobedonostsev, *Materialy*, delo 25, 12–14 (1705).

46. Cavalryman's wife: Pobedonostsev, *Materialy*, delo 43, 98. Peasant wife: *RIB* 25, no. 18, col. 19. Urban wife: *RIB* 25, no. 86, cols . 100–102.

47. Levy, "Women and the Control of Property"; Vladimirskii-Budanov, *Obzor*, 492–503.

48. Murdered husbands: *RIB* 2, no. 186, cols. 771–93 (1538); *Pamiatniki moskovskoi delovoi*, no. 245, 241–43 (1650). Family: *Pamiatniki moskovskoi delovoi*, no. 180, 199–200. Upkeep: *RIB* 14, no. 221, cols. 540–41. Exile: *Akty moskovskogo gosudarstva*, ed. N.A. Popov, vol. 1 (St. Petersburg, 1890), no. 686, 628. Abuse of daughter: *RIB* 25, no. 34, col. 36 (1627); *RIB* 25, no. 183, cols. 236–37 (1644).

49. *Domostroi. Po spisku Imp. Obshchestva istorii i drevnostei rossiiskikh*, Rarity Reprints, no. 18 (Letchworth, Eng., 1971), chaps. 38–39, 94–102. On husbands' authority over wives, see K. A. Nevolin, *Istoriia rossiiskikh grazhdanskikh zakonov*, pt. 1, in *Polnoe sobranie sochinenii*, vol. 3 (St. Petersburg, 1857), 75–84.

50. *RIB* 25, no. 99, col. 123. See also the complaint by a mother in 1627: *RIB* 25, no. 34, col. 36.

51. In addition to those complaints cited above, see *RIB* 25, no. 207, cols. 272–73 (1655); *RIB* 14, no. 342, cols. 739–40 (1645); *Moskovskaia delovaia*, pt. 2, no. 52, 68–69 (1655), no. 58, 72

father reported that he had had to rescue his daughter three times from crippling beatings by her husband and her father-in-law. The father won an out-of-court settlement whereby the guilty men agreed to support the injured woman for the rest of her life while she lived apart from her husband.[52] One woman in 1683 won a divorce because of her husband's abuse of her, even though she had been caught in adultery.[53] Similar instances show women defending their minimal rights as wives: a wife in 1629 sued her husband, who had abandoned her for maliciously incurring debts in her name and for beatings; a nun in 1632 sued her previous husband for assault and theft; and in several cases wives sued husbands for abandonment.[54] Women enjoyed and exercised the opportunity to defend themselves publicly from the harshest consequences of married life.

Women's high social esteem and their power to protect it, however, by no means subverted the patriarchal order of early modern Russia; indeed, it strengthened it. There is probably no better illustration of how pervasive patriarchy was in the Muscovite social as well as political order than the very institutions of honor that defended women's high status. Honor, linking the patriarchal world of social relations with the patrimonial world of politics, demonstrates their complete interdependence. In theory and practice Muscovite protections of honor affirmed male dominance in social and political life. Honor in Muscovy incorporated all the attributes of a good subject of Muscovy's patrimonial tsar—lawful behavior, loyal service to the tsar, tenacious defense of one's social position, Orthodox piety, and decorous personal behavior. It provided social integration: radiating down from the tsar through his palace to his officials and to the common people, honor united society like a family. At the same time protections of honor affirmed and encouraged conformity to a social community patriarchically structured: just as the tsar exerted patrimonial authority over his subjects, husbands and fathers exercised patriarchal control over their wives, children, daughters-in-law, servants, peasants, and other dependents.

Despite the honor they enjoyed, women—with the exception of those who lived in the interstices of patriarchy, nuns and propertied widowed mothers—remained throughout their lives dependents of men. Their dowry property reverted to their father if they died childless; their married property, though they often had a hand in managing it, remained ultimately the possession of the husband's clan. Numerous suits illustrate the degree to which

---

(1660), no. 61, 74 (1666); *Pamiatniki moskovskoi delovoi*, no. 128, 162 (1626), no. 200, 217–18 (1695).

52. *RIB* 12, no. 183, cols. 866–75.

53. *Akty, otnosiashchiesia do iuridicheskogo byta drevnei Rossii*, 3 vols. and index (St. Petersburg, 1857–1901), 2 (1864), no. 220, cols. 641–43.

54. Malicious debts: *RIB* 25, no. 77, cols. 88–90. Nun: *RIB* 25, no. 105, cols. 128–31. Abandoned wives: *RIB* 25, no. 225, cols. 305–6 (1659); no. 232, cols. 316–17 (1661).

women were subsumed in the male patrimony into which they were born or married: men sued on behalf of their women for dishonor; natal kinsmen sued to reclaim an abused daughter's dowry; in-laws sued widows for return of the deceased man's property; and daughters-in-law complained of ill-treatment by mothers-in-law.[55]

Even the solicitude shown victims of rape arose out of the demands of patriarchy: if a maiden lost her virginity, she could not be honorably married. Marriage was a potent tool for family alliances in the propertied strata, and for all economic strata an unmarried adult daughter was a burden. If a wife were raped or committed adultery, her progeny no longer guaranteed the perpetuation of her husband's bloodline. Furthermore, rape and insult to women were humiliations to the fathers and husbands whose failure to control and guard their women was thereby exposed. Conversely, women's modesty and fidelity brought honor to men and their clans. The church's avid persecution of illegitimate births and illicit sex also promoted patriarchy: prayers and christenings were withheld from unmarried mothers and their babies until the mothers testified that the pregnancy was caused by rape or otherwise-coerced sexual relations.[56] Here, in a patriarchal family's sense of its own honor, its distrust of women's sexuality, and its desire to perpetuate the male line, we find the rationale behind women's enhanced honor and status in Muscovy's patriarchal society.

In patriarchal societies women characteristically enjoy some special status as a counterpart to the controls to which they are subjected, controls intended to maintain male-dominated, household-oriented social structures. By according women high social esteem, patriarchal systems simultaneously give women real dignity—and the power to defend that dignity—and disseminate publicly values that shore up patriarchy. A woman is bound to the home and is expected to be modest and demure, obedient to the male head of household. If she conforms, she wins high dignity, and her reproductive capacity and status value are assured. By respecting women's high status, men in turn are reinforced in the paternalistic role of protector of women, children, and servants. Patriarchy, then, serves itself by serving women well. In the Muscovite case, however, it acted in a more humane way than it might have. Other patriarchal societies of the past —for example, in the Mediterranean and the Middle East—practiced seclusion, veiling, or physical mutilation to enhance and protect women's honor or gave women no legal recourse

55. *RIB* 25, no. 1, cols. 1–2 (1621); no. 5, cols. 6–7 (1626); no. 20, cols. 20–21 (1626); no. 61, cols. 70–71 (1628); no. 68, cols. 79–81 (1629); no. 100, col. 124 (1632). *RIB* 2, no. 206, cols. 946–49 (1642); no. 237, cols. 1016–17 (1637). *RIB* 14, no. 264, cols. 608–10 (1612). *Moskovskaia delovaia*, pt. 2, no. 58, 72 (1660); no. 61, 74 (1666). Titov, *Kungurskie akty*, no. 10, 19–20 (1670).

56. *Pamiatniki moskovskoi delovoi*, no. 174, 195–96 (1679); no. 183, 202 (1681); no. 218, 226 (1682). *RIB* 12, no. 212, cols. 988–90 (1690).

against the abuses of patriarchy.[57] In Muscovy only the most elite women were secluded, and they enjoyed with all Muscovite women the right to litigate against insult and physical abuse. When Muscovite law codes and litigations elevated women's honor, they were indeed enhancing women's status, giving them the only value patriarchy generally afforded women. When women (or men on their behalf) went to court to defend their honor, they were empowered to act on their enhanced status. The more women lived up to the standards of honor and the more they exercised the opportunity to defend their dignity, the more deeply ingrained the social values of Muscovite patriarchy became.

57. On the societal control of women outside Europe and the honor-and-shame ethic, see, among others, Yehudi A. Cohen, "Ends and Means in Political Control: State Organization and the Punishment of Adultery, Incest and Violation of Celibacy," *American Anthropologist* 71 (1969): 658–87; Jane Schneider, "Of Vigilance and Virgins: Honor and Shame and Access to Resources in Mediterranean Societies," *Ethnology* 10 (1971): 1–23; Nur Yalmon, "On the Purity of Women in the Castes of Ceylon and Malabar," *Journal of the Royal Anthropological Institute* 93 (1963): 25–58; J. K. Campbell, *Honour, Family and Patronage: A Study of Institutions and Morals in a Greek Mountain Community* (Oxford, 1964); *Honour and Shame: The Values of Mediterranean Society*, ed. J. G. Peristiany (Chicago, 1966); Hanna Papanek, "Purdah: Separate Worlds and Symbolic Shelter," *Comparative Studies in Society and History* 15 (1973): 289–325; Michelle Zimbalist Rosaldo, "Women, Culture and Society: A Theoretical Overview," in *Woman, Culture and Society*, ed. Michelle Zimbalist Rosaldo and Louise Lamphere (Stanford, 1974), 17–42; Nikki Keddie and Lois Beck, introduction to *Women in the Muslim World*, ed. Nikki Keddie and Lois Beck (Cambridge, Mass., 1978), 1–34; Ramon Gutierrez, "From Honor to Love: Transformations of the Meaning of Sexuality in Colonial New Mexico," in *Kinship Ideology and Practice in Latin America*, ed. Raymond T. Smith (Chapel Hill, 1984), 237–63; Gutierrez, "Honor Ideology, Marriage Negotiation and Class-Gender Domination in New Mexico, 1690–1846," *Latin American Perspectives* 12, no. 2, issue 44 (1985): 81–104; *Honor and Shame and the Unity of the Mediterranean*, ed. David D. Gilmore (Washington, D.C., 1987); and Patricia Seed, *To Love, Honor and Obey in Colonial Mexico: Conflicts over Marriage Choice, 1574–1821* (Stanford, 1988).

Through the Prism of Witchcraft: Gender and Social Change in Seventeenth-Century Muscovy

Valerie A. Kivelson

"A greater number of witches is found in the fragile feminine sex than among men; it is indeed a fact that it were idle to contradict, since it is accredited by actual experience."[1] This statement from a fifteenth-century Inquisition handbook on witches accurately expresses Western assumptions about witches. From New England to Poland approximately 80 percent of accused witches were female. The preponderance of female victims during the European witchcraft craze has piqued the interest of historians of women, raising the question of why women were singled out for persecution. Some analysts have interpreted the centuries of the European witchcraft craze as a particularly gruesome chapter in a long saga of concerted gynocide in history.[2] Anthropologically inclined historians have concluded that women suffered not because they were female but because they were a vulnerable, socially disadvantaged group or because they were somehow perceived as a threat to the established social order.[3] Still other scholars have proposed that the

Research for this paper was supported by grants from the International Research and Exchanges Board, the Fulbright-Hays Doctoral Dissertation Research Abroad Program, and the Mrs. Giles Whiting Foundation. I would like to thank Phil Ethington, Nancy Shields Kollmann, Tim Hofer, and Estelle Freedman for their help and suggestions.

1. Heinrich Kramer and Jacob Sprenger, *Malleus Maleficarum*, trans. Montague Sommers, in *Witchcraft in Europe, 1100–1700: A Documentary History*, ed. Alan C. Kors and Edward Peters (Philadelphia, 1972), 114.

2. See, for example, Andrea Dworkin, *Woman Hating* (New York, 1974), chap. 7; Mary Daly, *Gyn/Ecology: The Metaethics of Radical Feminism* (Boston, 1978), chap. 6.

3. Keith Thomas, *Religion and the Decline of Magic* (New York, 1971), 567; Christina Larner, *Witchcraft and Religion: The Politics of Popular Belief* (Oxford, 1984), 86; Brian P. Levack, *The Witch-Hunt in Early Modern Europe* (New York, 1987), 116–45; Carol F. Karlsen, *The Devil in the Shape of a Woman: Witchcraft in Colonial New England* (New York, 1987), 115; David Warren Sabean, *Power in the Blood: Popular Culture and Village Discourse in Early Modern Germany* (New York, 1984).

stereotyped image of witches as female, stemming from ancient beliefs in female susceptibility to evil, promoted the identification of women as witches.[4]

In the gender profile of accused witches Muscovite Russia presents the exception. The ratio of male to female witches in seventeenth-century Muscovy, nearly seven to three, reversed the typical preponderance, with men comprising the majority of accused witches. This anomalous finding allows us to test various theories of marginality and perceived social disruptiveness in explaining vulnerability to accusations of witchcraft.

A vast historical literature on witchcraft cases in England, Western Europe, and North America and a fledgling literature on Russian witchcraft permit an examination of Muscovite witchcraft in comparative perspective. Nikolai Iakovlevich Novombergskii, a Russian historian writing in the early twentieth century, and, more recently, the American scholar Russell Zguta pioneered the study of Muscovite witchcraft.[5] In addition, court records survive that document a sensational witchcraft case that paralyzed Lukh, a small town northeast of Moscow, between 1656 and 1660.[6] This essay employs evidence from the Lukh case to provide details in the broader picture of witchcraft practices in seventeenth-century Muscovy. The Lukh episode illuminates the internal dynamics of personality, authority, gender, and power within a single town, thus complementing Zguta's aggregate studies of Russia as a whole. For this investigation I have used the principal published source collections as well as scattered published and archival cases. The available sample includes only seventy seventeenth-century court cases involving 146 accusations.

OUTBREAK IN LUKH

On St. Nikolai's Day in the spring of 1656 a widow named Tat'iana was overcome by a strange fit while attending a church service. In delirium she began crying out that two other widows of Lukh and a townsman, Igoshka Salautin, had bewitched her with bread, over which they had cast a spell.[7]

---

4. Christina Larner, *Enemies of God: The Witch-Hunt in Scotland* (London, 1981), 85; H. C. Erik Midelfort, *Witch Hunting in Southwestern Germany, 1562–1684: The Social and Intellectual Foundations* (Stanford, 1972).

5. Russell Zguta, "The Ordeal by Water (Swimming of Witches) in the East Slavic World," *Slavic Review* 36 (1977): 220–30; "Witchcraft Trials in Seventeenth-Century Russia," *American Historical Review* 82 (1977): 1187–1207; "Witchcraft and Medicine in Pre-Petrine Russia," *Russian Review* 37 (1978): 438–48; "Was There a Witch Craze in Muscovite Russia?" *Southern Folklore Quarterly* 41 (1977): 119–28. Zguta relies for his source material primarily on the publications of Nikolai Iakovlevich Novombergskii: *Koldovstvo v Moskovskoi Rusi XVII veka* (St. Petersburg, 1906); *Materialy po istorii meditsiny v Rossii*, 4 vols. (St. Petersburg, 1905–7); *Vrachebnoe stroenie v do-Petrovskoi Rusi* (Tomsk, 1907).

6. Tsentral'nyi gosudarstvennyi arkhiv drevnikh aktov (TsGADA), fond 210, Prikaznyi stol, no. 300, fols. 1–89v.

7. Ibid., fol. 3.

Fits of bewitchment or spirit possession immediately spread to other townswomen. The women, in their testimony before a special investigator sent from Moscow, uniformly stated that they could not remember what they said and did while in the clutches of bewitchment. They remembered only standing in church when they began to feel faint and queasy. Their hearts started pounding as if about to explode, and chills, aches, and fevers wracked their bodies. When they reached their homes, they frequently encountered darkness, spinning walls, and great terror, which sometimes lasted several weeks.

Male witnesses, the husbands, fathers, and fathers-in-law of the afflicted women, provided more complete catalogues of symptoms. They lamented that their wives and daughters growled like bears, honked like geese, and barked like dogs. They cried out in the voices of wild beasts, birds, bears, hares, and cattle. They hiccuped, also "in voices." They ached and grimaced, fell to the floor, and called out mysterious accusations. In their madness they bit themselves and other people and said things "not pleasing either to God or to man."

Over the course of the next two years a total of thirty-five Lukh townspeople (thirty-three women and two men) displayed symptoms of possession, and another ten (all male) suffered from other forms of bewitchment, manifested as disease or impotence. In connection with the case fifteen husbands and fathers of victims and about seventy-five additional male witnesses from Lukh were questioned. At the beginning of the eighteenth century official censuses listed three hundred adult townsmen in Lukh.[8] Assuming that an equal number of women inhabited the town, those bewitched (forty-five) together with those questioned (ninety) represented more than one-fifth of the adult population of the town.

Accusations built incrementally, implicating a slowly widening circle of alleged sorcerers and witches. The denunciations gradually changed in nature from charges of folk healing to charges of casting spells and using evil incantations. Suspicions eventually converged on five men and their families. The broadest range of accusations revolved around the town healer, Tereshka Malakurov. Witnesses alleged that he kept charms, herbs, and talismans in his house and that many people went to him to be healed. Fed'ka Popov and the priest Matvei reported that they had paid Tereshka for medical consultations when their wives had been taken ill with demonic possession. The fact that he took money for his unsuccessful attempts to cure people counted strongly against him.

Igoshka and Ian'ka Salautin were accused of bewitching the wife of Luka Frolev, a Lukh resident. In her sickness Luka's wife cried out the words "master" and "guarantor" (*porutchik*). Her delirious words led Luka to

---

8. Ia. E. Vodarskii, *Naselenie Rossii v kontse XVII-nachale XVIII veka* (Moscow, 1977), 204.

identify the Salautins as the culprits "because I had a loan contract with him [Ian'ka], and his brother [Igoshka] was guarantor."[9]

Accusations then shifted from townspeople to outsiders, such as Arkhipko Fadeev, a monastic peasant, and Ian'ka Erokhin, a wandering minstrel (*skomorokh*). The minstrel was targeted for accusation after an altercation with Man'ka, daughter of a leading citizen and wife of a local fisherman. As Man'ka described the incident, her husband invited the minstrel to their home during the Lenten fast and ordered her to fetch some wine for the guest. She refused to do so. After that incident her kerchief disappeared and her fits began. The coincidence suggested that the minstrel had stolen the kerchief to cast spells over its owner.

The final person accused was an unlikely candidate, Fed'ka Vasil'ev, the son of a prominent townsman. His father, a shoemaker, served responsibly in official capacities and had never been known to cause trouble. Fed'ka was accused by a woman who cried his name while possessed but also when fully in control of her faculties. She asserted that he wore a cross under his heel, evidently a satanic fashion statement, and that he ran away and disappeared from the town as soon as she began to voice her charges.

All of the accused were imprisoned and questioned except for Fed'ka Vasil'ev, who vanished as soon as the situation grew dangerous and was not found for more than a year. All denied the sorcery charges at first questioning, admitting at most to healing epilepsy and curing hernias in small children "with words." They denied any knowledge of witchcraft practiced by themselves or anyone else, but several of them admitted that they served a magical function at weddings, warding off malign forces. A few of them confessed that they also knew how to cure impotence.

Several more rounds of torture, including beating, burning, and slow water torture, elicited from all except Igoshka Salautin complete confessions in conformance with the inquisitors' leading questions. Battered by his second ordeal in the torture chamber, Tereshka Malakurov confessed that he had learned sorcery from a horse doctor named Oska and that he was in the habit of chanting incantations to be carried off by the wind or by a stray dog. He attested that he scattered salt around the streets and crossroads, "and whoever comes along will be taken ill and will be overcome by misery and by trembling and will cry out with various voices, and others will hiccup and eat themselves and bite other people." In response to the inquisitors' questions Tereshka provided a remarkably practical motive for his sorcery: he explained that he had bewitched people for three years to make a living by charging to heal them, but then he was unable to cure them.[10]

Clearly under extreme duress the suspects not only elaborated on their

9. TsGADA, fond 210, Prikaznyi stol, no. 300, fol. 16.
10. Ibid., fol. 32.

own putative sorcery but also incriminated each other and named still more witches. Tereshka was tortured to such an extreme that he incriminated his wife Olen'ka as well. He confessed that he had taught her everything he knew and that she had carried spells out from the prison for him and had even worked her own curses independently. Olen'ka was duly imprisoned and tortured until she corroborated her husband's testimony in full. On July 27, 1658, in accordance with the tsar's order Tereshka Malakurov, Ian'ka Salautin, Arkhipko Fadeev, and Ian'ka Erokhin were executed. Olen'ka, Tereshka's wife, was buried in the earth, presumably up to her neck, in accordance with common judicial procedure for female felons. Igoshka Salautin refused to confess his guilt even after repeated torture and the execution of his brother. Fed'ka Vasil'ev had yet to be found.

The executions did not put an end to the matter. Igoshka Salautin, who had refused to admit guilt, was tortured again. His mother, the widow Nastasitsa, was arrested along with his brother Mit'ka. Each was tortured three times but refused to confess. A final surge of accusations ensued one year after the executions. This time charges revolved around the belated bewitchment of a little girl, also named Nastasitsa, Tomilo Ezhov's daughter:

> On June 23, 1659, . . . she says she came with loaves of white bread to the prison window and a hefty young fellow with red hair approached her. And she left that window and went to another, and that same fellow came up to her, and from that window smoke and wind hit her, and she was overwhelmed by misery, and when she reached home she began to ache and to cry out and she turned out to be just like the other bewitched women.[11]

The incident sparked a renewed epidemic of possession. Many of those who had recovered from their previous episodes, with the help of prayer and time, found themselves once more seized by fits and hysteria. Accusatory fingers pointed to the widow Nastasitsa Salautina and her two surviving sons, to Fed'ka Vasil'ev, who at last had been found and imprisoned, and to an assortment of other suspicious characters.

The records of the case come to an end after the transcripts of these people's denials, under repeated torture, of any wrongdoing. The documents register twenty-five accusations and five executions. Over the course of four years the hysteria in the town apparently spent itself.

PRECONDITIONS AND CAUSES OF WITCH HUNTING

A comparative examination of Russian witch hunting in relation to the West reveals broad similarities in political, religious, and procedural contexts. Within Western Europe witchcraft beliefs and practices varied greatly, but

11. TsGADA, fond. 210, Prikaznyi stol, no. 314, fol. 160.

generally the milder English and harsher Continental models provide the two poles. Russia fell between these extremes, sharing elements of both.

In her work on Scottish witchcraft Christina Larner distinguishes preconditions from immediate causes of witch persecution. Larner finds that witch persecution occurred only in places with basically peasant economies, where both elite and peasantry believed in witchcraft.[12] Several other factors predisposed areas to witch hunting, including changes in legal structure and organization, the rise of the nation-state, and an atmosphere of religious upheaval or the development of personal, internalized religion. The emerging consensus about witch hunting in Western Europe emphasizes the role of the state and of local secular authorities in encouraging witch hunting and demonstrates that witches served as convenient targets for establishing the authority and jurisdiction of the growing nation-states in the early modern period.

As to direct causes, detailed community studies have demonstrated that accusations of witchcraft formed just one weapon in an arsenal deployed in local conflicts. Given the basic preconditions, communities might manifest particular local tensions through witchcraft accusations, generally aimed at socially marginal or deviant people, who as outcasts or because of weak status could not successfully defend themselves against such charges.

In Muscovite Russia witch persecution began with a few highly visible political cases in the fifteenth century and escalated during the second half of the sixteenth century, reaching its peak in the second half of the seventeenth century, somewhat later than in most of Europe.[13] Zguta and others have maintained that Russian persecution of witches never reached the level of mass hysteria or devoured the number of victims its Western European counterparts did. This conclusion may be misleading, stemming from incomplete investigation of surviving archival materials.[14]

In Muscovy, as in the West, the seventeenth century witnessed tremendous growth of both church and state apparatuses. A conspicuously expanded bureaucratic presence in the countryside allowed the state to in-

12. Larner, *Enemies of God*, 193. In addition to Larner, this discussion relies primarily on E. William Monter, *Witchcraft in France and Switzerland: The Borderlands during the Reformation* (Ithaca, 1976); Midelfort, *Witch Hunting*; Alfred Soman, "Les procès de sorcellerie au Parlement de Paris (1565–1640)," *Annales: Economies, Sociétés, Civilisations* 32 (1977): 790–814; Robert Muchembled, *Sorcières, justice et société aux sixème et dix-septième siècles* (Paris, 1987); Karlsen, *Devil*; Sabean, *Power in the Blood*; Thomas, *Religion*; Alan Macfarlane, *Witchcraft in Tudor and Stuart England: A Regional and Comparative Study* (New York, 1970).

13. The apparent increase in cases in the second half of the sixteenth century noted by Zguta may merely reflect the general increase in surviving sources. It is likely however, that the frequency actually did increase with the expansion of state power and the judicial apparatus. Of approximately seventy cases I have examined, all but eight fall between the late 1640s and 1690.

14. Novombergskii's is the only systematic publication of documents on Muscovite witchcraft. I am convinced that the archives contain many other such cases.

trude increasingly in the lives of provincial subjects. Service and tax demands rose, and the 1649 law code institutionalized enserfment, which had been creeping into practice for the previous century and a half. Mid-century legislation tied townspeople as well as peasants to their communities. As part of a campaign to enforce social conformity, a series of decrees banned tobacco use, card playing, and excessive drinking, on penalty of exile to Siberia. Government monopolies regulated alcohol production.[15] The state made a claim to regulate even private conversations among its subjects through prosecution of "sovereign's word and deed" (*gosudarevo slovo i delo*) cases. Any act, comment, or even song that could be construed as remotely hostile to the tsar, whether a musketeer's tavern song or a peasant's empty curse, could land its perpetrator in court, facing harsh punishment.[16] In 1648 Tsar Alexis banned performances by minstrels, a group that challenged church and state prohibitions by wearing bright, provocative costumes, playing popular music, and wandering freely from place to place. In 1657 the church excommunicated all minstrels for their pagan tendencies and presumably also because their wandering violated the conventions of an immobile society.[17]

Witchcraft too fell under the expanded purview of the increasingly intrusive state. The church had long been concerned with stamping out witchcraft, considering it a lingering contaminant from pagan religion. Clerical disapproval is evident in surviving sermons and tales as well as in the records of the 1551 Stoglav Council, an important conference of the hierarchy of the Russian Orthodox church. From approximately that time the state began to share the church's concern about pagan survivals and to shoulder the responsibility for eliminating sorcery. In 1648 Tsar Alexis decreed that people who patronized sorcerers should be knouted and on repeated offense exiled. Five years later, in 1653, a harsher edict ordered the tools of black magic and the sorcerers who employed them burned.[18] Burning at the stake was only one of a number of possible punishments for a convicted witch. Others ranged from exile to live burial to nonspecific execution. Scholars have noted that states required significant resources to pursue, try, and punish witches on a wide scale. In Russia, as elsewhere, witchcraft persecution rose along with the unprecedented growth of the state's bureaucratic and judicial machinery.[19]

15. *Ulozhenie*, chap. 19, art. 19 (tying taxpaying townspeople to the towns where they have been living); chap. 25 (on production, sale, and consumption of alcohol and on drunkenness and tobacco).

16. Mark Charles Lapman, "Political Denunciations in Muscovy, 1600 to 1649: The Sovereign's Word and Deed" (Ph.D. diss., Harvard University, 1981).

17. Russell Zguta, *Russian Minstrels: A History of the Skomorokhi* (Philadelphia, 1978), 18, 60.

18. Novombergskii, *Koldovstvo*, nos. 14, 16, 17; Zguta, "Witchcraft Trials, 1190–95.

19. Larner, *Enemies of God*, 2; On Russian bureaucratic growth, see A. A. Zimin, "O slozhnenii prikaznoi sistemy na Rusi," *Doklady i soobshcheniia Instituta Istorii (Akademii Nauk)* 3 (1955): 164–76.

The judicial process in Russia had elements in common with both the European Inquisitorial and the gentler English mode of investigation. As in England, the initiative in filing suits against witches remained the prerogative of the community, not the church or state. Persons who felt themselves wronged by magic or local elders who feared for the safety of their communities filed complaints against sorcerers. In a typical example residents of Lukh implored the tsar and his officials to investigate episodes of possession among the townswomen, "so that we, your orphans, do not perish altogether because of them and so that we do not default on your sovereign's taxes and so that we do not die bitter deaths because of them."[20] State and society apparently shared a common concern over matters of sorcery. The state issued increasingly harsh decrees for dealing with practitioners of magic and urged ever-greater vigilance in combating the problem. Communities in turn proved cooperative in taking the initiative toward eradicating putative witches. It is difficult to evaluate the relative roles of the populace and the authorities in provoking the witch hunt, but some degree of collusion produced the actual trials.

Once a complaint was lodged by the public, the state took charge of the investigation. In Muscovy, as in most of continental Europe, torture could be applied in witchcraft cases, and confessions were wrung out of exhausted prisoners. Inquisitors interrogated suspects repeatedly, following an official list of questions: Who taught them witchcraft? Whom had they taught? What methods did they use? Who were their accomplices? Water torture, the rack, knoutings, scorchings with hot irons or flames, and rough shaking forced all but the strongest to implicate others. Frequently suspects later retracted their accusations of others, explaining that they had only named names to stop the pain. One woman entreated the authorities to release her sister, whom she had named earlier as a witch, explaining that she had thought her sister was dead and therefore safe from reprisals. Others named people in distant provinces or claimed not to remember their teachers' patronymics, perhaps to protect anyone they knew from sharing their ordeal. Those who managed to hold out against their tormentors and refused to confess actually stood a rather good chance of being let off on parole.[21]

If Muscovite witchcraft trials resembled Continental counterparts in the judicial process, in substance they bore more similarities to the English model, described by Keith Thomas and Alan Macfarlane.[22] Russian witchcraft trials placed far less emphasis on heresy and elaborate demonology than did either Continental or American trials. Black Sabbaths and night flying of European lore were unknown in the Russian countryside. Accusations of

20. TsGADA, fond 210, Prikaznyi stol, no. 314, fol. 165.
21. Protecting others: Novombergskii, *Vrachebnoe stroenie*, nos. 35, 20, 39; idem, *Koldovstvo*, nos. 7, 11, 66. Released on parole: idem, *Vrachebnoe stroenie*, nos. 20, 35, 39, 47.
22. Thomas, *Religion*, 435–586.

sorcery in Russia usually emphasized the hex (*porcha*) rather than satanism or heresy.

Most of the incantations that have survived rely on poetic nature imagery, perhaps preserving vestiges of pre-Christian pagan ritual. The transcript of a trial in Lukh in 1663 records the contents of a generic "woman letter" (*zhenskoe pis'mo*), a charm to make a woman fall in love with a man:

> I, slave of God, [say name] go out into an open field and as the moon shines on me and as the stars watch and hold fast to the moon, so let the female slave of God [say name] look at and hold fast to me. . . . In the sea-ocean lies a burning rock, and on that rock stands a tree. And when that tree is dry, it will wither away, just as that female slave of God will dry and wither for me. On that tree sits an iron man. He beats with his iron staff on the white-hot rock, and as the rock catches fire, so will that female slave of God catch fire for me carnally and fiercely.[23]

Despite the Christian tone lent by the recurrent phrase *slave of God*, the imagery in this passage, as in the majority of incantations, derives from the natural environment and from folklore. This category of spell relied on the power of analogy rather than the power of devils or deities to effect the desired results.

Although Zguta insists that diabolism was almost unknown in Russia, the texts of incantations copied into court records as evidence indicate that a sizable minority of sorcerers, such as Fed'ka Vasil'ev with his cross under his heel, did rely on satanic language and ritual to work their spells. One of the most dramatic of the satanic verses inverts the canonical affirmation of piety: "I renounce our creator, Christ-God, and the churches of God and the most holy liturgy and vespers and matins and all divinity and my father and mother and clan and tribe and swear allegiance to Satan and his beloved lackeys." The local governor who recorded these words added tantalizingly in his report to the tsar that "other sorcery is written in the letter that I do not dare write to you, Great Sovereign."[24]

As mentioned above, scholars of Western witchcraft associate the escalation in witch persecution with fundamental changes in religious climate and mores during the early modern period. An analogous spirit of religious revivalism gripped many parts of Muscovy in the late 1650s and early 1660s, the period of the Lukh witch scare. In particular, extreme religiosity swept the area around Lukh and Suzdal. During this period the forests surrounding Suzdal sheltered the visionary prophet Kapiton, a precursor of the religious extremists of subsequent decades. Pilgrims streamed into the area to consult with the great prophet. Kapiton was not the only attraction in the region for religious revivalists. In 1667 an awestruck resident reported that

23. Novombergskii, *Vrachebnoe stroenie*, no. 39.
24. Ibid.

an icon of the Holy Mother of God in the Church of the Resurrection of Christ in the town of Shuia, just outside of Suzdal, miraculously cured his wife's madness and fits. For the next few years worshipers flocked to the town to pay homage to the miracle-working icon of Shuia.[25] The second half of the seventeenth century also witnessed a serious rift within the Orthodox religious community, when a large group of schismatics rebelled against reforms of ritual and procedure initiated by the tsar and patriarch and broke away from the official church. Although none of the sources on witchcraft trials refers explicitly to the effects of the Great Schism, the same religious and political environment provided the background for both. This atmosphere of heightened religiosity accompanied the increased anxiety about bewitchment and sorcery.

THE GENDER OF WITCHES

Women comprised only 32 percent of the 136 accused witches in Russian cases examined here, whereas in Western Europe and North America on average 80 percent were women. The gender distribution in Lukh nearly replicated that of Russia as a whole.

The preceding analysis of religious and political conditions shows that the general environment that gave rise to the witchcraft scares was remarkably similar in Western Europe and in Muscovy. To explain the reversed gender distribution pattern, however, requires a search for differences. The most obvious difference lies in the Muscovites' institutionalization of enserfment and other policies meant to harden distinctions between social estates and tie the population down geographically, whereas Western Europeans enjoyed great mobility. Binding the population within particular taxpaying communities did not occur overnight with the *Ulozhenie* law code of 1649; rather, it happened gradually through the late sixteenth and first half of the seventeenth centuries, just as witchcraft accusations grew in frequency and number.

For Muscovite peasant women and townswomen enforced immobility appears to have reinforced the centrality of the extended family as the basic economic and social unit, thus strengthening whatever importance traditional kinship-based society accorded to women's positions as mothers and wives.[26] Some historians of Western Europe have suggested that Western women found themselves in more marginal positions and hence vulnerable to

---

25. V. Borisov, ed., *Starinnyia akty sluzhashchiia preimushchestvenno dopolneniem k opisaniiu g. Shui i ego okrestnostei* (Moscow, 1853), no. 99; idem., ed., *Opisanie goroda Shui i ego okrestnostei* (Moscow, 1851), no. 45.

26. On the effect of serfdom and the new hearth tax on the peasant family, see Richard Hellie, *Slavery in Russia, 1450–1725* (Chicago, 1982), 706–7; E. N. Baklanova, *Krest'ianskii dvor i obshchina na russkom severe, konets XVII–nachalo XVIII v.* (Moscow, 1976), 15–18.

TABLE 1.   Accused Witches by Sex

Location	Dates	No. of Men	No. of Women	% of Women
Russia	1622–1700	93	43	32
(Lukh)	1654–1660	16	9	36
France[a]	1565–1640	565	529	48
Geneva	1537–1662	74	240	76
New England	1670–1725	75	280	79
Southwest Germany	1562–1631	238	1,050	82
Scotland	1560–1727	242	1,491	86
England (Essex)	1560–1675	23	290	93

SOURCES. Lukh region: TsGADA (Moscow), fond 210, Prikaznyi stol, no. 300, fols. 1–89v.; N. Ia. Novombergskii, *Materialy po istorii meditsiny v Rossii*, 4 vols. (St. Petersburg, 1950–57), 4: 197–220; TsGADA, fond 210, Prikaznyi stol, stol'bets 17, fols. 54–57; *Starinnyia akty sluzhashchia preimushchestvenno dopolneniem k opisaniiu g. Shui i ego okrestnostei*, ed. V. Borisov (Moscow, 1853), no. 109; idem, *Opisanie*, nos. 45, 50. Russia: N. Ia. Novombergskii, *Koldovstvo v Moskovskoi Rusi: VII veka* (St. Petersburg, 1906); idem, *Vrachebnoe stroenie v do-Petrovskoi Rusi* (Tomsk, 1907), nos. 16–20, 35, 37–39, 41, 43, 47, 53. France: Alfred Soman, "Les procès de sorcellerie au Parlement de Paris (1565–1640)," *Annales: Economies, Sociétés, Civilisations* 32 (1977): 798–99. Southwest Germany: H. C. Erik Midelfort, *Witch Hunting in Southwestern Germany, 1562–1684: The Social and Intellectual Foundations* (Stanford, 1972), 181. New England: Carol F. Karlsen, *The Devil in the Shape of a Woman: Witchcraft in Colonial New England* (New York, 1987), 48–49, tables 1 and 2. All others: Brian P. Levack, *The Witch-Hunt in Early Modern Europe* (New York, 1987), 124, table 3.
   [a]Alfred Soman's figures for parts of France derive from the Parlement of Paris, which was primarily a court of appeal. He suggests that the high percentage of men in his sample may be a result of the greater tendency of men to appeal their cases, although he finds similar percentages among the few cases of first instance in his sample.

witch accusations because of the erosion of traditional community support systems.[27] Russian women, at the same time, may have found their situation within the family and the community increasingly stable. This divergence suggests a starting point for understanding the difference in gender of accused witches.

Addressing the question of why Western European witchcraft suspects were overwhelmingly female, scholars have noted the deeply ingrained misogyny of Western culture. Fear and suspicion of women as particularly susceptible to the temptations of evil date back at least to the Greeks and were reinforced by Christian doctrine. In the early modern period Western

27. On the erosion of traditional communities and its deleterious effects on women in the context of witchcraft trials, see Thomas, *Religion*, 553–56; Macfarlane, *Witchcraft*, 161; Carol Karlsen, review of *Salem Possessed*, by Paul Boyer and Stephen Nissenbaum, *Signs* 3 (1978): 703–4. For Macfarlane's retraction of the idea that changes in a traditional social structure accompanied the onset of the witch hunt, see Alan Macfarlane, *The Origins of English Individualism* (Oxford, 1978), 12, 59.

writers on witchcraft commonly dwelled on the insatiable female lust that predisposed women to make pacts with the devil and attend his midnight orgies.[28] As Christine Worobec indicates in her essay in this volume, Orthodox Christianity partook of much of the same ancient tradition of misogyny as the Western church and perhaps even expanded on it. Furthermore, folk proverbs display the hostility and distrust in Russian popular attitudes toward women.[29] Yet with this same cultural heritage of religious and popular misogyny Russia developed a dominant stereotype of witches as male.

The evidence that Russia and Europe shared a tradition of fear and distrust of female evil demonstrates that misogyny alone did not suffice to single out women as witches. Larner proposes that the Western misogynistic tradition produced a self-sustaining stereotype that maintained that "if you are looking for a witch, you are looking for a woman."[30] In Russia a different stereotype, reinforced by the accusation and conviction of predominantly male witches, determined that men, rather than women, were the first suspects in bewitchment cases.

THE PRACTICE OF MAGIC AMONG THE ACCUSED

The remainder of this essay examines four groups of participants—male and female purported witches and male and female accusers—in relation to their community and gender roles, the church and the religious environment, and the burgeoning bureaucratic state. Particularly within the category of accusers a striking pattern of differentiation of roles by sex emerges.

An analysis of those accused of witchcraft, both in Lukh and in Russia as a whole, poses the problem first of identifying why certain persons were likely targets and then differentiating the social profiles of male and female suspects. In Lukh the common characteristic uniting the suspects was social marginality or deviance from standards recently prescribed by the state, with healers mistrusted most of all. Folk healers came in for an especially hard time in the fight against sin and sorcery. Contemporary Russian science had no "professional" medical alternative to offer, and the populace consulted folk healers whenever illness struck.[31] The state clumped minstrels, vagrants, godless unbelievers, and folk healers all together in official decrees against

---

28. Kramer and Sprenger, *Malleus Maleficarum*, 114–45. Russian cases never refer to sexual relations with the devil, as is common in European lore.

29. Christine D. Worobec, "Accommodation and Resistance," 21.

30. Larner, *Witchcraft*, 85. Midelfort makes a similar argument about the power of stereotype in his *Witch Hunting*.

31. Priests apparently had some claim to a sanctioned right to practice healing. See Archpriest Avvakum, *The Life Written by Himself*, ed. and trans. N. Bronstrom (Ann Arbor, 1979), 65–66, 70.

undesirable elements.[32] In the eyes of tsarist officials all of these shady characters, whose powers derived from independent sources (magic or folk religion), posed a threat to the state's absolute control and its monopoly on
sources of cultural legitimacy.

Court records preserve testimony from twelve of the twenty-five Lukh
witches, and fragmentary biographical evidence survives concerning eight
others. Of these twenty people about whom we know more than just a name
and an accusation, at least nine, eight men and one woman, worked as healers. Five others were directly related to healers by blood or marriage. One
was a vagrant minstrel. Of the seventy cases from all over Muscovy analyzed
here, at least one-third involved charges against healers and their kinsfolk.
The overwhelming majority of accused healer witches insisted, even after
enduring the most gruesome tortures, that they administered a powder or
potion "meaning no ill, but to do good." Other endangered categories of
people included vagrants (*guliashchie liudi*), non-Russians, such as Mordvi-
nians and Tatars, and horse or cattle doctors, whose dealings in roots and
grasses brought them dangerously close to the shifting line between acceptable and illegitimate powers.[33]

Russian law acknowledged no particular distinction between white and
black magic, although the most common charges leveled in the seventeenth
century were directed against malefic or criminal sorcery (*vorovstvennoe vol-
shebstvo*), implying that the authors of the law acknowledged the existence of
some noncriminal variant. Suspicion, torture, and punishment of those healers who claimed prayer as their only tool did not differ to any measurable
extent from the treatment meted out to those who employed diabolical or
pagan incantations. In practice, however, most cases that came to trial involved accusations, if not confessions, of inflicting injury on others.

There is some evidence that personal grudges and dislikes, as well as social marginality, contributed to the likelihood that community members
would implicate a certain person. In the Lukh case one of the later suspects,
the deacon Ivan Ivanov, was an unpleasant drunk. Another Lukh resident,
Orinka, Matiushka Gor'ev's wife, was accused after displaying extreme arro-
gance in the face of the community's panic over witchcraft. She threatened a
group of women on the street, saying that she did not fear possession because

32. On healing in Muscovy, see Novombergskii, *Materialy*; idem, *Vrachebnoe stroenie*; idem,
Koldovstvo, esp. vi, ix, xviii–xxxii, and no. 14 (1648 decree). Rose L. Glickman believes that in
nineteenth-century Russia healers were quite distinct from witches; see "The Peasant Woman as
Healer" in this volume. On witchcraft and healing in the West, see Barbara Ehrenreich and
Deirdre English, *Witches, Midwives and Nurses: A History of Women Healers* (Old Westbury, N.Y.,
1973) 6–20; Daly, *Gyn/Ecology*, 223–92; Thomas, *Religion*, 177–211.

33. Itinerants: Novombergskii, *Koldovstvo*, nos. 2, 4, 19, 25, 27, 29; idem, *Vrachebnoe stroenie*,
no. 43. Foreigners: idem, *Koldovstvo*, nos. 4–5; idem, *Vrachebnoe stroenie*, no. 35; L. V. Cherepnin,
"Iz istorii drevnerusskogo koldovstva XVII v.," *Etnografiia*, 1929, no. 2, 90.

God loved her but that the others had reason to fear. In Komaritskii Province in 1648 a sexton and his wife brought on their accusation by uttering vicious threats at their neighbors. The woman was reported to have cursed an acquaintance with the uningratiating phrase: "Peasant, son of a whore, you will cringe at my feet!"[34] With few exceptions, however, accusers vented personal animosities only against people who otherwise fit the social profile of marginality and nonconformity.

Male witches frequently provided explanations for their magical dabblings reminiscent of Tereshka Malakurov's in the Lukh case. Like him, they harmlessly tried to make a living by curing the sick or telling a few fortunes. The financial theme carries through into many of the cases of male witches. For instance, a taverner alerted the authorities that a rival innkeeper in town had cursed him with many drunken customers to ruin his business. Second only to profit came sexual motivations: men often cast spells or used the services of sorcerers for lecherous purposes (*bludnye dela*). These "purposes" ran the gamut from attempts to entrap "anyone of the female sex whom I want, be it even my *boyarina*" to efforts by husbands to "live in counsel now and forever" with their wives and "live in love as of old."[35]

As was true with the men, more than one-third of the forty-three women charged with witchcraft in Muscovy admitted to practicing folk medicine for beneficial purposes but denied any evil intent. Those who did confess to casting spells for nonmedicinal purposes or to harm people seemed to use folk magic to compensate for their general powerlessness. According to testimony from accused female witches a large fraction were motivated to seek magical assistance by a desire for retribution or autonomy, themes that do not emerge in testimony from male suspects. In many cases female serfs, peasants, and servants resorted to spells to rid themselves of their masters and mistresses and their masters' agents. For example, in 1695 a household serf, Mashka, faced charges of trying to bewitch her owner, Semen Frolov. She admitted that a neighbor had given her an herb and had told her "to sprinkle it in Semen Frolov's food, and after that food, he, Semen, will not live to dominate her, Mashka." Court records state that a peasant woman recited a death sentence for her master's estate overseer over a hair taken from a corpse. A servant in a clerical household admitted that she slipped a log into an oven, intoning, "As this log is dead, so let the archpriest and his wife die." A case from Lukh Province elucidates how a woman might resort to witchcraft for vengeance and self-protection. Otniutka, a peasant woman belonging to a certain Artemii Volynskii, confessed to casting a spell after her husband was

---

34. Deacon: TsGADA, fond 210, Prikaznyi stol, no. 314, fol. 204. Orinka: ibid., no. 300, fols. 6–7. Sexton's wife: Novombergskii, *Koldovstvo*, no. 10.

35. Taverner: Novombergskii, *Koldovstvo*, no. 6. Sexual purposes: idem, *Vrachebnoe stroenie*, no. 18; idem, *Koldovstvo*, no. 25.

imprisoned in the master's house and held in irons. She admitted that she obtained some salt from a nearby supplier and scattered it with an incantation meant to rob the heart from her master's overseer and free her husband.[36]

Other confessions of female witches reveal the complexity of domestic relationships within the Muscovite home and the desperate lengths to which some women resorted in attempting to improve their lot. A household servant admitted that she had administered a magical potion in her mistress's food but with no intention to harm the mistress. The previous year, she explained, she had been caught stealing some crosses and rings from the household, and since that time her mistress had treated her badly. She claimed that she had procured a charm in hopes of restoring relations to their previous happy state, unaware that the potion would bring the mistress near death. A gentry woman in Murom confessed that she had placed coal, lumps of clay, kernels of grain, and dead mice in her in-laws' and her husband's beds. At first she maintained that the mice were meant to increase "masculine ferocity" and her other spells to heal diseases, but later she explained that she confessed to the crimes only to improve her standing with her husband's parents: "When I tell them I don't know anything [about the magical paraphernalia], they don't love me, but when I say something slanderous about myself, then they love me. So I slandered myself groundlessly."[37]

To increase their status in the home, women also resorted to a special, time-honored category of spells—the love potion. Many examples survive. Women who cast love spells seem to have been considered innocuous and were not prosecuted unless their potions took on a vengeful component. One of the most delightful relied on the force of analogy, a frequent trope for magical incantations: "As people look at themselves in the mirror, so may the husband look at his wife, and never tire of looking. As people love this salt in food, so may the husband love his wife."[38]

Of course, because prisoners testified under duress, the question arises of whether accused witches actually performed the rituals that were imputed to them, and whether they really thought they could work magic. Even if they never attempted to cast spells, their confessions revealed how close to the

---

36. Mashka: quoted in Cherepnin, "Iz istorii," 97. Archpriest: Novombergskii, *Koldovstvo*, no. 25. Oniutka: TsGADA, fond 210, Prikaznyi stol, no. 300, fol. 10. Other examples of women cursing their masters and mistresses: TsGADA, fond 210, Prikaznyi stol, no. 1225, fols. 6–7; Novombergskii, *Koldovstvo*, nos. 24, 26; Cherepnin, "Iz istorii," 99.

37. Thief: Novombergskii, *Koldovstvo*, no. 20. In-laws: idem, *Vrachebnoe stroenie*, no. 35.

38. Novombergskii, *Koldovstvo*, no. 33; idem, *Vrachebnoe stroenie*, no. 11; Elena Eleonskaia, "Zagovor i koldovstvo na Rusi v XVII i XVIII stoletiiakh," *Russkii arkhiv* 4 (1912): 611–24, 613; A. M. Astakhova, "The Poetical Image and Elements of Philosophy in Russian Exorcisms," *VII Mezhdunarodnyi kongress antropologicheskikh i etnograficheskikh nauk, 3–10 avgusta 1964 g.*, vol. 6 (Moscow, 1969), 268–69.

surface lay their hostility toward their masters and their desire to get even. Equally close to the surface lay a fear of domineering in-laws and a wish to improve their domestic situation. When forced to name even hypothetical victims, many women immediately thought of their masters or in-laws.

By contrast, there is clear evidence that healers and sorcerers did perform some rituals and practice some kinds of magic. The correspondence of detail in witnesses' testimony and the frequent recital of the chain of monetary exchange as magical ingredients passed from hand to hand make plausible the notion that sorcerers and witches practiced their craft and supported themselves with the patronage of a steady, believing clientele. In the Lukh case Tereshka Malakurov took money from his patients to effect a cure. In a case of attempted cursing and poisoning in Dobroe in 1676 officials found in the suspects' home "crushed grasses tied [with hair] in twelve knots, six little sacks of herbs, . . . a spell written in a little notebook, and a bunch of five different grasses."[39] Although most of the accused seem to have thought of themselves as healers rather than witches, many of them apparently did delve into the occult folk practices that the state and church condemned.

GENDER AND POWER RELATIONS IN WITCHCRAFT ALLEGATIONS

Whereas both the men and women accused of witchcraft were generally characterized by social marginality, their accusers played distinctly gendered roles. Men leveled charges of witchcraft when they felt their positions as heads of households to be diminished; women brought such charges to enhance their social standing or to be heard. Men blamed the interference of malign spells for three primary problems—impotence, hernias, and the affliction of their wives and children by spiritual possession. Every one of the male witnesses in the Lukh case expressed concern over one or more of these three categories of misfortune. Other regional witchcraft trials display some-what more variety, but the same patterns still dominate.

Impotence ranked among the difficulties most commonly blamed on witchcraft. About 10 percent of the cases examined here involved charges of causing impotence. The scale of each one of these cases was large, however, involving many self-proclaimed victims. In one case an entire district became so fearful of a local witch with a reputation for causing impotence at wed-dings that couples traveled to the next province to marry.[40] Healers who treated impotence fell under suspicion of having caused the condition in the first place. The testimony of the Lukh man Kiriushka Tret'iakov exemplifies this phenomenon. He announced that when he got married, "an unknown

---

39. Novombergskii, *Vrachebnoe stroenie*, no. 39; idem, *Koldovstvo*, nos . 26, 100.
40. Novombergskii, *Koldovstvo*, no. 10.

person bewitched me, and Arkhipko Fadeev cured me. Arkhipko confessed at that time, and many people brought charges of criminal activity against him in that matter."[41] The healer, witness to the man's humiliating limitation, fell victim to the patient's desire to explain away his shame. Arkhipko Fadeev, the peasant healer, had a large practice in treating both hernias and impotence. To his misfortune, when the possession of the widow Tat'iana sparked a witch scare in Lukh, a whole array of former patients lined up to testify against him.

Muscovites routinely attributed hernias to sorcery. Somewhat embarrassing in location and appearance, hernias were blamed on malicious intent. Many of the men who testified to personal encounters with evil magic complained that they had been afflicted by hernias and consulted healers who failed to rectify the condition and may even have invoked it.

Bizarre, unacceptable conduct on the part of the women or children under his authority also reflected poorly on a man. Aberrant female behavior indicated that the family patriarch had either lost control over his dependents or that he had failed to protect them from external assault.[42] For this reason men latched onto supernatural explanations of their wives' behavior.

Each of these three categories of concern among male accusers seems to relate to issues of masculine potency and control. Specifically sexual anxiety characterized the abhorrence of witches expressed by Western European men as well. Typical of Western writers on the subject, Heinrich Kramer and Jacob Sprenger, authors of the fifteenth-century *Malleus Maleficarum*, or *Hammer of Witches*, revealed an obsessive fear of castration and impotence through the machinations of witches. This preoccupation emerges most vividly in Kramer and Sprenger's extraordinary chapter "How, as it were, they Deprive Man of his Virile Member." The two Dominican inquisitors gravely recorded several remarkable incidents, including one in which

> a certain man tells that when he had lost his member, he approached a known witch to ask her to restore it to him. She told the afflicted man to climb a certain tree, and that he might take which he liked out of a nest in which there were several members. And when he tried to take a big one, the witch said: You must not take that one; adding because it belonged to a parish priest.[43]

Russian men's willingness to blame sexual impotence on witches fits a broader pattern of male witchcraft fears, with the single, striking difference

41. TsGADA, fond 210, Prikaznyi stol, no. 300, fol. 17.

42. On the Muscovite honor-and-shame ethic and its effects on men and women, see Nancy Shields Kollmann, "The Seclusion of Elite Muscovite Women," *Russian History* 10, pt. 2 (1983): 170–87; idem, "Women's Honor in Early Modern Russia," in this volume.

43. Kramer and Sprenger, *Malleus Maleficarum*, 145–54, esp. 151. Men could be blamed for causing impotence in the West as well, but usually those charges were not associated with witchcraft.

that during witchcraft scares Western men commonly displaced their anxieties onto "castrating women," whereas Russians generally put the blame on other men. The reason for this disparity is unclear. A simple explanation might be found in the fact that only male healers seem to have treated impotence. None of the female healers about whom I have found information was explicitly involved in treating male sexual problems, but my sample is small, including only twenty-four healers of either sex. The one woman charged with causing impotence—the one who drove her neighbors to the next province for their weddings—was not a healer. In fact, her own and her husband's testimony as well as that of witnesses suggests that she truly styled herself as a malevolent witch and threatened men around her with the curse of impotence.[44]

Women as well as men leveled charges of witchcraft in Lukh, but for the most part women identified suspects after fits of possession, whereas male witnesses rarely suffered possession. As was the case in colonial New England and elsewhere where spirit possession has been studied, women accounted for 94 percent, that is, all but two of the thirty-five people who were possessed in Lukh during the witch scare.[45] Contrary to what one might expect from instances of possession in the West, however, widows and young girls comprised a small fraction of the possessed in Lukh. By far the majority of women who suffered possession were married. Married women accounted for almost three-quarters of all possessed people. If we exclude men and girls, of the thirty-one adult women who were possessed, 84 percent were married. This figure probably closely approximated the percentage of adult married women in the population as a whole.[46]

Across a broad range of countries, cultures, and times, surrender to the forces of the irrational has provided the weak and downtrodden unusual opportunities for self-expression and self-assertion.[47] Irregular behavior sanctioned by culturally tolerated forms of possession can allow the oppressed, marginal figure to air grievances, gain attention and cautious respect, and sometimes obtain particular material benefits. In one African group,

44. Novombergskii, *Koldovstvo*, no. 10.

45. Karlsen, *Devil*, 224; Demos, "Witchcraft," 1315.

46. Figures on marriage and widowhood in the population at large are not available for the seventeenth century, but calculations by Peter Czap, Jr. for the late eighteenth century suggest that 84 percent would at least represent, and possibly overrepresent, the proportion of married women in the population. See his "Marriage and the Peasant Joint Family in the Era of Serfdom," in *The Family in Imperial Russia: New Lines of Historical Research*, ed. David L. Ransel (Urbana, Ill., 1978), 114. On percentages of widows, see Czap, "Marriage"; and cf. Levack, *Witch-Hunt*, 132; Larner, *Enemies*, 96.

47. On similar phenomena in different cultures, see Judith C. Brown, *Immodest Acts: The Life of a Lesbian Nun in Renaissance Italy* (New York, 1986), 60; and Carroll Smith-Rosenberg, "The Hysterical Woman," in *Disorderly Conduct: Visions of Gender in Victorian America* (New York, 1985), 208; Karlsen, *Devil*, 222–52.

anthropologist I. M. Lewis reported, possessed women demanded tribute in gifts and food from their intimidated husbands, thus routinely emerging from bouts of possession very fat.[48] In the cases Lewis examined, possession by spirits often enhanced women's power, particularly in the domestic sphere.

Testimony from the few unmarried possessed women in the Lukh investigation confirms Lewis's observation that the most "depressed and deprived" categories of people were subject to possession. One of the possessed was a crippled beggar girl. Several of the widows emphasized their straitened conditions, muttering, "I am a poor, simple person and don't go out anywhere with people and don't go around to feasts."[49] Possessed married women presumably expressed their own anger and dissatisfaction when they spoke in the voices of animals and hiccuped with rage. The same kinds of tensions over the distribution of authority in the household illustrated by the testimony of accused female witches in all likelihood characterized the households of the possessed as well. Judging by their susceptibility to possession, married women seem to have suffered as much from the domination of their masters and mistresses, parents-in-law, and spouses as widows and girls did from any potential vulnerability or social anxiety.

Muscovite townswomen and peasants played an active part in the social and economic lives of their communities, but within the household itself the wife's subordinate position produced stresses evident in the testimony of witchcraft trials. Emerging from the shadows of domestic subservience, the married women of Lukh found that their affliction placed them in the spotlight. The whole town discussed them, and grand officials from the capital listened to their every word. Their husbands, presumably eager to reestablish proper patriarchal order in their homes, lavished attention on them and vigorously prayed and petitioned on their behalf. Thus, possessed women gained uncharacteristic privilege and power through temporarily relinquishing self-control and succumbing to the anarchic forces of outside spirits or of the impulses of the unconscious.

The kinds of complaints that motivated men to presume themselves the victims of witchcraft matched a pattern very different from the complaints that drove their female counterparts to adopt the same role. The division of behavior by sex reflected relations of power in the society. Men had recourse to a somewhat wider variety of actions when asserting their already relatively privileged position. For the most part they required the assistance of supernatural forces to explain their predicament only when weakened or afflicted. Women, by contrast, faced a life of domestic subordination that could be

48. I. M. Lewis, "A Structural Approach to Witchcraft and Spirit-Possession," in *Witchcraft Confessions and Accusations*, ed. Mary Douglas (New York, 1970), 296, citing H. Stayt, *The BaVenda* (London, 1931), 305.

49. For example, TsGADA, fond 210, Prikaznyi stol, no. 300, fol. 20.

temporarily ameliorated if they turned to the empowering liberation of relations with the occult.

CONCLUSION

The political and religious climate of Muscovy in the sixteenth and seventeenth centuries, the height of the witchcraft scare, resembled that of contemporaneous Western Europe and New England in several key respects, namely, in the unprecedented expansion of the state in a quest to control its subjects' lives and maintain order, in the secularization of jurisdiction over the morality and conduct of the population, and in the heightened spiritualism and revivalist atmosphere of a religious community riven by reform movements. The Russian experience diverged most notably from that of the West in the preponderance of male witches. The dynamics of increasing social control may provide a significant, though unprovable, explanation for the greater tendency in Russia than in Europe to accuse men. In Russia prohibitions on social movement reinforced a closed community and extended family structure just as these were eroding in the West. By binding family members to their homes, enserfment and related limitations on voluntary mobility may have increased women's security within the household and thus decreased the likelihood that they would live as mavericks, healers, minstrels, or wanderers. Evidence from the trials confirms that fewer women than men were suspected on the basis of an itinerant life-style. Women would then have comprised a small fraction of social outliers, the major pool of witchcraft suspects. Not gender alone, but rather social marginality, in conjunction with a compelling stereotype of witches as male, appears to have been the critical factor in Russian witchcraft allegations.

Though the strengthening of traditional communities and extended families may have increased women's security, it did not add to their authority within the patriarchal household. The differences between male and female experiences of witchcraft reinforce the idea that Russian women chafed at their subordination to husbands, in-laws, and masters. Men relied on witchcraft accusations as crutches in times of weakness, whereas women leveled such accusations with the possibility of temporarily improving their personal status and correcting wrongs inflicted on them by others. Possession patterns in Lukh, when taken together with testimonial evidence from the trials, suggest that townswomen in Muscovy occupied a subordinate, restricted position in the private sphere of the household. From this inferior status women required an acceptable vehicle, such as spirit possession, for expressing dissatisfaction. As a shorthand formulation it may be possible to say that in Muscovite society lack of security produced witches, mostly male, and lack of authority produced accusers, both female and male.

A remarkable quote from one of the women accused of witchcraft in Lukh underscores the extent to which women were resigned to their exclusion from the male world of (relative) power and autonomy. Nastasitsa Salautina was the widowed mother of Ian'ka, Igoshka, and Mit'ka Salautin; the first had already been executed, the latter two were on trial for their lives. When asked whether she knew of any witchcraft performed by her sons, she replied, "I don't know of any violations of the witchcraft statute that my sons have committed . . . but I will not swear for them, because they are of the male sex, and I know what they are capable of but what exactly they do, I don't know."[50]

50. TsGADA, fond 210, Prikaznyi stol, no. 300, fol. 69.

Widows and the
Russian Serf Community

Rodney D. Bohac

Historical studies have typically presented two views of the Russian peasant widow. In one the widow is portrayed as impoverished, often alone, and vulnerable to the authority of men. Constantly subject to pressure from the male leaders of the village, widows often sought the protection of new husbands or, after the emancipation of the serfs in 1861, migrated to the cities. A second interpretation depicts widows as the most autonomous and influential women in the peasant community. They are shown managing households, for instance, and serving as healers and midwives.[1]

In fact, these two contradictory interpretations both contain truth. Peasant widows did face poverty, pressure to remarry, and social isolation. Yet some guaranteed their own subsistence, resisted male dominance, and exerted informal power within the household and community. The successful widows used or surmounted elements of the patriarchy, such as inheritance

1. Stephen P. Frank, "Popular Justice, Community, and Culture among the Russian Peasantry," *Russian Review* 46 (July 1987): 239–40, 261, describes widows who are accused of witchcraft, and Robert E. Johnson, *Peasant and Proletarian: The Working Class of Moscow in the Late Nineteenth Century* (New Brunswick, N.J., 1979), 56, describes young widows migrating to the city because of social isolation in the peasant village. Aleksandra I. Efimenko, *Izsledovaniia narodnoi zhizni*, vol. 1, *Obychnoe pravo* (Moscow, 1884), 96, also points out the widow's vulnerability. Samuel Ramer, "Childbirth and Culture: Midwifery in the Nineteenth-Century Russian Countryside," in *The Family in Imperial Russia: New Lines of Historical Research*, ed. David L. Ransel (Urbana, Ill., 1978), 218–35, mentions widows serving as midwives; and Barbara Alpern Engel, "The Woman's Side: Male Out-Migration and the Family Economy in Kostroma Province," *Slavic Review* 45 (Summer 1986): 257–71, describes widows as household heads. Peter Czap, Jr., "'A Large Family: The Peasant's Greatest Wealth': Serf Households in Mishino, Russia, 1814–1858," in *Family Forms in Historic Europe*, ed. Richard Wall, Jean Robin, and Peter Laslett (Cambridge, 1983), 119, and Steven L. Hoch, *Serfdom and Social Control in Russia: Petrovskoe, a Village in Tambov* (Chicago, 1986), 121, also discuss the ambiguities of the widows' position in the peasant village.

practices and limited access to public political life, that led to the suffering of other widows. Thus the system that constrained women's actions also presented opportunities to resist the patriarchy and exert influence within it.

In this essay I test this proposition by examining the lives of the serf widows of Manuilovskoe, a large estate belonging to the Gagarin family. Located 150 miles north of Moscow in Tver Province, Manuilovskoe contained nine villages and more than one thousand serfs in 1861. Like other peasants living in the non-black-earth region, the Manuilovskoe serfs employed the traditional three-field system of agriculture; they also turned increasingly to artisanal trades and migration to supplement their income in the nineteenth century. Work as carpenters, hemp scutchers, carters, and craftsmen helped the serfs pay *obrok* (money rent) to the Gagarins as well as raise the taxes they owed to the government.[2]

The communities of Manuilovskoe formed a hierarchy of organizations common among Russian peasants. At the base was the household, usually consisting of an extended multigenerational family and headed by a patriarch. Several households made up the larger peasant organization of the *mir*, or commune. At Manuilovskoe the *mir* consisted of all the households of the nine villages scattered across the estate. Each household was entitled to send one male representative to the *mir* assembly, the *skhod*, and it was in the meetings of the *skhod* that male serfs made the communal decisions crucial to the ongoing life of the estate. The *skhod* allocated farmland to individual households and set the tax and rent assessments for each household. It also elected peasant leaders, including an estate manager (*burmistr*), a trustee (*vybornyi*), and a small number of elders (*stariki*), who represented the community in dealings with the landlord. The estate manager was the most important of these officials. Because the Gagarins usually sent no overseer to Manuilovskoe, they depended on the manager to administer estate affairs and collect the *obrok*.

Serf women contributed significantly to Manuilovskoe's economy. In addition to carrying out household chores, spinning and weaving, and caring for children, they participated in agricultural work. Women tended livestock, raked hay, harrowed the fields, worked manure into the soil, and scutched hemp. Plowing remained the preserve of men, but largely because of custom, not because of any physical weakness on the part of women. It was not uncommon for other wealthy Tver landlords to hire women to plow their fields.[3]

2. For a fuller description of the Manuilovskoe economy, see Rodney D. Bohac, "Family, Property and Socioeconomic Mobility: Russian Peasants on Manuilovskoe Estate, 1810–1861" (Ph.D. diss., University of Illinois, 1982).

3. Ibid., 91–92; V. I. Pokrovskii, ed., *Istoriko-statisticheskoe opisanie Tverskoi gubernii v sel'sko-khoziaistvennom otnoshenii*, 2 vols. (St. Petersburg, 1879), 175, 214–17; V. A. Preobrazhenskii, *Opisanie Tverskoi gubernii v sel'sko-khoziaistvennom otnoshenii* (St. Petersburg, 1879), 467.

Because of serf women's contributions to the economy of the estate the community took women's labor into account when dividing the land and assessing each household's share of the *obrok* payment, but only if the women were married. Rents, taxes, and land allotments were calculated on the basis of the number of married couples (called *tiagla*, or work units) within a household. Single men were entitled to only one-half the allotment assigned to a husband and wife; unmarried daughters were not counted at all. The more married couples a household contained, therefore, the more laborers, landholdings, and wealth it enjoyed. To maintain high levels of labor and land, Russian serfs married their children at a young age and encouraged virilocal residence.[4]

But where did widows fit into a community so structured around the married couple? To answer this question, I will examine the records for Manuilovskoe estate compiled between 1810 and 1861. Over this half-century estate managers sent a steady stream of reports, ledgers, and household registers (*podvornye opisi*) to Gagarin family officials, who oversaw the activities of the estate from Moscow. The household registers and national censuses, or revisions (*revizii*), provide invaluable information about the estate's widows. The twelve registers and four revisions, which I will describe collectively as censuses, give basic demographic and ethnographic data about individual Manuilovskoe households, including their members' names, ages, marital status, and relationship to the household head. The registers also provide such detailed economic information as a household's *obrok* assessment, the size of its arrears, and the number of buildings and livestock it owned.[5]

The data gathered from these sources present some problems for analyzing the position of widows. The imperial government commissioned the revisions to determine assessments for military conscription and the head tax, both of which were based on the number of males. If a male listed in a revision did not appear in a subsequent one, the date of his departure from the revision rolls and the reason for it had to be listed. Because women were not drafted or taxed, the revisions did not record information about their movement and in some years did not list them at all. Thus when a woman disappeared from the Manuilovskoe censuses, I did not know whether she had died or moved off the estate. Unless additional evidence indicated other-

4. Hoch, *Serfdom*, 92–95.

5. Gagarin Family Papers, Tsentral'nyi gosudarstvennyi arkhiv drevnikh aktov (TsGADA) fond 1262, opis' 2, 1813 Household Register, delo (d.) 7192; 1823 Register, d. 7215; 1824 Register, d. 7219; 1826 Register, d. 7226; 1829 Register, d. 7240; 1833 Register, d. 7245; 1840 Register, d. 7256; 1851 Register, d. 7286; 1857 Register, d. 7320; 1860 Register, d. 7335; 1861 Register, d. 7338. The revisions are 1816 Revision, d. 7203; 1834 Revision, d. 7247; 1850 Revision, d. 7284; 1858 Revision, d. 7324. All Gagarin documents are from TsGADA, fond 1262, opis' 2; hence these will no longer be cited in source notes. Other terms used in archival citations include *list* (l.) and *obratnyi* (ob.).

TABLE 1.   Manuilovskoe Households Containing
Widows, 1813–61

Year	No.	%
1813	147	33.3
1823	147	29.3
1826	147	29.3
1829	121	20.7
1833	126	28.6
1840	125	36.0
1851	123	29.3
1857	122	19.7
1860	123	16.3
1861	132	13.6

SOURCE. Household registers and revisions.

wise, I assumed that those over forty years of age or those who had lived in a household for at least ten years had died. All others were coded as departing for unknown reasons; among them there may well have been some widows. Other widows, at least a dozen, may have gone uncounted because they died soon after their husbands. If both a woman and her husband died between censuses, there was no means of determining which partner died first. Nor was it always possible to determine exactly when a husband died. Eighteen men recorded in the 1834 revision as having died in 1821 turned up again in the 1823 and 1824 registers. In these and similar cases I recorded the date of the last appearance in the censuses as the year of death.

The incorrect recording of information by estate officials also affected age data. The ages of elderly women were especially problematical. The censuses recorded the age of the widow Fevrona Ivanova as sixty, sixty-three, and seventy in the 1813, 1816, and 1823 censuses, and fifty-two and fifty-four in 1826 and 1829. Mar'ia Sidorova's records presented even more difficulties. She was listed as seventy-nine and eighty-two years old in 1813 and 1816, as seventy in 1823, and as eighty in 1824. I arbitrarily handled this problem by using the age in the 1816 revision for women born prior to the first census in 1813. For those born after 1813 I used the age recorded in the first census in which they appeared. In any event, the age data do give a relative indication of age.

Despite these problems the censuses provide unique and revealing information about the nature of widowhood on Manuilovskoe estate. They indicate that many serf women faced widowhood. In 1851, 17.1 percent of Manuilovskoe women over the age of twenty were widows. In the censuses of the first half of the century, from one-fifth to more than one-third of the serf

TABLE 2.   Women on Manuilovskoe and Petrovskoe Estates, 1851
(percentages)

Age Cohort	Manuilovskoe			Petrovskoe		
	Married	Single	Widowed	Married	Single	Widowed
15–19	13.5	86.5	0.0	0.0	91.3	0.0
20–24	79.0	21.0	0.0	69.0	28.6	0.0
25–29	93.4	3.3	3.3	90.3	6.5	3.2
30–39	72.9	18.8	8.4	84.5	5.6	9.9
40–49	75.4	8.2	16.4	63.4	2.0	34.0
50–59	47.7	6.8	45.5	—	—	—
60+	23.0	7.7	69.2	—	—	—

SOURCE. Household registers and revisions.

NOTE. Data for the Gargarins' *barshchina* estate at Petrovskoe, Tambov Province, in 1850 are found in Steven L. Hoch, *Serfdom and Social Control: Petrovskoe, a Village in Tambov* (Chicago, 1985), 78. The remaining proportion of Petrovskoe women are *soldatki*, women whose husbands have been conscripted into the military. Because the percentages have been rounded off to the nearest tenth, they do not add up to 100 in all cases.

households contained widows (table 1). There was a widow in almost three-fourths (71.3 percent) of all the households at some point between 1813 and 1861. On Petrovskoe, a Gagarin estate in Tambov Province, the percentages of widows were higher, especially among women in their forties (table 2).[6] These inflated figures may have resulted from an epidemic or some catastrophic accident. The statistics from both estates confirm that middle-aged and elderly women often became widows.

Manuilovskoe serf women entered widowhood at a fairly early age. Almost a third of them were widowed in their thirties (table 3). Episodic crises partially account for high rates of widowhood among young women. In 1826 at least eleven men died from an epidemic while working on another of the Gagarins' estates. In the same year Manuilovskoe was suffering from the effects of four consecutive crop failures. Because hunger and disease were rampant in 1828, fifteen women under the age of forty became widows that year. War also raised the male death rate. The war against Napoleon in 1812 forced many men into the provincial militia; in 1812 six women in their thirties were widowed, in contrast to the usual annual figure of one or two.[7]

The high male mortality forced women, households, and the community to seek a variety of means to handle widowhood. All parties first faced the

6. Hoch, *Serfdom*, 78.

7. May 1826 Excerpt from the Ledger of Manuilovskoe Carpenters Sent to Moscow Province, d. 7225.

TABLE 3. Age at Entry into Widowhood, 1812–61
(percentages)

Age at Entry	1812–19	1820–29	1830–39	1840–49	1850–61	All Years
19–29	12.5	23.6	11.6	16.1	27.3	17.5
30–39	40.6	27.3	25.6	45.2	13.6	30.6
40–49	12.5	21.8	30.2	12.9	18.2	20.2
50–59	18.8	20.0	25.6	12.9	31.8	21.3
60–69	15.6	5.5	4.7	12.9	9.1	8.7
70+	0.0	1.8	2.3	0.0	0.0	1.1

SOURCE. Household registers and revisions.
NOTE. The total number of widows for the period 1812–61 was 183. Of them, 17.5 percent entered widowhood in 1812–19; 30.0 percent in 1820–29; 23.5 percent in 1830–39; 17.0 percent in 1840–49; 12.0 percent in 1850–61.

problem of providing subsistence for the new widow. Possible solutions included the widow's remaining in her husband's household, moving back to her natal family's household, or remarrying. Inheritance practices, a widow's age, and the presence of children affected the choice.

Manuilovskoe serf women possessed limited inheritance rights, as did most Russian peasant women. Russian peasants practiced a partible inheritance system in which all sons received an equal share of the father's property. On the Manuilovskoe estate this property included communal and purchased land, livestock, implements, buildings, and personal possessions. The daughter's share was composed of her trousseau and other possessions given to her when she married. The sons rarely took their share when they married. Instead they lived on with their wives in their parents' household while they worked to increase the worth of the family's possessions. After five to ten years, if enough capital had accrued and if they received permission from the landlord, they broke up or partitioned the household, usually into two new households.[8]

When a daughter married, she relinquished her rights to her natal household's communal and purchased land but in return gained rights to the property of her husband's family. These rights endured even after her husband died. A variety of factors may explain why Russian peasants, patriarchal in so many of their customs, allotted shares to widows. Some scholars argue that widows received a share because they had brought a dowry into the household. Dowries, however, may not have been common among Russian peasants. The peasants may have thought that widows had earned the right to a share by contributing their labor to the household economy. A widow's

8. Rodney D. Bohac, "Russian Peasant Inheritance Strategies," *Journal of Interdisciplinary History* 16 (1985): 23–42.

portion, which eventually devolved to her husband's direct male heirs, may further have served to protect male claims to the property from encroachment by distant relatives. But more obviously, the property provided support for a widow and her unmarried daughters.[9]

A widow who continued to live in her deceased husband's household was usually entitled to one-seventh of the household property. The portion was allotted to her for life. She was to use it to care for herself and any unmarried daughters and to provide dowries for them. When she died, what remained of her widow's portion devolved to her surviving unmarried daughters, who forfeited it to their father's male heirs when they married. Sons who did not want to look after their mothers and unmarried sisters were also obliged to provide them with a similar property share for their sustenance. When partitioning their household, Maksim Lavrent'ev's sons, for example, promised to provide their mother with an *izba* (a room or hut), a cow, a calf, a sheep, and a strip of land from each of their fields until her death. The widow Fedosa, age fifty, and her daughters, ages twenty and thirteen, received a more sizable one-seventh portion, including a new *izba* and agricultural buildings, a horse, a cow, a share of the grain reserves, and ten *desiatiny* (about twenty-seven acres) of purchased land.[10]

Widows with large property shares were sometimes coveted household members, helping male relatives extend their holdings. Newly partitioned households probably welcomed the opportunity to house a widow in return for possible control over her widow's portion. When his household partitioned, Mikhail Andreev invited his widowed aunt and nieces to live with him, so that he could manage her widow's share. He only lost control of it twenty-four years later, when he began to mistreat his spinster niece, the surviving heir to the widow's portion.[11]

In addition to exercising their own inheritance rights, widows also served as guardians of property for male relatives. It was particularly common for widows with small sons to play this role. These women usually did not receive a widow's portion but instead acted as trustees for their sons' property, which consisted of the deceased father's inheritance share. One *mir* directive placed Afima Ivanova in charge of her son's share. When he grew up, he was to care for his mother until she died. Then he would inherit the property.[12]

9. Efimenko, *Izsledovaniia*, 21–22, 68, 97; Margaret Jean Hay, "Women as Owners, Occupants, and Managers," in *Widows in African Society*, ed. Betty Potash (Stanford, 1986), 113, points out the role of widows as guardians of property.

10. 28 February 1833 Report, d. 7244, 1.45; 21 February 1812 Report, d. 7190, 1.5; 4 June 1857 Report, d. 7322, 1.16. Before the 1840s serfs did not use surnames. Instead their names consisted of a given name and a now-archaic form of patronymic (Ivanova, not Ivanovna). This is the form that will be used in this essay.

11. 26 July 1857 Report, d. 7322, 1.

12. 27 April 1821 Report, d. 7213. 1.83.

In most cases the widow's portion was insufficient for a woman to maintain her own independent household, especially if she was responsible for
small children. Her problems were compounded by the fact that the larger
community of the *mir* was often indifferent to her plight, if not actually preda-
tory in its efforts to gain control of her property. In other words, without the
protection of their own families many widows fell victim to the rapaciousness
of other families. Widows who headed nuclear-family households consisting
only of small children were especially vulnerable. The *mir* had the power to
lighten the tax burdens on such women, exempting them from all or part of
the *obrok* and from the head tax levied on their minor sons. This was a mixed
blessing, for those widows who no longer paid *obrok* lost their communal field
land and the grain produced on that land. The commune, saddled with
mutual responsibility for taxes, distributed its allotments to other, more productive households that could more easily meet their obligations to serf
owner and state. Getting control of the widows' land, not charity toward
them, was probably the chief motive for reducing the women's taxes.

Manuilovskoe records provide two examples of this sort of community
"aid." In 1811 Dar'ia Miniaeva and her "little orphans" petitioned the serf
owner Gagarin. "I'm a widow," she explained, "with small children. I had
two sons and four daughters." Her eldest son had died, and the surviving son
was only five years old. "Relieve me from *obrok*," she pleaded, "until my son
grows up." She finished by lamenting that *obrok* relief meant that her household would be without land. Another female petitioner, Stepanida Terent'-
eva, asked to be exempted from only one of her three tax units but also
worried about the loss of her field allotment. She claimed there would be
nothing left from which to feed her loved ones.[13]

Still more desperate was the situation of the widow Mar'ia Ivanova, who
complained to the Gagarins that the *mir* had taken not only her field land but
also her garden plot (*usad'ba*) within the village. The peasants grew vegetables, hemp, and flax and raised small livestock on these plots. Mar'ia Ivanova and her three children now controlled only the land on which her *izba*
stood. She asked to be relieved of the head tax and to have her garden returned to her. Other widows chose to bring male workers into their households as in-marrying sons-in-law or adopt adult sons rather than ask for tax
relief.[14] With male laborers they were less likely to lose their households'
land allotments to the commune.

The male leaders of the *mir* could also victimize a widow by refusing to
grant draft exemptions to her sons, thus permitting the young men on whom
the shrunken family depended for its livelihood to be taken away for lifetime

---

13. 2 May 1811 Petition from Dar'ia Miniaeva, d. 7189, 1.28; 7 February 1819 Petition from
Stepanida Terent'eva, d. 7216, 1.87.
14. January 1839 Petition from Mar'ia Ivanova, d. 7254, 1.28.

TABLE 4.   Widows' Movements according to Age at Entry into Widowhood, 1812–61 (percentages)

Age at Entry	Remain in Husband's Household	Remarry	Transfer and Remarry	Transfer	Destination Unknown
19–29	7.2	35.7	14.3	14.3	28.6
30–39	58.2	20.9	7.0	0.0	13.9
40–49	88.9	11.1	0.0	0.0	0.0
50–59	94.5	0.0	5.6	0.0	0.0
60+	93.3	0.0	6.7	0.0	0.0
All ages	66.4	14.8	6.7	2.7	9.4

SOURCE. Household registers and revisions.
NOTE. $N = 149$. The table's data do not include widows who appeared in the last register and had not yet moved.

service in the army. Varvara Gavrilova asked for a draft exemption in 1813 but was refused; the *mir* conscripted a son. Mar'ia Anafreeva's argument that she was a poor widow with small children also failed. The army took her eldest boy, a seventeen-year-old stepson. Only Domna Fedoseeva succeeded in getting a draft exemption, perhaps because she asked for only a short postponement of her son's enlistment.[15]

The pressure of the Manuilovskoe *mir* on women left without male defenders seems to have been effective: it drove women either to remarry, thus entering a new family that would protect them, or to flee the estate altogether. Deprived even of her garden, Mar'ia Ivanova dissolved her household and married a widower in another village. Stepanida Terent'eva tried to manage her small household for a few more years after her petition to the Gagarins but gave up in 1823 and ran away.

Owing to community pressure and economic hardships for a widow on her own, most Manuilovskoe widows remained with their husbands' families: two-thirds of those about whom we have information took this course (table 4). There they could be assured that their subsistence needs were looked after. Women over the age of thirty and those with children, especially sons, were highly likely to stay on with their in-laws (table 5). Remarriage was less an option for these women because of the complex property arrangements and often the financial losses that ensued when a woman moved out, taking her children with her.

A widow's remarriage created property complications for sons from her

15. 23 October 1813 Petition from Varvara Gavrilova, d. 7197, 1.47; 23 October 1813 Petition from Mar'ia Anafreeva, d. 7197, 1.48; 27 October 1813 Petition from Domna Fedoseeva, d. 7197, 1.11.

TABLE 5.   Widows' Movement According to Number of Widows' Children, 1812–61

Number of Children	Remained in Husband's Household	Remarried	Transferred	Locale Unknown
No children	6	8	7	3
One	19	9	3	4
Two	67	9	3	7
Total	92	26	13	14

SOURCE. Household registers and revisions.

first marriage. A son who followed his mother into her new husband's household took his father's inheritance share with him. Estranged from his natal family because his departure had cost them economically, the son could face problems in his new household as well. There he might lose control of his father's share to his stepfamily and hold uncertain claims to his stepfather's property.

Things were even more complicated for the progeny of a pregnant widow who chose to remarry before waiting out the pregnancy. A case of this kind occurred on Manuilovskoe in 1799. When Egor Dmitriev married Boris Nikitin's widowed sister-in-law, he had to promise Boris that if the pregnant widow had a son he would not demand an inheritance share for the boy. In other words, Boris Nikitin, not wishing to lose any family property, disinherited his brother's child. Despite the written agreement, twelve years later Egor Dmitriev claimed a right to some of Boris Nikitin's purchased land. It is not clear whether he received any land, but it is certain that Egor Dmitriev was not solicitous of his stepson's rights: he simply wanted to expand his own land holdings.[16]

Remarriage of women with daughters and no sons also presented difficulties. The records pertaining to Manuilovskoe estate suggest that bride-price was customary. Under bride-price the remarrying widow's daughters' own family would have been unwilling to have them move into a new household. They would not have wanted to forfeit any claims to the bride-price when the girls married.[17] Households were also reluctant to lose a remarrying widow's property portion, which was shared by her daughters. When a widow remarried, she took her share to her new household. Only when the widow died and her daughters remarried did the land revert to the first husband's brothers. Cases, however, demonstrate that married daughters could suc-

16. 9 April 1799 Marriage Agreement, d. 7189, 1.27; May 1811 Petition from Boris Nikitin, d. 7189, 1.23.
17. Hoch, *Serfdom*, 121; Efimenko, *Izsledovaniia*, 30.

cessfully lay claim to retention of the widow's portion. For example, when Avdot'ia Safronova remarried in 1762, her brother-in-law asked the *mir* to turn over to him that portion of his deceased brother's land Avdot'ia received as her widow's share. The *mir* agreed, but the serf owner at that time, P. V. Saltykov, overruled the decision, reassuring the widow that the land did not have to be returned until after her death. When Avdot'ia Safronova's daughter married, Avdot'ia, widowed again, moved into her son-in-law's household with her widow's share and remained there until she died. In 1811 her former brothers-in-law claimed the property. Her son-in-law refused to give it up, arguing that the land rightfully devolved to his wife after her mother's death and had been part of his property for thirteen years. When in another case, this time in 1813, heirs wanted a widow's share returned, the *mir* chose to compromise, dividing the land between the two claimants. In both cases a widow's remarriage resulted in her former brothers-in-law forfeiting property.[18] The ambiguities inherent in customary law encouraged male relatives to keep their brothers' widows at home, especially those with children, and dissuade them from remarrying.

Most of those widows who left their husbands' households were young. In the Manuilovskoe sample only three of the fourteen who moved in with other relatives and five of the thirty-two who remarried were over the age of forty. The rest were young women, three-quarters of whom moved out of their husbands' homes within four years of being widowed. Some of these women returned to households headed by members of their immediate family: four moved in with their fathers, and three with their brothers. The actual number of young women who made such arrangements may have been larger than my sample indicates, since at least fourteen women simply disappeared from the estate censuses (see table 4). Some of them may have moved in with relatives, some may have died, and some may have married men living in nearby villages not owned by the Gagarins.[19]

Among the relatively few older widows who left their in-laws' households, many seem to have been women who had no children remaining in that household. Most of them moved in with other relatives. One widow went to live with a brother, and another went to a cousin's home. These women remained in their new homes until they died. Only two women who moved in

18. 2 May 1811 Petition from Ivan Evdokimov et al., d. 7189, 1.26; 19 July 1811 Petition from Semen Gurianov, d. 7189, 1.31; 8 July 1813 Report, d. 7197, 1.20.

19. Manuilovskoe archives contain no records of petitions requesting marriage to outsiders, perhaps because the Gagarins were not concerned with the number of laborers they had on their *obrok* estate. The widows may also have simply left the estate to work elsewhere. Most of the departures of uncertain destination took place before 1833. The decade of the 1820s, with its crop failures and high mortality among male migrants, created many young widows, not all of whom would have had family protection. This need may have brought pressure on some to leave.

with other relatives had sons. Both of these women waited until their sons grew up and then, as trustees of the young men's inheritance, moved into already established households where there were no male heirs. The heads of these households adopted the widows' boys, making them the sole heirs to their households' property and gaining in return their labor and the use of their inheritance. Other widows who moved did so to join their newly married daughters. Two of these widows' daughters married young men who had recently become the heads of small households. When they moved in with their new husbands, they were accompanied by their widowed mothers and younger brothers. The brothers probably brought some property with them as well as their valuable labor power.[20]

Thus far the portrait of the widow's plight seems a dark one. If a woman managed to remain within her in-laws' household, she might endure the difficulties of widowhood with as much comfort and security as any Russian peasant knew. If she was left alone with young children and no adult males in her immediate family circle, her household would be beleaguered until she surrendered and dissolved it. Remarriage proved to be a satisfactory option mainly for relatively young widows.

But sheltering within her father-in-law's *izba* or fleeing to another village were not the only options open to a widow. The ambiguities and constraints of inheritance practices provided some enterprising widows with opportunities to resist male demands and sometimes to exert power within the household and community. Admittedly, it was a power often exercised indirectly, but in this it was not unlike the behavior of male serfs, who were as ostensibly powerless in their relationship to their masters as women were in dealings with men. Over time the Manuilovskoe serfs had devised a variety of tactics to resist and shape the Gagarins' decisions. They might delay carrying out an onerous demand by the landlord while declaring that they were doing their best. They might craft anonymous petitions.[21] Estate records suggest widows also maneuvered similarly oblique ways within the rules of a patriarchal order to mitigate the oppression in their lives.

Perhaps most empowering were women's property rights. Manuilovskoe records contain a variety of examples of serf widows taking advantage of their control over property to maximize their position within a household. When Ustina Ivanova's daughter married, she did not move out of her mother's house, as was customary. Instead her new son-in-law, Petr Avdeev, moved

    20. 18 October 1822 Report, d. 7214, 1.106 ob.
    21. Rodney D. Bohac, "Everyday Forms of Resistance: Serf Opposition to Gentry Exactions, 1800–1861," in *Peasant Economy, Culture, and Politics of European Russia, 1800–1921*, ed. Esther Kingston-Mann and Timothy Mixter (Princeton, 1991), 236–60. For discussions of the concept of resistance and the use of power in other patriarchal systems, see Natalie Zemon Davis, *The Return of Martin Guerre* (Cambridge, 1984); Davis, " 'On the Lame,' " *American Historical Review* 93 (June 1988): 572–603; and *Women and Power in the Middle Ages*, ed. Mary Erler and Maryanne Kowaleski (Athens, Ga., 1988).

in, probably so that there would be a man to work the household's land as well as act as its spokesman at meetings of the *mir*. Ustina Ivanova did not thereafter relinquish her power within the family circle, however. Estate records mention her arranging property transfers. In 1819, when the estate manager reported a land dispute, he stated that "Ustina and her son-in-law Petr Avdeev" had mortgaged a piece of land years before. His report also included a paraphrase of the elderly woman's testimony about the transaction. He recorded her words as "I and my son-in-law" mortgaged the land.[22] The listing of Ivanova as equal to the male head-of-household, who in the meantime had been drafted into the army, in something as important to the peasants as a land transfer attests to her continuing authority within the family.

Aksin'ia Petrova may have been another widow who protected herself from poverty and the encroachment of the *mir* by arranging for men to move in with her. Left to head a household without adult male workers, she proposed, or consented to a proposal, that her father and his family come to live with her. Her father benefited from the new arrangement too: he was able to leave his brother's household, taking with him his inheritance share. The *mir* and the Gagarins discouraged partitioning among brothers because the practice divided serf holdings into smaller, less viable economic units. By moving into his daughter's household, the father circumvented restrictions imposed by both *mir* and serf owners. Perhaps he coerced Aksin'ia Petrova into accepting him. By contrast, her role in the maneuver and her nominal control over her share of the household's property may have enhanced her influence.

Forceful women could also make their will felt when they decided to remarry. In 1811 Boris Nikitin complained to Gagarin officials in Moscow that he had offered to take care of his brother's pregnant widow and her new baby when it was born, but the sister-in-law had refused his proposal and remarried instead.[23] Mar'ia Anafreeva also exemplified an independent-minded woman who arranged her remarriage. As she explained later during an inheritance dispute, after her first husband died, she lived with his two brothers for two years. Forced to feed her two children "on her own" there, Mar'ia Anafreeva decided to leave. The estate manager and the *mir* permitted her to take her children's inheritance share and remarry. At age thirty-five she married a man fourteen years her junior, who was already a household head.[24] With her age, work experience, and control over her son's inheritance share, she likely wielded great influence in her new household.

---

22. 3 June 1819 Report, d. 7212, 1.5.
23. May 1811 Petition from Boris Nikitin, d. 7189, 1.23.
24. July 1815 Petition from Mar'ia Anafreeva, d. 7200, 11.38–39.

TABLE 6.   Relationship of Widow's New Husband to Household Head,
            by Widow's Age at Remarriage

| | Relationship to Household Head | | | | |
Widow's Age at Remarriage	Household Head	Eldest Son	Other Son	Other Relative	Total
20–29	3	1	3	0	7
30–39	9	3[a]	0	1	13
40–49	8	0	0	0	8
50–59	2	0	0	0	2
Total widows	22	4	3	1	30

SOURCE. Household registers and revisions.
[a] Includes one son-in-law (*zviat'*). The "other relative" is a cousin.

Few widows married younger men as Mar'ia Anafreeva did. Most widows married older men. Whereas the mean age difference between spouses in all Manuilovskoe marriages was only 1.3 years, for remarriages the gap reached an average of 8.1 years. More than one-half of the widows married men at least ten years older than they themselves. Studies of Central European peasants have suggested that such marriages could present problems for former widows. The women might become dependent on their new husbands in an effort to cope with new in-laws and stepchildren. In France, by contrast, folk sayings suggest husbands treated second wives better than their first.[25]

The documents from Manuilovskoe reveal little about relations between family members, save when those relations soured into conflicts that were brought to the attention of the Gagarins' officials. There is indirect evidence, however, that widows were maximizing the opportunities available to them when they remarried, even when—perhaps especially when—they married older men. Overwhelmingly they managed to choose husbands who were either heads-of-household or heirs to that position. This is true of women in all age groups, but it becomes universal in my sample for women over thirty (table 6). Both the head and the widow benefited from such a marriage: the head gained the widow's property and a wife who would supervise his daughters-in-law in their domestic chores; the widow became a senior woman, a position of authority and status within the family.[26]

25. Michael Mitterauer and Reinhard Sieder, *The European Family: Patriarchy to Partnership from the Middle Ages to the Present*, trans. Karla Oosterveen and Manfred Horzinger (Chicago, 1982), 65; Martine Segalen, *Love and Power in the Peasant Family: Rural France in the Nineteenth Century*, trans. Sarah Matthews (Chicago, 1983), 25–37.

26. Mary Matossian, "Peasant Way of Life," in *The Peasant in Nineteenth-Century Russia*, ed. Wayne S. Vucinich (Stanford, 1968), 17. The senior woman in the peasant joint family of

For some women marriage to a household head simply maintained their position, as their previous husband had also served as head. Instead of being demoted, these women moved into the senior position in another household. The rest of the widows went from a lower position, held when married to their first husband, to a higher status by marrying a household head or an heir to that position. Sometimes to enter such a marriage, the women moved into households with smaller holdings. Almost two-thirds, however, ended up in a household that owned the same or more property than their former in-laws. This evidence strongly suggests that the widows were participating in contracting these new alliances, choosing to leave their in-laws only when a better arrangement presented itself. The in-laws had little to gain when the women left; whether the widow married a household head or a junior son, the loss to the household she left was the same. For the woman, however, movement into a position of senior woman from widowhood represented an improvement, one worth the difficulties of separating from her first husband's family.

Widows did not have to restrict their ambitions to the post of a household head's wife. They could also aspire to be the head of a household. One-third (33.9 percent) of all households listed in Manuilovskoe records had a woman in the headship at some point between 1813 and 1861. The proportion of female household heads in any one census reached a high of 14.6 percent in 1851. (The percentages are 10.2 in 1813, 14.3 in 1823, 2.7 in 1826, 5.0 in 1829, 0.8 in 1833, 7.2 in 1840, 14.6 in 1851, 9.8 in 1860, and 13.6 in 1861.)[27] All of these women were widows. Some were more successful than others. Younger women tended to be in charge of poorer households, whose overall average holding of 2.6 horses was below the estate average. We have already seen how vulnerable such women were to village pressure, particularly if they had young children. But if a widow was older, if she had adult sons, and if her family had amassed some property, she might manage to be a secure, authoritative household head.

Most of the widows of Manuilovskoe who became household heads fit this description. Because they had been married to the household head, they had already served before their husbands' death as the senior woman in the family. Most had also been living in the household for a long period of time before becoming household head at a relatively late age. The mean age at reaching the headship was 54.9 years, and more than two-thirds became heads when they were over fifty. (On average men became household heads between the

nineteenth-century Italy played a similar role. See David Kertzer, *Family Life in Central Italy, 1880–1910* (New Brunswick, N.J., 1984), 33.

27. For each household in the census I designated the first person listed as the head. Widows served as household heads on other serf owners' estates as well. See A. Aleksandrov, *Selskaia obshchina v Rossii* (Moscow, 1966), 295–96; Hoch, *Serfdom*, 161; and Czap, "'A Large Family,'" 134.

ages of thirty-five and forty.) Among these older women, more than 80 percent had married sons, and almost one-half (44.1 percent) of these sons were thirty or older. Some of these households were quite wealthy by village standards: at least one-third of the widows headed households possessing four or more horses.

Not all of the women designated as household heads may have actually wielded the power normally allocated to a head. Ten of the thirteen widows who became household heads in 1823 had adult sons. Two of these sons had served as heads in the previous (1813) register; nine also served as village elders at some point between 1822 and 1824. Two sons, Abram Filipov and Ivan Martynov, had been active in community politics since 1816. Another son, Vasilii Sergeev, had served as the *mir* trustee (*vybornyi*). The mothers of these three men were listed as household heads. Because all were between seventy and seventy-five years of age, however, it may be that they held the title of head only as an honorific, as was sometimes the case for elderly men.[28]

By contrast, men in households headed by widows may have served as household representatives in male-dominated *mir* politics, while women ruled at home. In 1823, for instance, Lev Levlev served as an elder, but his mother, the family head, petitioned the Gagarins in a land dispute on the household's behalf. In another case Irina Nikitina petitioned for aid from the Gagarins when one of the women in her household gave birth to an illegitimate child. The estate manager questioned not Nikitina but her nephew, Anton Fedotov. Perhaps the manager went to Anton because he had served as a *mir* elder the year before in 1822. Seeking Anton Fedotov's corroboration of the widow's petition did not mean, however, that the official considered Anton to be the household head. When he wrote his report to Moscow, he described the nephew as "out of his aunt's household."[29]

Widows who were household heads engaged more frequently than any other group of women in the formal (and written) disputes of the community, usually over property or taxes. Young single women and married (not widowed) women never sent a petition appearing in Manuilovskoe archives. They were rarely even the subject of an estate manager's report. The widows sending petitions were either heads of households with no adult males or were remarried and involved in a property dispute. Often financial difficulties forced them to petition the *mir* and the Gagarins. We have already seen women pleading for tax relief or permission to bring a new male into the household. In 1817 Varvara Gavrilova asked that her family be freed from all

28. The data describing political officeholders came from numerous reports and ledgers from the 1820s.

29. 4 July 1823 Petition from Avdot'ia Titova, d. 7214, 1.158; 16 January 1823 Report, d. 7214, 1.133.

rent and taxes, but the Gagarins' officials ordered her to pay. She paid some of the rent but still owed twenty-five rubles when she again requested relief. Her second request led the Gagarins and the *mir* to halve her tax assessment of one unit and agree to pay the rent on her land until her grandson grew up. Varvara Gavrilova never mentioned that she owned two horses and had a married son, who was blind.[30] Mention of him could have influenced the response in two ways. His blindness may have led to rent relief, but his marriage may have justified a full *tiaglo* or tax burden. Instead she appealed to the *mir* as a widow, her best chance for receiving a lower tax assessment.

The tenure of these women as heads-of-household attests to the ability of some women to resist the pressure from village and family. They continued either to run their families or at least to live on in them as titular heads. Such widows were rare, but their existence demonstrates that a few women, by dint of luck, property, strength of character, or some combination of these, managed to carve out some autonomy for themselves amid the patriarchy of the *mir*. There is even one episode recorded in the Manuilovskoe documents in which widows resisted the pressure of estate managers as well.

Russian serf owners commonly demanded that young widows quickly remarry because unmarried women and men did not form full tax units and thus owed less in terms of obligations to their masters. The Iusupovs, a large family with property throughout Russia, required unmarried widows under forty years of age on their Smolensk estate to pay an annual tax of five to ten rubles. Serf elders on the Orlovs' estates were ordered to arrange marriages for their widows. Like these other magnates, the Gagarins sporadically carried out a policy of forced remarriages on their estates in Tambov and Riazan provinces.[31] In 1828 they decided to introduce such a policy at Manuilovskoe.

By 1828 the Manuilovskoe serfs had fallen far behind in their rents. The Gagarins sent an overseer, Ivan Ivanov, from Moscow to reorganize the estate and discipline the serfs. Ivanov ordered twenty-eight households to move to Nikolskoe, a Gagarin estate in Moscow Province. He placed two-thirds of the households remaining at Manuilovskoe on *barshchina*, a more onerous serf obligation than *obrok*. Ivanov also inspected the villages of Manuilovskoe to determine whether there were reasons other than simple sloth that explained the peasants' inability to meet their *obrok* payments. In September 1828 he reported to Moscow that he had found one problem—too many young widows. The widows, he declared, lived in their relatives' houses "for their own pleasure" and "do not do anything useful"; if these widows and all the unmarried girls among the Manuilovskoe serfs would

30. May 1817 Report, d. 7206, 1.94, 97.

31. Aleksandrov, *Sel'skaia obshchina*, 303; Hoch, *Serfdom*, 122; Peter Czap, Jr., "Marriage and the Peasant Joint Family in the Era of Serfdom," in Ransel, *Family in Imperial Russia*, 115, 120.

marry, twenty more work teams would be created, raising new revenue for the Gagarins. Ivanov then issued a draconian decree: either the widows would remarry, or they would be sent to work at a Iaroslavl paper mill. He also drew up a list of five widows who were ordered to move to Nikolskoe to marry men from the households he had deported there.[32]

By late October Ivanov was claiming great success for his program; he reported to Moscow that twenty-seven weddings would soon be performed. He did not report that the serfs were already deploying their time-honored defenses against him. None of the five women Ivanov had ordered to Nikolskoe had obeyed. Two managed to arrange quick marriages to widowers from Manuilovskoe. The other three simply ignored Ivanov. One waited five years and then remarried. The second stayed on in her son's household. The third woman probably hid or ran away, for she disappeared from estate records for four years after Ivanov's decree. The overseer did manage to find three other women to ship off to Nikolskoe, but they too managed to extract concessions from him. One of them refused to move unless her son accompanied her.[33] By October Ivanov was reduced to claiming credit for weddings that probably would have occurred without him, as autumn was the marrying season among peasants.

Manuilovskoe sources reveal the dangers to widows posed by the Russian patriarchy. The women faced poverty and social isolation, with little prospect of community aid. They remained dependent on male relatives, who sometimes tried to deprive them of their inheritance shares. They could be forced to marry men considerably older than themselves and to deal with resentful stepchildren. Yet some Manuilovskoe widows—and their numbers may have been small—used the inheritance practices, their seniority, and their children's support to resist the patriarchy or even to exert power. They took advantage of the property they controlled as trustees of their sons' inheritance shares or as holders of the widow's portion. After remarrying, they often served as the senior woman in their new family. And on their husbands' deaths the most assertive and able even became household heads. If Manuilovskoe widows could use the system to resist or achieve power, the other women whose voices were not heard in Manuilovskoe records may have also found ways to wield influence and protect themselves. The patriarchy, like all oppressive systems, was not without weaknesses, and the oppressed were not without means of recourse. The task remains to identify the extent of Russian peasant women's ability to resist the patriarchy and act within it.

32. 6 September 1828 Report, d. 7237, 1.16.
33. 23 October 1828 Report, d. 7237, 1.204; 1 August 1828 Report, d. 7237, 1.22.

Infant-Care Cultures in the
Russian Empire

David L. Ransel

In my explorations of the child welfare movement in Russia, I ran across an observation sometimes used by doctors and publicists in their arguments for urgent action to reduce the loss of life among Russian children. These writers pointed out that not only Western Europeans but even non-Russian peoples of the tsarist empire enjoyed lower infant mortality than did the Russians. It was not surprising to read that peoples living in the western borderlands of the empire, such as Finns, Estonians, and Jews, had better success than Russians in keeping their small children alive. Generally, the lowest rates of infant mortality in Europe were found among the peoples living in the northwest, and the rates increased as one moved to the east and southeast. Similarly, within Russia the highest rates of infant and childhood mortality were in the eastern provinces of European Russia. What struck me was the observation that in these eastern provinces the non-Russian peoples had low infant mortality by comparison with the Russians. A check into the source of these claims in the statistical compilations published by a leading demographer, S. A. Novosel'skii, revealed that in the late nineteenth century infant mortality among some of the non-Russian peoples of the Volga region was reported to be closer to that of the Balts, Finns, and Scandinavians than to that of the Russians living in the Volga basin.[1]

At first I suspected that the wide divergence in infant mortality among peoples living side by side was more an artifact of registration than a reflec-

Appreciation for financial support in connection with the research and writing of this chapter goes to the International Research and Exchanges Board, Indiana University, and the Woodrow Wilson Center.

1. For examples in the journalistic literature, see *Detskaia pomoshch'*, 1892, no. 13: 461–62; *Detskaia meditsina* 6, no. 3 (1901): 257. Statistics are in S. A. Novosel'skii, *Smertnost' i prodolzhitel'nost' zhizni v Rossii* (Petrograd, 1916), 144–46.

tion of real behavior. But checks on the reliability of the observation showed the differences in behavior to be authentic and substantial. In this preliminary study I can only remark on some of the findings and begin to shape hypotheses about the behavior and values that underlie them. For thorough analysis of infant mortality I would need to consider many variables, such as income, occupation, and female literacy, concerning which my information is now inadequate. I will limit analysis in this essay to comparisons between Russians and Volga Muslims, principally Tatars and Bashkirs.

THE RUSSIANS

The Russians are the nationality for which information is most plentiful, and they can therefore be used as the basis of comparison. In Russian compilations of the late imperial period the mortality rates were usually shown in aggregates that included the fifty provinces of European Russia. As late as the period 1887–96 childhood mortality (deaths of children up to five years of age) in this region was recorded as 432 per thousand live births. The actual rate may have been higher since infant deaths were not fully counted. More important, this average included large areas of non-Russian settlement—the Baltic provinces, Poland, and parts of the Ukraine—in which childhood mortality was lower than in Russia proper. If calculations were limited to the predominantly Russian provinces, they would show that as late as the last decade of the nineteenth century only about half the children survived to age five. An index of twenty-seven provinces of mainly Russian settlement that I constructed on the basis of compilations by V. P. Nikitenko for the years 1893–96 yields a mortality rate for ages 0–5 of 469 per thousand live births. Again, this figure understates the rate for Russians since it includes many non-Russians whose mortality was lower; but because the index excludes the worst years of famine, it may be a fairer assessment of ordinary mortality than figures cited (as they often are) for the whole decade.[2] At the high end of the childhood mortality range in the late nineteenth century were the provinces of Moscow and Saratov, in which 51.6 percent of the children died by age five; Tula Province, 52.4 percent; Nizhnii Novgorod Province, 53.8 percent; and Perm Province, 54.5 percent.[3]

In contrast to the childhood mortality rates, which were beginning to show improvement in this period, infant mortality (deaths up to age one) in these twenty-seven provinces stood at about one-third of all births and had remained at this level from the late 1860s (when records were first kept reg-

2. V. P. Nikitenko, *Detskaia smertnost' v Evropeiskoi Rossii za 1893–1896 god* (St. Petersburg, 1901), 226–29.

3. A. G. Rashin, *Naselenie Rossii za 100 let, 1811–1913 gg.* (Moscow, 1956), 198; *Detskaia meditsina* 6, no. 3 (1901): 257.

ularly) through the first decade of the twentieth century. This rate too is understated in view of the less-than-full accounting of infant deaths.[4]

The severity of infant mortality in late imperial Russia remained generally low in the western and southern provinces, shading into high rates in the central and eastern, and especially northeastern provinces of European Russia. The milder climate of the western and southern provinces might seem to have diminished the death rate. Other evidence, however, works against a climatic explanation. The annual bulge in morbidity and mortality among young children occurred not in the winter months but in mid- to late summer. Russian children were healthier in the cold months than in the warm ones.[5] Moreover, it was in the provinces of the northeast with their harsh weather that the contrast between infant mortality of the Russians and that of their non-Russian neighbors was greatest. Culture, not climate, played the larger role.

The disease environment into which children were born was much the same for all of the ethnic groups in the Russian empire. The difference in survival rates depended in large measure on the degree to which child care in the various cultures exposed infants to disease agents in their surroundings. Among the Russians this exposure was extraordinarily high.

The problems for Russian children began even before birth, if we are to believe the concerns voiced by the Russian medical community about the effects of alcohol consumption and syphilis on the health of the embryo and the developing fetus. It is difficult, however, to determine how much of this concern was attributable to the moral conceptions of Russian doctors and how much to observed behavior. Data on alcohol consumption by women are not well developed. Syphilis is better documented. In the late nineteenth century 8 percent of the children left at the Moscow Foundling Home suffered from syphilis. This special population was drawn primarily from the city and from towns and villages in the surrounding provinces. But syphilis was not confined to large urban areas. Its incidence was high in some provinces far removed from major population centers.[6]

4. Rashin, *Naselenie*, 194. My index of twenty-seven provinces for the years 1893–96, mentioned earlier, yields an infant mortality rate in these mainly Russian areas of 324 per thousand live births.

5. E. A. Osipova, "Neskol'ko statisticheskikh faktov otnositel'no smertnosti, rozhdaemosti i brakov v moskovskoi gubernii," *Chetvertyi gubernskii s"ezd vrachei moskovskogo zemstva* (Moscow, 1880), 116–19; *Detskaia meditsina* 6, no. 3 (1901): 257–58.

6. Some largely impressionistic evidence on female drinking can be found in *Trudy pervogo vserossiiskogo s"ezda po bor'be s p'ianstvom*, 3 vols. (St. Petersburg, 1910), 2: 569, 3: 1157, 1160; *Trudy kommissii po voprosu ob alkogolizme*, ed. M. N. Nizhegorodtsev (St. Petersburg, 1909), 3: 163–64. I am indebted to Patricia Herlihy for these references from her unpublished manuscript on the temperance movement in Russia. Syphilis was quite common in Russian villages. Though sometimes thought to follow migrant labor streams, high rates of syphilis could be found in regions with little migrant labor. See *S"ezd po obsuzhdeniiu mer protiv sifilisa v Rossii: Trudy* (St. Petersburg,

Apart from these dietary or disease effects, the heavy work load of women in the household, farmyard, and field may have hindered fetal development. The labor contribution of Russian women was crucial to the farm economy. According to a time-budget study done in the 1920s, Russian farm women spent nearly as many hours at agricultural labor (as distinct from household tasks) as did the men.[7] Pregnancy did not excuse women from working in the fields. Farm women often gave birth in a field or on the way home from the fields.[8] If at home, the birth took place either in the house or in the bathhouse, usually with the assistance of a village midwife or female member of the family with prior experience in birthing. To the extent that they had the time and energy, village women took precautions for the care of their babies. Their notions of hygiene were concentrated on removing potentially harmful human and spiritual agents. Even the use of the bathhouse, like the frequent use of a barn or other outbuilding when a bathhouse was unavailable, was not related to modern Western ideas about cleanliness but was a matter of ritual separation during a time of contamination and, even more, a protection from the influence of people with evil intentions. Village women believed that the fewer people who knew of the birth, the safer it would be for mother and child.[9] This belief had possible ancillary hygienic effects by encouraging the removal of some infectious agents. But hygiene in the modern sense was not known; until very late in the imperial era it was rare to find a village midwife who bothered to wash her hands before testing cervical dilation.[10]

Many practices of those assisting at a birth were intended to establish the newborn's proper relationship to authority and thus assist its growth. For example, women wrapped newborns in the coarse, unclean clothing of the

---

1897) for many references; V. I. Nikol'skii, *Tambovskii uezd, statistika naseleniia i boleznennosti* (Tambov, 1885), 280–84; M. Buch, *Die Wotjaken* (Helsingfors, 1882), 46, 52, 74. Russian doctors were convinced that syphilis traveled not only by sexual contact but by nonsexual contacts as well, especially in village conditions. See an interesting discussion of this issue by Laura Engelstein, "Morality and the Wooden Spoon: Russian Doctors View Syphilis, Social Class, and Sexual Behavior, 1890–1905," *Representations* 14 (1986): 169–208. Foundling-home statistics are reported in M. D. van Puteren, *Istoricheskii obzor prizreniia vnebrachnykh detei i podkidyshei* (St. Petersburg, 1908), 488–89.

7. A. Bol'shakov, *Sovremennaia derevnia v tsifrakh* (Leningrad, 1925), 100.

8. Typical of many reports of heavy summer labor and inadequate nutrition for women is that in Nikol'skii, *Tambovskii uezd*, 158–59.

9. A. O. Afinogenov, *Zhizn' zhenskogo naseleniia riazanskogo uezda v period detorodnoi deiatel'nosti zhenshchiny i polozhenie dela akusherskoi pomoshchi etomu naseleniiu* (St. Petersburg, 1903), 76; A. V. Balov, "Rozhdenie i vospitanie detei v poshekhonskom uezde, iaroslavskoi gubernii," *Etnograficheskoe obozrenie* 2, no. 3 (1890): 93–95; A. V. Balov, "Ocherki Poshekhon'ia," *Etnograficheskoe obozrenie* 14, no. 4 (1901): 118; E. A. Pokrovskii, *Fizicheskoe vospitanie detei u raznykh narodov, preimushchestvenno Rossii. Materialy dlia mediko-antropologicheskogo issledovaniia* (Moscow, 1884), 47–48. Pokrovskii reports on separation but rejects as a foreign import the notion of contamination.

10. Afinogenov, *Zhizn' zhenskogo naseleniia*, 77.

father in the expectation that it would make the child robust and win for it the love and goodwill of its father.[11] Baptisms in the home were sometimes performed in freezing rooms with icy water to duplicate the conditions in a church during the winter. Though primarily an expression of ritual conformity, this practice was also considered important for inuring the child to hardship. Across the northern and central provinces of Russia and in Siberia steaming infants in the bathhouse and flogging them with birch branches had the same goal of toughening up the children. These methods took their toll of infant life.[12]

The two most common causes of infant death were epidemic disease and intestinal disorders. There was little people could do to protect their children against epidemics, although the conditions of village life raised the level of exposure. Intestinal disorders were chronic, resulting from feeding practices and from what physicians who worked among the villagers described as neglect but would probably better be characterized as a sense of resignation about the fate of children. The farm families placed newborns in the only conditions they knew, the crowded village hut, where the infant hung suspended from a rafter in a fly-infested crib filled with dirty rags. The baby was either left among the rags and its own excrement or, more often, swaddled, but in either case it was washed infrequently. The water used in washing and feeding the baby came from the same supplies available for other household purposes.[13]

Most deadly were the feeding practices. Ethnographic accounts of village life usually state blandly that Russian mothers breast-fed their babies for three fasts (counting only the important ones of Lent and the Assumption), or for about a year and a half. Reports by doctors and officials working among the villagers paint a more complicated picture. During the summer months many women left their infants at home when they went to work in the fields; if they nursed them at all, they did so only early in the morning and late at night. This was especially true in the northern regions of European Russia, where the men left the villages to seek work elsewhere in the summer and the women managed the farms. But more important than whether the women nursed regularly, they very often placed their infants on solid food from the first days of life. This practice was required when the mothers were absent during times of field work and off-season jobs away from home; but

11. G. Popov, *Russkaia narodno-bytovaia meditsina* (St. Petersburg, 1903), 358; E. A. Pokrovskii, *Ob ukhode za malymi det'mi* (Moscow 1903), 13–20.

12. Pokrovskii, *Fizicheskoe vospitanie detei*, 77–78, 100–101.

13. Popov, *Russkaia narodno-bytovaia meditsina*, 352–61; S. Khotovitskii, "O nekotorykh pogreshnostiakh i predrassudkakh kasatel'no soderzhaniia detei v pervoe vremia ikh zhizni," *Trudy santpeterburgskogo obshchestva russkikh vrachei*, 1896, pt. 1: 160–66.

there was clearly more involved than the need imposed by the mother's absence since Russians fed solid food to infants even when the mother was at home and nursing. When asked why they did so, village women responded that a child could not survive on breast milk alone.[14] It is unclear if this belief was the result of projecting adult eating needs onto the baby or of assuming that the inadequate nutrition of lactating mothers made it difficult for them to sustain an infant. The villagers may even have understood that lactation drained the physical strength of poorly nourished women and made them less able to carry their usual work burdens. Connected with this physical consideration was a social one—the demands of other members of the household for the mother's services. Some sources note that members of the household resented the attention a mother gave to her newborn child because she could use it as an excuse for dropping other tasks.[15] Whatever the cause, the effects on the infants were clear. The solid food introduced gastrointestinal pathogens and led to diarrhea and rapid dehydration frequently ending in death.

Another deadly institution of Russian infant care was the *soska*. This instrument consisted of a piece of cloth filled with grain or other foods partially chewed by a member of the family and placed in the baby's mouth. It was often the first thing that entered the mouth of a newborn. A British doctor working in the Russian countryside reported the following scene shortly after he delivered a baby in a village home:

> Then in came the proud grandmother, chewing a rag in which was pocketed bacon rind and baked flour; this she was about to pop into the child's mouth to be the first intruding touch from the outside world when I stopped her, and asked her to consider whether it was as nice and clean a comforter as the mother's breast; and besides, had she not got pyorrhoea (her gums were awash with pus). . . . It was an ill-judged if not unkind interruption, because in any

14. The practice of early use of solid food was condemned by a Russian doctor as early as 1780: see Semen Zybelin, *Slovo o sposobe, kak predupredit' mozhno nemalovazhnuiu mezhdu prochimi medlennogo umnozheniia naroda prichinu, sostoiashchuiu v neprilichnoi pishche, mladentsam davaemoi v pervye mesiatsy ikh zhizni* (Moscow, 1780), 13–18. For the late nineteenth century, see Afinogenov, *Zhizn' zhenskogo naseleniia*, 99; Balov, "Rozhdenie i vospitanie," 99–100; P. F. Kudriavtsev, *Derevenskie iasli-priiuty v simbirskoi gubernii letom 1899 g.* (Syzran, 1900), 26; P. A. Peskov, *Opisanie durykinskoi volosti moskovskogo uezda v sanitarnom otnoshenii*, Sbornik statisticheskikh svedenii po moskovskoi gubernii, otdel sanitarnoi statistiki, vol. 1, sec. 3 (Moscow, 1879), 158–60; Popov, *Russkaia narodno-bytovaia meditsina*, 356. For additional sources and archival references to this behavior, see David L. Ransel, *Mothers of Misery: Child Abandonment in Russia* (Princeton, 1988), 269–70.

15. Popov, *Russkaia narodno-bytovaia meditsina*, 356; Leningradskii Gosudarstvennyi Istoricheskii Arkhiv (henceforth LGIA), fond 8, opis' 1, delo 187ch4, listy 183–84. Afinogenov, *Zhizn' zhenskogo naseleniia*, 99. For reports on the upper Volga region being compared here, see E. P. Busygin, N. V. Zorin, and L. I. Zorina, *Russkaia sel'skaia sem'ia Chuvashskoi ASSR (istoriko-etnograficheskoe issledovanie)* (Kazan, 1980), 53–55.

case the cosy rag would be thrust in the moment our backs were turned and by giving the babe something she had herself chewed she was in an animal sort of way binding her love to it as best she knew how.[16]

Although the doctor's remarks reveal both the city person's view of villagers as primitives and his failure to understand the woman's gesture as an assertion of her place (temporarily usurped by the doctor) in the birthing process, he did recognize the unfortunate effects of the *soska*. The Russian term for this instrument is usually misleadingly translated as "pacifier." It was meant to pacify, of course, but to do so in some measure by feeding the infant. It was part of the dietary regimen and regarded as an essential contribution to the baby's growth. In the summer, when the mother's help was needed in the fields, the *soska* was used almost continuously. Many times it was the child's only source of nourishment from early dawn until the return of the mother late in the evening.[17] Although the *soska* quickly putrefied and left around the baby's mouth a moldy residue that doctors recognized as a mark of bacteria likely to be causing the summer diarrhea fatal to many infants, village women evidently interpreted the residue as a positive sign, an indication perhaps that the baby was receiving the nourishment it required. They referred to the mold as a "flower in the mouth" and said that the baby's mouth was "blossoming."[18]

In an unfortunate conjuncture Russian infants had the least access to their mothers in the summer months, when gastrointestinal pathogens were most prevalent. In some parts of Russia in the late nineteenth century the murderous effects of summer outbreaks of disease and the absence of nursing mothers from the home reached astounding proportions. P. I. Zarin's study of one area of the Vereia District of Moscow Province revealed that 67 percent of the children born in the summer died within a month. In a study of the Borovichi District of Novgorod Province F. V. Giliarovskii found an even higher rate of death: 80 percent of the children born in the summer work season failed to survive.[19] To make matters worse, the seasonality of births in rural Russia aggravated the effects of this link between the absence of the

16. John Rickman, "Russian Camera Obscura: Ten Sketches of Russian Peasant Life (1916–1918)," in *The People of Great Russia: A Psychological Study*, ed. Geoffrey Gorer and John Rickman (New York, 1949), 50–51.

17. Pokrovskii, *Ob ukhode*, 41–46. Field reports of foundling-home officials are in LGIA, f. 8, op. 1, d. 187ch2, listy 242oborot, and d. 187ch4, listy 140–41. See also Balov, "Rozhdenie i vospitanie," 94.

18. From a study by Dr. N. E. Kushev of Saratov Province, 1879–88, cited in Nikitenko, *Detskaia smertnost'*, 30.

19. Zarin, "Bogorodskaia volost' vereiskogo uezda v sanitarno-statisticheskom otnoshenii," *Piatyi gubernskii s"ezd vrachei moskovskogo zemstva*, Protokoly zasedanii i trud (Moscow, 1881), 182–94; F. V. Giliarovskii, *Issledovaniia o rozhdenii i smertnosti detei v novgorodskoi gubernii* (St. Petersburg, 1866), 274.

mother and the prevalence of disease. Russian villagers were most active sexually in the immediate postharvest weeks of abundance, and conceptions in the late fall yielded a peak of births nine months later in July and August, just when the chances of the infants surviving were the poorest.[20] This unhappy combination of factors contributed greatly to Russia's high infant mortality.

The fatalism and resignation that shielded Russian parents from the potentially traumatizing impact of the carnage that surrounded them also must have served to increase the number of infant deaths. The loss of nearly half the children under the age of five made it impossible for parents to invest more than minimal emotional and physical energy in a child. Doctors who worked closely with the villagers remarked on the numbness of parents toward the death of children.[21] Proverbs and stories collected by ethnographers likewise reveal the emotional distance Russians put between themselves and the deaths of their children. A collection of sayings and proverbs about children features a number suggesting such a defense. "It's a good day when a child dies"; "Just as it's a good day when a child dies, it's an evil day when your wife dies"; "The death of a child is a mere chip off your knife blade, but that of a mom or dad leaves a gaping hole." Explicit in all these sayings is the valuelessness of an infant in comparison with a productive member of the household. "It's better to lose an egg than a chicken," another popular saying advised.[22]

One must use care in citing proverbs as evidence. Sayings can also be found that reflect the love Russian parents unquestionably felt toward their children. Yet the sayings quoted above point up an important reality about life in a village household. Members were evaluated in accordance with their current, past, and anticipated future contributions to the family. Resources were scarce and had to be allocated on the basis of such a calculation. The idea that all members of the household should receive equal treatment was foreign. In this calculation a certain number of children was essential to the survival of the household, and the parents did what they could to pull that number through. Mothers actively invoked or propitiated the many spirits with which the peasant world abounded and which could harm or protect a baby. The evil eye was considered an especially great hazard in the days following a baby's birth. Ill-intentioned people were the usual source of the

20. P. I. Kurkin, "Smertnost' malykh detei," *Publichnye lektsii* (Moscow, 1911), 28–31.

21. Examples are legion. A few references must suffice here: V. T. Demich, "Pediatriia u russkogo naroda," *Vestnik obshchestvennoi gigieny* 11 (1891): 127–28; P. Griaznov, *Opyt sravnitel'nogo izucheniia gigienicheskikh uslovii krest'ianskogo byta i mediko-topografii cherepovetskogo uezda* (St. Petersburg, 1880), 168 (reports of women who thanked God for taking their excess children); N. Zhbankov, *Vliianie otkhozhikh promyslov na dvizhenie narodonaseleniia kostromskoi gubernii po dannym 1866–1883 gg.* (Kostroma, 1887), 85; *Otchet moskovskogo vospitatel'nogo doma za 1869 god* (Moscow, 1870), 29–31.

22. T. Ivanovskaia, "Deti v poslovitsakh i pogovorkakh russkogo naroda," *Vestnik vospitaniia* 19 (1908): 124.

eye, but even friends and family might bring harm quite innocently by praising the baby unbetimes. Mothers already exhausted by the birth and their other responsibilities had to exert themselves further to guard against these dangers. When babies were ill, mothers used the traditional incantations and cures and called in village healers for additional remedies. (Many of these cures were of course harmful and merely sped the baby's death, but urban clinical medicine, to which peasants in desperation sometimes turned, could have similarly poor results before the 1880s.)[23]

Despite the desire and need for children the birth of a large number of them in a short time or the birth of children of the wrong kind (those that were weakly, misshapen, or crippled) could be a ruinous burden on a family. Some children were clearly regarded as more worthy of the investment of care than others. Women interpreted signs that allowed them soon after giving birth to gauge which babies were going to survive and which were not. If an infant looked odd, if it was too heavy, too pudgy, or too delicate, "the earth draws it back to itself," they said, and they assumed the child would die soon. If a baby developed too fast, or if it was too quiet, or if it stared too much at its surroundings, it was "not long for this world" (*ne zhilets na belom svete*).[24] Infants so labeled were not nurtured and protected to the same extent as those that seemed to have better prospects, and nature took its course. In some communities certain categories of children were simply not allowed to survive. Illegitimate children, though tolerated and nurtured in some villages, in others, if they managed to be born alive at all, did not last long.[25] Less valued children probably received much less attention and nursing from the mother because they were not considered worth the mother's lost work time. They were the children most likely to be turned over to old women or older siblings and fed on solid food more than the breast. This kind of differential nurturing leading to high death rates among certain categories of children has been observed in present-day peasant communities in the Third World. In these communities, just as in Russia one hundred years ago, outright infanticide is not culturally approved, but discriminatory treatment of

23. Balov, "Rozhdenie i vospitanie," 93–100; Demich, "Pediatriia"; Popov, *Russkaia narodno-bytovaia meditsina*, 357–62.

24. Balov, "Rozhdenie i vospitanie," 96, 99; the same was true of babies who did not cry at their baptism, according to Balov. He also notes (in "Ocherki Poshekhon'ia," 96, 100) the belief that babies born with their faces toward the ground (*litsom k zemle*) would not live long, a disturbing observation, since most babies are born face down (that is, facing the mother's spine). If Balov had this right, it would signify an excessive pessimism about the chances of an infant's survival. The belief does nevertheless fit with the notion of the earth pulling the child back to itself, the women naturally reading the face toward the ground as a desire of the child to return to the moist mother earth. Other examples in Afinogenov, *Zhizn' zhenskogo naseleniia*, 86–87.

25. In a twenty-year period (1836–55) in the town of Borovichi in Novgorod Province 2,138 illegitimate children were born, and not a single one survived. By contrast, religious schismatics and some other communities in Novgorod Province were more tolerant, and many of their illegitimate children survived. Giliarovskii, *Issledovanie o rozhdenii*, 338.

small children is prescribed.[26] It seems clear that late nineteenth-century Russian mothers made similar decisions about the allocation of their time and resources to their children. In the Russian case, as in that of back-country northeastern Brazil in the 1980s,[27] the decision seems to have been based more on the apparent hardiness of the child and the need for the mother's work services than, as in some other cultures, on the sex and birth order of the children.[28]

In Russia cultural beliefs no doubt helped to mask parental responsibility for the death of children and so made possible the continued psychic health of the mothers. The very folk beliefs that evidenced mothers' concern for their children, for example the need to ward off the evil eye or the actions of malevolent spirits, were likewise shields against feeling responsible for the death of children who may not have received adequate care. A mother may not have done everything necessary to propitiate the forces threatening her child; but who could realistically guard all the dozens of possible avenues by which harm could arrive? Ill luck would find a way, and, after all, it was God's will. The great uncertainty of survival of even valued children was another source of consolation in the loss of the less valued ones; who was to say that better care would have made any difference? Nevertheless, mothers could not avoid feelings of guilt, as is clear from stories told by villagers of dried-up milk flowing from the breast of a mother whose baby died while she was away and from tales of dead children appearing in the dreams of their parents when the parents were not remembering them in their prayers.[29] Some feeling of responsibility is vital to a sense of control and prevents a person from succumbing completely to despair.

To summarize, the circumstances surrounding the reproductive process in Russia, from poor prenatal care and the seasonal rhythms of work, conception, and birth to infant feeding practices and attitudes toward the death of

26. Susan C. M. Scrimshaw, "Infant Mortality and Behavior in the Regulation of Family Size," *Population and Development Review* 4, no. 3 (September 1978): 383–403; Monica Das Gupta, "Selective Discrimination against Female Children in Rural Punjab, India," *Population and Development Review* 13, no. 1 (March 1987): 77–100; Nancy E. Levine, "Differential Child Care in Three Tibetan Communities: Beyond Son Preference," *Population and Development Review* 13, no. 2 (June 1987): 281–304.

27. Nancy Scheper-Hughes, "Culture, Scarcity, and Maternal Thinking: Maternal Detachment and Infant Survival in a Brazilian Shantytown," *Ethos* 13, no. 4 (Winter 1985): 291–317.

28. The question of birth order in the survival of Russian children deserves further study. Scattered evidence I have seen shows the usual J curve of high mortality for the first birth, then a drop followed by gradually rising mortality in later births, but with remarkable distortion; for example, A. N. Antonov, *Smertnost' grudnykh i malykh detei, ee prichiny i mery bor'by* (Leningrad, 1931), 57; also note the comment on the Karamenko study in Nikitenko, *Detskaia smertnost'*, 21. Sex had been an important determinant in the decision to kill or abandon Russian children in the past (as was true of many other societies). See Ransel, *Mothers of Misery*, chap. 7.

29. Balov, "Rozhdenie i vospitanie," 99–100.

children—in short, the Russian infant-care culture—all conspired to raise Russian child mortality rates to among the highest recorded anywhere. When as many as half the children died before age five, the scene that Nina Berberova recalled from her childhood in a village north of Moscow must have been repeated in nearly every village of central Russia: "Every Sunday in the chapel there stood a row of small coffins containing the bodies of new-born infants—six, eight, sometimes even more. The infants were all alike, somewhat similar to dolls, somewhat to Easter suckling pigs."[30] A folk saying from the time expressed the reaction of people to this grim weekly display: "You can't make enough hay to supply an army, and you can't make enough babies to satisfy the Reaper."[31]

THE MUSLIM PEOPLES OF THE VOLGA

What first strikes one about the infant mortality statistics for the Muslim peoples of Russia is their improbability. In the empire as a whole in 1896–97 the infant mortality rate for Orthodox peoples was 284 deaths per thousand live births, wheras for the Muslim population it was 166.[32] The contrast is even more conspicuous if one looks at the statistics for regions in which large numbers of Orthodox and Muslim peoples lived in close proximity. For example, in Kazan Province at the end of the century mortality among the Orthodox in the first year was 304 per thousand live births and among the Muslims 161.[33] In Penza Province during the 1880s the infant mortality rate for Orthodox peoples outside the city of Penza was 342 per thousand live births, whereas for Muslims it was a mere 140.[34] However improbable at first sight, these figures meet basic checks for authenticity, such as age-appropriate sex ratios and comparisons of census data with household and family lists. The mullahs, who kept the registers of fertility and mortality for the Muslim peoples, evidently did their work conscientiously. A Russian doctor working in one area of Kazan Province did a check of these records over a twenty-seven-year period and found that "the very low figures shown for deaths of children are not a result of shortcomings or omissions in the records."[35]

Nearly everything about the Tatar demographic behavior differed from the behavior of the Russians, including patterns of marriage, conception, births, stillbirths, infant and child mortality, and age-specific mortality of

30. Nina Berberova, *The Italics Are Mine*, trans. Philippe Radley (New York, 1969), 17.

31. Ivanovskaia, "Deti v poslovitsakh i pogovorkakh," 1–2.

32. Novosel'skii, *Smertnost'*, 144.

33. Ibid., 145–46; *Detskaia pomoshch'*, 1892, no. 13: 461–62.

34. V. I. Nikol'skii, *Sanitarnoe issledovanie penzenskoi gubernii: Statistika naseleniia gorodov i uezdov za 10 let (1880–89 gg.)* (Penza, 1893), 56.

35. Sergei Ershov, *Materialy dlia sanitarnoi statistiki sviiazhskogo uezda* (St. Petersburg, 1888), 113.

TABLE 1.   Seasonality of Births (%)

	J	F	M	A	M	J	J	A	S	O	N	D
Orenburg Province												
Orthodox	**9.0**	8.2	8.4	7.5	7.6	8.4	**9.0**	8.9	7.6	**9.7**	8.8	7.0
Muslim	**11.7**	9.2	9.4	7.9	7.1	6.9	7.2	7.1	7.9	8.4	8.0	**8.9**
Sviiazhk District of Kazan Province												
Orthodox	**9.4**	7.7	7.1	6.7	6.9	8.6	**9.8**	9.0	7.9	**9.6**	9.7	7.3
Muslim	**11.8**	8.9	9.6	6.5	5.5	6.5	8.7	8.5	7.1	8.2	8.2	**9.9**

SOURCES. Orenburg—M. M. Kenigsberg, *Sanitarnoe sostoianie orenburgskoi gubernii po dannym estestvennogo dvizheniia naseleniia za trekhletie 1897–1899 g.g.* (Orenburg, 1901), 44; Sviiazhk—Sergei Ershov, *Materialy dlia sanitarnoi statistiki sviiazhskogo uezda* (St. Petersburg, 1888), 172.
NOTE. Highest percentages are in boldface.

women. Fertility of Muslims was below that of Russians, and the seasonality of Muslim births diverged sharply from that of the Orthodox population living in the same regions. Instead of a peak in births during the summer, which was characteristic of the Russians and exposed Russian infants to the most unfavorable environmental conditions for their survival, Muslims had the largest number of births in the winter. Muslims lost infants to death in the winter and early spring following the peak of births, but their losses were small compared to the Russians' devastating peaks of infant mortality in mid- to late summer. Table 1 indicates the difference in the seasonality of births in the two communities.

The explanation for these differences in the Russian patterns of infant mortality and those of the Tatars and Bashkirs is to be found largely in the treatment and behavior of women. Although much too little is known about these Muslim women, the records of officials and doctors who worked among them make clear that their behavior differed from that of Russian women. To begin with, Muslim women played a different role in the household economy. The wealthiest families could afford to cloister their women, but this practice was not typical. In most households the women were responsible for keeping up the home and its immediate surroundings, and they went to local markets. But in contrast to Russian women, only among poor families were Tatar women observed doing heavy field work or other arduous tasks outside of the home.[36] Among one Tatar ethnic group, the Mishari, in which women

36. A. A. Sukharev, *Kazanskie tatary (uezd kazanskii). Opyt etnograficheskogo i mediko-antropologicheskogo issledovaniia* (St. Petersburg, 1904) 39, observed women doing light field work. N. I. Vorob'ev, "Kazanskie tatary," *Materialy po izucheniiu Tatarstana,* ed. G. G. Ibragimov and N. I. Vorob'ev (Kazan, 1925), 2: 162, says they ordinarily did not work in fields.

regularly assisted with the field work, they were excused from heavy tasks beginning in the fifth or sixth month of pregnancy.[37] These practices could perhaps be regarded as a function of the economy more than of culture; by some reports Tatars were less heavily invested in agriculture and, having come to it more recently than Russians, preferred to rent out their lands and engage in commerce and service occupations in nearby towns. Despite such reports a great many Tatars were agriculturalists and yet maintained a sexual division of labor different from the Russians.[38] In the case of the Bashkirs, however, the economy was somewhat different. Many communities continued into the late tsarist era to lead a seminomadic life, spending a large part of the year following their herds to the hills and distant fields.

Superficially it might be thought that the use of alcohol would be lower among Muslims than among the Orthodox peoples and that this factor would influence prenatal and neonatal conditions favorably. The evidence, however, is mixed. By all accounts Volga Muslims did not observe the Islamic prohibition on alcohol. Muslim men drank, on occasion to excess.[39] Women were less often observed drinking, and their use of alcoholic beverages may have been confined principally to holidays. Still, to the extent they drank *kumys*, the homemade milk-based beverage of the non-Russian Volga peoples, they could have done themselves more harm than if they had drunk vodka, for chemical analysis of *kumys* showed it to contain toxins more potent than alcohol.[40]

The well-attested neatness of the Tatars may have played some role in the survival of their children. Muslims do a ritual cleansing several times a day before prayer, but there is no reason to believe it has hygienic effects (they may splash dirty water or even sand). Tatar women daily washed down the platforms that served as seats, tables, and beds in their homes, and they cleaned the floors once a week. The bathhouse was in frequent, often weekly, use, and in the baths Tatars were said to pluck out the hairs from their pubic region and underarms.[41] So a kind of cult of cleanliness reigned, which extended to the whitewashing of their homes several times a year and to small

37. R. G. Mukhamedova, *Tatary-Mishari* (Moscow, 1972), 174.

38. Sukharev, *Kazanskie tatary*, 47–50; L. F. Zmeev, *Medikotopograficheskoe opisanie i statisticheskii ocherk narodonaseleniia bugul'minskogo uezda samarskoi gubernii* (Moscow, 1883), 23.

39. Sukharev, *Kazanskie tatary*, 46. For an eighteenth-century report, see *Byt i verovaniia tatar sinbirskoi gubernii, v 1783 godu (Lz zapisok uezdnogo zemlemera Mil'kovicha)*, ed. N. Vinogradov (Kazan, 1905), 6. The German doctor K. Fuks, who worked among the Tatars in the first half of the nineteenth century, noted that village taverns on the Russian model were even then beginning to appear. K. Fuks, *Kazanskie tatary v statisticheskom i etnograficheskom otnosheniiakh* (Kazan, 1844), 5, 125.

40. V. D. Orlov, "'Kumyshka'—vodka Votiakov," *Vestnik obshchestvennoi gigieny, sudebnoi i prakticheskoi meditsiny* 9, no. 1 (1891): 79–93.

41. Vinogradov, *Byt i verovaniia*, 7; Sukharev, *Kazanskie tatary*, 30–32, 39; Afinogenov, *Zhizn' zhenskogo naseleniia*, 76.

daily tasks like milking, during which the women "wear large aprons, cleanse the udders with warm water, and cover the milk pail with a clean towel."[42] The regular washing of surfaces would have kept down summer dust-carrying pathogens and possibly washed away insects and insect eggs, but it is far from clear that before the use of water filtration and antisepsis these measures could have strongly contributed to protecting children from the disease agents in the environment.

More to the point, the period of confinement during childbirth for Tatar women extended considerably longer than for Russian women. Even poor families allowed women to rest for at least six days after giving birth. In wealthy families the period of confinement lasted for twenty days.[43] These periods of rest gave the women time to restore their energies, create an emotional bond with their babies, and establish a nursing regimen free from other demands and duties.

The key to the success of Volga Muslims in saving their infants was unquestionably their feeding practices. The women breast-fed their infants on demand for from one and a half to three years. This was an excellent regimen but still not the essential point, since Russian women, when possible, also breast-fed for a year or more. The determinant was that Muslim women did not introduce solid food until their children were well developed, usually not until the end of the first year of life, and then they began slowly with dairy products. It is true that modern pediatric practice recommends that properly developing babies past the fourth or fifth month should be given supplements to breast milk for optimal growth. But Muslim practices helped mitigate the effects of "weaning diarrheas" associated with the introduction of solid foods; these diarrheas were more dangerous the earlier the age at which they occurred.[44] The custom of these Volga Muslims not to introduce solid food and to keep their children exclusively on breast milk for at least a year, more than any other factor, accounted for the significant difference in infant mortality rates between these peoples and their Orthodox neighbors.[45]

The effect is easy to plot statistically. Until age one, mortality among Tatar children in the late nineteenth century was roughly equivalent to that in England, whereas the Russians living nearby showed rates of infant death from two to three times as high. Thereafter a reversal took place. In the age group one to five, after the Tatar mothers began placing their children on

42. Fuks, *Kazanskie tatary*, 27.

43. Sukharev, *Kazanskie tatary*, 41.

44. Clare E. Casey and K. Michael Hambidge, "Nutritional Aspects of Human Lactation," in *Lactation: Physiology, Nutrition, and Breast-Feeding*, ed. Margaret C. Neville and Marianne R. Neifert (New York, 1983), 230–31. For special problems of Third World women, see A. Chavez, C. Marinez, and H. Bourges, "The Role of Lactation in the Nutrition of Low Socio-Economic Groups," *Ecology and Food Nutrition* 4 (1975): 159–68.

45. For Muslim feeding practices, see Ershov, *Materialy*, 115–16; A. E. Romanov, *O zabolevaemosti naseleniia kuznetskogo uezda, saratovskoi gubernii* (Penza, 1883), 9.

solid food, the mortality of the children rapidly caught up with, and even surpassed, that of Russian children. Muslim children were no more immune to pathogenic organisms than were Russian children, and once exposed, they too suffered great losses. The deaths were even more numerous than they needed to be as a result of Muslims' poor access to medical services and common rejection of vaccination against smallpox.[46] Still, Muslims lost fewer children overall than did Russians. The worst mortality for Muslims came after age one, when children who had survived environmental assaults on their health thus far because of breast-feeding were exposed to the pathogens the Russian children had faced since birth.

A striking aspect of the comparison of these child-care cultures is the sharp divergence in practices of people living in close proximity. Russians and Tatars lived in seemingly tightly sealed, self-reinforcing cycles of fertility and infant mortality, and their practices did not appear to have had any marked influence on one another. With regard, for example, to the main killer of small children, intestinal disorders in the summertime, Russian and Tatar villages showed altogether different profiles. Russian children had a high incidence of such disease and Tatar children very low. It was not just that people living in the same province, or even in the next town or village, behaved differently. People of different ethnic groups living side by side in the same village operated under entirely different rules of behavior. A doctor in Kazan Province reported that in villages of mixed ethnic composition in the summer "every single Russian child suffers from diarrhea, whereas the Tatar children are all healthy. The Tatar mothers strictly avoid bottle feeding or solid food. Only in cases of extreme need do they use the so-called *al'va* [a pacifier made of fresh ingredients and heated before use, hence a less effective conveyer of pathogens than the Russian *soska*]."[47] A similar pattern of disease among children was found in Simbirsk Province, where Orthodox children ages one to ten suffered nearly twice the number of deaths from intestinal disorders as did Muslim children of that age group.[48]

What could have accounted for this difference in behavior between Russians and non-Russians? Social scientists are apt in these instances to propose a link between economic status and infant and child mortality. But if what is meant is a simple correlation between infant mortality and occupation or income, this type of explanation is unsatisfactory. I have examined the infant-care practices of Tatars and Bashkirs (as well as Volga Finns, who share some of the same behaviors) in several different locations and economic conditions, and they remain consistent. Similar feeding customs and in-

46. M. M. Kenigsberg, *O pagubnom vliianii kolossal'noi smertnosti detei i vysokoi rozhdaemosti v Rossii na proizvoditel'nye i ekonomicheskie sily strany i na kachestvennyi sostav armii* (Orenburg, 1910), 12.

47. Ershov, *Materialy*, 116.

48. Kudriatsev, *Derevenskie iasli-priiuty*, 19.

fant mortality rates prevailed among the settled Kazan Tatars and the seminomadic Bashkirs to the south.[49] Even as far away as the Belorussian city of Minsk, fifteen hundred kilometers from Kazan, an urbanized Tatar community that had resided separate from its ethnic cousins for centuries and no longer spoke the Tatar language nevertheless exhibited the same distinct patterns of demographic behavior as the Volga Muslims.[50] Limited data on infant care among Russian merchant families indicate that Russian behavior in this regard likewise cut across occupational and socioeconomic lines.[51]

The behavior of these Muslims seems to be not so much a response to immediate economic conditions as a deeply imbedded cultural pattern. Less certain is the source of this pattern and the motivation for continuing it. The doctors who worked among the Muslim peoples took the cause to be a strict Koranic injunction about the breast-feeding of children. According to the report of one doctor Muslim women enjoyed personal freedom and rights to property independent of their husbands. The one thing that the Koran allowed husbands to demand of their wives was the nursing of infant children, and this injunction therefore constituted a rule of some force.[52] A husband "owned" the milk of his wife.[53] A medical researcher in Orenburg Province attributed the success of Muslim child rearing to another Koranic rule that enjoined women to feed children with breast milk alone for a period of two years.[54] The Koran does contain a verse (2:233) to the effect that mothers should nurse children for two years, but it says nothing about omitting other foods and even includes loopholes that permit early weaning or use of a wet nurse. The injunctions mentioned by the doctors probably were local interpretations of the more broadly stated rule. Most other doctors and

49. Ershov, *Materialy*, 114–16; Nikol'skii, *Sanitarnoe issledovanie*, 54, 61–67; M. M. Kenigsberg, *Sanitarnoe sostoianie orenburgskoi gubernii po dannym estestvennogo dvizheniia naseleniia za trekhletie 1897–1899 g.g.* (Orenburg, 1901), 64–67.

50. The conclusion is drawn from data for the years 1877–86. A. A. Bekarevich, *K izucheniiu v mediko-topograficheskom i statisticheskom otnoshenii gubernskogo goroda Minska* (St. Petersburg, 1890), 38, 80–95.

51. P. V. Ivanov, *Materialy k izucheniiu goroda Penzy v mediko-statisticheskom otnoshenii* (St. Petersburg, 1903), 124–25; Kenigsberg, *Sanitarnoe sostoianie*, 101–2; S. G. Kassil', *Materialy k izucheniiu goroda Riazani v mediko-topograficheskom i statisticheskom otnoshenii* (Riazan, 1909), 157; V. I. Ornatskii, *Medikotopografiia i sanitarnoe sostoianie gubernskogo goroda Vologdy* (St. Petersburg, 1888), 78–80.

52. Sukharev, *Kazanskie tatary*, 40; S. I. Rudenko, *Bashkiry. Opyt etnologicheskoi monografii*, pt. 2 (Leningrad, 1925), 257–58.

53. The expression is from Vanessa Maher, who reports that in some Islamic societies a husband had to give permission for his wife to nurse someone else's child. Vanessa Maher, "Possession and Dispossession: Maternity and Mortality in Morocco," in *Interest and Emotion: Essays on the Study of the Family and Kinship*, ed. Hans Medick and David Warren Sabean (Cambridge, 1984), 107.

54. Kenigsberg, *Sanitarnoe sostoianie*, 102.

officials who reported on this aspect of life among the Volga Muslims also attributed the feeding practices to the Koran.[55] In doing so, they were undoubtedly passing on the reasoning of their Muslim informants and not simply plucking the explanations out of thin air. I suspect, nevertheless, that the informants themselves may have been unconsciously ascribing to religious sanction customary practices that predated the adoption of Islam. The most instructive approach is probably not to ask whether economics or religion most influenced the infant-care practices of these peoples but to examine the role religion played in rationalizing and sustaining customary practices and, in that connection, fixing the definition of the position of women in the economy and family life.

It seems clear that Muslims placed greater relative value on the reproductive role of women than did Russians and, by the same token, less relative importance on the productive functions. Women in both communities, with the exception of those at the highest socioeconomic levels, shouldered a heavy burden of both household and farm labor. Muslims, however, excused their women from many tasks several weeks before confinement, and they extended the period of rest and recuperation after a birth well beyond what the Russians did. Moreover, they excused women during menstruation from one of the most time-consuming tasks, food preparation.[56] Though principally a question of ritual contamination, this practice also revealed a reverence for the power and mystery of women's reproductive function. Another sign of this respect was the Muslim practice of building a wall of social separation between a young daughter-in-law and her new father-in-law. In Bashkir households the daughter-in-law was not to uncover her face in the presence of her father-in-law for a year after entering the home, and to reinforce this custom, she was to eat separately from him. This relationship in Russian village life was notorious for its abuse of the conjugal bond.[57]

For Muslim women themselves the relatively greater emphasis on their reproductive role has to be seen as a mixed blessing. They may have been relieved of some of their household and other tasks when these conflicted with their reproductive function, but the demands connected with birth and nurturing exacted a heavy price psychically and physically. A woman who did not produce children (the fault was assumed to lie with her) could be set

55. Among many other examples, see A. E. Romanov, *O zabolevaemosti naseleniia kuznetskogo uezda*, 9; Kudriavtsev, *Derevenskie iasli-priiuty*, 21.

56. P. S. Nazarov, "K etnografii bashkir," *Etnograficheskoe obozrenie* 2, no. 1 (1890): 190; Rudenko, *Bashkiry*, 258.

57. Nazarov, "K etnografii Bashkir," 189. See also Rudenko, *Bashkiry*, 258, 262. For a review of the evidence on Russian daughters-in-law, see Beatrice Farnsworth, "The Litigious Daughter-in-Law: Family Relations in Rural Russia in the Second Half of the Nineteenth Century," *Slavic Review* 45 (1986): 49–64.

aside easily by divorce or reduced in status (and access to food and other resources) by the husband's acquisition of an additional wife.[58]

The extended periods of lactation may also have taken their toll. They may provide an explanation for the unusually high mortality of Volga Muslim women in their childbearing years. In this regard a curious imbalance of a normal statistical pattern occurred. For most ethnic groups of the Russian empire higher survival rates of infants correlated with higher survival rates of women of childbearing age. But in the cases of the Tatars and Bashkirs that relationship did not obtain. Despite doing better than the Russians with their children, the women of these Muslim groups suffered significantly higher mortality rates in their childbearing years than did Russian women.[59] This statistic is all the more surprising in that Russian women endured a much higher number of births, with the attendant increased risks of maternal mortality. But extended lactation also carried risks, especially for poorly nourished women. Lactation requires a nutritional supplement of 550–600 calories a day, without which the nursing mother sacrifices her own reserves of energy and nutrients vital to her physical well-being.[60] Considering the poverty of most Volga Muslim households—observers agreed that these people were on average far worse off economically than their Russian neighbors[61]—it is unlikely that many of the lactating women among the Tatars and Bashkirs received the supplements they needed. Besides depleting the physical resources of women, lactation can invite invasion of pathogenic organisms through cracks in the areola opened by dryness or biting. Unfortunately, but revealingly, studies in the medical literature on the effects of breast-feeding have focused almost exclusively on the status of the infant, and little is known about the impact of breast-feeding on the health of mothers. Nevertheless, impressionistic evidence concerning Third World women indicates "prematurely aged appearance and a progressive weight loss with parity and age"; in addition to this general decline, repeated reproductive cycles carry the risk of specific deficiencies such as osteomalacia, anemia, goiter, and nutritional edema.[62] Although no more than a working hypothesis is possible until further research is done, it seems probable

58. Co-wives could not have equal standing. The husband normally placed one in charge, and only rarely was this the oldest wife. Reported in Nazarov, "K etnografii Bashkir," 191.

59. Discussion of normal correlation is in M. Ptukha, *Smertnost' 11 narodnostei Evropeiskoi Rossii v kontse XIX veka* (Khar'kov-Kiev, 1928), 35–36, and statistics, 31. A more detailed reckoning comparing Tatars and Russians in one district of Kazan Province can be derived from tables in Ershov, *Materialy dlia sanitarnoi statistiki*, 182–85.

60. Maher, "Possession and Dispossession," 109–11; Chavez, Marinez, and Bourges, "The Role of Lactation," 159–68; Casey and Hambidge, "Nutritional Aspects of Human Lactation," 211.

61. Nikitenko, *Detskaia smertnost'*, 24–25; Nazarov, "K etnografii Bashkir," 174–75; Ershov, *Materialy dlia sanitarnoi statistiki*, 93; Nikol'skii, *Sanitarnoe issledovanie*, 54.

62. Casey and Hambidge, "Nutritional Aspects of Human Lactation," 211, 227–28.

that prolonged lactation, added to the other burdens and deprivations endured by these Volga Muslim women, played an important role in their high rate of mortality during childbearing years.

CONCLUSION

An effort to sort out the causes for the differences in the infant-care cultures of the Russians and the Volga Muslims must begin with the assumption that their practices were adaptive or at least had been in the past. Since in the case of the Russians high costs were incurred in keeping women pregnant throughout their childbearing years and in supporting infants that would not survive to working age, the offsetting benefits must have been substantial. A series of proverbs, sayings, and direct rationalizations can be strung together to make a case that Russian villagers understood high infant mortality as a form of population control; but if birth control was their sole objective, a regime could have evolved that achieved the desired family size by less frequent pregnancies and better success with the children that were born, as happened among the Volga Muslims. Such a solution was probably less adaptive in the subsistence agricultural economy of the Russians, which left them vulnerable to periodic famines and epidemics. In those circumstances it was necessary to maintain high general fertility to replace sudden massive population losses. During more favorable times, when high fertility could threaten to exhaust the resource base, people could adjust by selecting through differential nurturing the most robust infants at or soon after birth. By the same token, contraception or abortion, two other methods of limiting the number of children, were less desirable because they disrupted the continuity of supply, threatened the health and even the life of the mother, and did not allow for selection by hardiness. But more study is required before we can say that population control through discriminatory treatment of infants was a cultural norm.

Whatever the cultural system may have prescribed, it is clear that by the mid-nineteenth century conscious choice, including the choice of illegal abortion, and the tyranny of work rhythms played a part for many Russian women in the loss of children. Giliarovskii, who recorded the demographic behavior of the common people in Novgorod Province from the 1830s to the 1850s, told of women who had had several abortions in a row because conception came at the wrong time, and birth would have interfered with their work. As a result the women harmed their reproductive organs and ended up with accompanying illnesses and the shame of having produced no children. Other women gave birth just before the work season and were therefore unable to breast-feed their babies. Because the mothers were not nursing, they conceived again at the end of the work season, so that another baby appeared at the beginning of the next work cycle, a process that repeated itself again and again. The women were pregnant much of the time, suffered from this burden and its attendant risks, and gave birth too often; moreover, most of the babies died.[63]

With regard to Muslim women, we might question whether in the circumstances of a sedentary economy their "more normal" infant-care was as adaptive as it had been under other conditions. They kept a large proportion of their children alive through the first year or two of life only to lose a high percentage of them in the next three to four years. Even if the total survival rate of their children was better than that of the Russians, their investment of food, clothing, time, energy, and emotional bonding must have been considerably greater for each surviving child. Could it be that their infant-care strategy was a holdover from a time when their people lived a nomadic life in which lower population density and a different diet gave their older children greater protection against disease? It seems clear, at any rate, that the reproductive function of Muslim women was relatively more valued than that of Russian women, whose reproductive and nurturant capacities were subordinated to their productive roles in the household economy.

Yet in an unusual trade-off Muslim women's greater confinement to the home and greater investment in their small children, though it may have benefited the children, was not especially healthy for the women themselves. The reasons for the high mortality of these women in the childbearing years is not altogether clear, but a number of factors, including the poverty of Volga Muslim communities, the ideological devaluation of women in Muslim societies, and the infant-care regime itself, with prolonged lactation under adverse dietary conditions, no doubt played an important part.

---

63. Giliarovskii wrote here that "all the babies" died—hyperbole, but only a slight exaggeration. His statistics, as reported earlier in this essay, indicate that about 80 percent of those born in the summer work season died. Giliarovskii, *Issledovaniia o rozhdenii i smertnosti*, lxxii–lxxiii.

1. Childbirth. From an illustrated manuscript of the life of St. Antonii Siiskii, sixteenth century. In the birth scene (upper left) a midwife attends the saint's mother, while the saint's father (upper right) waits in another building. The saint (lower left) is swaddled and lying in the distinctive Russian cradle, tended by a wet nurse. The saint's mother (lower right) presents him for baptism. The birth scene and the presentation scene are based on models from icons of the Virgin. From N. A. Bogoiavlenkii, *Meditsina u pervoselov russkogo severa* (Leningrad, 1966), 26.

2. Muscovy's tsaritsa and her attendants in public, late seventeenth century. From August Meyerberg, *Al'bom Meierberga: Vid i bytovye Kartiny Rossii XVII veka* (St. Petersburg, 1903).

3. A peasant woman outside her hut in a fishing village on the Volga River, late nineteenth century. Courtesy of Novosti from Sovfoto.

4 (opposite top). A peasant mother and child fetching water from a well outside their dwelling in Samara Province, late nineteenth century. Courtesy of Novosti from Sovfoto.
5 (opposite bottom). Peasant women and children, late nineteenth century. A few of the women are wearing factory-made *sarafany* (jumpers) and dresses. Courtesy of Museovirasto Historian Kuvo-Arkisto, Finland.

6. Peasant women pilgrims at the walls of the Ponetaevsky Monastery, late nineteenth century. Notice their leggings and bast shoes. Courtesy of Novosti from Sovfoto.

7. Migrant peasant women in late nineteenth-century Moscow. Courtesy of Novosti from Sovfoto.

8. Female peddler of kerchiefs, towels, and knitted socks in late nineteenth-century Moscow. The woman is wearing a factory-made dress. Courtesy of Novosti from Sovfoto.

9. Woman weaver, late nineteenth century. Notice the samovar and teapot in the background. From "Kustarnaia promyshlennost'," *Rossii: Zhenskie promysly* (St. Petersburg, 1913). Courtesy of Timothy Mixter.

10. A women's dormitory at the Trekhgornaia Textile Mill, c. 1900. Women workers sent factory scraps of cotton cloth back to their villages to be made into quilts for their beds. Courtesy of Novosti from Sovfoto.

11. An apartment of metalworkers of the Putilov plant in St. Petersburg, c. 1900. Courtesy of Novosti from Sovfoto.

14. The patriarch of the Russian Orthodox church blessing the Women's Death Battalion before they leave for the front, July 1917. Courtesy of Novosti from Sovfoto.

12 (opposite top). A food line, composed largely of women and children, in Petrograd in 1917. Food lines and rumors of food shortages helped spark the 1917 February revolution. Courtesy of Novosti from Sovfoto.

13 (opposite bottom). A largely middle-class demonstration in July 1917. The signs in the middle read "Power to the soviets of worker, soldier, and peasant deputies" and "Down with the ministers of the capitalists!" Courtesy of TASS from Sovfoto.

15. A panel design for Petrograd street decorations, celebrating the first anniversary of the October revolution, 1918. The angel's red clothing symbolizes her allegiance to the socialist revolution. Courtesy of Aurora Publishers, Leningrad.

16. A group of women delegates from different parts of the empire to the First All-Union Congress of Soviets, 1924. Courtesy of TASS from Sovfoto.

17. Literacy classes for women at the Krasnyi Bogatyr Works in Moscow, 1932. The booklet in the bottom left-hand corner is by Joseph Stalin. Courtesy of TASS from Sovfoto.

18. Instruction in breast-feeding for middle-class and working-class women, 1930s. Courtesy of Sovfoto.

19. Vera Mukhina's statue of the factory worker and the collective-farm worker, 1937. The female figure, representing the backward peasantry, is secondary to the male figure.

PART TWO

Transforming Tradition

Transformation versus Tradition

Barbara Alpern Engel

Even as they perpetuate it, women have always transformed tradition. What women learn from their mothers and fathers, their kin, and their culture, they reshape in the light of their own experience before they pass it along. But their legacy in the infinite variety of embroidery and handiwork, of folksongs and tales, engaged the attention only of ethnographers until social historians began to study them.[1] Because most historians of Russia have conceptualized transformation in terms of the public and the narrowly political, they have overlooked the role of women, who passed their lives in the private sphere of household, family, marriage, and motherhood. Even in much of the new social history historical actors have remained generically male. Outside the domain of women's history gender is a given, not an element in the construction of the historical subject, so that historians almost never stop to consider how, for example, being a male in a particular place, time, and culture might have shaped a worker's or revolutionary's consciousness and actions.[2]

Yet gender, or the social organization of sexual difference, shapes the experience of men as well as women. During most of Russian history, being male entitled a person to participate in public life, whereas being female

---

1. Soviet ethnographers were among the first to attend to peasant women's lives. See for example N. A. Minenko, *Russkaia krest'ianskaia sem'ia v zapadnoi Sibiri (XVIII–pervoi poloviny XIX v.)* (Novosibirsk, 1979); M. M. Gromyko, *Traditsionnye normy povedeniia i formy obshcheniia russkikh krest'ian XIX v.* (Moscow, 1986); T. A. Bernshtam, *Molodezh v obriadovoi zhizni russkoi obshchiny XIX–nachala XX v.* (Leningrad, 1988).

2. Partial exceptions are Reginald Zelnik, "Russian Rebels: An Introduction to the Memoirs of the Russian Workers Semen Kanatchikov and Matvei Fisher," *Russian Review* 35 (1976): 249–89, 417–47; and Stephen Frank, "Popular Justice, Community and Culture among the Russian Peasantry, 1870–1900." *Russian Review* 46 (1987): 239–66.

meant being relegated to household and family. Women's relations with the
state and the larger society were mediated by men, whom law and custom
empowered to speak for women. One sex was clearly superior to the other.
To call a man a *baba*, a woman, was a terrible insult. When women sought to
escape the "sphere described by nature and custom to the female sex," they
underplayed their femininity or disguised themselves as men.[3] Public space
was men's space: a woman who ventured forth alone and undisguised after
dark was at considerable risk of harassment. Yet the public and the private
are not separate worlds at all, as women's historians have increasingly
argued. They interact and intersect at many levels, and it is the seemingly
natural arrangements based on gender that often obscure the connections between them. Men's entitlement to public life derived partly from their control
of the women within their domain. At all levels of Russian society, authoritarian, hierarchical family relations that subordinated the young to their elders
and women to men reproduced and reinforced the authoritarian social and
political order. By fostering discipline and respect for authority on the personal level, the patriarchal family prepared people for social discipline and
respect for state authority. Women's subordination to men also played a key
role in maintaining social and political order, because the family stability
so essential to that order depended especially on husbands' authority over
wives.[4] Russian reformers and revolutionaries from the eighteenth through
the twentieth centuries were equally aware of the connection between domestic and public life. They knew that if Russia was to emerge as a modern,
westernized nation, it was not enough to reform its governmental and military institutions. Thoroughgoing change must also take place at home, within
the family that dominated the social and economic as well as personal lives of
most Russians.

Initial reforms affected aristocratic women, and they came from above.
Eighteenth-century rulers, beginning with Peter the Great, sought to destroy
the clan politics of the Muscovite period. When Peter ordered aristocratic
women to leave the seclusion of the *terem* and engage in the pleasures of social
life in 1718, he had more on his mind than giving his court some polish along
Western European lines. By breaking down the old Russian family regime,

3. Barbara Heldt, *Terrible Perfection: Women and Russian Literature* (Bloomington, Ind., 1987),
makes the point about insult. The quotation is derived from the translator's introduction to
Nadezhda Durova, *The Cavalry Maiden*, trans. Mary Fleming Zirin (Bloomington, Ind., 1988),
ix. To get around St. Petersburg at night, Sofiia Perovskaia and her friend Aleksandra Kornilova
often disguised themselves as boys. See the photograph in *Five Sisters: Women against the Tsar*, ed.
Barbara Engel and Clifford Rosenthal (New York, 1975), 215. An illuminating discussion of the
role of gender in structuring historical change is provided by Joan Scott, *Gender and the Politics of
History* (New York, 1988).

4. William Wagner, "The Trojan Mare: Women's Rights and Civil Rights in Late Imperial
Russia," in *Civil Rights in Imperial Russia*, ed. Olga Crisp and Linda Edmondson (Oxford, 1989),
79–80.

he hoped to weaken resistance to his demand that every nobleman serve the state and to foster the individual initiative essential to Russia's military and economic progress. At the same time Peter's reforms integrated upper-class women into the social life of the court and noble circles, for the first time providing them with freedom to choose their marriage partners. Once social interaction of men and women became the order of the day, education of elite women became a primary concern. Although acting according to a traditional definition of women's roles, Catherine the Great took steps to enlarge women's sphere and produce better wives and mothers. She established the Smolnyi Institute for Girls of Noble Birth in 1764 as well as public schools where girls of more humble background might obtain an education. These initiatives, which at first affected only a small number of women, represented the beginning of an uphill battle for women's education.

During the reign of the highly conservative Nicholas I (1825–55) the impetus for change passed from the autocracy to society. Russia's increasingly educated and westernized elite had hoped for liberal reforms, such as the rule of law (*Rechtsstaat*) and perhaps a constitution, from Nicholas's brother, Alexander I (1801–25), but Alexander had failed to grant them. Such men grew estranged, and on December 14, 1825, some of them attempted to take matters into their own hands by staging a coup d'état. Forces loyal to the new tsar, Nicholas I, easily crushed the attempt, which became known as the Decembrist uprising. Thereafter tight censorship and a ubiquitous secret police made activity in the public sphere both difficult and dangerous. Stimulated by the ideals of the German Romantics, and then by George Sand and the Utopian Socialists, male reformers and radicals turned inward to examine their own lives and reevaluate their personal relationships. This reflection led some of them to recognize the connection between the autocratic political order, which they opposed, and the patriarchal family that subordinated women and children to men. In reaction many of the leading male proponents of social and political change sought to democratize family relations. Starting in the 1830s, men of the intelligentsia tried to alter their personal relationships with women. First they exalted women and placed them on a pedestal; then, more successfully, they tried to create equality between the sexes. With a handful of noblewomen they debated in salons and on the pages of journals the legal and social status of women and the role women should play in transforming the family and regenerating a stagnant Russian society.[5]

5. J. H. Seddon, *The Petrashevtsy: A Study of the Russian Revolutionaries of 1848* (Manchester, 1985); Barbara Alpern Engel, *Mothers and Daughters: Women of the Intelligentsia in Nineteenth Century Russia* (New York, 1983); Richard Stites, *The Women's Liberation Movement in Russia: Feminism, Nihilism and Bolshevism, 1860–1930* (Princeton, 1978); G. A. Tishkin, *Zhenskii vopros v Rossii v 50–60 gg. XIX v.* (Leningrad, 1984).

We know most about the women who preferred leaving the domestic sphere to renegotiating relations within it. Even before men and women began elaborating the "woman question," a few remarkable women had taken matters into their own hands. In 1807 the noblewoman Nadezhda Durova fled her home near the Ural Mountains determined to escape her woman's lot. Disguising herself as a boy, she joined the Russian cavalry and served with distinction. In 1836 she published the journals she had kept during her years of service. By then other women writers had started to draw attention to the plight of the educated and able woman in a society that subordinated women legally to men, scorned their talents, and denied them any legitimate outlets outside the family.[6] In the early years of the reign of Alexander II (1855–81) more women turned from words to actions. Most of them were nobles, but they included Nadezhda Suslova, the daughter of a serf, who became one of Russia's first women doctors. Stimulated by articles on the woman question and by the turmoil surrounding the emancipation of the serfs in 1861, such women sought access to education, paid employment, and a role outside the household. From the ferment a feminist movement emerged. It quickly became the most effective advocate of women's right to higher education, helping gain for thousands of women the right to audit advanced lecture courses, receive medical education, and, at the end of the 1870s, attend a women's university (the *bestuzhevskie kursy*).[7]

Some women took their rebellion in a more extreme direction. In the late 1850s and early 1860s dozens of young women joined the nihilist movement. In the name of individual freedom they revolted against "family despotism." Daughters of nobles and government officials cropped their hair, dispensed with crinolines, and took to wearing blue eyeglasses and smoking in public as a declaration of independence from conventionally feminine dress and demeanor. Far more numerous were women revolutionaries, who alongside men pursued social justice and political change with propaganda leaflets or pistols in hand from the late 1860s onward. They were both more numerous and more prominent than women in the radical movements of Western Europe. Quite varied in their social origins, the majority nevertheless came from the same noble and bureaucratic background as the nihilist women, and all of them had received an education. They espoused an ideology of peasant revolution known as populism (*narodnichestvo*). During the 1870s they tried to use their knowledge to serve the peasants. Some worked among them as teachers, midwives, and medical aides. Others, disguising themselves as peasants, tried to rouse the peasantry to social revolution. Women also

6. On women writers, see Heldt, *Terrible Perfection*, and *Dacha na Petergofskoi doroge: Proza russkikh pisatel'nits pervoi poloviny XIX veka*, ed. V. Uchenova (Moscow, 1986).

7. Christine Johanson, *Women's Struggle for Higher Education in Russia, 1855–1900* (Kingston and Montreal, 1987).

figured prominently in populist organizations, where a few of them, like Vera Figner and Sofiia Perovskaia, assumed leadership roles. Profoundly unconventional in many respects, their experience nevertheless suggests the ways that tradition can empower as well as debilitate women. As a rationale for rebellion against the confining aspects of their traditional female role, women radicals and revolutionaries drew on feminine ideals of altruism and self-sacrifice that were rooted deep in the Russian past.

Industrialization and economic modernization, not ideology, would connect some peasant women to a larger world. In the decades that followed the emancipation of the serfs in 1861, Russia's network of railroads expanded, helping create a national market and erode village insularity. In the 1890s the Russian government undertook a policy of rapid industrialization that drew thousands of peasant workers to the factory or city for the first time. These processes affected peasant women slowly and unevenly because women were more likely than men to remain in their villages. In fact, the new demands that the emancipation placed on the family economy often increased women's responsibilities. Peasants experienced a growing need for cash to pay taxes and redeem their land as well as purchase consumer goods such as kerosene, nails, tea, and sugar. As a result, nonagricultural employment expanded. The need for additional income was greatest in the provinces of the Central Industrial Region, where by the 1880s agricultural production rarely sufficed even for family needs. From these provinces substantial numbers of peasant men traveled elsewhere in search of jobs, leaving women at home to take on their husbands' labor in addition to their customary work in the fields and the household.[8]

Women remained in the village also because the provisions of the emancipation made it difficult for peasants to give up their allotment of land and the tax responsibilities that went with it. Since women earned less than men in every trade and were assigned primary responsibility for child care, it made sense for them to take on men's tasks in the fields. And most women seemed to prefer the familiar village world. When they needed work outside the household, they sought it first in their own or nearby villages. This was true even of spinsters and widows, who were the most marginal persons in the village and only under certain circumstances had access to land in their own right.[9] One of the few trades they could control was healing, which had long provided single women with the means to support themselves outside of the patriarchal peasant household. Even as they continued to employ many of their traditional practices, toward the end of the nineteenth century

8. Barbara Alpern Engel, "The Women's Side: Male Outmigration and the Family Economy in Kostroma Province," *Slavic Review* 45 (1986): 257–71.

9. On peasant women's access to property, see Christine Worobec, "Customary Law and Property Devolution among Russian Peasants in the 1870s," *Canadian Slavonic Papers* 26 (1984): 220–34.

women healers began to adopt new medical techniques, such as the use of mercury to cure syphilis.[10] Household production of a range of goods provided another source of income for women. Peasant women had traditionally planted and harvested flax and hemp, then spun thread and woven cloth to make clothing for themselves and their family. To produce homespun flax and hemp for the market, as women increasingly did in the second half of the nineteenth century, was an extension of their customary role. So, in a different way, was taking in children from foundling homes in Moscow and St. Petersburg, nursing and raising them in return for cash payment.[11]

Working within the peasant household for an entrepreneur or factory added a new dimension to Russian peasant women's labor. In the decades that followed the emancipation, the number of women thus employed expanded rapidly. Working in their cottages, they unwound cotton for a factory or sewed kid gloves or rolled hollow tubes for cigarettes from materials distributed by an entrepreneur, who paid them for their work and sold the finished product. Even independent craftswomen such as lacemakers and stocking knitters often depended on middlemen to market their goods.[12] In many respects these women had the worst of both worlds. Their intermediary position between household and market left them vulnerable to exploitation by middlemen and, much more rarely, middlewomen (often widows), who took advantage of other women's inability to leave home to seek better terms. Nor did their work noticeably enhance their status at home. Connected to the market by virtue of their income-producing activities, they nevertheless worked within the traditional patriarchal household. So long as women remained in the village, patriarchal patterns continued to govern their lives. The vast majority of peasant women never left home.

Nevertheless, as the nineteenth century drew to a close, a growing minority of peasant women began to seek wages elsewhere. Even as the need for cash at home increased, it became ever more difficult to earn it in the village. Factories began taking over more and more of women's household trades, reducing what women could earn from them to the merest pittance. Unmarried women and widows, whose ties to household and village were the most tenuous, were the most likely to leave, but marriageable girls and even married women increasingly departed as well. Many went away temporarily, only for a season. Women from the same village or district might form artels (work collectives) and travel together to labor in other people's fields, cut

10. See the essay by Rose Glickman in this volume.

11. David L. Ransel provides a thorough account of the foundling trade in *Mothers of Misery: Child Abandonment in Russia* (Princeton, 1988).

12. On women's protoindustrial trades before the emancipation, see Edgar Melton, "Proto-Industrialization, Serf Agriculture and Agrarian Social Structure: Two Estates in Nineteenth Century Russia," *Past and Present*, May 1987, no. 115: 69–107; for the second half of the nineteenth century, see the essay by Judith Pallot in this volume.

peat in the swamps around Moscow, make bricks, harvest tobacco, or perform a variety of other poorly paid and backbreaking tasks. Women who worked year-round most often became domestic servants, but a growing proportion found work in factories; far smaller numbers of village-born women worked in urban crafts.[13] Most of these year-round migrants made their way to factory centers or the major cities, swelling the population of migrant peasants that constituted the majority of the population of Moscow and St. Petersburg at the end of the nineteenth century. By 1900 marriageable women aged sixteen to twenty-five comprised 17.6 percent of the peasant women in St. Petersburg.[14]

In the cities peasant women found difficult working and living conditions. Servants slept in corridors or in a corner of the kitchen; rarely did they have a room of their own. Without fixed working hours they were constantly at the beck and call of their masters. Factory women's working hours were better defined, but their day was long too. Before factory legislation mandated a workday of eleven and a half hours in 1897, women workers often labored fourteen hours a day, six days a week. Housing was scarce and outrageously expensive. Women workers either lived in factory dormitories, where dozens were crowded together in a single large room, or they rented a corner just large enough for their bed in an apartment. Factory women may have dreamed of a room of their own, but on their meager earnings it was an unattainable luxury.

Still, though her living and working conditions were often no easier than they had been in the village, the peasant woman who migrated to town or city experienced a new kind of independence. So long as she remained in the household of her father or husband, a woman's relations with the larger society were mediated by men. When she left her village on her own, she was no longer directly subject to patriarchal control. To be sure, peasant women often remained psychologically and legally tied to their village. Most working women sent a portion of their wages home, and they visited when they could. Marriageable women often planned to return, marry, and settle down when they had earned enough to pay for their dowry. Work left women little free time. Nevertheless, peasant women in the cities remained much freer than their rural sisters to court and to live as they chose.

It was the freedom, rather than its limitations, that most struck tsarist officials. The growth of prostitution served as its most visible and troubling symbol, and it moved the state to action. Suspecting all lower-class women on their own of "trading in vice," the state attempted to substitute for absent husbands and fathers its own patriarchal power. It created and elaborated a

13. Rose L. Glickman, *Russian Factory Women: Workplace and Society, 1880–1914* (Berkeley and Los Angeles, 1984).

14. *S.-Peterburg po perepisi 15 Dekabria 1900 goda*, fasc. 1 (St. Petersburg, 1903), 137–39.

network of laws to regulate prostitution and control venereal disease, laws that in fact affected all women of the lower classes. Even women who plied the trade casually and intermittently (or perhaps not at all) risked encountering the police and becoming registered as "professional" prostitutes, receiving a "yellow ticket" that clearly identified their trade. The "yellow ticket" licensed prostitutes to work at their trade but subjected them to police surveillance and medical supervision, allegedly to control venereal disease. Once registered as a professional prostitute, a woman on her own would no longer be her own mistress.[15]

The growing visibility of lower-class women in urban Russia elicited a response from intellectuals too. As increasing numbers of women penetrated into public and previously male space, the woman question took on new and complex life. But the political atmosphere in which people debated was different from what it had been in the immediate postemancipation era. In the 1860s and 1870s the struggle between state and society had been more explicitly political, involving feminist, liberal, and radical movements aiming to wrest from the autocracy some or all of its authority. In the politically repressive 1880s and 1890s political movements of this sort did not disappear, but their members experienced enormous difficulties expressing their ideas in print or acting on behalf of them. Intellectuals found it easier to contest the state in less direct, but nonetheless important ways. And there were many more intellectuals equipped to do so. The demands of an industrializing society had led to an expansion of both general and professional education. A new generation of educated persons, especially lawyers and physicians, asserted their right to operate outside state jurisdiction and have primary responsibility for the areas in which they claimed expertise.[16] Because of the gains of the feminist movement, some of these persons were women. They added a uniquely feminist perspective to debates conducted at conferences and meetings and on the pages of professional journals as well as popular publications.

Professional men sought greater rights for themselves, not for women, whose bodies became part of the terrain over which educated society struggled for power. Even as the basis of women's dependent status began to erode

15. Laurie Bernstein, "Sonia's Daughters: Prostitution and Society in Russia" (Ph.D. diss., University of California, Berkeley, 1987); Barbara Alpern Engel, "Prostitutes in Late Nineteenth Century St. Petersburg: A Personal and Social Profile," *Russian Review* 48 (1989): 21–44; Laura Engelstein, "Morality and the Wooden Spoon: Russian Doctors View Syphilis, Social Class, and Sexual Behavior, 1890–1905," *Representations* 14 (1986): 169–208, and "Gender and the Juridical Subject: Prostitution and Rape in Nineteenth Century Russian Criminal Codes," *Journal of Modern History* 60 (1988): 458–95; Richard Stites, "Prostitute and Society in Pre-Revolutionary Russia," *Jahrbücher für Geschichte Osteuropas* 31 (1983): 348–64.

16. On the consequences of professionalization, see Nancy M. Frieden, *Russian Physicians in an Era of Reform and Revolution, 1856–1905* (Princeton, 1981), and Richard Wortman, *The Development of a Russian Legal Consciousness* (Chicago, 1976).

as a result of women's migration, jurists revising laws treating sexual crime and prostitution denied women agency and ensured that individual autonomy remained a male preserve. When they discussed abortion and infanticide, the only forms of birth control women had, male physicians and jurists, like tsarist officials, expressed anxieties about uncontrolled women. Professional men differed from government authorities in seeking to substitute their own authority for the power of the patriarchal state. Male physicians who opposed official regulation of prostitution, for example, argued that medical authority must replace it.[17] By contrast, educated feminist women often defended lower-class women, contending, for example, that women had the right to make their own reproductive choices regardless of their social status. Yet feminists, like professional men, sometimes denied lower-class women agency. In their campaign to abolish the yellow ticket, feminists tended to stress women's victimization. According to this perspective women of the lower classes did not choose prostitution from among the limited options available to them; rather, thousands "perished" as a result of their youth and inexperience, often because they had been seduced and abandoned by men.[18] This language of victimization served a political function. In Russia, as elsewhere in Europe, feminists who found in the subjection of lower-class women to regulation a metaphor for every woman's lack of social and political rights rallied to the cause of abolition.[19]

The lack of basic rights for women seemed all the more glaring after 1905. In that revolutionary year workers, students, and intellectuals joined forces to wrest from the autocracy civil rights and political representation. Feminists provided generous support for the liberation movement. Even as they intensified their efforts to attain women's suffrage, most leaders of the women's movement embraced the idea that women's liberation was inseparable from the liberation of society as a whole. Women campaigned alongside men for political change. The revolution of 1905 revivified Russian feminism and brought new recruits to its ranks.[20] But feminist support for the liberation movement, so generously given, was rather less generously returned. When the revolutionary upheaval subsided, only men had gained the vote in the new quasi parliament, the imperial Duma. This left women in the position of lobbying the men who had once been their equals in political powerlessness as well as their allies in political struggle. The liberal Kadet

17. See the article by Laura Engelstein in this volume; also Engelstein, "Gender and the Juridical Subject."

18. Mariia Pokrovskaia provides the clearest example of this sort of thinking. See her "Bor'ba s prostitutsiei," *Zhurnal Russkago Obshchestva okhraneniia narodnago zdraviia*, (1900), no. 4: 417. For evidence that women became prostitutes for more complex reasons, see Engel, "Prostitutes."

19. Bernstein, "Sonia's Daughters."

20. Linda Harriet Edmondson, *The Feminist Movement in Russia, 1900–1917* (Stanford, 1984).

party, which dominated the first Duma, was divided over the issue of women's suffrage. Because of their working-class orientation parties of the left, although staunch advocates of women's rights, were, with the notable exception of the Labor Faction (*Trudoviki*), suspicious of "bourgeois feminism" and reluctant to support it.

But women themselves did not always agree about how they wanted to transform their lives. The years following 1905 saw a proliferation of feminisms and a fragmentation of women's efforts as the feminist movement lost members and momentum. Many working-class women gave their loyalty to socialist parties more readily than feminist ones. During 1905–6 feminists had tried hard to bridge the vast social chasm that separated educated women from their laboring sisters, but their efforts rarely succeeded for long. By 1908 all but a handful of feminists, Mariia Pokrovskaia most notable among them, had abandoned the effort to reach lower-class women.

Socialist parties were no more prepared than feminist ones to fight for the needs of working-class women. This reluctance was despite the prompting of women leaders such as Aleksandra Kollontai, who attempted to build a movement of women workers within the Social Democratic movement. When women workers articulated their own needs on the pages of socialist newspapers, men managed to ignore them.[21] Unable to overcome their views of women as backward and inferior, the male leadership of socialist parties remained largely unresponsive to working-class women's attempts to transform their own lives.

The outbreak of World War I mobilized Russian women at unprecedented levels. New jobs opened up in the factories that men abandoned for the front; women of the upper classes volunteered and found work nursing and gathering clothing and medical supplies; in the absence of men, peasant women shouldered all the responsibility for field work or traveled for the first time to cities in search of employment. Overall, war brought women more hardship than rewards.[22] Nevertheless, World War I helped prepare the way for the more profound transformations that the Bolsheviks would undertake after 1917. It blurred gender boundaries and undermined traditional society still further, bringing hundreds of thousands, perhaps millions, of women into public life for the first time. Many of these women held positions formerly occupied by men. At the same time the upheavals that accompanied the war created an undercurrent of nostalgia, a longing for the way things used to be in the comfortable, patriarchal past. Many men shared this feeling; probably many women did too. During the 1920s this nostalgia would fuel resistance to further changes in people's personal lives.

21. Barbara Evans Clements, *Bolshevik Feminist: The Life of Aleksandra Kollontai* (Bloomington, Ind., 1979); Glickman, *Russian Factory Women*; Stites, *Women's Liberation Movement*.

22. See the essay by Alfred Meyer in this volume.

As wives and mothers, those most traditional of female roles, working-class women initiated the actions that culminated in the fall of the autocracy on International Women's Day, February 23, 1917. In Russia, as elsewhere in Europe, lower-class women customarily acted as guardians of the community by assisting each other in times of need, and they took primary responsibility for maintaining everyday life by obtaining fuel, food, and shelter for their families. The war had severely undermined women's ability to fulfill these roles, prompting them to call a meeting for "bread and peace" and organize a strike in the textiles mills of Petrograd (formerly St. Petersburg) for February 23. The response was enormous. Over the next few days, as hundreds of thousands of men joined in, the women's protest turned into a full-scale revolution, forcing Nicholas II to abdicate on February 25.[23]

The short-lived Provisional Government that replaced the tsar satisfied the feminist demand for suffrage on July 20. It also granted women the right to serve as attorneys as well as to act as jurors, and it gave them equal rights within the civil service. These actions won the Provisional Government the cautious support of the feminists. But the revolution brought lower-class women neither the bread nor the peace they had demanded in February. As a result, they became more responsive to the organizing efforts of the Bolshevik party, which made "peace, land, and bread" its slogan.

On October 23–24, 1917, the Bolsheviks came to power, bringing with them a thoroughgoing agenda for social and economic change that included transforming working women's lives.[24] In the socialist society they would build, women would be full and equal participants in productive labor. Socialism would relieve women of household tasks such as child care, laundry, and cooking. The initial steps seemed promising. The Bolsheviks published a family ode in 1918 that equalized women's status with men's, removed marriage from the hands of the church, allowed a marrying couple to choose either the husband's or the wife's surname, and granted illegitimate children the same legal rights as legitimate ones. Divorce, virtually impossible in the tsarist period, became easily obtainable. In 1920 abortion became legal if performed by a physician. The Women's Bureau (Zhenotdel) was established in 1919 as a result of the efforts of Bolshevik women such as Aleksandra Kollontai and Inessa Armand. During the 1920s it conducted propaganda among working women and attempted to bring women into the revolutionary process and promote their equality in public and private life.

These woman-oriented initiatives from above helped foster the mobilization of lower-class women from below. Ardently defending their own and

23. Temma Kaplan, "Women and Communal Strikes in the Crisis of 1917–1922," in *Becoming Visible: Women in European History*, ed. Renate Bridenthal, Claudia Koonz, and Susan Stuard, 2d ed. (Boston, 1987), 429–51.

24. On women's mixed response to the Bolshevik takeover, see Barbara Evans Clements, "Working Class and Peasant Women in the Russian Revolution," *Signs* 8 (1982): 215–35.

their children's interests, women took active part in debates over the New Family Code of 1926. The code proposed to make divorce still easier to obtain and provide women living with men in de facto unions with the same legal protections as women in registered marriages. Women opposed these provisions, asserting that they would encourage male irresponsibility and further erode their fragile family economy. Lower-class women were equally involved in the struggle to obtain birth control and acquire broader access to abortion during the 1920s. They made abundantly clear that they preferred to control their own fertility.[25]

But even in the 1920s waves of change hit an undertow of conservatism that indicated the tenacity of tradition at almost every level. The conservatism is evident in revolutionary iconography, through which the Bolsheviks sent women mixed messages. Even as the Bolsheviks attempted to transform women's roles and free them from the family, they perpetuated images that undercut their efforts by portraying women as helpers of men and as Mother Earth.[26] There was considerable opposition to women's emancipation from men within the party and even more opposition outside of it. Opposition was most violent among the Muslims of Central Asia. In the second half of the 1920s the Bolsheviks launched a campaign against forced marriage and polygamy, and they encouraged Muslim women to unveil. Bloody riots erupted in response to this attack on traditional male privilege. Men harassed and sometimes raped unveiled women. Between March 1927 and December 1928 about eight hundred women activists and rebels against tradition were murdered. The Bolsheviks were forced to retreat.[27]

Social and economic circumstances did not favor women's emancipation. Peasant women in villages little affected by revolutionary change continued to have illegal abortions to hide their "shame," much as peasant women had done before the revolution. Moreover, at least as much as war, the disorder of the 1920s prompted lower-class women to long for more stability.[28] Despite party pronouncements on equality women remained vulnerable both personally and economically. Millions of women had lost husbands to war and revolution; men who survived sometimes abandoned their aging wives for younger women. Rates of female unemployment remained high through the 1920s. Revolutionary transformation did not end most women's loyalty to

25. Wendy Goldman, "Freedom and Its Consequences: The Debate on the Soviet Family Code of 1926," *Russian History* 11 (1984): 362–88, and her article in this volume.

26. See the essay by Elizabeth Waters in this volume.

27. Gregory Massell, *The Surrogate Proletariat: Moslem Women and Revolutionary Strategies in Soviet Central Asia, 1919–1929* (Princeton, 1974).

28. For the effects of war on women, see Barbara Evans Clements, "The Effects of the Civil War on Women and Family Relations," in *Party, State, and Society in the Russian Civil War: Explorations in Social History*, ed. Diane Koenker, R. Gregor Suny, and William Rosenberg (Bloomington, Ind., 1989), 105–22.

the family and especially to their children. However, food shortages, poor housing, lack of job opportunities, and especially family instability made women's traditional responsibilities considerably harder to fulfill. The deserting husbands and short-term unions that led some women to seek abortion prompted others to demand more-conservative family policy to ensure their ability to provide for their children. Instead of unions easily contracted and dissolved they wanted strong and stable marriages.

By the end of the 1920s the party leadership had grown more traditional too. Aleksandra Kollontai was out favor and Joseph Stalin increasingly in command. The declining birth rate, which was blamed on too many abortions, raised concerns about the labor force of the future. The soaring divorce rate of the 1920s seemed to threaten a society about to undergo the rigors of rapid industrialization. In the 1930s the government reversed many of its earlier policies concerning women and family life. In 1930 the Zhenotdel was shut down, its task completed, according to government propaganda. In the mid-1930s, as women entered the wage-labor force in unprecedented numbers, abortion was made illegal, homosexuality became for the first time a crime, divorce grew difficult and expensive to obtain, and the distinction between legitimate and illegitimate children was restored. Equally significant, the family was officially rehabilitated and labeled socialist, and the emancipation of women was declared achieved. All political challenges to the Stalinist synthesis of transformation and tradition were suppressed. The proletarian women who had spoken out in defense of their own interests during the 1920s were silenced, and issues relating to women's liberation disappeared from the political agenda.

The Peasant Woman as Healer

Rose L. Glickman

In Solzhenitsyn's small masterpiece *Matryona's Home*, Matryona, a peasant woman in a remote Russian village, tells the narrator that all of her six children had died mysteriously, without symptoms of disease, before they reached the age of six months.

> The village had decided that there was a curse on Matryona. "Yes, there was a curse on me," Matryona said, obviously convinced of it herself. "They took me to a nun to be cured. She gave me something to make me cough, then waited for the curse to jump out of me like a frog. Well, it didn't. . ."[1]

Matryona was attempting to cure her affliction by turning to a folk healer, a *znakharka*, the sole medical practitioner in the Russian countryside for centuries and the primary and preferred medical practitioner even when professional medical personnel appeared after the emancipation of the serfs in 1861. Solzhenitsyn's story takes place in 1953. Matryona, roughly sixty years old, would have been a young woman in the 1920s and 1930s. As studies of the peasantry in those decades reveal, folk medicine was still alive and well in the Russian countryside. Folk healers remained, as they had been before the revolution, a powerful and pervasive presence in peasant culture as midwives, abortionists, and curers of every kind of physical and mental dysfunction, often to the despair of the professional medical establishment.

Healing was regarded as an occupation—as a profession or craft—by both the peasantry and officialdom. Indeed, the 1897 census defined folk

The author gratefully acknowledges the American Council of Learned Societies for support in the research and writing of this study.

1. Alexander Solzhenitsyn, "Matryona's House," *Stories and Short Prose*, trans. Michael Glenny (New York, 1971), 31.

healers as a distinct group in the population, characterized by the way it made a living. Although there were male healers (*znakhari*), the overwhelming majority of healers was female.[2] In this study I therefore refer to the healer as female, making the appropriate gender distinctions where they are relevant. For peasant women, more than for men, healing was a unique category of work, providing them with rewards, both material and nonmaterial, that no other endeavor in peasant culture afforded.

Survival in a largely subsistence agrarian economy, where the household produced most necessities, depended on the indivisible contribution of all able-bodied family members. What specifically was women's labor contribution? In the domestic domain the woman, as in most peasant cultures, had the sole responsibility for child care. Child care, however, was tucked into the crevices of her work obligations in the hut and its environs and in the fields. In addition to working the kitchen garden, caring for the smaller livestock, and preparing and preserving food, the peasant woman hauled wood and water and maintained the hut. It was her duty to clothe herself, her husband, and her children and accumulate dowries for her daughters. She not only spun, wove, and sewed the clothing but also often had full responsibility for the flax field or the sheep that provided her with raw material.

The boundaries of gender in the domestic sphere were impermeable: men did not do women's work in the hut and its environs. Field work was another matter. Women had always shared the field work with men, and their share increased throughout the nineteenth century, especially where declining agriculture encouraged men to seek nonagricultural work in cities and factories (*otkhod*). General, theoretical, and ideological studies of peasant life often made neat distinctions between men's and women's field work that disintegrate under scrutiny. True, custom frequently allocated certain separate work for men and women in the fields, but necessity undermined these distinctions: reports from all corners of the Russian empire attest to women's participation in heavy field work and to the interchangeability of men's and women's field work. Further, women as well as men engaged in domestic craft production (*kustar'*) in the many areas of Russia where peasants could not live by agriculture alone. Peasants fully acknowledged the importance of women's labor contribution to the household. "We need a wife and a horse equally," a peasant explained to a researcher in 1880. "A muzhik cannot survive long without both. If the housewife dies, you must find another. If the horse croaks, you must get another. To live on the land the muzhik must have a horse and a wife."[3]

In a curious break in logic common to many peasant societies, there was

2. Without exception all the sources cited in this study, as well as all the material I have used but not cited, attest to the predominance of women among healers.

3. M. K. Gorbunova, "Po derevniam," *Otechestvennye zapiski*, 1881, no. 9: 25.

an enormous imbalance between the acknowledgment of women's contribution to household survival and their rewards. In return for their labor women normally had the right only to maintenance. Although women's rights to their dowry were largely protected by tradition and fiercely defended by women themselves, the contents of the dowry did not support life. Land supported life, and peasant customary law dictated the devolution of land and its essential accoutrements to men alone (except, rarely, when the commune conceded a widow the right to use her dead husband's land during her children's minority). Women were denied direct access to land, the fulcrum of peasant culture on which all rewards, status, and power turned. From birth through old age male kin—fathers, brothers, and sons—and the male community mediated women's access to subsistence. Even as changing economic conditions in the postemancipation period accorded more women greater daily responsibility for tilling the soil, customary law steadfastly withheld from them an independent claim to land. Hence it followed that, as one prominent student of peasant life summarized, "[the woman] may not participate in the governance of household affairs. . . . In the final analysis, she is considered beneath any adult male."[4] Similarly, in the rough democracy of the commune, comprising male heads-of-household, "to act according to woman's reason, to listen to [her], is not done . . . and therefore the *skhod* [village assembly] does not take the woman's voice into account in making decisions."[5] The woman's subordinate position in household and community was reflected in a variety of personal and social relations. For example, wife beating was ubiquitous and within broad limits sanctioned by customary law. The father-in-law's imposition of sexual relations on the daughter-in-law, though considered a sin, was sufficiently widespread to merit a separate word in the Russian language—*snokhachestvo*.[6]

The foregoing account is, of course, schematic and static. It does not take into account individual personalities and special relationships between kin and within the community. Nor does it reveal the plethora of minute variations in customary communal arrangements across the Russian empire. It does, however, broadly describe the harsh, dependent, and exclusionary conditions of most peasant women's lives and the low esteem in which women

    4. Aleksandra Efimenko, *Izsledovaniia narodnoi zhizni*, vol. 1, *Obychnoe pravo* (Moscow, 1884), 76.
    5. S. Ia. Kapustin, "Obzor materialov po obshchinnomu zemlevladeniiu, khraniaiushchiisia v Vol'nom ekonomicheskom obshchestve," *Russkaia mysl'*, 1890, no. 1: 30.
    6. This account of women's work and place in peasant society is based on Rose L. Glickman, "Women and the Peasant Commune," in *Land Commune and Peasant Community in Russia: Communal Forms in Imperial and Early Soviet Society*, ed. Roger Bartlett (London, 1990), 321–38, and idem, *Russian Factory Women: Workplace and Society, 1889–1914* (Berkeley and Los Angeles, 1984). See also Barbara Alpern Engel, "The Women's Side: Male Outmigration and the Family Economy in Kostroma Province," *Slavic Review* 45 (1986): 257–71, and the essay by Judith Pallot in this volume.

were held in late imperial Russia and through the early decades of the Soviet period. All the more significant and interesting, then, was the position of the *znakharka*.

In principle, practitioners of folk medicine fell into two categories— healers (*znakharki*) and witches (*kolduny*). Both derived their powers from an interplay of mundane skill and supernatural forces. Healers, mainly female, derived their powers from God or his entourage of saints and performed only beneficial, curative services, whereas witches negotiated with unclean spirits and visited on their victims physical and mental illness as well as other forms of malevolence, mischief, and misfortune. In contrast to the Western European and American experience, most "professional" witches—those who consciously and deliberately practiced witchcraft—were male.[7] Among alleged witches, ordinary people who claimed no special powers but were accused of sorcery by their neighbors, there were probably as many women as men.[8]

In practice, the distinction between healer and witch was sometimes blurred, for the Russian spiritual universe was characterized by a duality or ditheism in which Christianity and paganism coexisted quite comfortably, melding into an inextricable amalgam of beliefs. As Solzhenitsyn described Matryona:

> However, this did not mean that Matryona was really a fervent believer. If anything, she was a pagan and, above all, superstitious: if you went into the garden on St. John's day, that meant there would be a bad harvest next year; if a storm was whirling the snowflakes round and round, it meant that someone had hanged himself; if you caught your foot in the door, it meant a visitor. For as long as I lodged with her, I never once saw her say her prayers or cross herself. Yet she always asked for God's blessing before doing anything and she invariably said "God bless you" to me whenever I set off for school. . . . There were ikons in the cottage. On ordinary days they were unlit, but on the eve of feast days and on the feast days themselves Matryona would light the ikon lamp.[9]

Thus the peasant spiritual universe was a busy, crowded, and eventful place, where God, saints, and angels jostled unclean spirits, all of whom intervened in human affairs and could be invoked to intervene through the

7. According to S. A. Tokarev, in the Ukraine there were two or three female witches in every village. The vastly greater number of female witches there than among the Russians was the consequence of the influence of Western Europe through Poland on the Ukraine. He does not, however, distinguish between "professional" witches and "alleged" witches. See S. A. Tokarev, *Religioznye verovaniia vostochnoslavianskikh narodov XIX–nachala XX veka* (Moscow, 1957), 28–29.

8. N. A. Nikitina, "K voprosu o russkikh koldunakh," *Sbornik Muzeia antropologii i etnografii*, 1928: 303; Nikolai Rudninskii, "Znakharstvo v Skopinskom i Dankovskom uezdakh, Riazanskoi gubernii," *Zhivaia starina*, 1886: 195–97; Russell Zguta, "Witchcraft Trials in Seventeenth-Century Russia," *American Historical Review* 82 (1977): 1187–1207.

9. Solzhenitsyn, "Matryona's House," 23–24.

good (or bad) offices of healers and witches.[10] Official Orthodoxy was uncomfortable with popular ditheism, but on the village level it was sanctioned by representatives of Christianity, unlike in Western Europe, where the priest regarded the healer as a rival.[11] As we have seen, Matryona's healer was a former nun. More often than not, the village priest shared his flock's belief in the *znakharka*'s ability to invoke divine spirits to cure as well as its belief in the witch's ability to inflict harm, readily advising his parishioners to turn to the *znakharka* or using his own Christian powers to exorcise a bewitchment.[12] The priest's treatment of the afflicted did not differ significantly from the healer's. A priest informant from Tomsk Province described his ministrations to a peasant woman who refused to go outside to milk the cow lest she encounter "unclean spirits" seeking to bewitch her:

> For my part. . . I could not refuse an afflicted one. I read and sang [from the prayer book] for two days consecutively with exorcising prayers. Finally, I ordered her, against her will, to drink from a glass of consecrated oil . . . ; when she drank the oil, there jumped out of her a carp . . . , a small mouse, and six frogs. They were all rotten and putrefying. Since then she is well and healthy.[13]

The healer was the main agent of cure, the priest only an episodic curer, as were transients, wanderers, and pilgrims, who, in contrast to the practice in Western Europe, were accepted in Russia, dispensing cures in exchange for a night's lodging and a meal. Finally, the holy fool, a mentally retarded or otherwise neurologically disturbed person, was considered blessed by God and capable of episodic curing as well.[14] In extreme cases of persistent illness that *znakharki* appeared powerless to relieve, peasants might even turn to witches for medical help, albeit apprehensively.[15] The nebulous area between healing and witchcraft was sometimes manifested in a witch's conver-

---

10. L. I. Min'ko, "Magical Curing (Its Sources and Character, the Causes of Its Prevalence)," *Soviet Anthropology and Archeology* 12, nos. 1–2 (1973), no. 3 (1973–74); Nikitina, "K voprosu o russkikh koldunakh," 334; Zguta, "Witchcraft Trials." For a detailed and informative description of the spirits in whom Russian peasants believed, see Linda Ivanits, *Russian Folk Belief* (London, 1989).

11. See, for example, Keith Thomas, *Religion and the Decline of Magic* (New York, 1971), 267.

12. G. Kovalenko, "O narodnoi meditsine v Pereiaslavskom uezde, Poltavskoi gubernii," *Etnograficheskoe obozrenie* (henceforth *EO*), 1881: 141–42; A. A. Levenstim, *Sueverie i ugolovnoe pravo* (St. Petersburg, 1899), 50; T. Popov, *Russkaia narodno-bytovaia meditsina po materialam etnograficheskogo biuro V. N. Tenisheva* (St. Petersburg, 1903), 61; D. Ushakov, "Materialy po narodnym verovaniiam velikorussov." *EO*, 1896: 165.

13. L. V. Ostrovskaia, "Mirovozrencheskie aspekty narodnoi meditsiny russkogo krest'ianskogo naseleniia Sibiri vtoroi poloviny XIX veka," in *Iz istorii sem'i i byta Sibirskogo krest'ianstva v XVII–nachale XX v.: Sbornik nauchnykh trudov*, ed. M. M. Gromyko (Novosibirsk, 1975), 137.

14. Wayland Hand, *Magical Medicine* (Berkeley and Los Angeles, 1980), 51; Popov, *Russkaia narodno-bytovaia meditsina*, 74; M. K. Gerasimov, "Materialy po narodnoi meditsine i akusherstvu v Cherepovetskom uezde, Novgorodskoi gubernii," *Zhivaia starina*, 1898, p. 1: 159.

15. Popov, *Russkaia narodno-bytovaia meditsina*, 59.

sion from malevolence to benevolence, from a covenant with unclean spirits to the invocation of God, the Mother of God, and the saints to cure rather than summon up illness. In 1926, for example, an anthropologist discovered in Nizhnii Novgorod Province a former practicing witch, Mariia Sherstiukova, who, having passed her demonic powers on to someone else, now attended church, performed funeral rites, and treated patients with herbs and chants. Her previous affiliation with unclean spirits did not prejudice the local peasants against her, and she was fully accepted as a *znakharka*.[16]

The medical practitioner of last resort was the professionally trained doctor. These preferences were in perfect harmony with the peasant belief system. For the most part peasants did not acknowledge physical or natural causation of illness. They believed that illness was due to interference in bodily or mental function by either divine or unclean forces. God, it was believed, was especially quick to punish peasants with illness for working on holy days or otherwise neglecting their observance, although these transgressions by no means exhausted the behaviors that could elicit divine retribution.[17] Whatever the transgression and whatever the supernatural intervention, treatment had to address itself to the cause and be of equal or superior strength.[18] To be sure, peasants acknowledged natural causes for certain physical afflictions—broken bones or dislocated limbs, burns, snakebites, even syphilis. Miscarriage could be a punishment for the mother's sins—not observing the fasts or having sexual relations with her husband on holy days—but heavy lifting, excessive work, or beatings were blamed as well.[19] Peasants rejected the idea that contagion played a role in most epidemic diseases (with the notable exception of cutaneous symptoms like boils), at least as modern science has explained it. The animistic notion of physical and emotional dysfunction as something material that could be brought on by the wind, called up by the word, or transmitted by a glance or touch is a kind of acknowledgment that infectious disease can be communicated through objects of common use, but it could only be prevented or cured by nonmaterial means.[20] Though illnesses with physical causation could be treated with mundane remedies, the curative properties of herbs or other natural substances were enhanced, indeed invoked, by the *znakharka*'s specialized knowledge of charms and chants and her ability to transform neutral elements such as water and fire into curative agents.

16. Nikitina, "K voprosu o russkikh koldunakh," 301–3.

17. Kovalenko, "O narodnoi meditsine," 143. For the importance that peasants attributed to work prohibitions on holidays, see M. M. Gromyko, *Traditsionnye normy povedeniia i formy obshcheniia russkikh krest'ian XIX v.* (Moscow, 1986), esp. 125.

18. Popov, *Russkaia narodno-bytovaia meditsina*, 49.

19. Ibid., 326.

20. Ostrovskaia, "Mirovozrenchenskie aspekty narodnoi meditsine," 134; Ushakov, "Materialy po narodnym verovaniiam velikorussov," 169.

Znakharki were highly specialized according to ailments.[21] Bonesetters only set bones, toothache specialists treated only toothaches. One observer reported a healer who cured nothing but ruptured belly buttons.[22] Other *znakharki* specialized in the method of treatment and used only charmed water or fire or steam for a variety of afflictions; some cured by frightening the illness out of the patient's body or transferring the illness from the human body to an animal or an inert object such as a stone. Some healers were internists who recommended ingesting remedies ranging from herbs to mercury compounds. Others specialized in prophylactic measures intended, for example, to guard against a potential epidemic. Bloodletters only bled and cupped; they and specialists in plants and herbs were the least likely to rely heavily on magical ritual.[23] But all healers to some degree accompanied their treatment with chants, invocations, and suggestion and, however mundane the treatment, surrounded the procedure with mystery. Most villages and districts had sufficient numbers of healers to satisfy most needs, although in exceptional cases peasants might travel far beyond their usual venues to seek a renowned specialist.

Who was the healer? How did she acquire and apply her skills? What was her position in the peasant community? In the late 1890s a physician-researcher in a central Russian village interviewed a *znakharka*, Marfa, whom he described as an intelligent, bold, and energetic old woman. How did she become a *znakharka*? he asked.

"I remained a widow with six small children, so I had to feed myself somehow."

"Did you learn to cure from someone?"

"It's from God."

"Did you begin to cure immediately?"

"How can you do it immediately? No, little by little. It happened that I was treated myself and saw how others cure. So, I watched closely and began to cure myself: I learned from others."

"Do you treat with herbs?"

"With herbs, with sayings, and I wash with magical water."

"Would you tell anyone these sayings?"

"Why not? It's not sinful. I get this from God. So, I went among the holy and asked, is it a sin to heal? The old men said, not at all, it's not a sin. You see, I had a dream. . . . I was in a room and a girl came into the room with a book in one hand and a jug in the other. She looked into the jug and then into the book. Then she says three times, no, it's not a sin. I asked Father Ambrosia about the dream. He said, It's alright, it's given from God. The monks, the most holy of them, also said it was alright."[24]

---

21. Popov, *Russkaia narodno-bytovaia meditsina*, 56; Gerasimov, "Materialy po narodnoi meditsine i akusherstvu," 159.

22. Popov, *Russkaia narodno-bytovaia meditsina*, 179.

23. Ibid., 78.

24. Ibid., 60–61.

Marfa's story illustrates several characteristics common to most *znakharki*. With the exception of fortune-tellers, who were often young women, the *znakharki* were elderly. Peasants believed that age conferred on healers wisdom inaccessible to the young.[25] Given the short life expectancy of peasants in prerevolutionary Russia, healers might be forty years of age, but most were older.

Almost without exception the *znakharka* was landless. Strictly speaking, of course, all women were landless. But women such as Marfa were without fathers, husbands, or sons through whose access to land they could derive subsistence, or they were daughters or wives of landless peasants. In other words, the *znakharka* had to provide for herself, and often for her children or grandchildren as well, without the support of the traditional peasant household.

For the most part healing was not initially a calling. It was a profession (or trade) that women chose out of need and the absence of alternatives. Male healers often adapted the skills of other professions to healing, so that among male healers were former horse doctors and shepherds or former soldiers who had been medical aids in the army.[26] Men had a certain advantage in that literacy among male peasants, although low, was significantly higher than among female peasants. Some men apparently had access to old herbaries that had been in vogue in the sixteenth and seventeenth centuries.[27] Women did not have the kinds of prior training that served them subsequently as healers. Many *znakharki* picked up some knowledge casually in the normal course of their lives. For example, in remote areas of Russia, like Siberia, young unmarried women frequently traveled from their own villages, where there were no churches, to attend services in neighboring or even distant villages and exchange "recipes," as it were, for healing.[28] And since every peasant was treated by healers many times in his or her life, there was a common lexicon, albeit primitive compared to the *znakharka*'s, to which further mundane knowledge would be added as well as the more important knowledge of chants and invocations. Often healing skills were first acquired by direct observation and later augmented by study and experimentation. "My father's sister healed," another healer reports. "So I imitated her, and I imitated my grandfather who was a soldier and then began to heal. So now

25. Ibid., 51; Gerasimov, "Materialy po narodnoi meditsine i akusherstvu," 158.

26. The shepherd's success in finding appropriate food for his flock, keeping it together, and protecting it against wolves was considered extremely responsible and skilled work requiring magical rituals—sometimes, but not always, aided by a priest. Therefore, he "knew words" and could transfer this knowledge to healing. See Tokarev, *Religioznye verovaniia vostochnoslavianskikh narodov*, 31–32.

27. V. Demich, "Ocherki russkoi narodnoi meditsiny," *Vrach*, 1889, no. 7: 183; Popov, *Russkaia narodno-bytovaia meditsina*, 74.

28. Aleksei Makarenko, "Materialy po narodnoi meditsine Ushurskoi volosti, Achinskogo okruga, Eniseiskoi gubernii," *Zhivaia starina*, 1897, p. 1: 57–58.

when I give a patient some kind of medicine and he feels better, I use the medicine a second and a third time."[29] The healer's skills could be passed from mother to daughters or daughters-in-law and often were.[30] Transmission of healing skill and knowledge was actually more common among male healers in parts of Russia where a particular kind of healing was performed only by men who routinely passed the profession on to their sons. Witches always kept their skills in the family, passing them on to children or spouses. In the absence of kin, witches could confer their powers through an inanimate object like a stick or stone, which, placed on a path, would be picked up by an innocent and unsuspecting recipient.[31] The difference between healers and witches was that healers bequeathed their knowledge, by teaching or example, whereas witches bequeathed their occult power.[32]

Marfa's account demonstrates the church's sanction of the invocation of God, saints, angels, and, conspicuously, the Mother of God for healing. Concomitantly it illustrates her conviction that in addition to practical skills she had special ones that derived from righteous sources. "I am also a healer," claimed another *znakharka* from Marfa's region. "I help in my own way; I wash with water. My deceased mother taught me. It's not witchcraft, my daughter, she said to me, but God's work, because it works through prayer. She gave me a tiny figure of the Mother of God, called Siropitatel'nitsa, and told me to dip it into water to make the water holy and to cure by washing with this water."[33] Marfa's willingness to repeat her chants openly was characteristic of the *znakharka*, who believed that because her powers were of divine origin she had nothing to hide. Witches, by contrast, jealously guarded their chants, depending as they did on mystery, fear, and intimidation to impress their patients.

The most ubiquitous healer, because most peasant women had recourse to her many times in their lives, was the peasant midwife, or *povitukha* (also called *povival'naia baba* or *babka*). (I will refer to her in Russian to distinguish her from the *akusherka*, the professionally trained, licensed midwife, who was rarely a peasant.)[34] The *povitukha* required something more than the talents of the ordinary *znakharka*. Virgins, no matter how old, could not be midwives. Further, a *povitukha* had to have had children, living or dead, although one with many live children (not a usual occurrence among the Russian peasantry, among whom infant mortality was extremely high) had demon-

29. P. Bogaevskii, "Zametki o narodnoi meditsine," EO, 1889, no. 7: 101.

30. Popov, *Russkaia narodno-bytovaia meditsina*, 61.

31. Nikitina, "K voprosu o russkikh koldunakh," 306.

32. Ushakov, "Materialy po narodnym verovaniiam velikorussov," 180.

33. Popov, *Russkaia narodno-bytovaia meditsina*, 61.

34. Samuel Ramer, "Childbirth and Culture: Midwifery in the Nineteenth Century Russian Countryside," in *The Family in Imperial Russia: New Lines of Historical Research*, ed. David L. Ransel (Urbana, Ill., 1978), 218–35.

strated that she knew how to *babnichat'* (do a *babka*'s work). Normally, a woman who illegally cohabited with a man could not practice midwifery; in exceptional circumstances, however, she could redeem herself in the eyes of the community by long cohabitation. In other words, a *povitukha* had to have a spotless sexual history. She also had to have a reputation for selflessness. A *povitukha* was a healer, one observer commented, but not every healer could be a *povitukha*: "The *povitukha* has the most honored place in peasant society; her calling and type of knowledge is completely different from the calling and the knowledge of the ordinary healer."[35]

To heal was not a way to get rich. The *znakharka* took what the family could afford, usually payment in kind—a loaf of bread, five eggs, a length of cotton or wool. In the mid-1870s a *zemstvo* physician reckoned that on the average a healer earned about five rubles a year in cash.[36] The *znakharka* lived no better than the ordinary peasant, especially if healing was the only source of subsistence, and she sometimes had to supplement it by begging, hiring herself out to do field work during the harvest season, or both.[37] It appears that in certain parts of Russia male healers with a specialty like curing snakebites could command considerably greater remuneration, such as sacks of flour, and had less need to supplement their incomes with other kinds of work.[38]

Most of what we know about folk medicine comes from the reports of rural *zemstvo* doctors, ethnographers, geographers, biologists, and local priests and schoolteachers. Scientists and casual reporters were in the main fairly neutral and occasionally were rather positive about folk medicine and its practitioners, like the biologist who discovered 125 efficacious herbs in a *znakharka*'s arsenal and enthusiastically applauded her for using them intelligently.[39]

Zemstvo physicians, an extremely valuable source, are another matter. Doctors, like healers, did not practice medicine among the peasantry to get rich, although generally their incomes were adequate by the standards of professional medicine at the time.[40] They were, however, massively over-worked. To practice medicine in the countryside among the peasants re-quired enormous dedication and was rewarded with enormous frustration.

35. Makarenko, "Materialy po narodnoi meditsine," pt. 1: 95, pt. 2: 384; Popov, *Russkaia narodno-bytovaia meditsina*, 342.

36. Kovalenko, "O narodnoi meditsine v Pereiaslavskom uezde," 147; Nikitina, "K voprosu o russkikh koldunakh," 303; K. Tolstoi, *Vospominaniia zemskogo vracha* (Moscow, 1876), 30. In Dr. Tolstoi's region *zemstvo* doctors earned twelve hundred rubles a year; a licensed midwife earned on the average 240 rubles a year. Ibid., 30, 83. See also Nancy Frieden, *Russian Physicians in an Era of Reform and Revolution, 1856–1905* (Princeton, 1981).

37. Bogaevskii, "Zametki o narodnoi meditsine," 101; Kovalenko, "O narodnoi meditsine v Pereiaslavskom uezde," 147; Nikitina, "K voprosu o russkikh koldunakh," 303.

38. Kovalenko, "O narodnoi meditsine v Pereiaslavskom uezde," 147.

39. Ostrovskaia, "Mirovozrencheskie aspekty narodnoi meditsiny," 125.

40. Frieden, *Russian Physicians*, 47–48, 218–20.

The extremely sparse distribution of *zemstvo* physicians in rural areas dictated a daunting work load. In 1897 the ratio of doctors to patients for seventeen *zemstvo* provinces was one to 24,977.[41] To be sure, the situation varied significantly from province to province and even within a province. In Moscow Province in 1898, for example, one district had one doctor for every eight thousand inhabitants, whereas another had one for every twenty thousand. But for the conscientious doctor—and most *zemstvo* doctors were dedicated and idealistic—trying to treat peasants was like cleaning the Augean stables.[42] Further, as rationalists, "men of science," they were appalled by, and constantly struggled with, the peasants' ignorance and superstition as well as the filth, poverty, and poor diet they were powerless to influence. But physicians were mainly frustrated by competition from the *znakharka*. This competition was not, as it often was in Western Europe, over income, for the *zemstvo* doctor received his salary from the *zemstvo* regardless of how many patients he treated.[43] Rather, it was over concern for the well-being of the peasantry, which the doctor believed he was more capable of enhancing than the *znakharka*.

Without exception doctors bitterly complained about the peasants' preference for the folk healer. "In the countryside there is not a single sick person who sooner or later would not turn to his *znakharka*," laments a *zemstvo* physician with nine years of experience, relating the following anecdote from his rural practice. He asked a woman whom he had treated for syphilis with mercury how she felt. She replied that his medicine had not helped her. The doctor, surprised, pointed out to her that her nose ulcers were cured. "True," replied the *baba*, "but it was not your medicine. [They disappeared] because our *baba-znakharka* taught me to smear them with saliva."[44]

Fortunately, doctors make their attitudes sufficiently clear for us to separate prejudice and rancor from reality in their accounts. The doctor who systematically refers to the healer's patients as victims or describes the *znakharka* as avaricious, stupid, and deliberately deceitful is an angry man; his descriptions of folk medicine are likely to be selectively negative.[45] When a doctor attributes the *povitukha*'s "ineffective, superstitious, and coarse methods" to her belief that God's curse on Eve made it a sin to alleviate the woman's pain, you know that this doctor is blaming the healer—as if she

41. Ibid., 158.

42. Ibid., 94.

43. For example, see Jean-Pierre Goubert, "The Art of Healing: Learned Medicine and Popular Medicine in the France of 1790," in *Medicine and Society in France: Selections from the "Annales Economies, Sociétés, Civilisations,"* ed. Robert Forster and Orest Ranum (Baltimore, 1980), 1–23.

44. Rudninskii, "Znakharstvo v Skopinskom i Dankovskom uezdakh," 169–70.

45. Ibid., passim.

were the inventor of these beliefs and practices instead of the translator of normal peasant convictions into life.[46] As one doctor exhorted his colleagues, it was essential to study *znakharki*, for "to fight the enemy successfully one must know his strengths and weaknesses."[47]

To be sure, to the modern ear descriptions of some of the healer's methods are horrendous. The healer's wanton use of toxic substances, especially mercury compounds, frequently led to the patient's death. Doctors as well as *znakharki* treated syphilis with mercury, but circumspectly. As one doctor commented, when a syphilitic patient came to him after having been treated by a *znakharka*, he never knew what to cure first, the mercury poisoning or the syphilis.[48] Vodka and steam baths, a common treatment for many illnesses, often drove the patients to a state of exhaustion from which they could not recover. It is difficult to disagree with the doctor who called the woman in childbirth a "veritable martyr" when the *povitukha* stuffed rags into her anus to prevent the baby from coming out the wrong passage, encouraged her to vomit, made her jump repeatedly from a bench, and hung her upside down by the feet.[49] Nevertheless, some doctors grudgingly conceded that for all their filth, ignorance, and superstition, *znakharki* actually did some good or at worst did no harm. Even the most reproachful doctors approved of some of the *povitukha*'s birthing methods,[50] and others agreed with a modern investigator of midwifery who said, more poetically, "Lowly she may have been and inept she often was, but it was scarcely her fault. Her not very clean hands guided countless millions of babies into this world."[51] One doctor acknowledged that "in most cases the *znakharki* deal beautifully with fractures and dislocations" and commended them for having the good sense not to undertake surgery.[52]

Far more than the actual efficacy or harmfulness of folk cures, peasant ignorance, the power of tradition, or the scarcity of doctors accounted for peasants' preference for healers over doctors. In reality, professional medicine of the late nineteenth and early twentieth centuries was powerless before many illnesses. Many efficacious treatments prescribed by doctors were simply impossible to apply in the conditions of peasant life—appropriate diet and bed rest, for example, not to speak of higher standards of cleanliness and

46. Demich, "Ocherki russkoi narodnoi meditsiny," 227.

47. Gerasimov, "Materialy po narodnoi meditsine i akusherstvu," 158.

48. Rudninskii, "Znakharstvo v Skopinskom i Dankovskom uezdakh," 176.

49. Demich, "Ocherki russkoi narodnoi meditsiny," 227; Gerasimov, "Materialy po narodnoi meditsine i akusherstvu," 177; Popov, *Russkaia narodno-bytovaia meditsina*, 11.

50. Demich, "Ocherki russkoi narodnoi meditsiny," 226; Tolstoi, *Vospominaniia zemskogo vracha*, 96; Popov, *Russkaia narodno-bytovaia meditsina*, 66–67.

51. Thomas Rogers Forbes, *The Midwife and the Witch* (New Haven, 1966), ix.

52. Tolstoi, *Vospominaniia zemskogo vracha*, 66–67.

hygiene. Further, the peasant wanted a quick cure and could always find a *znakharka* who would promise and sometimes actually deliver.[53] The *znakharka*'s failures did not blemish her reputation nor undermine the peasants' faith in her competence. Peasants were fatalistic about death. They believed that each person had an allotted time to live and that healing helped only those whose time was not yet up.[54] They were not so tolerant of the doctor's failures, however, which destroyed whatever little trust they may have had in him. For the doctor was like a benevolent colonist, an intruder from a foreign culture: "Although he is not a bureaucrat [*chinovnik*] or a landowner [two of the peasants' least favorite types], he is nonetheless a stranger."[55] The Russian peasantry had little reason to trust the good intentions of the representatives of urban educated society. The doctor-patient relationship is just another manifestation of the chasm between the two Russias, the urban educated population and the peasantry. However well-intentioned the doctor and however he tried to understand the peasant, science more often than not prevailed over sympathy. A good example of the insensitivity of the medical profession to peasant culture was the *akusherka* or, as the peasants called her, the *beloruchka* (literally, woman with white hands).[56] Usually young, probably unmarried and childless, and from the urban educated stratum, the *akusherka* violated every peasant criterion of who should help bring a child into the world. Similarly, during epidemics representatives of the medical establishment enforced immediate burial of the victims of cholera to prevent contagion. Absolutely correct from a medical and hygienic point of view, this practice trampled and abused the peasant tradition of the open casket and impeded the creation of a trusting relationship between doctors and peasants.[57] As one extremely dedicated doctor concluded after six grueling years of service, "The [provincial] doctor can earn the people's trust only at the cost of his entire life, complete self-sacrifice, and at that only if he has to cover a very small region."[58]

What the healer had that the doctor did not was time, compassion, and the implicit trust of her patients. The *znakharka* usually made house calls and listened endlessly, attentively, and empathically to the patient's complaints.

53. Tolstoi, *Vospominaniia zemskogo vracha*, 68; Rudninskii, "Znakharstvo v Skopinskom i Dankovskom uezdakh," 173; Popov, *Russkaia narodno-bytovaia meditsina*, 152; E. Ia. Zalenskii, *Iz zapisok zemskogo vracha* (Pskov, 1908), 9.

54. Tolstoi, *Vospominaniia zemskogo vracha*, 73, 132; Kovalenko, "O narodnoi meditsine," 145; Popov, *Russkaia narodno-bytovaia meditsina*, 52; V. N. Bondarenko, "Ocherki Kirsanovskogo uezda, Tambovskoi gubernii," *EO*, 1890, no. 3: 86.

55. Popov, *Russkaia narodno-bytovaia meditsina*, 50.

56. Ibid., 342.

57. Nancy Frieden, "Child Care: Medical Reform in a Traditional Culture," in Ransel, *Family in Imperial Russia*, 239–40.

58. Tolstoi, *Vospominaniia zemskogo vracha*, 48, also 20–21, 370.

After childbirth the *povitukha* remained for three days to care for mother and infant. The healer had a profound belief in her powers, natural and supernatural. She understood, however inarticulately, the healing power of persuasion and the beneficial effects of relieving tension, and she had a capacious bag of tricks for soothing the patient, even using what one doctor compared to hypnotic suggestion as understood by contemporary neuropathology.[59] The "soothing human qualities of talk and sound especially valued in . . . [an] oral culture" were prized above the professional physician's nostrums and frequently inapplicable advice.[60] As one ethnographer summarized the *znakharka*'s virtues and appeal:

> The majority of village "dukhtari" and "dukhtarki" [a play on the word *doktor*], as they are jokingly referred to, are without question good, pleasant, and talkative people. They are living books of village news and stories of past and current life. They offer masses of facts about illnesses and about unusual recoveries, convincing the patient that his illness is not unique, that similar misfortunes, inevitable physical suffering, befall everyone on this earth; that to "sit around and moan" is pointless, since so-and-so had such-and-such an illness and recovered completely.[61]

Peasant women's options for independent survival outside the household were limited at all points in their lives and more so as they aged. They could, of course, abandon the village entirely for work in the city or factory, as increasing numbers of women did at the end of the nineteenth and beginning of the twentieth centuries. They could "leave the world" (*uiti ot mira*) and out of profound piety enter convents or other kinds of women's religious communities.[62] Market conditions permitting, women could engage in *kustar'* production. Whether they kept their earnings or threw them into the family coffers depended on local custom and individual family need. *Kustar'* production, engaging mainly peasant women within the household, also provided a precarious but independent existence for some women outside of the house-

---

59. Popov, *Russkaia narodno-bytovaia meditsina*, 63, 66. For a thoughtful and provocative discussion of the relative merits of "primitive" and modern psychotherapy, see Thomas, *Religion and the Decline of Magic*, 206.

60. Barbara Kerewsky-Halpern, "Healing with Mother Metaphors: Serbian Conjurers' Word Magic," in *Women as Healers, Cross Cultural Perspectives*, ed. Carol Shepherd McClain (New Brunswick, N.J., 1989), 119.

61. Makarenko, "Materialy po narodnoi meditsine," 384.

62. N. Dobrotvorskii, "Krest'ianskie iuridicheskie obychai: Po materialam sobrannym v vostochnoi chasti Vladimirskoi gubernii (uezdy Viaznikovskii, Gorokhovetskii, Shuiskii i Kovrovskii)," *Iuridicheskii vestnik*, May 1889, 270; Brenda Meehan-Waters, "Peasant Women and the Development of Women's Religious Communities in Russia: A Case Study, 1864–1917" (Unpublished paper); Meehan-Waters further elaborates in *Forgotten Russia: Popular Piety and Women's Religious Communities, 1764–1917* (Forthcoming).

hold, often spinsters or widows, and a rather comfortable income for a tiny minority among them who abandoned production to become middlewomen between producer and market.[63]

The independent *kustar'* worker and the *znakharka* had in common several characteristics and circumstances that set them apart from ordinary peasant women. Both functioned outside of the household and in many cases outside of the commune as well. Both worked not for a household, dependent on and subordinate to male kin, but in the modern sense of the word; they exchanged a skill for remuneration in the marketplace for the sake of their own survival.

Yet the *znakharka* had characteristics that set her apart from all peasant women. Healing had always been a woman's remunerative occupation and as such was anomalous in peasant culture. Further, healing was a kind of social insurance. The mother who gave her knowledge to her daughter knew full well that several decades might pass before the daughter could use her skills or, indeed, that she might never use them.[64] But it was a legacy of potential welfare in need and in old age, for widowed and elderly women without male kin, along with orphans, were often among the poorest members of the peasant community. Whether the commune decided to provide for them depended on an enormous variety of local customs and on the economic and human resources of the commune. The healing profession thus compensated for the absence of a household and of the support or concern of the commune. The healer was autonomous but not isolated. She remained very much within the peasant community but transcended the domestic domain to establish networks within that immediate community and sometimes beyond it. In a culture, like many others, that held women in low regard, it conferred on women stature, respect, and esteem they could acquire in few other ways.

63. See Glickman, *Russian Factory Women*, chap. 2; idem, "Women and the Peasant Commune," 23–25.

64. Karewsky-Halpern, "Healing with Mother Metaphors," 120.

Women's Domestic Industries in Moscow Province, 1880–1900

Judith Pallot

A characteristic feature of nineteenth-century industrialization in Russia was that much of it took place in the countryside in small factories and workshops or directly in peasant huts. These peasant manufactures (*krest'ianskie promysly*) were different from traditional peasant craft industries that served local markets, used local raw materials and household labor, and were part of the "natural economy" of the peasants. The new peasant manufactures were associated with the economic changes taking place in the nineteenth century. Improvements in transport and the expansion of demand for consumer goods meant that the goods peasants produced could reach national, and even international, markets. By the second half of the century peasant manufacturers were linked into complex networks of raw-material suppliers and retailers organized from the cities. The system that this mobilization of rural labor represented can be described as *protoindustrialization*, using the term first coined by Franklin F. Mendels in his work on the early stages of industrial development in Europe.[1] A feature of the protoindustrial household was that its income derived from both agricultural and a variety of nonagricultural sources, including domestic manufacturing. In Russia such households were found in large numbers in the forested northern and central provinces, where poor agricultural resources and land shortage meant that households could be supported by agriculture for an average of four and a half months a year.[2] The manufactures in which households engaged in these regions fell roughly into three groups, each differing from the others in the degree of

---

1. Franklin F. Mendels, "Proto-industrialization: The First Phase of the Industrialization Process," *Journal of Economic History* 32 (1972): 241–61.
2. "Promysly i nezemledelcheskie zarabotki krest'ian moskovskoi gubernii 1898–1900 godu," in *Statisticheskii ezhegodnik moskovskoi gubernii za 1900* (Moscow, 1900), 1.

independence the producer had. The first group consisted of manufactures most like the traditional craft industries, in which households used family labor to manufacture items for which they produced or bought raw materials themselves. The second was manufactures in which the peasant worked under contract to a merchant who did the marketing and supplied raw materials. The third was industrial work in which labor was contracted by factories or their "putters-out" to complete a single stage of a production process at home, an arrangement that contemporaries referred to as the domestic system of large-scale production.

Of the thousands of domestic industries recorded by nineteenth-century investigators, those in which women made up most of the labor force were disproportionately concentrated either in the third group or in the second, in which there were particularly large numbers of middlemen. The reasons for this concentration are not hard to find since rural women constituted the section of Russia's growing industrial labor force most vulnerable to exploitation by industrial or merchant capital. They were relatively immobile, which limited their ability to "vote with their feet" if they did not like their working conditions; they were provided with their basic needs in food and shelter by the household, which gave entrepreneurs an excuse to pay them a less-than-subsistence wage; their children made up an additional labor force for which the entrepreneur did not have to pay, and they were unprotected by factory legislation.[3] Wherever the circumstances of the peasant economy dictated that women household members be deployed into the domestic manufacturing sector, such women found themselves having to work long hours at repetitive jobs for little reward. In this respect Russian rural women seem to have shared the experience of women in domestic industries throughout northwest Europe. Ivy Pinchbeck, one of the first investigators to explore the conditions of women's work in the early stages of industrialization, described the role of women in English protoindustrial households as "immobile," "dependent," and characterized by "drudgery and monotony."[4] Other authors writing on preindustrial Europe have echoed this general conclusion, although there is some disagreement about whether protoindustrialization increased or decreased women's job choices and their economic indepen-

3. The tsarist government did not intervene in the labor market and industrial relations in a systematic way until after 1905. But some steps were taken before then. A labor code was issued in 1886 requiring all workers to be given a written contract and wage book by their employers. Legislation in 1897 limited the workday to eleven and a half hours, and in 1903 legislation was passed providing compensation for industrial accidents. None of this legislation applied to workers in domestic industries, that is, to people employed outside factories. See Peter Gatrell, *The Tsarist Economy, 1850–1917* (London, 1986), 95–96.

4. Ivy Pinchbeck, *Women Workers and the Industrial Revolution*, 1750–1850 (London, 1931; repr. London, 1981).

dence compared with previous periods or with peasant women in purely
agricultural regions.[5]

In this essay I explore how the growth of capitalism in domestic industries affected women's lives in Moscow Province in the last two decades of the
nineteenth century. I have chosen Moscow Province because it was here that
industrialization and urbanization were most advanced and, consequently,
that large changes were taking place in women's lives. I am not arguing,
however, that Moscow Province was a prototype for other regions of domestic
manufacture emerging in Russia at that time. As Pat Hudson has observed
with respect to English industrialization, "advanced" forms of the putting-out
system with well-developed regional specialization of labor and a high degree
of labor dependency often proved to be a developmental dead end.[6] In the
case of Russia it is difficult to determine what the long-term outcome of involvement in domestic manufacture would have been for women since the
1917 revolution changed the whole sociopolitical context of protoindustrialization. It is possible, however, to come to some conclusions about the direction
in which developments seem to have been propelling women in the final
decades of the tsarist regime. I have used two principal sources. The first is a
survey made in 1880 by the statistical department of the Moscow provincial
zemstvo into women's domestic industries in the province.[7] The second is the

5. In addition to Pinchbeck, *Women Workers*, other classic statements about the impact of
industrial capitalism on women's work are in Louise A. Tilly and Joan W. Scott, *Women, Work
and Family* (New York, 1978); Alice Clarke, *Working Life of Women in the Seventeenth Century* (London, 1919); and Roberta Hamilton, *The Liberation of Women: A Study of Patriarchy and Capitalism*
(London, 1978). The view in these works—that the net effect of industrialization was to reduce
the economic importance of women's labor and restrict their work opportunities—has been
challenged. See, for example, Chris Middleton, "Women's Labour and the Transition to Preindustrial Capitalism," in *Women's Work in Pre-industrial England*, ed. Lindsey Charles and Lorna
Duffin (London, 1985), 181–206. Writing from a Marxist perspective, Middleton argues that the
development of capitalism in preindustrial peasant communities could result in greater flexibility in labor deployment strategies of households than has previously been thought. She does not
see women's labor being marginalized at this stage of capitalist development.

6. Pat Hudson, "Proto-industrialization: The Case of the West Riding Wool Textile Industry in the Eighteenth and Nineteenth Centuries," *History Workshop* 12 (Autumn 1981): 37.

7. In the 1880s the newly formed local authorities (*zemstva*) conducted a series of investigations into peasant handicrafts in the provinces of Central Russia. The investigators described the
origins of each handicraft industry, the villages in which they were practiced, the acquisition of
raw materials, the precise processes involved in manufacture, and the arrangements for marketing. One aim was to discover which manufactures were worthy of support and further development. The authors of these studies were normally political populists and saw domestic industries
as an example of the "natural economy" of the peasant household. One of the volumes on
Moscow Province was devoted to "women's industries," and its author was a woman, M. K.
Gorbunova. Gorbunova included just nineteen domestic industries in the volume—those in
which women made up the whole labor force. For the other, more numerous industries in which
women made up a portion of the labor force, other volumes have to be combed. Gorbunova's

analysis of the 1898–1900 Moscow Province household census results made by the statistician P. A. Vikhliaev.[8]

THE DEVELOPMENT OF DOMESTIC INDUSTRY
IN MOSCOW PROVINCE

Moscow Province lay at the heart of the Central Industrial Region.[9] Its preeminence as an industrial center dated back to the reign of Peter the Great, but even before the Petrine reforms craft production had become a major economic activity of peasant households. Woodlands and other locally occurring natural resources supplied raw materials for the manufacture of a range of consumer items, but it was the absence of restrictive guilds and lagging handicraft production in the cities that provided the real stimulus for their development. Households on *obrok* (quitrent) were particularly noted for crafts, and in the eighteenth century those households were among the wealthier in the province, able to buy leather boots and consumer items.[10] By the turn of the century the multioccupational household was the most common type in the province, and the number of domestic manufactures in which they engaged had proliferated. Among the more than one thousand domestic manufactures recorded by nineteenth-century investigators were activities as diverse as glass bead, cloth, guitar, toy, felt boot, and abacus manufacture, bark, reed, and straw basket weaving, and the painting of lithographs and wrapping paper.[11] Members of households engaged in such manufactures divided their time between farming for three or four months in the summer and manufacturing during the rest of the year. Men and women used their time differently, however. Women had domestic obligations to

---

study is in *Zhenskie promysly moskovskoi gubernii*, vol. 4 (Moscow, 1882). It was also published in *Sbornik statisticheskikh svedenii po moskovskoi gubernii. Otdel khoziaistvennoi statistiki*, vol. 7, pt. 2 (Moscow, 1879–82).

8. P. A. Vikhliaev, *Moskovskaia guberniia po mestnomu obsledovaniiu, 1898–1900*, vol. 4, pt. 2 (Moscow, 1908). Vikhliaev was a leader of the Social Revolutionary party and a noted statistician. The first twenty years of his working life were spent in the *zemstva*, first as an agronomist and later as a statistician and economist. He was particularly interested in the problems of the peasantry and organized a number of investigations of peasant agronomy and economy in Moscow Province. The investigation he conducted in 1898–1900, one volume of which dealt with domestic industries, was a household statistical survey using data gathered over a two-year period from key respondents in the villages. The results were presented in tabulated form by village and, for three districts, were disaggregated by socioeconomic status of household.

9. This region consisted of Tver, Smolensk, Vladimir, and Moscow provinces as well as the northern districts of Tula and Kaluga provinces.

10. Jerome Blum, *Lord and Peasant in Russia from the Ninth to the Nineteenth Century* (Princeton, 1967), 303.

11. Judith Pallot and Denis Shaw, *Landscape and Settlement in Romanov Russia, 1613–1917* (Oxford, 1990), 221.

fulfill, which reduced the hours they could spend at their crafts; these obligations included cleaning and maintaining the hut, grinding grain to make bread, preparing food daily, and tending livestock. In the spring the need to prepare the hemp field further cut into the time women had for crafts. By contrast, men were freer in the winter to pursue their crafts, but they had to give them up earlier in the spring with the onset of plowing. The precise sexual division of labor in households was affected by their size and composition; for example, the allocation of work to male and female household members was rather more fluid in small households than in large ones. Apart from differences in the time given to agriculture and manufacturing, there was also a rough division of labor in the crafts practiced by men and women. Because they had responsibility for clothing family members, women were traditionally associated with spinning, carding, and weaving, whereas men were more likely to work with wood, metal, leather, and stone.

By the last two decades of the nineteenth century these divisions of labor had broken down in many peasant households. M. K. Rozhkova, in her history of the formation of the working class in Moscow Province, describes the changes that brought about this disintegration.[12] Some traditional crafts, such as spinning, died out because of mechanization; other changes involved the development of labor migration (*otkhodnichestvo*), which took household members away from their villages for protracted periods to work in the factories of Moscow. This latter process was most evident in the western *uezdy* (districts). By contrast, in the east of the province an expansion of the number of textile mills turned Bronnitsy and its neighboring districts into a continuous belt of weaving and related domestic manufactures. Elsewhere, the range of craft industries proliferated in response to the growth of urban and rural markets. These changes could not help but have an impact on the sexual division of labor in households, yet their effects were unevenly distributed geographically.

DISTRIBUTION AND RATES OF PARTICIPATION

According to Vikhliaev's calculations, 98 percent of peasant households in Moscow Province in 1898–1900 (26.4 percent of adult women and 53.3 percent of men) were involved in supplementary employment.[13] Women showed a tendency to stay in their own villages, whereas many men found employment away from their home working either in Moscow, in one of the growing number of "factory villages" in the province, or in some itinerant trade. Commitment of married women to daily household tasks must partly explain

12. M. K. Rozhkova, *Formirovanie kadrov promyshlennykh rabochikh v 60–nachale 80kh godov XIX v.* (Moscow, 1974).

13. Vikhliaev, *Moskovskaia guberniia*, 37.

TABLE 1. Place of Employment of Peasants Involved in Side Employment
in Moscow Province, 1898–1900

| | % of Peasants Working | | % of Peasants Working Outside Home Village | | | |
	In Own Village	Outside Own Village	In Own District	In Moscow or St. Petersburg	In Other Provinces	Else-where
Women	68.6	31.9	48.7	37.3	2.7	11.3
Men	26.5	76.0	36.9	48.0	4.9	10.2

SOURCE. P. A. Vikhliaev, *Moskovskaia guberniia po mestnomu obsledovaniiu 1898–1900*, vol. 4, pt. 2 (Moscow, 1908), 37.

this difference. When they did work beyond the boundaries of their native village, women ventured less far afield than men, as table 1 shows.

Child labor was widespread in the province. Table 2 illustrates two aspects of this phenomenon: first, the share of the total labor force made up of minors, and second, the percentage of each age cohort involved in nonagricultural labor. The high activity rate of young girls is immediately striking. In Bronnitsy District nearly one-quarter of all girls under twelve years of age were employed in manufacturing (as against 10 percent of boys in the equivalent age group), and among the thirteen- and fourteen-year-olds the proportion was two-thirds.[14] In all three districts the proportion of women engaged in supplementary employment fell off in the 18–45 age group, but the proportion of men increased. A reasonable explanation for this difference is women's assumption of the full round of household duties when they married.[15]

Another feature revealed in table 2 is that the percentage of women in all age groups working in nonagricultural employment varied between districts more than did the percentage of men, a finding that suggests women's deployment into manufacturing was sensitive to local factors. Vikhliaev, in his analysis of this finding, settled on relative land shortage or abundance as the chief differentiating factor.[16] The districts in which women's involvement in

14. The low participation of boys does not mean that their labor was not being used; where they did not help with domestic industries, they were engaged in a variety of tasks around the farm, such as scaring crows from sown fields and clearing stones.

15. In Moscow District 84.1 percent of rural women were married by the age of twenty-five and 45 percent by the age of twenty. Calculated from *Sbornik statisticheskikh svedenii po moskovskoi gubernii: Moskovskii uezd, svedeniia o narodonaselenii i ego dvizhenii za 1869–1873 goda* (Moscow, 1877), 212–19.

16. In Bronnitsy District, for example, the average per capita amount of land for households in which women were employed in one of the main domestic industries was between 0.46 and 0.78 *desiatiny*. This compared with more than one *desiatin* for households with typical male industries, such as silverwork (1.13) and tailoring (1.03). See Vikhliaev, *Moskovskaia guberniia*, 596.

TABLE 2. Age Distribution of Workers in Domestic Industries in Three Districts of Moscow Province, 1898–1900

	% Distribution of Workers by Age						% of Cohort Workers by Age					
	Under 12 yrs.	13–14	15–17	18–45	46–60	>60	Under 12 yrs.	13–14	15–17	18–45	46–60	>60
Bronnitsy District												
Males	1.8	3.8	9.1	64.9	15.6	4.8	8.8	54.1	83.0	90.2	79.0	42.7
Females	7.2	6.9	12.7	59.5	8.1	5.6	24.2	64.9	76.7	55.5	32.2	18.7
Moscow District												
Males	1.1	3.1	8.6	66.5	16.4	4.3	4.8	37.9	68.4	82.1	71.5	37.4
Females	5.1	5.5	11.1	60.3	10.2	7.8	18.9	57.3	77.5	60.1	45.2	28.4
Volokolamsk District												
Males	1.2	2.7	8.8	66.8	16.2	4.3	5.5	32.9	72.8	82.9	67.5	29.5
Females	4.2	5.3	12.8	62.3	8.3	7.1	6.8	23.2	36.5	26.3	15.1	9.7

SOURCE. P. A. Vikhliaev, *Moskovskaia guberniia po mestnomu obsledovaniiu 1898–1900*, vol. 4, pt. 2 (Moscow, 1908), 37, 46.

manufacturing was at its highest were those in which farms were below the average size for the province. They described an arc stretching from the northeast to the southwest and included the districts around Moscow. In these districts peasant households in which women were involved in one of the main domestic manufactures were also those with the least amount of land. Underemployment of labor on the land seems, therefore, to provide one explanation for the development in this part of the province of domestic industries, in particular those requiring a large influx of cheap labor.[17] But there are other explanations for differences in the level of female participation in domestic industries. As Gay Gullikson has observed in her work on Auffay in seventeenth- through nineteenth-century France, the failure of most studies to consider the gender of participants in domestic manufacture has obscured the variety of conditions that could give rise to protoindustrialization.[18] In Moscow Province factors such as distance from the capital and the pattern of communications and physical resources, which affected entrepreneurs' decisions about where to site factories, determined the range of employment opportunities available locally to the peasantry. In the eastern districts the presence of textile mills scattered throughout the area allowed both women and men to work in domestic manufacture while continuing to farm. By contrast, in the western districts the absence of such opportunities and the development of high levels of labor migration in which men were the principal participants meant that women there had to assume responsibility for an ever wider range of jobs on the farm.

In her essay on the impact of capitalism on the division of labor in proto-industrial households, Chris Middleton has identified what she describes as two "modal types" of adaptation to the growth of manufacturing. The first describes the situation in which, because of male household members' involvement in industry, women are forced to expand their range of work on the farm, which they might combine with supplementary employment in some home-based manufacture. The second modal type describes the opposite situation: women withdraw from agricultural work to concentrate exclusively on domestic manufacture. In both cases the preexisting division of labor is replaced by another, different division of labor but one in which male and female spheres of activity remain separate.[19] Both patterns could be

17. This conforms with Joan Thirsk's explanation for the development of domestic industries in preindustrial England. See Joan Thirsk, *The Rural Economy of England* (London, 1984), 217–33.

18. Gay L. Gullickson, *Spinners and Weavers of Auffay: Rural Industry and the Sexual Division of Labor in a French Village, 1750–1850* (Cambridge, 1986), 198.

19. Chris Middleton, "Women's Labour," 196. Middleton's argument begs the question of whether the division in the agriculturally based preindustrial household was as inflexible as is often assumed. Martine Segalen, using evidence from France, argues the case for flexibility, trying to show that men and women regularly shared jobs normally ascribed to one gender or the other. See Martine Segalen, *Love and Power in the Peasant Family: Rural France in the Nineteenth Century*, trans. Sarah Matthews (Oxford, 1983), 96–111.

observed in Moscow Province, the tendency being toward the former in the western districts and toward the latter in the eastern districts, but deviations from the two modal types were even more common. As peasant manufacturing developed in the province, the range of men's and women's activities in the household became more symmetrical; tasks previously done by either men or women could now be done by both, and both partners added domestic manufactures to their repertoire of jobs.[20] The development of domestic manufacturing in Moscow Province led to a broadening of women's range of activities contributing to household survival.

THE CHARACTERISTICS OF WOMEN'S INDUSTRIES AND THEIR DEVELOPMENT

Diversification in the jobs women and men did in peasant households did not, of course, mean that the level of exploitation to which each gender was subjected by emergent capitalism was the same; symmetry did not necessarily bring with it equality. In fact, as contemporary sources show all too clearly, where domestic manufactures were concerned, women were forced to work on the lowest status and least well remunerated domestic manufactures. There were nineteen domestic industries out of the thousand recorded for Moscow Province that were dominated by women, that is, where women made up the bulk of the labor force and where the acquisition of raw materials and marketing were organized mainly by women. These manufactures ranged from basket weaving, which involved rather small numbers, to bobbin winding, in which thousands were employed.[21] Other manufactures were defined as male by contemporary investigators, even though women could make up a substantial part of the labor force, as in weaving. In these industries the control of raw-material supply and marketing was usually in the hands of men. In some, usually specialized industries or those involving protracted periods away from home, women constituted a minority of the labor force. These included tailoring, wood carving, and metalworking. Because of

20. In his seminal article on protoindustrialization Hans Mendick shows that the exchange of roles between genders was not unusual in Germany. See Hans Mendick, "The Proto-industrial Family Economy: The Structural Function of Household and Family during the Transition from Peasant Society to Industrial Capitalism," in *Essays in Social History*, ed. Pat Thane and Anthony Sutcliffe, vol. 2 (Oxford, 1986), 23–52.

21. The nineteen domestic manufactures and the numbers of women employed in them in 1880 were: lacemaking, 959; gold-thread embroidery, 47; knitting, 12,240; making fishnets, 373; weaving *lapti* (bast sandals), 87; making reins, 204; plaiting peasant boots from leather strips (*pletenie chun'*), 53; gold-lace making, 330; making frills and edgings, 378; glove making, 3,025; the assembly of *papirosy*, 8,765; beadwork, 125; belt making, 574; straw-hat making, 42; sewing string bags, 25; knitting scarfs, 42; bobbin winding, 10,004; sewing heels on stockings, 12; finishing machine-made knitwear, 29. The most obvious omission from the 1880 volume on women's industries was cotton weaving, which was included in a separate volume, *Promysly moskovskoi gubernii*, pt. 5 (Moscow, 1879–1882).

their emphasis on manufacturing, *zemstvo* surveys in the 1880s did not include wet-nursing or domestic service among domestic occupations they investigated, despite their importance as a source of supplementary income for peasant women. As David Ransel, author of a major work on Russia's foundling-home system, has shown, abandoned babies were farmed out by the authorities to peasant women in rural districts in return for a monthly payment, linen, and clothing.[22] These women came predominantly from the families of poor households in the central and western districts of the province, where other opportunities for earning nonfarm income were limited and women had assumed full responsibility for farming as their menfolk took part in *otkhodnichestvo*. Wet-nursing an orphaned child was more compatible with farming than were some other domestic industries; and if the baby survived, it would eventually provide additional labor on the land.

Among the domestic industries involving manufacture, four were large employers. These were cotton weaving, bobbin winding, the assembly of mouthpieces for cigarettes, and knitting. In 1898–1900 these industries employed 84,862 women of working age.[23] Because these manufactures have rarely been described in the English-language literature, I include here an account of how they originated and changed in the last two decades of the nineteenth century.[24]

Cotton weaving was the largest employer of women in the province, providing work for 28,350 in 1898–1900. Most cotton handweaving took place directly in peasants' huts, although increasingly it was facing competition from mechanized factory production. Women were also employed in other types of handweaving, such as of silks, brocades, and velvet, but in much smaller numbers. The pattern of male domestic weaving was the exact opposite of that for women: men dominated the labor force in the production of silk, velvet, and brocade but were a minority in cotton handweaving. This division of labor reflected differences in the earnings associated with the domestic manufacture of the high-value and the cheaper cloths. The average monthly wage of a cotton weaver was three to four rubles. By contrast, velvet, silk, and brocade weavers could expect to earn an average of six rubles over an equivalent period. Vikhliaev characterized the situation among the domestic handweavers thus: "Work in cotton cloth production is least well rewarded. This is adequate for women workers but is unsatisfactory for the male population, which has wider opportunities for using its labor power."[25] In fact, women were relatively recent recruits to cotton weaving. Previously

22. David L. Ransel, *Mothers of Misery: Child Abandonment in Russia* (Princeton, 1988).

23. Calculated from Vikhliaev, *Moskovskaia guberniia*, 349, 448.

24. The principal Western source dealing with women's domestic industries in imperial Russia is Rose L. Glickman, *Russian Factory Women: Workplace and Society, 1880–1914* (Berkeley and Los Angeles, 1984).

25. Vikhliaev, *Moskovskaia guberniia*, 456.

men had made up most of the labor force, but they left when competition from mechanical looms drove down prices for cotton cloth. A similar substitution of female for male labor had taken place in the first half of the nineteenth century when the production of broadcloths and woolens began to be mechanized. By the 1880s weaving these cloths had largely transferred to factories.

The retreat of men from cotton working was accompanied by their physical withdrawal from the peasant hut to work on looms in rural workshops (*svetelki*) or on mechanical looms in factories. Rural workshops were purposely built to accommodate the large silk-weaving looms, and they were more spacious and airier than the normal hut of the domestic weaver. In an industry not noted for good work conditions, the workshops were at the more acceptable end of the scale. Alternatively, men who abandoned domestic cotton weaving sought more regular and better paid work in textile factories. This shift generally involved a change from hand to mechanical weaving, but because many of these factories were local, it did not necessarily mean that peasants had to quit their village. Table 3 compares the place of work of male and female weavers in Moscow Province in 1898–1900.

The division of labor in weaving in rural Moscow Province in the last two decades of the nineteenth century can thus be said to have determined the conditions of work of the weavers, their access to modern technology, and their wages. On balance it worked to the disadvantage of women. Commenting on the tendency to explain a similar division of labor among weavers in the Auffay in terms of the degree of physical difficulty of weaving different types of cloth, Gay Gullikson has written, "The difference in strength requirements . . . was slight, however, and the assertion of male superiority was far more important in the emergence of this new sexual division of labor than was physical strength."[26] The same process seems to have been at work in the textile districts in Moscow Province, where the argument that household duties forced women to stay at home or that the silk looms were too large for them is insufficient to explain their concentration in the technologically least advanced sectors of cloth production.

Bobbin winding (*razmotka bumagi*) was another branch of the textile industry that took place directly in peasant huts. The job of the bobbin winder was a simple one. Skeins of cotton had to be wound onto bobbins for use on hand looms. The tools the bobbin winder needed for her task consisted of a rotating spindle on which the skein was fixed, a cylinder to hold the bobbin, and a wooden baton. When the worker hit the cylinder to make it spin, the cotton was wound onto the bobbin. Once all the bobbins had been filled, they would be exchanged for a new batch of skein and empty bobbins. In 1898–1900 there were nearly thirty thousand bobbin winders in Moscow Province, all

26. Gullickson, *Spinners and Weavers*, 109.

TABLE 3. Percentage of Rural Weavers Engaged in Factory and Domestic Labor in Moscow Province, 1898–1900

	Cottons			Woolens			Silks		
	Female	Male	Total	Female	Male	Total	Female	Male	Total
Factory	40.8	63.5	51.9	73.4	88.0	82.8	28.0	32.4	30.5
Domestic	54.1	32.0	43.3	26.6	12.0	17.2	67.2	57.6	61.8
Combination	5.1	4.5	4.8	—	—	—	4.8	10.0	7.7

SOURCE. P. A. Vikhliaev, *Moskovskaia guberniia po mestnomu obsledovaniiu 1898–1900*, vol. 4, pt. 2 (Moscow, 1908), 455.

but two thousand of them women. As in cotton weaving, mechanical processes had been developed for bobbin winding; but because women's labor could be bought so cheaply (by 1900 the weekly earnings in Serpukhov District were less than eighty kopeks), textile factories continued to employ domestic bobbin winders in the last decades of the century. In fact, between 1880 and 1900 there was a more than twofold increase in the number of bobbin winders.

The assembly of *papirosy* shells (*verchenie patronov*) was the third largest women's domestic industry. The manufacture of *papirosy* (Russian cigarettes with cardboard mouthpieces) expanded in the last two decades of the century, the number of women employed rising from 8,767 in 1880 to 16,594 in 1898–1900. The domestic worker's task consisted of gluing cigarette papers into cylinders and then inserting a cardboard filter into these. The *papirosniki* who did this work received boxes of two thousand pieces of paper machine-cut into squares and equal numbers of cardboard mouthpieces, plus starch for the glue. As in the other domestic industries, the materials were obtained directly by the women themselves from the factories or via intermediaries. After finished batches were checked for quality and spoiled filters discarded, payment was made for the remainder. In 1896 the gluing of cigarette papers was mechanized and transferred to factories, but the insertion of the mouthpieces continued to be done by hand in the peasants' huts. One result of the increased productivity of labor in producing the cylindrical papers was a much-expanded demand for domestic workers to finish the process. Simultaneously, however, weekly wages of *papirosniki* fell by more than half, from one ruble thirty kopeks to sixty kopeks a week over the twenty-year period.

Knitting was the least well remunerated of the mass domestic manufactures involving women. It differed from the three already considered in that it did not form an extension of factory production. Women sought out their own suppliers of material and their own customers for knitted garments. Knitting was a traditional craft that developed in peasant households as a by-product of making sheepskins. Discarded wool was spun into thread and knitted into thick socks to go inside the peasants' bark shoes. Men as well as women and children knitted for family consumption. By the end of the nineteenth century the former craft character of the industry had been transformed. The market for knitted goods was now in the towns, where the fashion for wearing shoes and boots created a demand for stockings and socks made out of fine wool or cotton. A market for fine knitted gloves and scarves also developed. Another change was that men no longer knitted because of the low prices paid for knitwear in the saturated market. Indeed, with average weekly earnings of hand knitters falling to below fifty kopeks a week by the end of the century, the reluctance of peasant men to spend their time knitting is understandable. Women also sought to escape knitting if they could, but with 12,455 engaged in hand knitting in 1898–1900, it remained one of the more important domestic manufacturing activities for women in the province. Women's persistence with such an unlucrative activity can in part be explained by the fact that compared with other domestic industries, knitting could be relatively easily meshed with jobs that had to be done around the farm: "Women knit continuously, everywhere, on their way to town, traveling in a cart, walking across the fields: They do not have to spend a lot of money to start up in knitting, they do not need a lot of working capital, they do not need any particular aptitude, they do not need any imagination or dexterity; from the age of five or six years they begin to knit to earn just a few kopeks a week."[27]

At the end of the nineteenth century knitting machines appeared in the traditional knitting villages, but only the wealthier families could afford them. Some small knitwear factories were established employing five to six women, each earning on average three to four rubles a month. These workshops were generally under the direction of women, but the machines were owned by men. An 1880 comment on this arrangement is instructive: "The machines are always worked by the women, although the peasant head of the family considers himself owner of the enterprise. This is as it should be; he, the peasant, bought the machine; he also buys the material and sells the finished product."[28]

Knitting was not the only domestic industry in which women were excluded from the new technologies. In weaving, men dominated work with mechanical looms, and in the domestic manufacture of braid the advent of mechanization resulted in an industry that formerly was exclusively female becoming male.[29] Once a manufacture was mechanized, it seems it was seen by the working population as a "new" occupation for which a differently composed work force was appropriate. The transfer of some manufactures to large factories where regular wages could be earned no doubt contributed to such changes in perception, but they were also indicative of women's marginalization in the labor process. However, on this latter point it must not be forgotten that some women were able to profit from the changes and rose to become managers of new enterprises responsible for organizing the work of the more junior household and nonhousehold members. Inevitably, it was in the more prosperous households that were able to afford the new technologies that such women were found.

27. *Zhenskie promysly*, 4: 104.

28. Ibid., 4: 150.

29. Ibid., 4: 49. Authors working on Third World development have observed that men appropriate new technologies. This tendency is attributed to extension services that target men, even though women may be equally involved in farming or crafts. See Esther Boserup, *Women's Role in Economic Development* (London, 1970). For the Soviet Union, see Susan Bridger, *Women in the Soviet Countryside* (Cambridge, 1987). Bridger shows that rural men have prior calls over machines in the Soviet Union.

Other domestic industries than the four already considered provided employment for women in Moscow Province, but apart from wet-nursing, none approached the same scale. Where they occurred, these other domestic manufactures could dominate a locality. The domestic gold-lace industry, for example, was found in four contiguous villages in Zvenigorod District, and fishnet manufacture was prevalent in nine adjacent villages in Mozhaisk District. These and similar manufactures tended to use intermediaries to supply raw materials and to market produce, although there were exceptions. The fishnet makers prepared flax they had grown themselves for their nets (but relied on itinerant traders to buy up the finished product), and in nearly all industries there were persons who would journey to market to sell their manufactures. In certain industries, such as lacemaking, straw plaiting, and decorative beadwork, a woman might rise from the ranks to become a trader, journeying to market to sell produce for her co-villagers and obtain raw materials. Contemporary commentators give contradictory assessments of these people, referring to them as female kulaks but also acknowledging that a division of labor between marketing and manufacture was necessary in villages located a long way from town. Some became well known to Moscow merchants. In the gold-lace industry, for example, the four principal Moscow merchants, all of them men, would give out thread only on the recommendation of the "senior" gold-lace maker, Aksin'ia Arkhipova, who effectively controlled lace manufacture through a network of subcontractors in the lacemaking villages.

THE WORKING DAY AND THE WORKING YEAR

The rhythm of work in domestic industries was tied to the farming calendar. By the last two decades of the nineteenth century the length of the working year for women in domestic industries was highly variable, lasting from five and a half months for fishnet makers to ten and a half months for the *papirosniki*. If we subtract church holidays and Sundays, women in the four main industries would normally spend between 160 and 170 days at their work. The short working year for the women fishnet makers came about because in the villages where this industry was found, all male peasants from the age of nine or ten were absent as tailors, returning only for church festivals and the hay harvest. Women had to do all the work in the fields and farmyard, which included plowing, carrying wood, carting manure, sowing and harvesting flax, and looking after large and small livestock. The time they had for making fishnets was thus limited to the period before the onset of the spring plowing and after the sowing of the winter field in the autumn. Similarly, in the districts where farming was relatively successful and land holdings above average, the working year in domestic industry for women was comparatively short because their labor was needed early in the season in the fields.

Cotton weavers in the western districts of the province worked for only seven
months of the year, whereas their counterparts in the east worked at their
looms for nine or more. As was to be expected, it was in the eastern districts
that women worked for more than nine months of the year in domestic industries. In these districts women in farming households spent the short summer
break from domestic manufacture bringing in the hay harvest and collecting
berries and mushrooms from the woods.

During the period of the year when they were engaged in domestic manufacture, women worked continuously, breaking only on rest days and when it
was necessary to pick up more materials and deliver finished work. The
length of time taken in trips to market varied between industries. Gold-
thread embroiderers from Zvenigorod District would take three days for the
round trip to Moscow, but they made the journey at fairly infrequent intervals.
By contrast, the *papirosniki* had to make weekly journeys to paper factories
because of the bulkiness of the product. When not on the road, women
began work early every morning and continued until late at night. The *papirosniki* started at 6:00 or 7:00 A.M. and finished between 9:00 P.M. and midnight. With breaks for meals, they could expect to sit at their work for thirteen and a half hours a day. Cotton weavers generally began their working
day earlier, at 4:00 A.M. They then worked for seven or eight hours, with a
single twenty-minute break for breakfast, until midday, when they would
stop work to prepare and eat lunch and do other jobs about the house; then
they would resume work at their looms until 9:00 or 10:00 P.M. On average,
women put in a twelve-hour day at their looms, but the workday could increase to fourteen or more hours before Easter, when everyone wanted to
earn more for the holiday. And the pace of work was by no means leisurely:
the women had to "spare no effort" to earn their three to four rubles a
month.[30] The 1880 survey of women's domestic industries gives the following description of the average day of a woman in the knitting villages:

> In the autumn, after all the field work has been finished, women begin at day-
> break; they see to the livestock, bring in the firewood, fetch the water, sweep up
> the inside of the hut, light the stove, and begin to prepare the meals and bake
> bread. If the woman has a baby, she has to bathe it and comb its hair. . . .
> Having cleaned themselves up, mother and daughters sit down to their work—
> to spin thread and to knit. They break for lunch, but after lunch the same work
> begins again and continues until the early evening, when it is time to see the
> livestock again—to milk the cows and to water and feed them. And after that
> they continue with the same work. Once evening comes, they have supper, and
> in some places the girls gather together to work in different huts.[31]

30. Vikhliaev, *Moskovskaia guberniia*, 485.
31. *Zhenskie promysly*, 4: 146.

Even on market days women hand knitters continued their work on the journey to town, as the following extract records: "You see women carrying whole bundles on their backs with pitchers, bottles, and liter vessels full of cream and milk, and at the same time in their hands there are socks and they are knitting."[32]

Children's work hours did not differ much from their mothers'. Indeed, in some cases teenage girls put in much longer hours since they had fewer interruptions. Children under fourteen generally started work later and finished earlier than older girls and were given the easier work to do. Even the youngest member of the household could expect to spend the greater part of her waking hours at work once she had been taught the appropriate skills. Girls in the households of bobbin winders would begin approximately on their sixth birthday, whereas in the knitting industry eight-year-old girls were expected to knit one pair of socks a day. An 1880 investigator wrote, "As soon as a young girl has learned how to knit stockings, she is forced to spend most of her day knitting. [Her parents] gradually increase the amount of work she has to do and punish her severely if the work is not done."[33] Russian peasants do not seem to have been noticeably more demanding of their children than parents elsewhere in rural Europe. Even in nineteenth-century England glovers began work at the age of eight or nine and plaiters at the age of three.[34]

The long hours that women and children put into domestic industries naturally affected their health. The *papirosniki* could be easily recognized by "their emaciated physiognomy, sluggish gait, apathy and nervousness, and the other signs of bad health";[35] wet-nursing was popularly linked to the spread of disease and child neglect.[36] The long hours of repetitive labor were exacerbated by the unhealthy conditions that existed in some domestic industries. Cotton weavers in particular had to put up with overcrowding and pollution. One author likened women cotton weavers to "pariahs who have been cast...onto the bottom rung of the social ladder and burdened by chronic boredom and slow physical growth."[37] Long hours were feared to "exhaust the strength of future mothers," but the greatest concern was expressed about child labor. Apart from the physical and psychological damage done to children forced to sit inside all day at a repetitive task, long hours

32. Ibid., 4: 143.

33. Ibid., 4: 145.

34. Jennie Kittering, "Rural Industries," in *Village Life and Labour*, ed. Raphael Samuel (London, 1975), 118–19.

35. Vikhliaev, *Moskovskaia guberniia*, 350.

36. Ransel, *Mothers of Misery*, 278–83.

37. P. Belov, "Kartina kustarnogo proizvodstva v sele Cherkizova moskovskogo uezda," *Mir bozhii* 6 (1900): 34.

cut into school attendance. Girls were particularly affected because such
large numbers of them worked from an early age in domestic industries. High
rates of female illiteracy were a problem in the knitting and lacemaking
villages, where even the more successful female entrepreneurs could neither
read nor write.

Poor remuneration for women in domestic manufacture was compounded
by the fact that women were paid at irregular intervals and often in goods
rather than money. All the different types of intermediaries with whom the
women had to deal—putters-out, itinerant traders, and Moscow merchants—were guilty of depressing the value of women's already meager
earnings in this way. In 1880 the cotton weavers in Volokolamsk District
reported to *zemstvo* investigators that they had not received money wages in
the past three years. In the words of one woman, "You go and ask for money
and the boss says to you, 'What do you need money for? I have everything
you could want—take it.' They pay with red cotton thread, head scarves,
salt, sugar, groats—only never with money!"[38] Needless to say, the value of
the goods thus used in payment was calculated at inflated prices.[39] To keep
wages low without losing their labor force, factories varied their method
of payment of women outworkers. Thus in *papirosy* manufacture buyers
would switch at intervals between paying women in cash and kind. For the
women there was always the possibility that their next payment would be in
cash, which would deter them from looking for a new employer.

Women had some weapons with which to fight back. Most commonly they
tried to retain for their own use some of the materials they were supplied.
These could then be sold or worked on prior to sale. For example, one of the
sources of yarn for the stocking knitters around Moscow was cotton
sold them by bobbin winders. The practice suppliers introduced of weighing
batches of materials they issued could not combat such theft, as in each
industry women found ways of cheating the scales. Knitters, bobbin winders,
and weavers would soak their yarn in salty water to increase its weight or
would pack finished items in such a way as to disguise loose work. Coopera-
tion was another method women had of resisting middlemen, but in the
nineteenth century it does not seem to have been much developed. Women
workers were prepared to help each other out in various ways, however.
Papirosniki would pass on work to friends or relatives if they were unable to
fulfill orders themselves, and in other industries women would recommend
one another to Moscow traders and agree to answer for the standard of the
recommendee's work. Although it was common practice in all domestic industries trading through Moscow for wholesalers to take securities in lieu of
the materials they gave out, in a number of women's industries no such

---

38. *Zhenskie promysly*, 4: 55.
39. Ibid., 4: xi, 33.

security was demanded, and the word of a regular contact was sufficient for materials to be issued to a newcomer. These practices are not easy to interpret (they might indicate the power of a few "female kulaks" over their neighbors), and in any event they made little impression on the relatively powerless position of women workers in domestic industries.

WOMEN'S DOMESTIC MANUFACTURES AND THE HOUSEHOLD ECONOMY

Despite the low pay the contribution that women's earnings in domestic manufacture made to peasant household income was far from trivial. The 1880 survey found that women earned more than one and a half million rubles annually, double the value of the redemption payments due from each male soul in Moscow Province. The figure has to be treated with caution since estimates of the number of women involved in different industries were often approximations and did not include the earnings of women cotton weavers or women who "assisted" in the predominantly male domestic industries. The practice of paying in goods that did not correspond in value to quoted rates of pay adds a further element of doubt about the figure. At the end of the century the contribution from the four main women's industries was somewhere in the region of two and a quarter million rubles.[40] These earnings were concentrated in the poorer districts, where they must have played a role in the economic survival of peasant households, as was recognized at the time. Thus in the main regions where women assembled *papirosy* it was said in 1880 that "it is only the women who feed us here."[41] And in an instructive reversal of the "normal" state of affairs, the birth of a girl was welcomed with greater enthusiasm than that of a boy in the lacemaking villages.

The nineteenth-century investigators of domestic industries were unable to make up their minds about whether their earnings gave women economic independence. With wages below the subsistence minimum the independence earned must have been limited. Married women employed in one of the main industries were generally able to retain their earnings. However, unmarried women or women who assisted in one of the male manufactures might not be paid, their share of earnings going directly into the household budget. One way that parents attempted to keep control over their children's earnings was to ask employers to pay them in goods, which were easier to keep track of than cash. Married women were expected to use their earnings to fulfill their traditional tasks of clothing and feeding the family, but any left

40. This figure assumes monthly average earnings of three rubles over nine months for the eighty-five thousand women engaged in the four main domestic industries in 1898–1900.

41. *Zhenskie promysly*, 4: 217.

over could be used to purchase luxuries such as tea. The deployment of women in domestic manufacture thus had a potentially contradictory impact on the peasant economy. On the one hand, women's earnings must have helped some households continue farming; on the other, manufacture exposed young women and men to a wider society, and that exposure might lead to their seeking more-permanent employment and alternative life-styles outside farming. Contemporary investigators voiced fears about the potential disruption to the family of some young peoples' involvement in domestic industries. For example, female knit workers in villages surrounding Moscow were said to have "disruptive" attitudes compared with the "sober" and "industrious" behavior of knit workers in the depths of the province. In knitting villages near the city young women reportedly broke from their work to drink tea at frequent intervals and expected to be bought "nice dresses" for their trips to market. As early as the 1870s such demands were being held responsible for family breakups, rising violence against women, and the permanent departure of increasing numbers of young women to the city.[42] These accusations echo the Victorian English concern with declining morality among young women in domestic industries; glovers were said to be of "rather easy virtue," and plaiters were condemned for their "immorality" by the Agricultural Employment Commission of 1867–69.[43] These fears seem to reflect a similar ambiguity on the part of Russia's educated about the passing of agrarian society.

The data available at the turn of the century show rates of household survival in the domestic manufacturing districts in Moscow Province to have been geographically differentiated. The largest numbers of households to give up working their land were found in the districts to the east and south of Moscow in those places where both male and female household members were employed in domestic industries. By 1900, 20–25 percent of resident households in the main textile districts in the east of the province had ceased to work their land, hiring it out to neighbors or returning it to their communes. This figure does not include households that had quit their villages altogether at an earlier date.[44] The rate of the abandonment of farming fell off sharply to the west of Moscow, to as low as 5–6 percent in Dmitrov and Volokolamsk districts. It would be tempting to ascribe these differences to the rate of women's participation in domestic manufacture since, at least as far as the official figures are concerned, between one-third and one-half of the total female population was engaged in manufacture in the east of the prov-

42. Ibid., 4: 148. In the introduction to this volume Gorbunova listed the adverse consequences of involvement in domestic industries on women. These included poor education and the loss of traditional skills, such as how to make clothes for their families, forcing them to purchase clothes for their families.

43. Kittering, "Rural Industries," 118, 126.

44. Pallot and Shaw, *Landscape and Settlement*, 236.

ince compared with less than 10 percent in the west; it might have been that the deployment of women in domestic manufacture represented the final stage in the transformation of peasant into proletarian.[45] But caution is needed in accepting this thesis. First, the classifications used by investigators in the nineteenth century mean estimates of the number of women in domestic manufactures are inaccurate and unreliable. Second, as Vikhliaev showed in his analysis of the 1899 census data, size of landholding was also a crucial determinant of a household's ability to continue farming. It was the combined misfortune of a small landholding and low-paid work in domestic manufacture (households with the smallest landholdings were able to command the least remunerative jobs in industry) that resulted in the failure of the poorest farms. Hence households with larger landholdings were not necessarily bound to follow their unfortunate neighbors into liquidation just because their womenfolk were engaged in domestic manufacture. Indeed, women's earnings made an important contribution to household income and played a crucial role in household survival.

CONCLUSION

In the final decades of the nineteenth century women involved in domestic manufactures came to occupy the lowest rung in the hierarchy of industrial workers in Russia. They constituted a source of labor that, unprotected by factory legislation, was both cheap and captive. The low status of women in the industrial labor market at that time is demonstrated by their involvement in precisely those domestic manufactures most vulnerable to competition from mechanization and factory production. In the short term the introduction of machines drove women workers' wages down, and in the long term it resulted in the loss of work altogether. Peasant men seem to have been complicitous in these changes, excluding women from the higher-paying and more stable manufactures. It would be a mistake, however, to assume that the experience all women had of the domestic industrial sector was the same. Some women, albeit few, were engaged in manufactures for which a future market seemed relatively secure; others lived in places where a switch to an alternative source of supplementary employment was fairly easy to make; yet others rose to become entrepreneurs themselves. Like peasant households in general, therefore, those in which women's manufactures were developed could be differentiated from one another by wealth and status. However, the fact remains that the poor predominated among women domestic manufacturers.

45. It was Lenin's thesis that industrial labor must prevail over agriculture as capitalism developed. Many villages would lose their agricultural function and become industrial settlements populated by the newly formed proletariat. Ibid., 218–20.

It is less clear what impact women's involvement in domestic manufacture had on their status in peasant society. For households that retained land, the contribution women made either from earning money in domestic manufacture or from taking over all the farming tasks was obviously essential to their survival. Yet the complementarity of women's and men's work that was necessary to such household survival was not matched in other spheres; women continued to be debarred from inheriting land and from participating in the communal *skhod* and certain aspects of social life. Gullikson's words about protoindustrialization in Auffay are appropriate here: "The evidence reveals a culture that valued male work more highly than female work and provided more leisure and status consumption for men than for women, despite the importance of women's earnings to their families and to the entire region."[46] The last two decades of the nineteenth century involved women in Moscow Province in new forms of production, but this involvement did not put them on an equal footing with men. As Rose Glickman has shown in her study of women in the factory, the inequalities were reproduced again in the urban setting.[47]

46. Gullickson, *Weavers and Spinners*, 85.
47. Glickman, *Russian Factory Women*.

Abortion and the Civic Order:
The Legal and Medical Debates

Laura Engelstein

In the years following the 1905 revolution the Russian intelligentsia, both political and professional, felt itself and the nation in crisis. Revolutionary and parliamentary politics alike had failed to alter the basic structure of the regime or resolve pressing social problems. Those problems seemed, if anything, to have grown more acute. Observers complained of a general moral decline. Working-class families, so it was said, had fallen into disarray as fathers took to the bottle, children took to the streets, and adolescents turned to petty crime and prostitution.[1] Meanwhile privileged youth spurned political tracts in favor of pornography and books on the so-called sexual question.[2] Abortion was on the rise: women, it was said, rejected motherhood in favor of pleasure and career.[3]

In a world that seemed to have lost its moral cohesion, professionals and civic activists joined in the discussion of intimate as well as public norms. The change in women's roles and in their sexual behavior occupied the atten-

---

1. On the new views of crime in this period, see Neil B. Weissman, "Rural Crime in Tsarist Russia: The Question of Hooliganism, 1905–1914," *Slavic Review* 37 (1978): 228–40; Joan Neuberger, "Stories on the Street: Hooliganism in the St. Petersburg Popular Press," *Slavic Review* 48 (1989): 177–94. On adolescent prostitution and crime, see M. K. Mukalov, *Deti ulitsy: Maloletnie prostitutki* (St. Petersburg, 1906); B. Bentovin, "Spasenie 'padshikh' i khuliganstvo: Iz ocherkov sovremennoi prostitutsii," *Obrazovanie*, 1905, no. 11–12, pt. 1, reprinted in *Torguiushchie telom: Ocherki sovremennoi prostitutsii*, 2d ed., rev. (St. Petersburg, 1909); I. M. Faingar, "Detskaia prostitutsiia," *Vestnik psikhologii, kriminal'noi antropologii i pedologii* 10, no. 3 (1913).

2. On the sexual indulgence of educated youth, see M. A. Chlenov, *Polovaia perepis' moskovskogo studenchestva i ee obshchestvennoe znachenie* (Moscow, 1909), 76–77, 86–87. On the shift from politics to sex, see A. S. Izgoev, "Ob intelligentnoi molodezhi," *Vekhi: Sbornik statei o russkoi intelligentsii*, 2d ed. (Moscow, 1909), 104.

3. M. M. Isaev, in *Otchet X obshchego sobraniia russkoi gruppy mezhdunarodnogo soiuza kriminalistov, 13–16 fevralia 1914 g. v Petrograde* (Petrograd, 1916), 282.

tion of participants at a conference on women that convened in St. Petersburg in 1908 and at another on prostitution in 1910.[4] Whereas infanticide
had been a concern of medical and legal communities for decades,[5] discussion of abortion and artificial birth control first appeared in the professional
press in the 1890s and remained sporadic before 1905.[6] It was in the years
preceding World War I that the question of abortion came to the fore in
medical and legal circles. The subject offered professionals the opportunity to
express fundamental ideas about the construction of the civic order, the
proper exercise of public authority, and the relationship between private life
and social organization.

The abortion debate was not a back-alley affair. The opening sallies were
fired in April 1910 at the eleventh congress of Russia's leading medical association, the Pirogov Society, which since its founding in 1885 had
spearheaded the profession's drive for disciplinary autonomy and become the
focus of its oppositional political activity during 1905. This round was followed by a discussion at the fourth congress of Russian gynecologists and
obstetricians, meeting in St. Petersburg in December 1911.[7] The latter occasion attracted 320 participants and was chaired by Dmitrii Ott, the interna-
tionally renowned director of the Imperial Gynecological Institute and con-
sultant to the medical council of the Ministry of Internal Affairs.[8] Various

4. See *Trudy pervogo vserossiiskogo zhenskogo s"ezda pri russkom zhenskom obshchestve v S.-
Peterburge 10–16 dekabria 1908 goda* (St. Petersburg, 1909), and *Trudy pervogo vserossiiskogo s"ezda po
bor'be s torgom zhenshchinami i ego prichinami, proiskhodivshego v S.-Peterburge s 21 po 25 aprelia 1910 goda*,
2 vols. (St. Petersburg, 1911–12).

5. Some early examples include M. G., "O detoubiistve," *Arkhiv sudebnoi meditsiny*, 1868,
no. 1, pt. 2: 21–55; A. Zhukovskii, "Detoubiistvo v Poltavskoi gubernii i predotvrashchenie
ego," *Arkhiv sudebnoi meditsiny*, 1870, no. 3, pt. 2: 1–13.

6. For example, A. G. Boriakovskii, "O vrede sredstv, prepiatstvuiushchikh zachatiiu,"
Vrach 14, no. 32 (1893): 886–87; S. V. Filits, "Sovremennaia polovaia zhizn' s meditsinskoi
tochki zreniia," *Meditsinskaia beseda* 14, no. 3 (1900): 65–80; E. Katunskii, "K voprosu o prave
roditelei na zhizn' ploda," *Meditsinskaia beseda* 14, no. 7 (1900): 177–84; I. V. Platonov, "Ob"ekt
prestupleniia izgnaniia ploda," *Vestnik prava*, 1899, no. 7: 155–67.

7. On the eleventh congress, see T. O. Shabad, "Iskusstvennyi vykidysh s printsipial'noi
tochki zreniia," in *Trudy XI Pirogovskogo s"ezda*, ed. P. N. Burlatov (St. Petersburg, 1913),
3: 214–17; and "Iskusstvennyi vykidysh s printsipial'noi tochki zreniia," *Sibirskaia vrachebnaia gazeta*, 1911, no. 10: 115–16. On the fourth congress, see "Protokol zasedaniia IV s"ezda Obshchestva rossiiskikh akusherov i ginekologov," *Zhurnal akusherstva i zhenskikh boleznei*, 1912, nos. 3–4:
386–88, 539–48; S. Aleksandrov, "Chetvertyi s"ezd rossiiskikh ginekologov i akusherov v
S.-Peterburge, 16–19 dekabria 1911 goda," *Prakticheskii vrach*, 1912, no. 1: 15–16; I. P. Mikhailov-
skii, "Chetvertyi s"ezd obshchestva rossiiskikh ginekologov i akusherov (Spb. 16–19 dekabria
1911 g.)," *Sibirskaia vrachebnaia gazeta*, 1912, no. 4: 44–47.

8. On Ott, see *Rossiiskii meditsinskii spisok, izdannyi Upravleniem Glavnogo Vrachebnogo Inspek-
tora Ministerstva Vnutrennykh Del na 1916 g.* (Petrograd, 1916), and *Biographisches Lexikon der hervor-
ragenden Ärzte der letzten fünfzig Jahre (1880–1903)*, ed. I. Fischer, 2d and 3d eds. (Munich and
Berlin, 1962), 2: 1158–59.

local medical societies also drew up position papers,[9] and the Pirogov Society
again debated the question at its twelfth congress in the early summer of
1913.[10] In February 1914 the Russian Group of the International Union of
Criminologists discussed the matter at its tenth national convention.[11]

A professional interest in abortion did not distinguish Russian physicians
and criminologists from their colleagues abroad. In Germany, England,
France, and the United States abortion and birth control became contested
social issues in the late nineteenth century and into the twentieth.[12] What is
of interest in the Russian discussion is the way in which medical and legal
issues were mapped onto the local political and cultural terrain. The implications of the question were not narrow. To listen to the Russians argue over
abortion is to hear an exchange on basic principles of public authority and
civic life. Opinions on women's control over their reproductive lives constituted not only a critique of the existing political order but also a blueprint for
a new and better one. Indeed the physicians, criminologists, and jurists engaged in this exchange examined three distinct models of social organization:
one in which the state imposes norms of private conduct through the repressive action of the law; one in which society exerts preemptive restraint
through the exercise of professional expertise; and one of individual self-
regulation, in which private decisions determine personal choice.

9. For example, see the report from the Urals by A. V. Linder, in "Protokol zasedaniia IV
s"ezda," 545–46; on Omsk, see "Doklad komissii po bor'be s iskusstvennymi vykidyshami
Omskogo Meditsinskogo Obshchestva XII-mu Pirogovskomu s"ezdu vrachei," *Obshchestvennyi
vrach*, 1913, no. 6, otdel 6: 683–92.

10. *Dvenadtsatyi Pirogovskii s"ezd. Peterburg, 29 maia–5 iiunia 1913 g.*, vyp. 2 (St. Petersburg,
1913); also I. I. Binshtok, "Dvenadtsatyi Pirogovskii s"ezd i uchenie Mal'tusa," *Prakticheskii
vrach*, 1914, no. 9: 123–27; E. L. Stoianovskaia, "Otchet: 12-yi Pirogovskii s"ezd, otdel akusherstva i zhenskikh boleznei, 2-oe zasedanie 1-go iiunia," *Russkii vrach* 12, no. 28 (1913): 1010–12.

11. See *Otchet X obshchego sobraniia*, 233–55, 272–333, 354–400. An account of this meeting
also appeared in "Desiatyi s"ezd russkoi gruppy mezhdunarodnogo soiuza kriminalistov," *Pravo*, 1914, no. 10: 809–40.

12. See Angus McLaren, "Abortion in England, 1890–1914," *Victorian Studies* 20 (1977):
379–400; "Abortion in France: Women and the Regulation of Family Size, 1800–1914," *French
Historical Studies* 10 (1978): 461–85; *Birth Control in Nineteenth-Century England* (New York, 1978);
and *Reproductive Rituals: The Perceptions of Fertility in England from the Sixteenth Century to the Nineteenth
Century* (New York, 1985). See also Patricia Knight, "Women and Abortion in Victorian and
Edwardian England," *History Workshop* 4 (1977); 57–68; R. P. Neuman, "The Sexual Question
and Social Democracy in Imperial Germany," *Journal of Social History* 7 (1974): 271–86; idem,
"Working-Class Birth Control in Wilhelmine Germany," *Comparative Studies in Social History* 20
(1978): 408–28; James Woycke, *Birth Control in Germany, 1871–1933* (London, 1988); Carroll
Smith-Rosenberg, "The Abortion Movement and the AMA, 1850–1880," in *Disorderly Conduct:
Vision of Gender in Victorian America* (New York, 1985); and James C. Mohr, *Abortion in America: The
Origins and Evolution of National Policy, 1800–1900* (New York, 1978).

THE STATUS OF ABORTION IN RUSSIAN LAW

Infanticide and abortion were linked in the legal and forensic literature as two forms of murder both defined in relation to female criminal agency.[13] The code defined infanticide as an unpremeditated form of murder since the guilty mother was presumed to have acted impulsively, under the pressure of overwhelming emotion, in an abnormal physical and mental state occasioned by "shame and fear" or in the commonplace anguish of postpartum distress. By contrast, abortion was defined as a premeditated act, a crime of choice, not desperation, and hence from the legal point of view less excusable and more reprehensible than infanticide.[14]

The abortion statute did, however, recognize a distinction between the woman's role and that of outside parties. Lawmakers argued that it was necessary to retain the concept of abortion as murder because the fetus "still belonged to the human race...even though [it was] not yet completely developed";[15] but they established milder penalties for those performing an abortion with the mother's consent or for the mother who performed it herself.[16] Though the motive of shame and fear, said to mitigate the crime of

13. For a comparison of existing legislation on abortion in other states, see Gustav Radbruch, "Abtreibung," in *Vergleichende Darstellung des Deutschen und ausländischen Strafrechts. Vorarbeiten zur Deutschen Strafrechtsreform*, ed. Karl von Birkmeyer et al., 15 vols., Besonderer Teil, vol. 5 (Berlin, 1905), 159–83. Russians were aware of the differences in Western legislation on the subject; see *Ugolovnoe ulozhenie: Proekt redaktsionnoi komissii i ob"iasneniia k nemu* (St. Petersburg, 1897), 6: 104–7.

14. Articles 1451 and 1461–62 in *Ulozhenie o nakazaniiakh ugolovnykh i ispravitel'nykh 1885 goda* (henceforth *Ulozhenie* [1885]), ed. N. S. Tagantsev, 11th ed., rev. (St. Petersburg, 1901), 665 ("shame and fear"), 670–71. On prevalent attitudes toward the two crimes, compare, for example, physician D. N. Zhbankov's denunciation of abortion as an upper-class indulgence with his insistence on the "abnormal," "fatal" circumstances driving women to infanticide: "K voprosu o vykidyshakh," *Prakticheskii vrach*, 1914, no. 31: 423–25; no. 32: 432–34; no. 33–34: 442–44; no. 35–36: 452–54; no. 37–38: 463–67; and "O detoubiistve," *Prakticheskii vrach*, 1909, no. 17: 316.

15. See note to articles 1867–69 justifying the provisions of the 1845 code: *Proekt ulozheniia o nakazaniiakh ugolovnykh i ispravitel'nykh, vnesennyi v 1844 godu v Gosudarstvennyi Sovet, s podrobnym oznacheniem osnovanii kazhdogo iz vnesennykh v sei proekt postanovlenii* (henceforth *Proekt* [1844]) (St. Petersburg, 1871), 618. The 1845 code was not substantially altered until 1917 despite various amendments and a revised edition of 1885.

16. According to the 1845 code, anyone convicted of performing an unwanted abortion would lose all civic standing and could be sentenced to six years (up to ten if the woman died) of the most severe form of penal servitude. They might in addition be subjected to branding and the lash if they belonged to the unprivileged ranks, which were liable to corporal punishment. Abortion by the mother or with her consent also entailed loss of civic rights but only exile or resettlement in Siberia (and the lash in appropriate cases). The 1885 edition (which followed the elimination of corporal punishment from the criminal code) lowered the penalties to loss of rights plus simple penal servitude (again six to ten years) where consent was absent; loss of rights and up to six years of corrective incarceration for the woman or her assistant, with additional time for highly trained personnel. See *Ulozhenie o nakazaniiakh ugolovnykh i ispravitel'nykh* (henceforth *Ulozhenie* [1845]) (St. Petersburg, 1845), 494–95 (articles 1932–34; *Ulozhenie*

infanticide, was not written into the abortion law, it was considered grounds for leniency in that case as well. The authors of the code explained their indulgence toward the mother on the grounds that popular opinion did not consider abortion a serious offense "because the child in the womb does not yet seem alive; because it cannot itself be attached to life nor be the object of other people's tenderness and attachment; because many consider (however erroneously) that not wanting it to be born is virtually the same as not wanting children in the first place; and because even the tenderest of parents do not regret an accidental miscarriage the way they do the death of a newborn child."[17]

Criminal agency in both infanticide and self-induced abortion was limited to women in their capacity as mothers, acting independently and privately in relation to their own children, and the penalties were virtually the same.[18] By employing professional aid, the mother became part of a wider social network and enhanced her power to control her reproductive life. Even when women sought assistance, however, the full force of the law was directed not against them but against those who helped them. As agents with greater freedom to act and to control their actions, abortionists had more chance of succeeding and less excuse for wanting to do so.

The statute especially restricted the right of trained personnel to substitute their own professional judgment for the woman's expressed desire. Though all abortion was illegal, practitioners could not be held additionally responsible for the pregnant woman's injury or death should they have performed the operation at her request—only if they had taken the decision on their own.[19] Such cases might include destruction of the unborn child as a result of procedures employed during delivery while the mother was unconscious or otherwise unable to consent.[20] Paradoxically, the legal risks were greatest when the operator was actually trained for the job. The lawmakers explained their attempt to control the activities of "doctors, obstetricians,

---

(1885), 670–71 (articles 1461–63). The loss of all rights attached to one's juridical status, known as civic death, barred the condemned from ever regaining his or her place in society.

17. *Proekt* (1844), 618 (note to articles 1867–69).

18. Women in both cases lost all civic rights and would spend a minimum of four years in corrective incarceration; the maximum was slightly higher for infanticide (six as opposed to five years). Compare articles 1451 (infanticide) and 1462 (self-induced abortion), *Ulozhenie* (1885), 664–65, 671.

19. Senate decision no. 18 (1904), in *Resheniia ugolovnogo kassatsionnogo departamenta pravitel'-stvuiushchego senata za 1904 god* (Ekaterinoslav, 1911), 39–40.

20. One physician explained that such crude procedures were most often employed by rural practitioners, who operated under primitive conditions: Katunskii, "K voprosu o prave roditelei na zhizn' ploda," 184. For a legal critique of this strict provision, explaining why explicit consent was not always possible to obtain, see A. A. Ginzburg, "Izgnanie ploda," *Zhurnal ministerstva iustitsii*, 1912, no. 7: 54–55.

midwives, and pharmacists," able by virtue of their skill to avoid being caught (since they in fact did less physical damage), on the grounds that in practicing abortion, qualified personnel violated professional principles and abused the public trust.[21] Conviction for performing an abortion with the woman's consent might carry a penalty of more than six years in corrective incarceration.[22] Even a proposed revision of the existing criminal code, published in 1903 though never adopted, retained this antiprofessional bias, though it lessened the severity of punishment.[23] This situation goes far toward explaining why the medical profession, obstetricians in particular, rallied to the cause of abortion reform.

Here the Russians differed markedly from their colleagues in the West. In both England and the United States laws against abortion increased in severity during the nineteenth century, largely at the initiative of physicians seeking to enforce their professional authority at the expense of female autonomy in reproductive affairs.[24] In Russia, by contrast, the desire to enhance their professional standing led physicians to demand either the reduction of existing legal sanctions against abortion or outright decriminalization, stressing the convergence, rather than conflict, between women's interests and their own. Such a stance reflected the awkward position of the Russian medical profession. Ill-paid, overworked, dependent on state support and public employment, and suffering from low social esteem, physicians resented state intrusion, repudiated the regime's high-handed administrative methods (including the liberal use of penal sanctions in everyday affairs), and identified with the cause of the powerless—whether peasants or women. Relatively privileged though they might be, especially in cultural terms, these doctors maintained a posture of critical caution in relation to the administrative state that deprived them of professional and civic autonomy. Their distrust was mitigated by the improvement in the nation's political situation after 1905 and by the disillusionment of many physicians with radical tactics and populist dreams, but it was never entirely overcome.[25]

21. Articles 345 and 346: *Svod zakonov ugolovnykh* (St. Petersburg, 1835), 121; article 1934: *Ulozhenie* (1845), 495; motive in note to draft articles 1867–69 in *Proekt* (1844), 618; additional explanation in *Ugolovnoe ulozhenie* (1897), 6: 167.

22. See articles 1462 and 1463 in *Ulozhenie* (1885), 671.

23. *Ugolovnoe ulozhenie* (1897), 6: 167; *Ugolovnoe ulozhenie, Vysochaishe utverzhdennoe 22 marta 1903 goda* (St. Petersburg, 1903), 177 (articles 465 and 466). These statutes eliminated loss of rights from the penalties imposed.

24. See McLaren, "Abortion in England," 389–94, and *Reproductive Rituals*, 129, 137–44; Knight, "Women and Abortion," 62–63; Smith-Rosenberg, "Abortion Movement," 217–44; and Mohr, *Abortion in America*, 147–57, 160–64. By the end of the century, however, many European physicians had accepted the legitimacy of performing abortions for medically indicated reasons: McLaren, "Abortion in France," 470–72.

25. For the general picture of the Russian medical profession, see Nancy Mandelker Frieden, *Russian Physicians in an Era of Reform and Revolution, 1856–1905* (Princeton, 1981); for the

THE MEDICAL SIDE

Physicians at the eleventh Pirogov Society congress in 1910 stressed that abortion, once the privilege of the well-to-do, had reached "epidemic" proportions and was now common in all social classes. Often victims of poverty and economic exploitation, sometimes victims of rape by "hooligans" and violent mobs (*pogromshchiki*), women seeking abortion seemed to be suffering not only the age-old burden of moral opprobrium but also the specific hardships of the post-1905 years.[26] The main speaker at both the 1911 meeting of gynecologists and the twelfth Pirogov Society congress in 1913 was obstetrician Lazar Lichkus, director of a St. Petersburg maternity clinic.[27] On each occasion he was joined at the podium by a legal expert and other obstetricians—in 1911 by professor Iulius Iakobson, board member of Prince Ol'denburg's children's shelter and senior staff physician at the St. Petersburg Institute of Gynecology and Midwifery, along with junior professor Liudvig Okinchits; and in 1913 by Iakob Vygodskii, from a Jewish hospital in Vilnius.[28]

Nine physicians spoke out at the 1913 Pirogov Society congress session on abortion. Four were women, five came from the provinces, five worked for *zemstva* (local government assemblies) or municipal hospitals, a number (like Lichkus himself) had obviously Jewish names, and all but two were between thirty and forty years of age and had completed their training within the past

---

post-1905 modifications, see John F. Hutchinson, "'Who Killed Cock Robin?' An Inquiry into the Death of Zemstvo Medicine," in *Health and Society in Revolutionary Russia*, ed. Susan Gross Solomon and John F. Hutchinson (Bloomington, Ind., 1990), 3–26.

26. Shabad, "Iskusstvennyi vykidysh" (1913), 214–17, and "Iskusstvennyi vykidysh" (1911), 115–16.

27. The texts of Lichkus's talks were reprinted in *Russkii vrach*: L. G. Lichkus, "Vykidysh s sudebno-meditsinskoi tochki zreniia," *Russkii vrach* 11, no. 4 (1912): 109–18, and "Iskusstvennyi prestupnyi vykidysh," *Russkii vrach* 12, no. 39 (1913): 1358–66. For an acrimonious exchange with an opponent of his position, see N. Khokhlov, "Po povodu postanovleniia Otdela akusherstva 2-go iiunia na 12-m Pirogovskom s"ezde 'Ob iskusstvennom prestupnom vykidyshe,'" *Russkii vrach* 12, no. 29 (1913): 1048–49; L. Lichkus, "Vynuzhdennyi otvet na korrespondentsiiu N. I. Khokhlova: Po povodu postanovleniia Otdela akusherstva 2-go iiunia na 12-m Pirogovskom S"ezde, 'Ob iskusstvennom prestupnom vykidyshe,'" *Russkii vrach* 12, no. 33 (1913): 1181–82; N. Khokhlov, "Pis'mo v redaktsii," *Russkii vrach* 12, no. 38 (1913): 1341–42.

28. For the texts of their talks see V. L. Iakobson, "Sovremennyi vykidysh s obshchestvennoi i meditsinskoi tochki zreniia," *Zhurnal akusherstva i zhenskikh boleznei*, 1912, no. 3: 305–18; L. Okinchits, "Kak borot'sia s prestupnym vykidyshem," *Zhurnal akusherstva i zhenskikh boleznei*, 1912, no. 3: 319–32; and Ia. E. Vygodskii, "Iskusstvennyi vykidysh s obshchestvennoi i vrachebnoi tochki zreniia," *Dvenadtsatyi Pirogovskii s"ezd*, 375–77. The legal scholar who spoke at the gynecologists' convention was M. P. Chubinskii. For the text of his talk see M. P. Chubinskii, "Vopros o vykidyshe v sovremennom prave i zhelatel'naia ego postanovka," *Zhurnal akusherstva i zhenskikh boleznei*, 1912, no. 4: 461–86; and M. Chubinskii, "Istreblenie ploda i problema ego nakazuemosti," *Iuridicheskii vestnik*, 1913, no. 2: 112–35.

fifteen years. The two speakers represented a slightly older generation: born in the 1850s, they had completed their studies by 1882. Both attacked existing laws, Lichkus calling for a broader range of legitimate abortion, Vygodskii for outright decriminalization. In the discussion two women, Liubov' Gorovits from St. Petersburg and Kseniia Bronnikova, a senior staff physician at the St. Petersburg Imperial Maternity Clinic, energetically denounced the antiabortion laws as a violation of women's rights; Nadezhda Bezpalova-Letova, a staff physician at the Rostov municipal hospital, believed women's equality would solve the abortion problem; and a fourth woman, Nadezhda Zemlianitsyna from Perm Province, insisted on the criminality of abortion and defended the importance of motherhood.[29]

Both the gynecologists' congress and the gynecological section of the Pirogov Society voted to recommend that the government decriminalize abortion.[30] Not all physicians accepted these positions, and the debate spilled over into the medical press. Most professional commentators agreed with the opinion voiced at the medical conventions that abortion was a problem physicians and jurists must address because in recent years it had been dramatically on the rise, in Russia as well as in Europe, despite the existence of repressive laws. The Russian incidence was said to have started its climb in the mid-1890s, with the intensification of industrial and urban development, and to have skyrocketed following the 1905 revolution.[31] One physician drew the analogy between 1905 and the French Revolution of 1789, which, she declared, had also produced an upsurge of abortions.[32] Not only was this rise in itself an ominous sign, but it increased the disjuncture between formal legal principles and both medical and judicial practice: physicians found themselves more often engaged in criminal activity, and the courts came up against the force of contrary public opinion and social reality.[33]

29. For details of the discussion see *Dvenadtsatyi Pirogovskii s"ezd*, 84–88, 210–13, 375–77; and Stoianovskaia, "Otchet: 12-yi Pirogovskii s"ezd," 1010–12. Biographical information from *Rossiiskii meditsinskii spisok . . . na 1894 g.* (St. Petersburg, 1894) and *Rossiiskii meditsinskii spisok . . . na 1916 g.* (Petrograd, 1916).

30. Gynecologists' decision cited in N. Vigdorchik, "Vrachebnye otkliki: Ereticheskie mysli o prestupnykh vykidyshakh i o preduprezhdenii beremennosti," *Prakticheskii vrach*, 1912, no. 15: 242. Pirogov resolution cited in V. D. Nabokov, "Desiatyi s"ezd kriminalistov," *Pravo*, 1914, no. 9: 663. Also quoted in Sergei Iablonovskii, "Prava nerozhdennykh," *Russkoe slovo*, 1913, no. 129 (June 6): 2.

31. This opinion was universal; see Iakobson, "Sovremennyi vykidysh," 310–112; also O. P. Pirozhkova, "K voprosu o vykidyshe," *Zhurnal akusherstva i zhenskikh boleznei*, 1912, no. 4: 520, 522; Vigdorchik, "Vrachebnye otkliki," 243; "Doklad komissii," 683; L. G. Lichkus, "Iskusstvennyi prestupnyi vykidysh," *Russkii vrach* 12, no. 39 (1913): 1359.

32. O. P. Pirozhkova, in Aleksandrov, "Chetvertyi s"ezd," 16.

33. On the impossibility of enforcing the law because it conflicted with social practice, see G. Ia. Zak, "Umershchvlenie ploda i ugolovnoe pravo," *Pravo*, 1910, no. 46: 2751–52; no. 47: 2840; also Dr. Brodskii, in Shabad, "Iskusstvennyi vykidysh" (1913), 216; and congress resolution in Aleksandrov, "Chetvertyi s"ezd," 16.

Since the law targeted both the pregnant woman and the medical practitioner as perpetrators of the crime, arguments for legal reform took two directions—in defense of women's rights to physical self-determination and of physicians' rights to make technical decisions on professional grounds. Physicians were unanimous in wishing to substitute their trained judgment for the blanket repression of the law, which, they believed, succeeded only in creating a truly criminal underground of incompetent and unlicensed operators and increasing the dangerous effects of abortion. Many jurists likewise called for legalization in all, or almost all, cases, in the name of individual liberty, juridical secularism, and social welfare. Only a few voices in either exchange spoke for women's absolute right to make personal choices—and many of these speakers were women.[34] Both professional communities thus rejected the first of the three models (social control through legal repression), preferred the second (public self-regulation through expert intervention), and hesitated before the third (individual self-determination, in this case by women).

Physicians who demanded reform of the existing law (model 1, modified to accommodate the principle embodied in model 2), as well as those who wished to remove abortion from the criminal code altogether, sanctioned the right of properly qualified medical personnel to perform abortions for medically appropriate reasons. In rejecting the statutory limitations on this authority, the second group did not necessarily define the formal mechanisms through which it would be exercised. Most relied on moral assurances. "Let the physician's high calling be society's best guarantee that such operations will not be undertaken lightly," urged the Omsk Medical Society. "For indeed society and the state entrust him with the life and health of all their members."[35] Very few of the Russian physicians who engaged in these debates, whether at the conventions or in the general or medical press, maintained that abortion was under all circumstances morally and medically objectionable.[36]

34. For example, women physicians K. N. Bronnikova and L. M. Gorovits at the twelfth Pirogov congress: see discussion in *Dvenadtsatyi Pirogovskii s"ezd*, 212–13, and a hostile account in Khokhlov, "Po povodu postanovleniia Otdela akusherstva," 1048. Also Pirozhkova, "K voprosu o vykidyshe," 523, and M. I. Pokrovskaia, "K voprosu ob aborte," *Zhenskii vestnik*, 1914, no. 4: 102–5. On the legal side, see St. Petersburg attorney F. A. Vol'kenshtein and another participant in the 1914 criminology congress named Oks, in *Otchet X obshchego sobraniia*, 327, 380–81; and M. L. Oleinik, "Prestupnyi abort v doktrine i zakonodatel'stve," *Trudy kruzhka ugolovnogo prava pri Spb. universitete*, ed. M. M. Isaev (St. Petersburg, 1913), 138.

35. "Doklad komissii," 690.

36. The most categorical denunciations of abortion I have found are K. V. Goncharov, *O venericheskikh bolezniiakh v S. Peterburge (po statisticheskim dannym Alafuzovskoi muzhskoi i Kalinkinskoi zhenskoi gorodskikh bol'nits)* (St. Petersburg, 1910), 118, and A. Kalinkovitskii, "Eshche ob iskusstvennom vykidyshe (V zashchitu amfibiopodobnogo zarodysha)," *Vrachebnaia gazeta*, 1913, no. 43: 1533–36, both of whom deplored all but the strictest medically indicated abortions. Gon-

Disagreement arose, rather, over two points—whether abortion should be decriminalized across the board, thereby allowing both women and doctors the freedom to make decisions without fear of reprisal; or whether the law should merely establish a range of cases, to be identified by trained practitioners, in which abortion would be permitted. Those who accepted the second alternative went on to differ as to what criteria should delineate tolerated and prohibited interventions. Even in cases of therapeutic abortion based on strictly medical considerations (the health and welfare of mother or child) there was room to disagree. More controversial, however, was the issue of so-called social abortion—whether physicians were ethically justified in terminating a normal pregnancy the healthy mother was unwilling to bring to term because of the nature of her life circumstances.

Feminist principles sometimes, but not always, induced physicians to support decriminalization (the third model). Feminist public-health activist Mariia Pokrovskaia denounced the abortion laws as an unwarranted restriction on female autonomy and called for full decriminalization on the grounds that women only, not physicians, were in a position to judge the legitimacy of their own needs. There was no absolute standard, she declared, against which to weigh individual claims. Invoking "the example most often cited in defense of antiabortion laws—the high-society lady devoted to pleasure . . . who does not want children," Pokrovskaia denied that such a woman's motives were any less valid than those of an overburdened peasant wife. "Since the society lady risks her life in resorting to abortion, she obviously considers the birth of the child worse than death itself. Her arguments may seem pitiful to us, but to her they have enormous meaning."[37] Pokrovskaia did not approve of abortion, which she viewed as a consequence of society's "abnormal" indulgence in sexual pleasure for its own sake, but she defended rationally controlled reproduction as essential to "racial hygiene"—the production of better-quality children.[38] The concept of voluntary motherhood (*soznatel'noe materinstvo*), by which women regulated pregnancy in the interests of more-effective mothering and greater personal independence, belonged to the rhetorical arsenal of Western as well as Russian feminists of the time.[39]

charov had served briefly as a *zemstvo* physician before taking up service in military medicine, eventually joining the faculty of the Academy of Military Medicine. Kalinkovitskii was a Jewish *zemstvo* physician in Poltava Province. See biographical note to Goncharov's book, 152–53, and *Rossiiskii meditsinskii spisok* (Petrograd, 1916).

37. Pokrovskaia, "K voprosu ob aborte," 103.

38. Ibid., 105.

39. Rosalind Pollack Petchesky, *Abortion and Woman's Choice: The State, Sexuality, and Reproductive Freedom* (New York, 1984), 41. In England feminists promoted voluntary motherhood, but few defended either contraception or abortion: McLaren, *Birth Control in Nineteenth-Century En-*

Pokrovskaia's colleague in public health, Dmitrii Zhbankov, did not adopt this concept. A leader in the *zemstvo* medical community and the Pirogov Society, he shared Pokrovskaia's commitment to women's rights and women's education, her hostility to regulated prostitution, and her antipathy to the idea that sex was meant for anything but procreation, but he did not agree that women had the right to make their own reproductive choices. To him the upper-class lady wanting to abort represented all that was corrupt, self-indulgent, and self-destructive about what he called the post-1905 "abortion era." Women could not achieve equal rights, he warned in a 1914 article, unless they rejected the emphasis of contemporary culture on artificial (that is, nonreproductive) sexual gratification and returned to their "natural" function—motherhood, not sex—eschewing birth control as well as abortion.[40] Moreover, Zhbankov was virtually the only professional engaged in these debates who cited the opposition of the Orthodox church to abortion in defense of his own highly moralistic views.[41]

Like Zhbankov, many physicians interpreted the increased abortion rate since the 1890s in class and political terms. Most attributed the post-1905 rise to a combination of cultural and economic crises: on the one hand, the urban working class was finding it harder to make ends meet and adopting supposedly upper-class habits of family regulation for economic reasons; on the other hand, the so-called moral decline following the collapse of revolutionary hopes had increased the public's interest in sexual expression and lessened regard for traditional sexual ties.[42] Abortion itself was said to be a product of capitalist relations, the movement to decriminalize it a foreign

---

gland, 197–99; Judith R. Walkowitz, "Male Vice and Feminist Virtue: Feminism and the Politics of Prostitution in Nineteenth-Century Britain," *History Workshop Journal* 13 (1982): 92; and Mohr, *Abortion in America*, 111–12. Russian examples defending both include E. Zinov'eva, "V zashchitu prav rozhdennykh: Pis'mo v redaktsiiu," *Sovremennyi mir*, 1913, no. 8: 250, 252–56; and Sof'ia Zarechnaia, "Neomal'tuzianstvo i zhenskii vopros," *Zhenskoe delo*, 1910, no. 27–28 (August 10): 10–12. Both of these writers, unlike Pokrovskaia, identified themselves as socialists. On the ambivalent attitudes of European socialists toward abortion and birth control, see Neuman, "Sexual Question and Social Democracy" and "Working-Class Birth Control"; and Angus McLaren, "Sex and Socialism: The Opposition of the French Left to Birth Control in the Nineteenth Century," *Journal of the History of Ideas* 37 (1976): 475–92.

40. Zhbankov, "K voprosu o vykidyshakh," no. 31: 425 ("abortion era"), no. 32: 432–33, no. 33–34: 444, no. 35–36: 452 ("natural"), no. 37–38: 467.

41. Zhbankov, "K voprosu o vykidyshakh," no. 35–36: 452.

42. Ia. Falevich, "Itogi Tomskoi studencheskoi polovoi perepisi: Doklad, chitannyi 18 fevralia 1910 g. na zasedanii Pirogovskogo Studencheskogo Meditsinskogo Obshchestva pri Tomskom Universitete," *Sibirskaia vrachebnaia gazeta*, 1910, no. 28: 330; Iakobson, "Sovremennyi vykidysh," 310; "Doklad komissii," 684; V. A. Brodskii, "Iskusstvennyi vykidysh s meditsinskoi i obshchestvenno-ekonomicheskoi tochek zreniia," *Vrachebnaia gazeta*, 1913, no. 18: 660, no. 20: 711–12; Pirozhkova, "K voprosu," 521–22; N. A. Vigdorchik, "Detskaia smertnost' sredi Peterburgskikh rabochikh," *Obshchestvennyi vrach*, 1914, no. 2: 247.

idea.[43] The most advanced nations (France and the United States were always cited in this regard) and the most cultivated classes were said to practice abortion at the highest rates.[44]

Infanticide, by contrast, was the more likely resort of peasant women.
Criminal data seemed to confirm the contrast between the backward countryside and the sophisticated town—the one subject to the tyranny of nature
and the desperation born of ignorance and need, the other substituting culture for nature and rational control for the elemental expression of emotion.[45]
Though some physicians (as well as criminologists) admitted abortion was
"not peculiar to any specific social group,"[46] their rhetoric betrayed the
power of the stereotype. According to them, aborting mothers included, in
declining order of symbolic prominence, "the high-society lady accustomed
to luxury who need not worry about her daily bread, the prostitute seeking
a living on the streets, as well as the housemaid and the woman factory
worker."[47] One physician hostile to decriminalization insisted that "real"
proletarians were interested in the right to motherhood, not abortion.[48]

The same rhetoric characterized contemporary medical discussions of
birth control. (Abortion was sometimes castigated by opponents of contraception as its "most loathsome form.")[49] Contraception was a foreign idea,[50] a

43. See Binshtok, "Dvenadtsatyi Pirogovskii s"ezd," 124; Vigdorchik, "Vrachebnye otkliki," 242–43 (ironic reference to belief in foreign origins); L. Rutenberg, "K voprosu o sovremennom vzgliade na dopustimost' sotsial'nogo vykidysha," *Vrachebnaia gazeta*, 1916, no. 31:
489; S. Elpat'evskii, "Samoistreblenie chelovechestva: Po povodu s"ezda kriminalistov v Peterburge," *Russkoe bogatstvo*, 1914, no. 4: 267.

44. On France and the United States (the first said to be dying out, the second to be a
hotbed of abortion), see Lichkus, "Iskusstvennyi prestupnyi vykidysh," 1359–60; also Zhbankov, "K voprosu o vykidyshakh," no. 32: 433–34, and Gei, in *Otchet X obshchego sobraniia*, 328.
On the prevalence of abortion among the educated, see, among others, Oleinik, "Prestupnyi
abort," 118.

45. On this sociological contrast, see Lichkus, "Iskusstvennyi prestupnyi vykidysh," 1358;
also Vigdorchik, "Detskaia smertnost'," 245; Oleinik, "Prestupnyi abort," 112, 118; and Chubinskii, "Vopros o vykidyshe v sovremennom prave," 470. For data on rural and urban court
cases, see M. N. Gernet, *Detoubiistvo: Sotsiologicheskoe i sravnitel'no-iuridicheskoe issledovanie* (Moscow, 1911), 143. On the calculated nature of contraception and abortion, see Elpat'evskii,
"Samoistreblenie chelovechestva," 269. Europeans made the same urban-rural comparison: see
Knight, "Women and Abortion," 58, and McLaren, "Abortion in France," 475.

46. Zak, "Umershchvlenie ploda," no. 46: 2751. Among others who believed that abortion
occurred among all social classes are Iakobson, "Sovremennyi vykidysh," 312; Oleinik, "Prestupnyi abort," 110; Dr. Rappoport, in Shabad, "Iskusstvennyi vykidysh" (1913), 215; and
Elpat'evskii, "Samoistreblenie chelovechestva," 266–67.

47. Zak, "Umershchvlenie ploda," no. 46: 2751.

48. I. I. Binshtok, "Eshche o nakazuemosti aborta," *Prakticheskii vrach* 13, no. 15 (1914):
215.

49. Filits, "Sovremennaia polovaia zhizn'," 73.

50. Boriakovskii, "O vrede sredstv," 887.

product of capitalism,[51] more prevalent among the educated classes[52] and less among the common folk too busy with work to think much about sex in the first place.[53] In a positive vein it was regarded as a means for women to gain access to "freedom and all the benefits of science, culture, and civic life [*obshchestvennaia zhizn'*]."[54] As working people gained cultural skills, they also used more-rational means of regulating their reproductive lives. "The only people who still produce children without restraint," wrote Dr. Sergei Elpat'evskii in 1914, "are those at the very bottom level of society [*nizy obshchestva*]—in particular the Russian peasants. That is," he corrected himself, "they used to." He admitted that contraceptive devices were now available in provincial pharmacies, where they sold like hotcakes.[55]

Public-health physician Natan Vigdorchik of St. Petersburg offered similar observations on the behavior of urban workers in 1914. "The more educated members of the proletariat [*bolee kul'turnye sloi*] more often use abortion than the less educated. This is indeed a universal phenomenon, that all types of artificial birth control travel the rungs of the social ladder from top to bottom."[56] In switching from abortion to contraception, the Russian working-class elite was only following the example of its more sophisticated comrades abroad.[57] Working women had a particular interest in limiting family size. "No sooner does the first ray of consciousness penetrate into this dark life," the physician went on, "than women begin to look for some way to lighten the double load imposed on them by nature and society."[58]

These were the views, however, of a physician who accepted the fact that Russia was changing. By contrast, the anticapitalist bias of many of his colleagues cut two ways. The morally objectionable aspect of abortion could be attributed to the materialist individualism of capitalist society and of the spoiled rich (urban middle-class women indulged vanity and the desire for pleasure, and doctors turned a profit from the women's selfish desires); its morally excusable side could be explained as a response to the suffering engendered by that same society (working-class women were forced to abort to protect the welfare of their other children; unwed working girls turned to abortion to protect their honor against hypocritical bourgeois contempt and to keep their jobs). In another way this argument should have undermined

51. "Po voprosu o neomal'tuzianstve," *Sibirskaia vrachebnaia gazeta*, 1908, no. 38: 411.
52. For contraceptive use among the male student body, see Falevich, "Itogi," no. 22: 270, no. 23: 271, no. 27: 318.
53. Filits, "Sovremennaia polovaia zhizn'," 65, 79.
54. "Po voprosu o neomal'tuzianstve," 411.
55. Elpat'evskii, "Samoistreblenie chelovechestva," 269–70.
56. Vigdorchik, "Detskaia smertnost'," 247.
57. Ibid., 248.
58. Ibid., 250.

the very grounds for the Russian abortion debate in the first place, but here logic did not win out. For if birthrates were falling in most of Europe, to the point where France thought itself to be dying out, the same could not be said for less-developed Russia, where abortions may have been rising but fertility was still holding its own.[59] "It is true," admitted one staunch enemy of abortion, whose spread he attributed to the baneful effects of feminist agitation, "that Russia's population continues to increase at a very high rate, despite our fantastic mortality level. No matter how far the abortion epidemic may spread, Russia will not soon find itself in the position of France." He nevertheless opposed the practice on the grounds that abortion destroyed the physical and psychic health of individual women.[60]

The Russian anxiety over abortion reflected more the nation's cultural than its demographic transformation. Commenting on the call of the 1911 gynecological congress for legalized medical abortion and its endorsement of birth control, the same Natan Vigdorchik noted that attitudes had only recently changed. Not so long ago, he commented ironically, "who in Russia would have dared come to the defense of those 'disgusting sores of capitalism'?" But now "Russian physicians, those same Russian physicians, of whom it is always said that they are steeped in the highest idealism, that they hold high the banner of social responsibility [*obshchestvennost'*], . . . speak openly before all of Russia . . . advocating (how dreadful!) the decriminalization of abortion and artificial contraceptive means!" Vigdorchik argued that the shift in attitude simply reflected the realities of current medical practice. Could the sharp rise in abortions be explained only by the role of "special underground doctors, unscrupulous has-beens who sell their expertise for criminal ends? Nothing of the sort. [Abortions are performed by] the most ordinary physicians, your good friends and comrades, people you admire."[61]

Vigdorchik's contention that abortion was endemic and in fact accepted by most (male) members of society, who did not think their doctors criminal for performing abortions on sisters, mothers, and wives,[62] was reiterated by the Omsk Medical Society in its report to the 1913 Pirogov Society congress. The report emphasized that women in particular accepted the termination of pregnancy in its early stages as an everyday occurrence, without feelings of remorse. Vigorously endorsing women's right to seek abortion for "social" causes (illegitimacy, rape, large families, need to keep working), the Omsk Society insisted both on the right of the medical profession to corporate

59. Lichkus, "Iskusstvennyi prestupnyi vykidysh," 1359.

60. Binshtok, "Eshche o nakazuemosti aborta," 213–15.

61. Vigdorchik, "Vrachebnye otkliki," 242–43. Vigdorchik's remarks were warmly endorsed by the *Siberian Medical Gazette*: "V zashchitu aborta i preduprezhdeniia beremennosti," *Sibirskaia vrachebnaia gazeta*, 1912, no. 17: 209–10.

62. Vigdorchik, "Vrachebnye otkliki," 244.

autonomy and on women's right to voluntary motherhood.[63] The doctors thus saw their own desire for self-governance reflected in the situation of their female patients.

In addition to decriminalization the society called for extensive social measures to support mothers, families, and children and for reform of existing laws on marriage, divorce, and illegitimacy.[64] However, not all physicians who endorsed such practical prescriptions and the accompanying social critique also accepted the demand for full decriminalization. Lazar Lichkus, for example, believed the law should continue to prosecute irregular abortionists even as it allowed physicians to take the necessary medical steps. "Doctors," he asserted, "stand closer than anyone else to the population and can better understand its needs."[65] It could well have been countered that untrained abortionists, especially in the countryside where the job was done by trusted peasant women, were closer to the people than any physician could be. And indeed, the nature of popular attitudes toward abortion (invoked, for example, by the framers of the 1845 criminal code) was difficult to determine.[66] Despite such objections the organizations representing the profession as a whole took more radical stands. Most important, gynecologists associated with the influential Pirogov Society believed they best served the public welfare by opposing the abortion law outright.[67]

THE LEGAL SIDE

In February 1914 the Russian Group of the International Union of Criminologists, an association of lawyers, legal scholars, and specialists in crime of varied political views, meeting in St. Petersburg, echoed the Pirogov Society's stand on decriminalization.[68] By that time there was general agreement in the legal community that reform was overdue. Even the Ministry of Justice favored a drastic reduction in the penalties imposed, including an end to the loss of civic rights entailed in all cases. The ministry continued, however, to think that physicians and midwives deserved special chastisement for their

63. "Doklad komissii," 684, 687–88, 690.

64. Ibid., 691.

65. Lichkus, "Iskusstvennyi prestupnyi vykidysh," 1366.

66. For example, one ethnographic study maintained, on the one hand, that peasants denounced abortion as ungodly and, on the other, that they employed folk abortive practices that did not usually work, leaving infanticide as the only option: T. Popov, *Russkaia narodno-bytovaia meditsina: Po materialam etnograficheskogo biuro kn. V. N. Tenisheva* (St. Petersburg, 1903), 326–29.

67. Resolution cited in Nabokov, "Desiatyi s"ezd kriminalistov," 663, and Iablonovskii, "Prava nerozhdennykh," 2.

68. On the politics of this group, see S. S. Ostroumov, *Prestupnost' i ee prichiny v dorevoliutsionnoi Rossii*, 3d ed. (Moscow, 1980), 197.

role.[69] But the government did not speak in one voice on this question. The highly placed, politically conservative professor of gynecology Georgii Rein, also a member of the State Council, headed a special commission appointed by the Minister of Internal Affairs in 1912 to review public-hygiene legislation. The Pirogov Society was not represented on this commission, which set out to replace the services of *zemstvo* and community physicians with a centrally administered medical regime that would subordinate the profession to the state bureaucracy. The outbreak of war prevented the plans from being adopted, but Rein's intentions were already well known by 1913.[70] As part of its recommendations, the commission defended existing criminal penalties for abortion.[71] Precisely because reform seemed to be in jeopardy and because neither the draft criminal statutes of 1903 nor the proposal of the Ministry of Justice had resolved all the relevant questions, the criminologists felt their deliberations to be of immediate practical import.[72]

The sessions opened with two keynote addresses—one urging decriminalization, by sociologist Mikhail Gernet; the other calling for retention of the law in modified form, by Evgenii Kulisher, a St. Petersburg attorney who served on the editorial board of the group's journal.[73] Fourteen people spoke on each side of the question—thirteen jurists (including one woman) and one physician (also a woman) for decriminalization, ten jurists (including one woman) and four physicians (all male) against.[74] The female physician was the same Liubov' Gorovits who had argued passionately at the 1913 Pirogov Society congress for women's right to make their own reproductive decisions, and she once again gave a ringing defense of the dignity and moral value of freely chosen motherhood.[75] Without changing his earlier support for broadening the legal grounds for abortion, Lazar Lichkus found himself in

69. "Khronika," *Pravo*, 1913, no. 16 (April 21): 1024.

70. On the role and politics of this commission and on Rein's views, see John F. Hutchinson, "Politics and Medical Professionalization in Russia after 1905" (Unpublished manuscript), 12–30, and Hutchinson, "'Who Killed Cock Robin?'" 19–20. I would like to thank Professor Hutchinson for making his unpublished manuscript available to me.

71. The commission's proposal slightly reduced the weight of the penalty for self-induced abortion but left the other penalties unchanged and thus significantly more onerous than those provided in the 1903 reformed code. On the proposal, see Pokrovskaia, "K voprosu ob aborte," 102.

72. On the inadequacy of the 1903 code, see Ginzburg, "Izgnanie ploda," 53.

73. Biographical information on Gernet is available in the introduction to *Izbrannye proizvedeniia*, ed. M. M. Babaev (Moscow, 1974), 8–37. For the text of his talk, see M. Gernet, "Istreblenie ploda s ugolovno-sotsiologicheskoi tochki zreniia," *Vestnik prava*, 1914, no. 3: 233–38.

74. Beginning in 1906, women were allowed to study law but were prevented from practicing as attorneys: Linda Harriet Edmondson, *Feminism in Russia, 1900–1917* (Stanford, 1984), 147–48.

75. The text of Gorovits's remarks is in *Otchet X obshchego sobraniia*, 291–97; for her tone and audience response, see A. Trainin, "Na s"ezde kriminalistov: Fakty i vpechatleniia," *Russkoe bogatstvo*, 1914, no. 4: 261.

the company of the distinguished obstetrician Dmitrii Ott in defending Kulisher's more cautious position. Altogether six professors of law weighed in on Kulisher's side, against three on Gernet's. The eminent State Council member and criminal law expert Senator Nikolai Tagantsev spoke against decriminalization. The group's executive committee was split, six to two, in favor of reform, not legalization, but in the end the congress as a whole voted thirty-eight to twenty, with three abstentions, to eliminate abortion from the criminal code.[76]

The proceedings themselves were passionate in tone, and the public reaction was more emotional still. "The February congress has become the center of public attention," wrote Aron Trainin, one of Gernet's supporters, in April 1914. "In the daily press and the thick journals, at lectures and fashionable debates, the congress's basic resolutions are discussed with unflagging passion."[77] The vote to decriminalize abortion had "made a terrible impression on wide reaches of the public," commented a physician that same year.[78] Gernet himself counted seventeen published responses by physicians and legal experts, thirteen in his favor.[79] Defeated opponents of the adopted resolution called it irresponsible and demagogic; the right-wing press denounced it as a machination of the Jews.[80]

Above and beyond its engagement with the particulars of the abortion question, the debate represented a split within progressive educated society.

76. *Otchet X obshchego sobraniia*, 400; G. N. Shtil'man, "Abort na s"ezde kriminalistov," *Pravo*, 1914, no. 10: 777. Also see the intelligent summary by a Gernet supporter, Trainin, "Na s"ezde kriminalistov," 256–62. Proceedings of the abortion debate appear in *Otchet X obshchego sobraniia*, 233–55, 272–333, 354–400. The sources do not indicate the identities of all sixty-one voters. For biographical information on the speakers, see "Imennoi ukazatel'," *Dvenadtsatyi Pirogovskii s"ezd*, xv–xviii; *Rossiiskii meditsinskii spisok, na 1894 g. . . . na 1916 g.* (St. Petersburg, 1894, 1916); "Spisok chlenov Russkoi gruppy Mezhdunarodnogo Soiuza Kriminalistov k 4 ianvaria 1909 goda," in *Russkaia gruppa Mezhdunarodnogo Soiuza Kriminalistov: Obshchee sobranie gruppy v Moskve, 4–7 ianvaria 1909 goda* (St. Petersburg, 1909), vii–xx; "Spisok chlenov Russkoi gruppy Mezhdunarodnogo Soiuza Kriminalistov k 21 aprelia 1910 goda," *Russkaia gruppa Mezhdunarodnogo Soiuza Kriminalistov: Obshchee sobranie gruppy v Moskve, 21–23 aprelia 1910 goda* (St. Petersburg, 1911), viii–xxiv; "Spisok chlenov Russkoi gruppy Mezhdunarodnogo Soiuza Kriminalistov na 1 ianvaria 1914 goda," *Otchet X obshchego sobraniia*, 34–48 (also in *Zhurnal ugolovnogo prava i protsessa*, 1913, no. 4: 136–44); "Spisok deistvitel'nykh chlenov Iuridicheskogo Obshchestva pri Imperatorskom S.-Peterburgskom Universitete so vremeni uchrezhdeniia Obshchestva," *Iuridicheskoe obshchestvo pri imperatorskom S.-Peterburgskom Universitete za dvadtsat' piat' let (1877–1902)* (St. Petersburg, 1902), 115–25; and *Ves' Peterburg na 1913 god: Adresnaia i spravochnaia kniga g. S.-Peterburga* (St. Petersburg, 1913).

77. Trainin, "Na s"ezde kriminalistov," 248.

78. Elpat'evskii, "Samoistreblenie chelovechestva," 262.

79. M. N. Gernet, "K voprosu o nakazuemosti plodoizgnaniia: Otvet moim kritikam," *Vestnik prava*, 1914, no. 16: 489.

80. Objections by the group's chairman, V. D. Nabokov, appear in *Otchet X obshchego sobraniia*, 395, and Nabokov, "Desiatyi s"ezd," 656–57; reply in Gernet, "K voprosu o nakazuemosti plodoizgnaniia," 489.

On the one side stood an alliance of liberal and socially conservative reformers who viewed the law as a repository of absolute standards, alien to any particular views, whether overtly religious values, the political aims of the absolutist state, or progressive social ideals. They argued that abortion, as a form of murder, occupied a legitimate place in the secular statutes. On the other side stood a mixture of left-leaning liberals and reform socialists who challenged the possibility of legislating such absolute distinctions and made social policy their ultimate concern.[81] No outright revolutionary or ardent reactionary entered the lists, and the range of desired practical alternatives was not wide: no one wanted to increase existing penalties;[82] no one justified abortion as a positive good;[83] all favored better welfare services, increased medical intervention, and attention to female exploitation and women's rights. Conflict arose over the role of the law and the state in regulating individual conduct, setting ethical norms, and ensuring social justice—that is, over the same political and philosophical issues with which the physicians were engaged.[84]

Members of the more radical camp pursued a number of arguments, attacking the use of repression (model 1) and invoking the right to personal self-determination (model 3).[85] Under the first rubric they challenged the very basis of existing law, denying that abortion was murder, since the fetus was incapable of independent life. An antiabortion physician who invoked the pathetic "squeak" of a four-month-old fetus being expelled from the womb as an argument in defense of the law aroused cold skepticism from his opponents, who insisted the supposedly criminal act did not have a legally recognizable object.[86] Any other claim smacked of religion or fantasy, not science, they said.[87] To condemn abortion in absolute moral terms as a form of murder, as the law's defenders did, should logically prevent them from endorsing the operation in exceptional cases for medically or socially valid motives, as some still wished to do. In terms of criminal agency (the other

81. The two figures representing this split were the liberal Kadet V. D. Nabokov (father of novelist Vladimir Nabokov), later a member of the Provisional Government who left the country after the Bolshevik revolution, and the socialist Mikhail Gernet, who stayed on to become a respected Soviet legal sociologist. On Nabokov, see N. I. Afanas'ev, *Sovremenniki* (St. Petersburg, 1909), 1: 187; on Gernet, see note 73 above.

82. Elpat'evskii, "Samoistreblenie chelovechestva," 274.

83. Trainin, "Na s"ezde kriminalistov," 259–60.

84. For a concise and subtle account of the issues at stake, see Trainin, "Na s"ezde kriminalistov," 258–61.

85. Aside from Gernet, those who spoke for decriminalization were I. B. Fuks, A. I. Gillerson, S. M. Khlytchieva, S. A. Iznar, V. N. Novikov, Oks, I. I. Torkhovskoi, A. N. Trainin, F. A. Vol'kenshtein, L. M. Zaitsev, professors V. D. Pletnev, N. N. Polianskii, and P. P. Pustoroslev, and the physician L. M. Gorovits. Their arguments are recorded in *Otchet X obshchego sobraniia*.

86. This exchange is in *Otchet X obshchego sobraniia*, 284–85, 315.

87. *Otchet X obshchego sobraniia*, 316.

necessary component of a crime) opponents of the law questioned the presumption of malicious intent. One speaker even presented abortion as a laudable moral choice reflecting the pressure of a responsible guilty conscience. Another wondered why the statute on infanticide seemed more sensitive to women's legitimate motivations than the abortion law.

Assailing the law from the social rather than the juridical perspective, some speakers on the radical side claimed the statute was unfair to the poor. With medically supervised abortion illegal, poor women were more likely than wealthy ones with personal connections to resort to underground practitioners, incurring greater physical risks and therefore also legal risks when the mishaps came before the courts. The decriminalizers insisted as well that laws must rest on strictly secular and absolute juridical principles. Moral values (let alone religious ones) had no place in modern legislation, they felt, since moral norms were not universal but varied from culture to culture and class to class. Not every nation considered abortion murder, and the attitude of the "people" or the "public," even in one's own land, was notoriously hard to pin down. That people had the absolute right to control their private affairs (in the case of women, to make their own reproductive choices) meant the state had no business regulating intimate conduct or subordinating personal behavior to national policy goals. Political motives for encouraging population growth had no place in a modern state under the rule of law (the entire congress shared this objection). In any case, they were sure that decriminalization would have no negative demographic consequences, since the instinct for motherhood was stronger than any law.[88]

Speakers on the other side of the debate, defending the retention of a modified antiabortion law, also adopted some of the positions articulated by opponents of the law—that the existing statute was unfair; that the state should offer positive inducements to motherhood in the form of social services; and that strictly medical indications were not the only valid grounds for abortion to be sanctioned by law.[89] However, they disagreed with the decriminalizers on the following points. First, all maintained that abortion was in fact murder, at least in the later stages of pregnancy, and that the law must defend the sanctity of human life. To allow exceptions, they argued, was not inconsistent with the legal recognition of mitigating circumstances. For example, it was not always a crime to kill a grown person. Second, they all attributed a moral function to criminal law, though in varying degrees. However secular, some said, the law still embodied moral values recognized

88. These same arguments also appear in Oleinik, "Prestupnyi abort," 140–44, 148–49.

89. Aside from Kulisher, those who wanted to keep abortion a crime were S. A. Drutskoi, E. A. Dubosarskii, N. S. Tagantsev, T.O. Zeilinger (a woman), professors M. P. Chubinskii, M. M. Isaev, P. I. Liublinskii, V. N. Shiriaev, A. S. Zarudnyi, and A. A. Zhizhilenko, and physicians M. N. Briukhatov, G. Gei, L. G. Lichkus, and D. O. Ott; see *Otchet X obshchego sobraniia.*

by society at large. Others went further and insisted laws must actively encourage moral behavior, both condemning murder and shaping the limits of
permissible sexual conduct. A few gravely warned that legal abortion would
lead to general debauch (in both sexual and social terms) and the collapse of
all moral standards, though even these persons refrained from speaking in
religious terms.[90] Third, speakers on this side tended to think motherhood
was in need of legal underpinning. "Women," said one, "are changing before
our very eyes," and motherhood itself was in danger of extinction.[91] Paradoxically, therefore, the side that defended women's autonomy in reproductive affairs imputed to women a natural inclination toward motherhood;
those who worried about the social consequences of such autonomy saw
motherhood as a social construct rather than a natural urge and hence as
something in need of public endorsement.

Even before the vote the eminent liberal jurist Vladimir Dmitrievich
Nabokov, who had presided over the session, charged Gernet and his followers with behavior unbecoming a scholarly gathering.[92] He feared a resolution
in favor of decriminalization would diminish the group's prestige. Too radical to affect policy decisions, it would remain without issue (*besplodna*—an odd
term to use in the context of abortion, *izgnanie ploda*).[93] Nabokov was not in
fact afraid of taking controversial stands on sexual issues. He had earlier
faulted the 1903 draft code for penalizing homosexual relations between con-
senting adults on the grounds that no one's rights or welfare were adversely
affected.[94] By contrast, in the case of abortion he maintained that individual
interests (those of the fetus) were indeed at stake since the decriminalizers
failed to confront the problem of third-trimester operations.[95] Not all liberals
agreed, however, that the legal protection of individual rights necessitated an
antiabortion statute.

Gernet, for his part, insisted that the issue was one of neither morality nor
legal principle but class politics. Worried that the woman of comfortable
means might indulge her vanity at the expense of maternal obligation, his
opponents lost sight of the real victim of the abortion laws—the poor work-

90. For the development of this conservative position on the function of the law and on the
sexually dangerous consequences of decriminalization, see Platonov, "Ob"ekt prestupleniia
izgnaniia ploda," 163–64. But even Platonov did not advocate stricter penalties: ibid., 176.

91. Isaev, in *Otchet X obshchego sobraniia*, 282.

92. Nabokov's closing remarks, in *Otchet X obshchego sobraniia*, 395.

93. Nabokov, "Desiatyi s"ezd," 666–67.

94. V. D. Nabokov, "Plotskie prestupleniia, po proektu ugolovnogo ulozheniia," *Vestnik
prava*, 1902, no. 9–10, reprinted in *Sbornik statei po ugolovnomu pravu* (St. Petersburg, 1904), 99–
125. Nabokov translated the section on homosexuality for Berlin sexologist Magnus Hirschfeld's
journal of sexual science and homosexual liberation: Vladimir V. Nabokov, "Die Homosexuali-
tät im Russischen Strafgesetzbuch," *Jahrbuch für sexuelle Zwischenstufen* 5, no. 2 (1903): 1159–71.

95. *Otchet X obshchego sobraniia*, 397.

ing woman.[96] Strictly speaking, this was not true. Those who argued for keeping abortion on the books did not necessarily deny the unfairness of the law, nor were they attempting to combat the rising incidence of the crime by making the punishment worse. Rather, as in the case of infanticide, they argued for the importance of mitigating circumstances, for attention to the particulars of each case.[97] Despite their refusal to take the final step and emancipate women from legal tutelage over their bodies, one need not doubt the sincerity of their professed interest in the fate of the poor, who were traditionally the objects of compassion and social concern, as contemporary attitudes toward infanticide made clear.

What concerned defenders of the law was the threatening implications of the third model—a weakening of the intelligentsia's moral and professional authority over the lower classes, and the acceptance of educated women as free agents and civic equals. Nabokov, for example, favored equal rights for women before the law but stopped short of endorsing women's suffrage.[98] Class politics may have been at issue in the abortion debate, but not in the sense Gernet had in mind. The antidecriminalization rhetoric suggests that symbolically abortion did not represent a problem of poor women in the traditional sense but of women who had greater resources at their command. Peasant wives, as everyone knew, continued to bear too many children and dispose of unwanted ones after they were born. It was urban working women and women of the debaters' own social milieu who ended their pregnancies before anyone was the wiser.

Abortion was the product of choice, not of desperation; it symbolized female autonomy and rendered women inaccessible to public control. It became a mass phenomenon when poor women shifted in large numbers from traditional agricultural roles to jobs in cities, losing the moral innocence they seemed to have enjoyed as village wives and daughters subject to male discipline and abuse. Meanwhile educated women were questioning their domestic obligations, some even wanting a role in public life.[99] One university student, when asked why he and his wife used contraceptive devices, said that pregnancy "removes women from political and intellectual life and prevents them from being members of society."[100] The abortion debate empha-

96. Gernet, in *Otchet X obshchego sobraniia*, 387; Gernet, "K voprosu o nakazuemosti plodoizgnaniia," 491.

97. The case for individualized application of the law was made with particular emphasis by eminent legal scholar M. P. Chubinskii, in *Otchet X obshchego sobraniia*, 376–77; see also his speech to the gynecological congress: Chubinskii, "Vopros o vykidyshe," 475.

98. Edmondson, *Feminism in Russia*, 50, 66–67.

99. The connection between increased abortion, the improved position of women in society, the movement of peasant women to the cities, and the principles of women's rights is made explicitly in Elpat'evskii, "Samoistreblenie chelovechestva," 270–71.

100. Falevich, "Itogi," no. 28: 330.

sized the dangerous consequences of women's liberation, however imperfect it might still have been.

Who was it that spoke most vociferously for reproductive freedom at the professional meetings? "Precisely the women doctors," noted a male colleague. "At both the Pirogov and the criminologists' congresses," he continued, "the women who took part were the most cultivated [*naibolee intelligentnye*], the most select of women, and, one must assume, of a mature age. There is no reason to believe they were wild fanatics or emotionally perverted types; they without doubt constituted a female intelligentsia, the defenders, to a certain degree, of women's interests."[101] They expressed the "individualism" of women recently freed from complete dependence on men by the increase in civic and economic opportunity.[102]

A 1913 short story by Ol'ga Runova called "Nothing Sacred" (*Bez zaveta*), published in the thick journal *Contemporary World*, supplied at least one anti-abortion physician with a literary portrait of women who aspired to sexual autonomy.[103] Assembled in the gynecological clinic of the fictitious Dr. Rasmussen, Runova's female characters reinforced the dominant iconography of the woman who wished to control her reproductive life: eager for pleasure, excitement, fashionable clothes, and sexual attention, they all had jobs to keep as well as husbands and lovers to entice. They used contraceptives and thoughtlessly turned to abortion, knowing it was something all women accepted, even peasant wives and respectable mothers worried about pregnant teenage daughters. Physicians, Runova realized, played a central role in women's lives by regulating their sexuality. Thus the patients both feared and idolized the powerful figure who held their sexual fate in his hands. Disabused of the political illusions he had entertained in 1905, Dr. Rasmussen punished his patients for denigrating motherhood—woman's true calling, in his view—by performing hysterectomies without their consent.

Physicians could narrow or expand the range of women's choices but ultimately could not control them. "Before becoming lawyers, judges, or professors," Rasmussen admonished, "[women] should fight for the right to be mothers."[104] The young heroine of "Nothing Sacred," the wife of a provincial railroad engineer, is briefly impressed by the doctor's traditionalistic

101. Elpat'evskii, "Samoistreblenie chelovechestva," 265.

102. Ibid., 267, 271.

103. Ol. Runova, "Bez zaveta: Rasskaz," *Sovremennyi mir*, 1913, no. 10: 29–69. Ol'ga Pavlovna Runova (née Meshcherskaia, b.1864) was one of a number of women writers in this period whose fiction described the attempts of young women to lead professionally and sexually autonomous lives. She regularly contributed fiction to the liberal and progressive journals. Her stories were collected in 1916 under the title *Lunnyi svet* (Moonlight). I would like to thank Charlotte Rosenthal for providing me with this information about Runova, which she has gathered in the course of compiling a dictionary of Russian women writers. The story is cited in Binshtok, "Dvenadtsatyi Pirogovskii s"ezd," 123.

104. Runova, "Bez zaveta," 65.

fervor but cannot renounce the lover whose attentions relieve the boredom of married life. Rasmussen believed she should return to her stolid husband and the tedium of provincial life; she ought to have resisted the allure of the big city, which she observed from the clinic window. "There the street seethed with life," Runova wrote. "The marquees of the movie houses sparkled; the trams purred as they hurried by; . . . loud and triumphant sounded the brief, sonorous tunes of the automobiles, bearing the happy and gay to unknown destinations."[105] In this world of commercial delights, artificial lighting, and hectic, unfocused movement, sexual pleasure often avoided reproductive consequences, husbands lacked authority, and even prestigious physicians found their advice ignored. The real problem with which abortion confronted physicians, as Zhbankov in his anxiety saw, was the moral and political crisis—coded in sexual terms—of educated men faced with workers and women challenging established patterns of cultural and civic control in an increasingly less predictable social and cultural environment.

105. Ibid., 47.

The Impact of World War I on Russian Women's Lives

Alfred G. Meyer

There is a small but growing literature dealing with the relationship of wars to women's lives. The topic is of considerable intrinsic interest since wars are crisis situations that affect all aspects of social life, including the sexual division of labor: as men leave for the front, women must replace them. To feed themselves and their children, the wives of breadwinners called to service must seek employment even if they have never done so before. Meanwhile, entire lines of work related to the production and distribution of goods or services associated with the peacetime economy may disappear "for the duration," spelling massive unemployment. If these include professions with a large number of women workers, the sudden unemployment affects women particularly harshly. Altogether, wars are not just military events but inevitably involve the so-called home front. With men in the field of battle, women are drawn into public life in far greater numbers than in peacetime. If the enemy manages to invade a country, many severe dislocations and hardships may result that effectively wipe out some of the differences between front and rear, with drastic consequences for the women "at home."

Wars also challenge conventional gender consciousness and self-consciousness, especially the view that men engage in action, that theirs are the heroic virtues of courage and strength, whereas women's role is to weep and to wait, to comfort the sick, the crippled, and the dying, but to refrain from participating in the great decisions and the violent action. Wars may reveal the folly of the stereotype. Many men are sensitive, averse to violence, brutality, and killing, and many women may have all the traits of the activist, the

I wish to thank June Pachuta Farris, for her generosity in sharing with me her vast bibliographic knowledge; Sara Gray, for assisting me in gathering statistical information; and the Center for Russian and East European Studies, University of Michigan, for financial support.

capable manager, or even the warrior. The shock of battle experiences can bring into the open men's sensitivity and aversion to war as well as create opportunities for women to prove themselves as fighters. The absence of men certainly gives women in many situations more autonomy than they previously enjoyed.

For women, therefore, wars are periods of extraordinary stress. Wars confront them with problems they may not have had to face before, with deprivations and disasters that often seem beyond human endurance. Yet in light of the hardships faced by the soldiers at the battlefront, the sacrifices made by women are easily slighted. Wars also provide women with unprecedented opportunities for activities from which in peacetime they are excluded and for behavior previously considered unfeminine. Hence they can facilitate progressive leaps in women's emancipation from stifling traditions and conventions. Consider the upper- or middle-class young lady who became an army nurse in World War I. Why did she join? From patriotism or some other moral compulsion, from a sense of adventure, or from a wish to escape a confining home?[1] Whatever her motives, by volunteering for such service she defied all the conventions of her late-Victorian upbringing. She entered an overwhelmingly male society. Her duties involved dealing with the naked bodies of men in their prime and with grime, pus, and blood. If she served at or near the front or in a contagious disease ward, she placed her life in just as much danger as did any soldier. She had to endure hardships and bear those of others. To show weakness was a luxury she could not afford.[2]

The adjustment to this situation is illustrated in the memoirs of an upper-class woman who served as a nurse at the front. She relates that she acquired a pair of sturdy peasant boots and a man's leather jacket, rather unladylike clothing. "With God's help," she writes, "my transformation went well, the feminine in me decreased more and more, and I did not know whether to be sad or glad about this."[3] Russian women, said the editor of a journal dealing with women's roles in the war, will face the task of seeing that after the war they maintain their places as active participants in social life; they will show that they are fearless and strong, with forceful hands and souls of steel. "We will lose our dainty looks but gain experience and strength."[4]

Dainty looks, squeamishness, and helplessness were of course traits associated with, and inculcated in, upper- and middle-class women. The deeply ingrained patriarchalism of working-class and peasant culture notwithstanding, that statement cannot be applied to lower-class women. Indeed, as I will demonstrate in this essay, the war affected Russian women in many different

1. V. V. Brusianin, *Voina, zhenshchiny i deti* (Moscow and St. Petersburg, 1917), 31–32.
2. Lidiia Zakharova, *Dnevnik sestry miloserdiia na peredovykh* (Petrograd, 1915), 116.
3. Ibid., 13.
4. A. K. Iakovleva, *Zhenshchina i voina* (1915).

ways, depending on their class, status, and even geographic location. For
instance, the hunger riots that broke out during the war (not only in Russia
but also in France, Italy, and Germany) were primarily riots by working-
class women, for reasons that will become obvious.

As the exigencies of war drew large numbers of women into the work force
and into public life, the women's movement used this mobilization as an
argument in support of its demand for equal rights as citizens. Although the
war thus served as an opportunity for feminists to press their demands, it
also presented women's movements with a profound dilemma. Throughout
Europe and North America the women's movement, for reasons that need
not be developed here, was associated with pacifism. But almost everywhere
the patriotic fervor that gripped the nations involved in the war caused a
deep split in women's organizations between those that supported the war
effort and those that were determined to fight for a peace of reconciliation—
or for any peace at all. For the former, their patriotic stance at times required
substantial adjustments of many other political attitudes—be it postponement of their demand for equal rights, the abandonment of previously professed attitudes of admiration for the culture of a country with which they
were now at war, or a shift in position on matters related to sexuality and
motherhood. Again, these dilemmas were more pronounced in the upper-
and middle-class women's movement than in that of the working class.

In this essay I will present a preliminary report based on research that has
not exhausted the available resources. I will begin with a summary of the
disruptions the war brought about, both for society as a whole and for
women in particular. This section will be followed by a discussion of changes
in the gender division of labor and of women's participation in various kinds
of volunteer work. I will end with a tentative assessment of the long-range
consequences of this episode for the role of women in Russia after 1917.

ECONOMIC AND SOCIAL IMPACT OF THE WAR

The most immediate impact of the onset of war was the drainage of manpower. In the first five months of the war Russia mobilized more than five
million men into the armed forces, and by March 1917 the number mobilized
had risen to more than 14 million—estimates vary from 14,175,000 to
14,923,000.[5] Those figures represent a staggering, sudden loss of men in their
prime, most of whom must be assumed to have been in the work force as
wage earners or agricultural producers. One author states that the number of
men called up for military service represented 36 percent of the male popula-

    5. Stanislas Kohn, *The Cost of the War to Russia: The Vital Statistics of European Russia during the
World War, 1914–1917* (New Haven, 1932), 15; *Rossiia v mirovoi voine, 1914–18 gg. (v tsifrakh)* (Moscow, 1925).

tion of working age.[6] Staggering, too, were the losses in life and limb these men suffered. The estimates again vary: figures for Russian casualties range from about 7.3 million to almost 8.5 million; they include those killed, those missing, those wounded, and those gassed.[7] But they do not seem to include military manpower losses due to illnesses not caused by enemy action except those suffering psychological breakdown (shell shock). Nor do these figures include civilian losses resulting from the war.[8]

In addition to depriving Russian society of so numerous a work force, the war necessitated profound changes in the country's economy. Entire industries came to a standstill or were drastically reduced—among them the garment industry and luxury trades of all sorts, wholesale and retail trade, commerce, and various kinds of office work. In all these trades female labor had been employed in large numbers, and these women suddenly found themselves unemployed. The virtual death of rural cottage industries, especially those working with tobacco, robbed many rural women of wages they had hitherto received. The prohibition against the sale of alcoholic beverages, decreed in August 1914, sharply lowered employment in restaurants and bars,[9] although because of increased home brewing, it probably did not appreciably curb alcoholism.

The mobilization of male breadwinners and the loss of previous employment opportunities spelled destitution for women throughout the empire. In areas close to the front there were other hardships. Massive destruction of dwellings, crops, and possessions forced millions of people to flee from the enemy with little more than the clothes on their backs. Rape seems to have been a relatively frequent occurrence in areas near the front.

The situation of hundreds of thousands of soldiers' wives was desperate. The families of reservists called up for service were entitled to a small monthly assistance, as were families of soldiers on recovery furlough after discharge from a military hospital. War widows and the families of crippled soldiers apparently were due a small pension. In some cities these inadequate welfare payments were supplemented by money from the city treasury,[10] but that too was very little and subject to the whim or the goodwill of local authorities. No such assistance was provided in the countryside or to the wives of men who had not seen peacetime service.[11] Many women therefore sought employ-

6. Lewis H. Siegelbaum, *The Politics of Industrial Mobilization in Russia, 1914–17* (London, 1983), 152.

7. Kohn, *Cost of the War to Russia,* 135

8. For additional figures on military casualties, see Zlata I. Lilina, *Soldaty tyla—zhenskii trud vo vremia i posle voiny* (Moscow, [1918?]), 83.

9. Ibid., 30; Elena Gal'perin, *Zhenshchina-krest'ianka v nyneshnei voine i reforma volostnogo samo-upravleniia* (Moscow, 1916), 8; *Zhenskii vestnik,* 1914, no. 10: 215ff.

10. *Zhenskii vestnik,* 1915, no. 3: 62–63.

11. Ibid.

ment. What kind of employment was available to them, and how well prepared were they for it?

The question is not easily answered. A small portion of women crowding
into urban employment offices may have been workers' wives who had not
previously held jobs. Many more may have been married or single women
whose jobs had disappeared or peasant women newly arrived in the city.
Others may have been unskilled women entering the labor force for the first
time; if they had work experience, it was in the village, and the habits and
skills of urban life were new to them.

An editorial from October 1914 in the feminist journal *Zhenskii vestnik* expressed the exasperation of people working in employment offices but may
also reflect unjustified middle-class condescension toward the poor. It discusses an article by a Ms. Kotliarevskaia entitled "Nerazrabotannye": "She
has taken this well-chosen term from a simple woman who, when asked what
she intends to do in the capital city, replied, 'I am a person whose potential
has remained undeveloped [*Chelovek-to ia nerazrabotannyi*].'" Kotliarevskaia
states that these days she meets such "underdeveloped" women by the hundreds in the Petrograd child welfare office, even though one cannot deny that
they possess intelligence and talent:

> What is awful and painful is that they themselves rarely are conscious of their
> own lack of development. . . . They apply for jobs as nursemaids, servants,
> seamstresses, floor sweepers, and laundresses, but they do not know how to do
> any of these things. They actually do not even know how to do laundry or wash
> floors. "I don't know how to cook, I don't know how to look after children, I
> don't know how to polish things," is what they are saying. Ninety percent of
> them are illiterate and have never held a pen in their hands. They are scared of
> everything new. . . . They are afraid to leave their children in a shelter. . . .
> They say, "When my husband comes back, he will give me hell and ask me
> why I gave the child away," or "When the children grow up, they will upbraid
> me, [asking] why I kept them in an orphanage."

The editorial adds that "underdevelopment" is not confined to women of the
lowest classes but is found also among the upper strata. Women of the intelligentsia may have some education, but they lack practical skills and are
therefore ill equipped to work where their talents may be most needed. "How
many hapless mothers are there today who until now have been living under
the tutelage of a husband but are now obliged to struggle independently for
the survival of their children?" continues the writer of the editorial. "With
horror they realize that they are not capable of doing that because they lack
the experience and the skills, so they let their hands sink down, and the
family will perish."[12]

"The war must teach women a lot. It will also have to open their eyes to

12. Ibid., 1914, no. 10: 219–20.

their condition."[13] This statement is echoed many times in women's journals, often coupled with the suggestion that the reason Russia was woefully unprepared for the many emergencies created by the war was that it had kept women and non-Russians from using their talents by denying them access to education and careers.[14] This middle-class feminist complaint should not imply that the portrait sketched above was representative of Russia's lower-class women in general; nonetheless, the difficulties that many women must have faced in finding suitable employment may in part have been the result of systematic undereducation. And surely, the writer who argued that the war had brought women out of their "pale of settlement" in the social division of labor was overoptimistic.[15]

Indeed, article after article in *Zhenskii vestnik* emphasized how poorly prepared Russian women were for any public role. They were repeatedly portrayed as without legal rights, especially against their husbands; they were said to be largely illiterate, undereducated, unskilled, helpless, fearful, and subject to fierce sexual harassment. In April 1915 the journal published an interesting imaginary sequel to Ibsen's *Doll's House*. In this story Nora cannot make it alone and is destitute. She does find work, but it is a dead-end job that neither makes use of her skills nor rewards her appropriately.[16]

The loss of male workers was most immediately and acutely evident in the villages, and it led to the rapid feminization of agricultural work. In the towns and cities the employment of women in jobs hitherto considered suitable only for men proceeded much more slowly and reluctantly. The first reports in women's journals talk about messengers, porters, mail carriers, and streetcar conductors—jobs that were taken over by women, often the wives of men who had previously held them. The hiring of women in Warsaw as truck drivers in the fall of 1914 was regarded as extraordinarily unconventional.[17] More women than previously were now employed in white-collar jobs as accountants, secretaries, telegraph operators, primary-school teachers and—very reluctantly and slowly—as secondary-school teachers. As employees of the railroad system they entered both office work and blue-collar work and by the summer of 1916 constituted 35 percent of all railroad employees. In the metalworking industry women constituted 3 percent of the work force in 1913; by April 1916 that proportion had risen to 18 percent. In the Moscow region 115,000 women were employed in industry, among them 20,000 metalworkers.[18]

As early as 1915 women began to work in mining operations under-

13. Ibid.
14. *Zhenskoe delo*, 1915, no. 23: 19–20.
15. Nikolai N. Ardashev, *Velikaia voina i zhenshchiny Rossii* (Moscow, 1915) 11.
16. *Zhenskii vestnik*, 1915, no. 4: 94.
17. *Zhenskoe delo*, 1915, no. 10: 17.
18. *Zhenskii vestnik*, 1917, no. 2: 31.

ground, as did juveniles twelve years or older; in Kharkov women joined the fire brigades. As the war dragged on, even greater numbers of women and children were hired in industries that had hitherto been almost exclusively male—munitions, chemicals, cotton, and coal. In Russian industry as a whole the proportion of women rose from 26.6 in 1914 to 43.2 percent in 1917;[19] in Petrograd the number of women in the metalworking industry increased sixfold.[20] Similar proportional increases of female labor occurred in woodworking and leatherworking.[21] Only begrudgingly did universities and polytechnical institutes, in response to the growing need for trained personnel, begin to accept female students.

At first, women were employed chiefly in the most unskilled jobs.[22] In time, however, they were set to work with machinery and in various skilled jobs, and they were found suitable. As usual, they received lower wages than did men for similar work. In some industries women were paid no more than about 35 percent of what men were paid.[23] The justifications advanced for this discrepancy have a familiar ring: whereas for men the wage work they do is their principal duty as breadwinners, for women it is supplementary or temporary activity; further, women are less well trained and change jobs more frequently. The employers got away with this discrimination because far fewer working women than men belonged to trade unions. One contemporary commentator complained that the Social Democratic movement, its leaders, and the rank-and-file workers paid little attention to the plight of women workers and made little attempt to mobilize women. Meanwhile, the exodus of working men to the military services weakened their union and party organizations.[24] So, of course, did government repression.

The interest of destitute women in work of any kind and the factory owners' interest in profits thus supported each other: for women wage work was a necessity; for management it provided economic advantages. Men working in essential industries were exempt from service at the front.[25] But that exemption made them dependent on employers, who could raise work demands and lower wages. Any working man protesting against this treatment could be sent to the army.[26] Since women had always been paid less than men, male workers regarded the employment of women as a threat and

19. S. A. Smith, *Red Petrograd* (New York, 1983), 23.
20. W. Bruce Lincoln, *Passage through Armageddon: The Russians in War and Revolution, 1914–1918* (New York, 1986), 107. See also Diane Koenker, "Urban Families, Working-Class Youth, and the 1917 Revolution in Moscow," in *The Family in Imperial Russia: New Lines of Historical Research*, ed. David L. Ransel (Urbana, Ill., 1978), 292.
21. Smith, *Red Petrograd*, 23.
22. Ibid., 24–25.
23. Lilina, *Soldaty tyla*, 44. For additional figures, see ibid., 38–42.
24. Ibid., 115–17, also 102–3.
25. Siegelbaum, *Politics of Industrial Mobilization*, 152–54.
26. Ibid., 41.

sought to eliminate it.[27] At a time when employers could punish a rebellious worker by sending him to the front, this "proletarian anti-feminism"[28] is likely to have intensified.[29]

The conditions under which women in industry worked during the war were harsh. A decree dated October 19, 1915, suspended many provisions for the protection of women and young people working in industry,[30] making it possible for women and juveniles to be employed in coal mining and similarly hazardous or heavy labor. Meanwhile, the factory inspectorate was drained of personnel, so that industrial safety laws still on the books were not enforced.[31] Industrial medical facilities, too, were depleted of whatever scant personnel they had had in peacetime; hence medical services in factories seriously deteriorated. The report about one factory, in which a single doctor handled up to five thousand ambulatory patients a month, may have been an extreme case.[32] But from many parts of the empire public-health insurance agencies (*bol'nye kassy*) reported that women in industry required medical attention more frequently than men.[33] The number of workdays lost to illness rose steeply; and again the number of women reporting ill was disproportionately high;[34] in some cases the health insurance agencies ran out of funds.[35]

It quickly became apparent that the Russian government was woefully unprepared for the disasters of the war, and the population, by now predominantly female, paid the price in many ways. Housing conditions deteriorated, especially in working-class districts;[36] inflation rose rapidly, matched by a similarly rapid fall of real wages, with resulting deficiencies in nutrition; gross inadequacies in medical services and medical supplies developed, made worse by bureaucratic interference in medical practices.[37] Another catastrophe for which the authorities were entirely unprepared was the flood of refugees pouring into the country ahead of the advancing German, Austrian, and Turkish armies. More than ten million people fled helter-skelter, often without possessions or money. They brought with them cholera, typhus, and dysentery. They had no place to go and sought shelter wherever they could

27. For instance, see Iu. Delevskii, "Bor'ba s zhenskim trudom v rabochem dvizhenii," *Russkoe bogatstvo*, August 1914.

28. Werner Thönnessen, *The Emancipation of Women: The Rise and Decline of the Women's Movement in German Social Democracy, 1863–1933* (Frankfurt, 1973).

29. Smith, *Red Petrograd*, 175–76.

30. Siegelbaum, *Politics of Industrial Mobilization*, 154.

31. *Pirogovskii s"ezd vrachei i predstavitelei organizatsii zemstv i gorodov* (Petrograd, 1916), 54.

32. Ibid., 55.

33. Ibid., 53

34. Lilina, *Soldaty tyla*, 77–80.

35. Ibid.

36. *Pirogovskii s"ezd*, 51–53.

37. Lilina, *Soldaty tyla*, 38 n. 1, 54 n. 1; Lincoln, *Passage through Armageddon*, 374; *Pirogovskii s"ezd*, 57–59, 7–8, 32.

find it; railroad stations and abandoned factory buildings became their homes. There was no provision to feed them. Often they carried no identification documents with them and hence had trouble finding work except in the countryside. They were easily exploited, and many of the women turned to prostitution. In their flight from the enemy, parents and children often became separated.[38] The fact that many of them were non-Russian and non-Orthodox doubtless made things even more difficult for them.

Children and juveniles without a parental home roaming the streets were a familiar sight even before the war; they were known as *besprizornye* (neglected ones) or *nechie deti* (nobody's children).[39] During the war their numbers increased alarmingly. Not only were they swept into the interior with the wave of refugees; many of them had been abandoned when the only adult in the home, their mother, had gone to work.[40] Other children ran away from home or from harsh masters to whom they had been given into apprenticeship. They survived by becoming newspaper vendors or joining street gangs that trained them to be burglars, pickpockets, and pimps.[41] Juvenile delinquency, crime, and prostitution spread rapidly and widely. "We are raising a whole generation of criminals," complained one women's journal,[42] and the authorities demanded that more prisons be built to house juvenile offenders. In sum, the war intensified problems related to child abandonment, neglect, and delinquency. These are matters of concern to fathers as much as to mothers; yet the war gave rise to so many women who, at least for the duration, were single mothers that in the short run it was predominantly a mothers' problem.

THE IMPACT OF THE WAR IN THE COUNTRYSIDE

The Russian village was drained of its male work force more quickly and more thoroughly than was the Russian city. Of the more than fourteen million men mobilized by 1916, ten million were peasants.[43] In the summer of 1914, 38 percent of all provinces in the empire had reported no labor shortage or only a negligible labor shortage during the harvest. By 1916 about half of the provinces registered an acute shortage of hands, and the other half reported a "medium" shortage of labor during the harvest.[44] With the men of military age gone, the people left to do the field work were women, children, and the elderly. In general, women had been used for field work in the

38. *Zhenskii vestnik*, 1916, no. 2: 32–35; *Pirogovskii s"ezd*, 32–35.
39. *Deti i voina: Sbornik statei* (Kiev, 1915), 6; also *Zhenskoe delo*, 1914, no. 10: 1–2; 15 May 1914, no. 23: 10–13.
40. *Zhenskii vestnik*, 1914, no. 10:220.
41. *Deti i voina*, 8–20.
42. *Zhenskoe delo*, 1915, no. 22:1–3.
43. Siegelbaum, *Politics of Industrial Mobilization*, 152.
44. P. B. Struve, *Food Supply in Russia during the World War* (New Haven, 1930), 301.

past, but certain tasks had been reserved for men. Women had harvested crops and, where draft animals were lacking, pulled plows. But they had not guided the plows, and they had not had a say in planning and management. Now suddenly they were obliged to do everything, and with greatly reduced resources. Not only was there a lack of hands; draft animals too had been taken away by the army. The country suffered a massive loss of meat and dairy animals due to enemy action and army requisitioning. Farm implements had largely been imported from Germany, and when they broke down, they could not be replenished. Domestic implement factories mainly switched to the production of war material. Smithies and repair shops were short of coal. The transport system was in disarray.[45] Out of 2,500 flour mills in 1916, 1,650 stood idle for lack of coal or grain.[46] Related to all these shortages, both as cause and as effect, was a rapid decline in farmed acreage. The severe inflation that began soon after August 1914 hit the countryside painfully. Everything needed, from hired hands to seed grain and draft animals, was in short supply.

The shortage of human labor was aggravated in areas close to the theaters of operation by the fact that many farm women were drafted to dig trenches and build military fortifications.[47] To be sure, the labor shortage was relieved somewhat by the use of prisoners of war as farm helpers, mostly on large estates. Estimates of the number of prisoners so employed range from 260,000 to 380,000—insignificant in any event. Of the millions of refugees that streamed into the interior, some must have found work in the countryside as well.

At a women's congress held in late April 1916 in Moscow a delegate argued in favor of a reform to recruit women into democratized *volost'* administrations. In support of her plea she cited the success with which women had managed to carry on in agriculture. She began:

> In the spring of 1915 the Kiev provincial *zemstvo* did an economic survey of the households of men called into service. A great deal of effort was devoted to this, the work was done carefully and quickly, data were collected from every district. But a year has gone by, and all this precious material lies around unprocessed, because the *zemstvo* refused to appropriate the 6,000 rubles required for this. After this should one be astonished that the survey which included 155 questions did not contain a single question about the effect of the war on the increased use of female labor in the peasant household? Those who came out against this limited themselves to pointing out that this should be taken for granted: once the men are gone, peasant women have no other recourse except to do the men's work.[48]

45. Siegelbaum, *Politics of Industrial Mobilization*, 148–51.
46. *Pirogovskii s"ezd*, 55.
47. Gal'perin, *Zhenshchina-krest'ianka v nyneshnei voine*, 8.
48. Ibid., 1–2.

In her presentation, citing a wealth of local sources from all areas of the empire, the speaker gives Russian farm women high marks for the resoluteness with which they undertook to carry on this work, for the intelligence and resourcefulness with which they went about it, and for the side effects of this effort in changing rural women's self-consciousness. According to her sources, women quickly learned all necessary operations and often showed themselves less tradition-bound than the men, hence readier to try innovative methods and up-to-date machinery. She further credited women with initiative in counseling each other and starting cooperative ventures and work teams.[49] In many places women assumed police functions and joined fire brigades. Moreover, throughout the empire reports had come in about village women's new interest in becoming literate, and some were hired as scribes in *volost'* administrations.[50] Altogether, the speaker sang the praises of those whom many Russian sophisticates had held in contempt as *temnye baby* (uneducated women): "This time of tribulation has tremendously raised the demands made on people. And these demands must be met by the dark, downtrodden [*zabitaia*] woman of the village who at the moment when our country was in need took upon herself the full weight of the great and serious cause."[51]

How generally this success of village women was appreciated is difficult to ascertain. Although feminists applauded them and used their effort as an argument to give them their due voice in organs of self-government, many a male peasant may have felt threatened by this feminization of what had been his preserve. This attitude is suggested by occasional reports that when the husband returned from the war, the old tyranny and beatings resumed.[52] They confirm the impression I have gained from many countries and different periods that in rural cultures violence against women increases when, in the course of modernization or war, women obtain opportunities for work that has hitherto been closed to them or in some other way begin to find alternatives to the traditional way of life and its pattern of subordination.

WOMEN AT THE FRONT

Many, if not all, nations have their stories and legends about heroic women who in times of war joined the ranks of the warriors, donned soldiers' uniforms, and with sword or rifle in hand fought to defend their country. During World War I women in Great Britain, France, and the United States implored their governments to let them serve in the armed forces. (I am not

---

49. See also *Zhenskii vestnik*, 1915, no. 10: 159.
50. Gal'perin, *Zhenshchina-krest'ianka v nyneshnei voine*, 9ff.
51. Ibid., 11.
52. E.g. *Zhenskii vestnik*, 1915, no. 4: 94.

aware of similar efforts by women in Germany.) In both the United States and Great Britain auxiliary services for women were in fact created, though with obvious reluctance. But these servicewomen were strictly barred from frontline or combat duty.

Russia, too, had its tales of women soldiers. Under Catherine II a women's military company was formed "from noblewomen and the daughters of the Balaklava Greeks." It seems to have been some sort of Potemkin village, created indeed by Potemkin, to impress or amuse the visiting emperor Joseph II, and it existed only for about two months.[53] A gentry woman who managed to enlist in a cavalry regiment during the Napoleonic Wars, was decorated for bravery and promoted to officer's rank by Alexander I, and retired as a cavalry captain has left a vivid account of her army career.[54] Women are said to have participated in battles during the Crimean War.

In 1914 many Russian women seem to have been eager to follow these examples. To judge by the journal accounts, they came from all classes and included princesses, peasant women, and middle-class secondary-school students. The stories one reads in these journals follow a persistent pattern. Singly or with a companion, a young woman cut off her long hair, perhaps darkened her complexion, smoked cigarettes to roughen her voice, acquired a uniform, and then tried to enlist in an army unit. In some cases the woman tried to serve in the same unit as her husband. The method of recruitment must have been extraordinarily haphazard; for even though many of these women were rejected, a surprisingly high number eventually succeeded in joining a fighting unit (though not always on the first try). Apparently, it required no more than the consent of a company or regimental commander for the volunteer to find herself enrolled in his unit.[55] Many of these female soldiers earned decorations for bravery and promotions as noncommissioned officers. Many were wounded or killed in battle. Exact numbers are impossible to ascertain; but even if they were only a few dozen, the phenomenon of women soldiers in battle does not seem to have occurred in any other country during World War I (except for a Scottish woman who fought in the ranks of the Serbian army with great distinction).

Women of wealth managed to join the army in their own fashion. Princess A. M. Shakhovskaia, a licensed pilot, was accepted as a military pilot. A wealthy woman in Kharkov donated her automobiles to the army and par-

---

53. Aleksandr Bogdanov, *Voina i zhenshchina* (Petrograd, 1914), 29–30.

54. Nadezhda Durova, *The Cavalry Maid: The Memoirs of a Woman Soldier of 1812*, trans. John Mersereau, Jr., and David Lapeza (Ann Arbor, 1988).

55. For a number of such stories, see *Zhenskoe delo* and *Zhenskii vestnik*, 1914–16; also M. Artamanov, "Devushka-dobrovolets," *Zhenskoe delo*, 1916, no. 17:8–9; Brusianin, *Voina, zhenshchiny i deti*, 104–8. See also S. I. Nikoforov, *Zhenshchiny geroi na voine, ili Znai nashikh bab!* (Odessa, 1914), about a group of peasant women who took a group of enemy soldiers prisoners.

ticipated in frontline reconnaissance on horseback and in one of her automobiles; by August 1915 she had earned three medals.[56] Russian feminists
differed sharply in their attitudes toward these warrior women. *Zhenskii vestnik*, a radical feminist journal affiliated with the progressives, expressed
approval;[57] but *Zhenskoe delo*, a "ladies'" journal, suggested that the fighting
forces were not a suitable place for women.[58] War, as one author correctly
observed, promotes courage and fear, selfishness and solidarity, hatred and
compassion, toughness and softness. It promotes heroism and brings out the
best in men, women, and children. But it also brutalizes and brings out the
worst in them.[59] In condemning Russian "amazons" for abandoning their
femininity, the editors of the journal indicated that women's calling is to be
compassionate, helping, and healing; hence when men become soldiers,
women should become nurses. Indeed, at the beginning of the war so many
women sought to serve as nurses with the troops that large numbers had to
be turned down.[60]

Theoretically, nurses were to be found no closer than three to four miles
behind the front, in mobile field hospitals; divisional and regimental aid stations were to be staffed by male physicians or physicians' assistants (*fel'd-
shery*). But in fact nurses routinely moved up to the regimental aid station and
often functioned as litter bearers in the front line. At times they were even
sent into no-man's-land between the front lines to pick up the wounded.[61]
Russian army nurses shared all the hardships of the soldiers, suffering significant casualties from enemy fire.[62]

THE RESPONSES OF PRIVILEGED WOMEN TO THE WAR

There seems to have been a broad consensus among commentators that all
the disasters of the war—labor shortages, the high number of casualties and
refugees, deficiencies in countless necessities—caught the authorities of the
empire unprepared. The official bureaucracy was ill equipped and often unwilling to deal with the many emergencies.[63] But they were also reluctant to
encourage or permit citizens' organizations to do the necessary work. They

---

56. Ardashef, *Velikaia voina i zhenshchiny Rossii*, 13; *Zhenskoe delo*, 1915, no. 24:17.

57. *Zhenskii vestnik*, 1914, no. 11:234–35; 1914, no. 9: 199.

58. *Zhenskoe delo*, 1915, no. 20:1–3; 1914, no. 21:17.

59. Brusianin, *Voina, zhenshchiny i deti*.

60. Bogdanov, *Voina i zhenshchina*.

61. Lidiia Zakharova, *Dnevnik sestry miloserdiia na peredovykh pozitsiiakh* (Petrograd, 1915), 118;
Brusianin, *Voina, zhenshchiny i deti*, 109ff; Bogdanov, *Voina i zhenshchina*, 20–23.

62. *Zhenskoe delo*, 1914, no. 20:1–3; 1915, no. 21:17. For a fictionalized account of the hazards
faced by nurses on the western front, see Helen Zenna Smith, *"Not So Quiet . . .": Stepdaughters of
War* (London, 1930).

63. *Zhenskoe delo*, 1915, no. 13:7; *Pirogovskii s"ezd*.

were loath to collaborate with the cooperative movement[64] or with the industrial business community[65] and refused permission to the Pirogov Society, an organization of Russian physicians, to hold a conference on the medical problems created by the war. The conference, originally planned for May 1915, did not manage to meet until a year later.[66] Similarly, some bureaucrats refused to let the physicians of the Union of Zemstva administer inoculations to frontline troops or establish its own hospitals for sick and wounded soldiers.[67] Furthermore, government authorities were slow to appropriate funds to cope with immediate emergencies and showed themselves reluctant to relinquish bureaucratic control over *zemstvo* and other civic organizations.[68] In complaining about this situation, many commentators deplored the fact that Russians lacked the habit of community participation or grassroots initiative (*obshchestvennaia samodeiatel'nost'*), but they also noted that the bureaucrats' distrust of all citizens' participation frustrated any attempt to solve pressing problems.[69] As a result, the tsarist government turned out to be less successful in devising and imposing systematic control over the affairs of the home front than were the governments of Germany, France, or Great Britain.[70] Citizens' volunteer efforts were also ineffective— timid, disorganized, often chaotic, and wasteful, the results pitifully inadequate.[71] The overall impression is one of much brave talk and relatively little action.

Nonetheless, citizens did respond to the emergencies that the war had created by volunteering their time, energy, and resources for a wide variety of tasks.[72] To judge by the articles in women's journals, Russian women offered their services and their resources for numerous volunteer activities—cutting bandages, sewing and knitting clothing for the troops, preparing food packages for soldiers, staffing traveler aid stations, tea rooms, soup kitchens, and similar facilities for soldiers in transit, and organizing hospitals, rest homes, shelters, orphanages, and other facilities for the wounded, the crippled, and the homeless.

As in all countries that went to war in 1914, activists in the Russian women's movement adduced these contributions that women were making to

64. *Zhenskoe delo*, 1915, no. 15:2–4.

65. Siegelbaum, *Politics of Industrial Mobilization*, 156–210.

66. *Pirogovskii s"ezd*, introduction.

67. Ibid., 5.

68. Ibid., 4–6.

69. *Zhenskoe delo*, 1915, no. 16:1–2, 17; no. 7:1–5, no. 18:1–2, 16; Bogdanov, *Voina i zhenshchina*; Siegelbaum, *Politics of Industrial Mobilization*, 210.

70. Siegelbaum, *Politics of Industrial Mobilization*, 156–58.

71. *Zhenskii vestnik*, 1915, no. 7–8:133, 135; *Zhenskoe delo*, 1916, no. 24:19; 1914, no. 23:16.

72. Vserossiiskii zemskii soiuz, *Sobranie upolnomochennykh gubernskikh zemstv v Moskve 7–18 sentiabria 1915 g.* (Moscow, 1916), 24, 31, 37, 42; *Pirogovskii s"ezd*, 14ff.

the war effort as arguments in favor of extending the rights of women in many different areas—citizenship rights, legal equality with men, access to educational institutions and careers, and sexual equality (including aid for single mothers), to mention only the most prominent ones. Arguments of this kind seem to have found little encouraging echo either among the authorities or even in the male intelligentsia.[73] A public meeting that sought to discuss the women's question more positively (some well-known speakers came out in favor of extending women's rights) was dispersed by the police.[74] Meanwhile, the Ministry of Internal Affairs announced that it was considering allowing women to be elected to city dumas,[75] and in the summer of 1915 the emperor recognized women's contributions to the war effort by creating a new medal for women, the St. Olga Medal.[76]

Once in a while the women's journals would report that yet another institution of higher learning was cautiously opening its doors to women or that some job hitherto considered a male preserve was being made available to women. At the same time, there were occasional warnings that after the war, when the men came back, there would be fierce conflict and strong attempts to return women to the home; the hymns of praise now sung to heroic women would then turn into hymns of hate.[77]

CONCLUSION

Wars and other times of national emergency promote unity where there was disunity. They force people who have hitherto fought each other to forget their enmities and join forces in a great common cause. Numerous voices in all the countries at war chimed in with this sentiment, and the women's journals of Russia joined the chorus. Many editorials suggested that the time had come to surmount class barriers and ethnic divisions.[78] But the practice often lagged far behind such preachings. My impression is that in no major country did it lag farther behind than in Russia, in contrast to what happened, say, in Germany. The German home front saw a great deal of fruitful collaboration between Social Democratic and bourgeois women's organizations—something unthinkable before 1914.[79] Some of this collaboration was encouraged, some of it discouraged, by the military authorities. In my as yet incomplete research I have seen no evidence of similar

73. *Zhenskoe delo*, 1916, no. 4:12–15.

74. Ibid., no. 7:13.

75. *Zhenskii vestnik*, 1916, no. 1:12.

76. "Znak otlichiia Sviatoi Ravnoapostol'noi Kniagini Ol'gi," *Zhenskii vestnik*, 1916, no. 1.

77. T. Druzhinina-Skodalupi, "Voina i zhenskoe dvizhenie," *Zhenskoe delo*, 1916, no. 13:1–4.

78. E.g., Bogdanov, *Voina i zhenshchina*, 31–32.

79. Marie-Elisabeth Lueders, *Das unbekannte Heer: Frauen kämpfen für Deutschland, 1914–1918* (Berlin, 1936).

class collaboration in wartime Russia, partly, of course, because the Social Democratic activists were in exile, in hiding, in prison, or in Siberia, and many of them opposed the war and therefore would have nothing to do with those who supported it.

Moreover, although brave progressives preached the bridging of class divisions and ethnic antagonisms, the war often served to exacerbate them. The national emergency may at first have promoted patriotism and self-sacrifice, but in the long run material needs encouraged blatant and aggressive selfishness. The unpreparedness and inefficiency of the bureaucracy, the reluctance to deal effectively with unprecedented emergencies, and the unwillingness to allow grass-roots initiatives to organize—all these factors helped discredit the existing system and go far in explaining the ease with which a seemingly minor food riot led to its rapid disappearance.

By the beginning of 1917 people were desperate in their attempt just to survive. They no longer expected relief from the authorities. They also no longer could expect genuine collaboration from people outside their own group or class. Some writers added that the fierce struggle for mere survival was also destroying the sense of comradeship among women workers.[80]

In reading some of the women's journals published during the war years, I have been struck by the mounting evidence of growing class division and class antagonism. People in high places behaved as if there were no needs or emergencies. People of wealth—old-established or newly-acquired through war profiteering—flaunted their riches and displayed their luxuries. *Zhenskoe delo* resolutely championed feminist demands—equal rights, access to education and careers, and an end to the double standard of sexual behavior. But its editorials opposed women joining the industrial work force and lobbied forcefully against the unionization of women workers.[81] Its fashion pages, up to the very moment of the revolution, featured female garments that were conspicuously wasteful of material; its advertisements displayed expensive cosmetics; and its housekeeping page gave recipes for pineapple desserts and other items that must have been unobtainable in wartime Russia.[82] A corset, said one of its editorials during the war, should not be bought ready-made but should always be custom-fit; and not to wear a corset at all was the mark of a provincial hick.[83] High-society life went on with its horse races, balls, theater, opera, and ballet. All this profligacy was noticed by the poor. It was lampooned in articles and cartoons in the press and may also have been obvious to those on the front.

80. *Zhenskii vestnik*, 1917, no. 2:14.
81. *Zhenskoe delo*, 1916, no. 15:15.
82. Ibid., no. 20:17.
83. Ibid., 1914, no. 20:34. For a better discussion of the life of luxury in the midst of misery, see A. Epifanskii, "Zhenskii trud v dni velikoi voiny," ibid., 1916, no. 20:8–10, and M. Stoianovskaia, "Khvosty i khvosty," ibid., 1917, no. 3:2–4.

Early in the war *Zhenskoe delo* featured a lady's letter to her husband at the front. In it the wife allowed the man vicariously to share the family's idyllic life, the nice development of the children, the wife's undaunted courage in coping and in doing her extra bit for the war effort. It was a letter designed to reassure the warrior in the field that the home front was well taken care of and that the domestic hearth he was protecting was in good shape. By the end of 1916, if not before, such morale-building letters had been replaced by letters in which women complained about their difficult lives, their loneliness, their tiredness, and their despair. At least one author I have read believes that such letters contributed significantly to the demoralization of the army, to massive desertions, and to the collapse of the tsarist regime.[84] One should not, I believe, underestimate this contribution to the revolution made by Russia's women.

84. Tat'iana Aleksinskaia, *Zhenshchina v voine i revoliutsii* (Petrograd, 1917).

The Female Form in Soviet Political Iconography, 1917–32

Elizabeth Waters

According to the catalogue of the All-Union Philatelic Exhibition held by the Commissariat of Communication in 1932, "stamps reflect the social structure, the economy, and the political order of a given country."[1] Not only do they document an epoch, notes the catalogue; they also constitute a weapon in the class struggle and as such are used by governments to further their interests: in the West they are part of a system of oppression and exploitation, and in the Soviet Union they advance the cause of liberation and socialist construction. Even a theme such as women, the catalogue maintains, at first glance completely "innocent" and "apolitical," reflects the class nature of society; Soviet stamps are "the only ones in the world to feature a working woman and peasant woman against an industrial or agricultural background rather than some titled female idler."[2]

This thesis of congruence between political iconography and political institutions is not something to which Soviet scholarship has turned its attention either at the time of the Philatelic Exhibition or subsequently. Neither stamps, nor coins, nor monuments, nor posters have been examined in any detail either as documents of an epoch or as weapons in the class struggle; still less has the meaning of the female form in such political imagery been considered. The aim here, then, is not to fill gaps or address shortcomings in any existing literature, much less to overset an established orthodoxy, but rather to begin a discussion already opened by historians and art historians working in other national cultures about the social and political significance of the female form in official iconography. That subject must be of impor-

---

1. *Filateliia: Vsesoiuznaia filatelicheskaia vystavka Narodnogo Komissariata Sviazi SSSR* (Moscow, 1932), 12.
2. Ibid., 11.

tance to those who do not share the view that "women" is, even at first glance, an innocent and apolitical category.[3]

An examination of the first fifteen years of Soviet political iconography prompts a number of questions. What was the range of female imagery used by the Bolsheviks, in what quantity were these images produced, and in which genres of political iconography did they appear? Did the location, frequency, and shape of images change over time, and if so, was this change a result of direct government intervention or of the conscious or unconscious response of artists to policy demands? Were images of women designed to be role models, ideal types of womanhood, and if so, what do they tell us about Bolshevik perceptions of gender difference?

The February revolution of 1917 swept away not only the tsarist autocracy but also its symbolic order: flags and banners were torn down, double-headed eagles wrested from their perches, and portraits of the tsar destroyed. The Bolsheviks understood the power of symbol to convey and reinforce political messages, and when they came to power in October, they were quick to develop their own system of emblems and devices: committees for the erection of monuments and the production of posters were set up, and competitions were held for the design of a state flag, a seal, an emblem, and new coins and stamps. Though the new symbols were to be aesthetically pleasing as well as politically correct, the government from the first showed itself loath to take artistic risk, choosing images that were conventional and realistic rather than avant-garde and original. Two well-known artists, members of the modernist school, Natan Alt'man and Sergei Chekhonin, were declared winners of the stamp competition organized by the Commissariat of Enlightenment (Narkompros) in 1918, but their entries were not recommended for issue;[4] designs by I. Puni for the seal of the Soviet of People's Commissars and by Sarra Lebedeva for a one-ruble coin were also rejected.[5] There was little

---

3. For a discussion of women in socialist iconography, see Eric Hobsbawm, "Man and Woman in Socialist Iconography," *History Workshop Journal*, 1978, no. 6: 121–37; Maurice Agulhon, "On Political Allegory: A Reply to Eric Hobsbawm," *History Workshop Journal*, 1979, no. 8: 167–73; S. Alexander, A. Davin, and E. Hostettler, "Labouring Women: A Reply to Eric Hobsbawm," *History Workshop Journal*, 1979, no. 8: 174–82; and M. Agulhon, *Marianne into Battle: Republican Imagery and Symbolism in France, 1789–1880* (Cambridge, 1981). The most comprehensive study of women and allegory is Marina Warner, *Monuments and Maidens: The Allegory of the Female Form* (London, 1985). Though there is as yet no Western study of Soviet iconography, a number of recent books have tackled related themes: Christel Lane, *The Rites of Rulers: Ritual in Industrial Society—the Soviet Case* (Cambridge, 1981); Nina Tumarkin, *Lenin Lives! The Lenin Cult in Soviet Russia* (Cambridge, Mass., 1983); Peter Kenez, *The Birth of the Propaganda State: Soviet Methods of Mass Mobilization, 1917–1929* (Cambridge, 1985); *Bolshevik Culture: Experiment and Order in the Russian Revolution*, ed. Abbott Gleason, Peter Kenez, and Richard Stites (Bloomington, Ind., 1985); and Richard Stites, *Revolutionary Dreams: Utopian Vision and Experimental Life in the Russian Revolution* (New York, 1989).

4. See I. Ia. Vaks, *Narisoval khudozhnik marku* (Moscow, 1978), 59–60.

5. The designs of Alt'man, Chekhonin, Puni, and Lebedeva are reproduced in P. N. Shterenberg, "Otchet o deiatel'nosti Otdela Izobrazitel'nykh Iskusstv Narkomprosa," *Izobra-*

public discussion in the party or the artistic community about why political iconography should adopt certain styles; presumably it was felt that imagery ought to be comprehensible to the masses and ought not to shock public taste or alienate public opinion. A few of the posters produced during the civil war were the work of prominent artists who made no attempt to hide their avant-garde allegiances—El Lissitsky' s *Beat the Whites with the Red Wedge* is the most famous example[6]—and some of the country's best-known sculptors, including I. Shadr, M. Manizer, and V. Mukhina, worked on public monuments. But for the most part, political iconography was not characterized either by innovation or by excellence, its producers—almost all of whom were, like other artists, male[7]—belonging to the rank and file of the profession.

Political iconography produced in the Soviet Union between 1917 and 1932 can be divided into three categories, each with its own conventions and purposes. The first category comprises the paraphernalia of statehood, such as the Soviet flag and emblem, whose design never varied. The second includes stamps, coins, and bank notes—official icons with a national circulation, whose design changed regularly, though infrequently. Public monuments and posters belong to a third category—the monuments semi-permanent and usually of unique design, the posters short-lived and mass-produced, but both having educational as well as symbolic meaning. Whereas the design employed in icons of the first category was exclusively inanimate and therefore need not be considered here, the human form was sometimes used on stamps, coins, and bank notes and almost always found in monumental and poster art; it was much more likely to be male than female.

The political iconography produced in the years immediately after 1917, when revolution and civil war gripped the country and the state propaganda and agitational system was still in the process of formation, already showed this preference for the male form. A poster by A. Aspit, *A Year of Proletarian Dictatorship*, takes as its central figures a male worker with hammer and a male peasant with sickle, shown against the background of a mass demonstration streaming through a triumphal arch.[8] A government medal minted to commemorate the second anniversary of the October revolution has on its obverse a male allegory of the new society, recognizable as such not by his clothes—in fact he wears a loincloth—but by the hammer he carries in one

---

zitel'noe iskusstvo, 1919: 50–81; see also V. Karlinskii, "Pochtovye marki RSFSR 1917–1921," *Sovetskii kollektsioner*, 1966: 25.

6. *El Lissitzky: Life, Letters, Text* (London, 1965), no. 40.

7. Several prominent members of the avant-garde were women. Many of them, including Liubov' Popova and Varvara Stepanova, were committed to applied art, designing dress fabrics and stage sets; but with the exception of Sarra Lebedeva they do not appear to have shown any interest in political iconography.

8. S. Petrova, *Plakaty strany sovetov* (Moscow, 1977).

hand and the sheaf of wheat in the other, by the factory and cornfield in the background, and by the encircling slogan "Proletarians of all countries, unite."[9] The worker in Matvei Manizer's bas-relief, executed in 1920 for the Petrovskii Passage in Moscow, is likewise male: clad in minimal classical drapery, he leans forward, one hand on his chin in the pose of Rodin's *Thinker*, the other gripping a wheel.[10] One of the first set of stamps issued by the Russian Soviet Federal Socialist Republic (RSFSR) in August 1921— the only one of the five to include a human figure—represented "Liberated Labor" as a young man stripped to the waist, sword in hand, kneeling over the slumped body of the dragon he has slain.[11]

In all these cases, and in the many more that could be cited, it was the male figure that was chosen to personify the Bolshevik regime. The reason might seem a simple one: the October revolution, after all, was largely a male event,[12] and those virtues the Bolsheviks admired—singleness of purpose and strength of will—were traditionally understood as male attributes to be represented most convincingly by the male figure. It was only natural, surely, that the symbolic order hammered into shape in the heat of a civil war should be a masculine one and that patterns of signification thus established should persist for many years. This argument has something to commend it, but it does not take into account the convention within Western art of representing liberty and the nation (in times of war as well as peace) as a woman or the practice, dating back to the eighteenth century, of deploying the female figure as an allegory of revolutionary struggle and revolutionary government. There was in existence then a distinct tradition of female iconographical representation from which the Bolsheviks could have borrowed. In fact they did borrow from it, but sparingly and not for long. A closer look at the history of the allegory in Soviet political iconography provides some clues as to the wider context in which male personification came to be preferred.

The Russian revolutionary movement had not countered the symbols of tsarist power with any elaborate iconographical system of its own. The intricately embroidered banners of some Western trade unions, for example, had

9. M. German, *Sertsem slushaia revoliutsiiu* (Leningrad, 1980), nos. 383–84.

10. *Sovetskoe izobrazitel'noe iskusstvo* (Moscow, 1977), no. 127. The platform on which the worker's right foot rests is engraved with a hammer and sickle; the instruments are not crossed, as subsequently became standard, but are positioned at some distance from each other, the mouth of the sickle facing to the right.

11. *Catalogue spécial de timbre-poste* (Paris, 1956), 32.

12. The Bolshevik party was with few exceptions led by men, and as contemporary photographs suggest, men were more frequently involved than women in the mass demonstrations and meetings of the revolutionary period. The party gave men the credit for the development of culture and society in the past as well as in the present: of the twelve monuments erected in Moscow between 1917 and 1919, only one (to Sofiia Perovskaia) commemorated a woman's contribution. See "Otchet o deiatel'nosti," 71.

no parallel in prerevolutionary Russia.[13] Such incriminating evidence would have been dangerous in a country where unions were banned or heavily policed; even after 1905 demonstrators usually carried a simple strip of red cloth, either unadorned or painted with slogans.[14] The making of a revolutionary iconography came with February 1917, and as part of this process the female allegory, which tsarist iconographers had on occasion used, was appropriated for the cause of freedom and the republic. The Petrograd Izhora Works paraded a banner decorated with a woman in national costume: a (male) worker is smashing the iron bands that chain the maiden to the rocks, and the sun shines in the background.[15] Another banner, carried in the capital on May Day, sported an imposing female figure of indeterminate derivation and a building, of equally vague lineage though smaller in scale, illustrating the slogan "All hail the socialist republic."[16] Tokens produced by the Provisional Government also featured female personifications of liberated Russia and of revolution. In one a woman dressed in national costume is holding a pennant and standing on what is apparently a pile of chains; in another she is wearing a classical tunic and a laurel wreath and carrying a banner and a shield bearing the inscriptions "All Hail the Democratic Republic" and "Free Russia"; in a third the debt to the French revolutionary tradition is clear from the woman's Phrygian cap and bared right breast.[17]

The October revolution did not immediately banish the female form from political iconography. One of the panel designs for street decorations in Petrograd to mark the first anniversary of the October revolution in 1918 included two female angels with trumpets, their allegiance to socialism clearly indicated by their red garments and the red banner one of them holds in her hand. In another such design two women in long flowing robes hover, as in a Chagall painting, above a procession, their revolutionary meaning fixed by the hammers and banners held aloft by the demonstrators.[18] The cover of a photo album on the history of the revolution published by the Third International in 1920 is illustrated by a female figure in Grecian robes, her right hand carrying a hammer, her left hand pointing forward toward the sun.[19]

13. See J. Gorman, *Banner Bright: An Illustrated History of the Banners of the British Trade Union Movement* (London, 1973).

14. Thus, paradoxically, while the banners of highly literate British workers depended for their effect largely on the visual image, in semiliterate Russia it was often the word that remained central.

15. On display at the State Museum of Revolution, Moscow, February 1988.

16. E. B. Fainshtein, *V mire otkrytki* (Moscow, 1976), 53.

17. Robert Werlich, *Russian Orders, Decorations and Medals* (Washington, 1968), 98–99, figs. 264, 258, 256.

18. German, *Serdtsem*, nos. 179, 182, 180.

19. *Proletarskoe foto*, 1932, no. 11:11.

The same year a poster issued in Ekaterinburg, a town in the Urals, depicted Soviet power as a woman who provides the people with "shelters" and "free canteens" and rids them of their enemies—the bourgeois, the general, the kulak, and the priest—reinforcing the image with the slogan "To some Soviet power is a loving mother [*rodnaia mat'*], to others a wicked step-mother."[20] The monument to the constitution erected on Soviet Square in 1918–19 is perhaps the most important example of the female allegory in Bolshevik political iconography since it was located in the very heart of the new capital and clearly intended as a lasting statement of the ideas of the new regime.[21] The monument consisted of an obelisk fronted by a sculpted figure of a woman whose extended arm and bared legs proclaim her allegorical status.[22] The trend, however, was away from representing nationhood, liberty, and revolution by the female form. In 1921 a poster could still put a raised sword in the hand of its central female figure, a working woman in contemporary dress;[23] but as nonallegorical representations became the norm, such devices were perceived as incongruous and abandoned.

A number of reasons can be suggested for this rejection of the female allegory. Changes in artistic styles and tastes cannot be discounted. Across the Western world the classical tradition, and with it the female allegory, had been under attack for many decades, and in Russia the revolution served to weaken an already precarious hold. However, male figures executed in the classical style continued to appear for a number of years: in 1927, for example, A. Matveev produced a sculptural group entitled *October*, consisting of three nude figures, identifiable as worker, peasant, and soldier only by their accoutrements—one holds a hammer, the second has a beard, and the third wears a Budennyi helmet and carries a rifle.[24] In other words, particular reasons for the rapid disappearance of the female allegory have to be distinguished from those responsible for the more gradual decline of the classical tradition as a whole. The popularity of the female allegory in the iconography of those socialist movements and parties dismissed by the Bolsheviks as reformist quite possibly redounded to its discredit. An even more serious objection was no doubt the use to which it had been put by "bourgeois," "capitalist" governments. At home there was the example of the Provisional

---

20. B. S. Butnik-Siverskii, *Sovetskii plakat, 1918–1921* (Moscow, 1960), 167, no. 270.

21. The monument, built of plaster of paris, deteriorated rapidly and was dismantled in the late 1930s. In 1954 the square was filled with a monument of an altogether different type—Iurii Dolgorukii astride a horse, commemorating the eight hundredth anniversary of Moscow; it was made of more-permanent materials and is still going strong.

22. *Istoriia russkogo iskusstva*, vol. 11 (Moscow, 1957), 149.

23. Butnik-Siverskii, *Sovetskii plakat*, no. 530.

24. *Istoriia russkogo iskusstva*, 11: 431.

Government and the White Army,[25] and abroad, during World War I, the belligerent nations had tapped the female allegory for all the martial enthusiasm and patriotic fervor it was worth.[26]

The implication for iconography of the shift in the political thinking of the Bolsheviks at the beginning of the 1920s also has to be considered. As the civil war came to a close, the realities of Russian backwardness could no longer be ignored. The economy was in ruins and the people demoralized. In the spring of 1921 the party voted for the New Economic Policy (NEP), a partial return to capitalist economic mechanisms, and came to terms with the prospect of a lengthy period of transition. Optimism gave way to caution. Visions of the socialist millennium vanished under the press of mounting problems. In Western socialist iconography the allegorical woman was usually reserved for evocation of the harmonious society of the future;[27] suitable to symbolize vague and abstract ideals of social harmony, the female form was apparently judged inadequate to convey the everday concerns and struggles of the working class. It would seem likely that in Soviet Russia this same distinction operated, enabling allegory to survive the era of war communism, when predictions of the rapid storming of the communist heaven were current, but not the transition to NEP.

The Bolsheviks had come to power in 1917 with the emancipation of women on their agenda. As Marxists, they believed that change in the ownership of the means of production signaled a transformation of social and cultural life and with it the end of women's subordination. Aleksandra Kollontai, a prominent Bolshevik and a longtime advocate of women's rights, predicted new harmonious relationships between women and men based on the equality of the sexes in economic and public life. Lenin, the leader of the party, damned the drudgery of housework and looked to its future abolition. The women's department (Zhenotdel), set up in 1919 to further the cause of female emancipation, was committed to improving women's position in the worlds of work and politics and encouraging the establishment of public amenities such as canteens and crèches that were envisaged as eventual

25. Denikin's army produced a poster, *Victim of the International*, in which Russia, in the guise of a young woman in the traditional headdress (*kokoshnik*), is threatened by "bestial commissars." See *Vystavka: Plakat i listovka grazhdanskoi voiny* (Moscow, 1926), 10–11. Several of the nations newly liberated from the Russian empire made use of the female form in their political iconography: the stamp designs of Georgia (1919–20), Latvia (1919–20), and Poland (1921) featured woman as allegory of the nation. See V. V. Popov, *Katalog i opisanie pochtovykh marok* (Kiev, 1922–23), 92, 118–20, 106.

26. See the posters reproduced in Joseph Darracott and Belinda Loftus, *First World War Posters* (London, 1972), 71; also Maurice Rickards, *Posters of the First World War* (London, 1969), nos. 26–27, 30–31, 35–38.

27. Gorman, *Banner Bright*, 122–23.

substitutes for the individual domestic economy. With the introduction of
NEP these ambitious plans were abandoned, and talk of the rapid and complete emancipation of women ceased. Nonetheless, commitment to the principle of equality for women remained, and as the regime consolidated itself, a
wide range of policies was implemented to improve the status of women.

Paradoxically, this proliferation of campaigns to "draw women into industry" and "raise the proletarian consciousness of women" may well have
served to exclude the allegorical woman from iconography. It introduced the
possibility that the female image would be interpreted as a real woman
rather than an allegory and that its presence at the center of the iconographical system would therefore be rejected as inappropriate. For all that
Bolshevik ideology proclaimed the equality of the sexes, in practice men were
expected to monopolize the revolutionary virtues of militancy and political
consciousness, and women to incline toward backwardness. For all that
women's rights were part of the Bolshevik program, they were seen as a
secondary matter, subordinate to the political and economic struggles of the
(male) working class. Bolshevik Marxism viewed change first and foremost
in terms of production: the worker and the factory took the center of the
revolutionary stage. By the same token domestic life was on the periphery: if
home and family were transformed as a by-product of revolution, well and
good; if not, there was no point in a special allocation of time and energy to
their reform, as other issues took precedence.[28]

This ordering of priorities returns us to the original proposition—that the
Bolsheviks preferred an iconography peopled by men because the revolution
was largely a male event and was perceived as such by those who commissioned and those who designed the symbols of the new regime. Unconscious
assumption of the masculine universal had not in the past prevented governments and revolutionary movements from adopting the female allegory; but
the Bolsheviks, who came to power at a time when this particular artistic
device was losing its force and in a country where it had never been strong,
were unlikely to resist the trends toward nonallegorical representation, particularly since their ideology foregrounded the factory and industrial work
and privileged the public over the private. The party was predisposed to
adopt a masculine political iconography, and circumstances conspired to
encourage that choice.

The creation of the Union of Soviet Socialist Republics (USSR) at the end
of 1922 resulted in an increase in the output of political icons as the govern-

28. For a discussion of Bolshevik ideology and government policies during the 1920s, see
Richard Stites, *The Women's Liberation Movement: Feminism, Nihilism and Bolshevism, 1860–1930*
(Princeton, 1978); Barbara Evans Clements, *Bolshevik Feminist: The Life of Aleksandra Kollontai*
(Bloomington, Ind., 1979); Beatrice Farnsworth, *Alexandra Kollontai: Socialism, Feminism and the
Bolshevik Revolution* (Stanford, 1980); W. Berelowitch, "Modèles familiaux dans la Russie des
années 1920," *L'évolution des modèles familiaux dans les pays de l'Est européen et en URSS* (Paris, 1988).

ment sought to strengthen its hold. The new Soviet coins (like the new state emblem) incorporated inanimate objects in their design, including a red star, a rising sun, and a hammer and sickle; in addition (unlike the new state emblem) they featured for the first time in the history of postrevolutionary numismatics the human figure. A modern Soviet numismatist, A. A. Shche-lokov, makes the following comment:

> For the first time . . . . coins carried images of people who with their own hands created and grew the earth's riches, instead of the profiles of emperors and empresses. Thus on the silver ruble of 1924 we see a worker and peasant stand-ing side by side. We gather from the arrangement of the figures that the worker is calling the peasant to the new life, and the rising sun is lighting the path to the industrial town.[29]

Though Shchelokov does not mention it, the worker and peasant on the silver ruble were both male, as indeed were the other "images of people" to appear on coins during the NEP period—a peasant sowing seed on a gold chervonets minted in 1923[30] and a blacksmith on a fifty-kopek piece issued between 1924 and 1927.[31] The first standard, mass issue of stamps released at the end of 1922 and the beginning of 1923 likewise dealt in "images of the people" that were exclusively male, featuring designs based on a set of three sculptures of the male figure by I. Shadr—a worker, a Red Army soldier, and a peasant.[32] Similarly, when E. Gintsburg designed his *Memorial to G. V. Plekhanov*, he took a male worker to symbolize the proletarian revolution: a man in the dress of industrial labor, with one hand on a hammer, the other holding a red flag, stands ready for action below the lectern from which "the father of Russian Marxism" is speaking to his imaginary audience.[33]

Poster art, however, on which the Bolsheviks relied heavily in their bid to gain popular support for their policies, did not confine itself to the male image. During World War I all belligerent nations had made abundant use of this medium, and Soviet Russia continued to do so even after peace had been restored, producing posters that promoted a wide variety of Bolshevik virtues from economic productivity to literacy and health. Since the posters aimed at changing lives, they sought to offer a range of images that would strike chords of recognition and empathy and inspire trust and emulation. Almost all the posters of the civil war had been addressed to men and

29. A. A. Shchelokov, *Monety v SSSR* (Moscow, 1986), 9.

30. I. G. Spassky, *The Russian Monetary System* (Amsterdam, 1967), 239. The gold chervonets was minted by the RSFSR, not the USSR.

31. Spassky, *Russian Monetary System*, 240–41; Fred Reinfeld, *Catalogue of the World's Most Popular Coins* (London, 1967), 226.

32. *Sovetskie pochtovye marki* (Moscow, 1958), 9; for a photo of the sculptures, see German, *Serdtsem*, nos. 372–74.

33. *Istoriia russkogo iskusstva* 11: 39.

peopled by men;[34] those produced during NEP were more likely to include women among the workers of the new Soviet world.[35]

One well-known poster by N. Kogout, produced in 1920, illustrates the slogan "By force of arms we have smashed the enemy. With our hands we will get bread. All hands to work. Comrades." It has two large-scale figures working an anvil against a backdrop of factories and small-scale renderings of workers.[36] Though the proletarians in the background are all male, one of the two central figures is a woman, creating the impression that the project of economic restoration is an enterprise to which both sexes contribute. The composition and the graphic design of the poster are stylized (a discarded Budennyi helmet lies at the man's feet, three rifles defy the laws of gravity to support each other in an upright position at his side; the anvil is decorated with a hammer and sickle), but the clothes the workers wear are copied faithfully from contemporary life. The woman, who is drawn in red, white, and black, wears a blouse and a long skirt covered with an industrial apron, and her hair is hidden under a red scarf. Though the apron was not to prove a prerequisite for the image of the *proletarka* (working woman), the kerchief tied at the nape of the neck and the color red became her chief iconographical attributes. Kogout's heroine was also typical in her youth and the concentration with which she grips the tongs. The Bolsheviks saw the younger generation as their natural constituency; hence the women in Soviet political iconography of the 1920s tended to be in their twenties. The dedication and militancy of these ideal women were indicated not only by the factories, banners, and slogans that surrounded them but also by their earnest gaze and pugnacious stance, arms held uncompromisingly in the air or extended insistently in the desired political direction. Never as frenzied as Marianne, the allegorical centerpiece of the French revolutionary imagery, these female figures expressed a disciplined political temperament suitable to followers of scientific socialism.

In Kogout's poster the woman takes second place to the man; it is he who occupies the dominant left side of the poster and wields the all-important hammer, chief symbol of the proletariat. He is active, she passive. The *pro-*

34. Butnik-Siverskii, *Sovetskii plakat*, has entries on 3,694 posters, fewer than forty of which are addressed to women or feature women centrally in the graphic composition.

35. Civil-war posters have been reproduced in a number of publications: *Plakaty pervykh let sovetskikh vlasti (1918–1922 gg.)* (Kazan, 1958); Butnik-Siverskii, *Sovetskii plakat*; G. Demosfenova, A. Nurok, and N. Shantyko, *Sovetskii politicheskii plakat* (Moscow, 1962); N. Baburina, *Sovetskii politicheskii plakat* (Moscow, 1984); G. Piltz, *Russland wird rot: Satirische Plakate 1918–1922* (Berlin, 1977); S. White, *The Bolshevik Poster* (New Haven, 1988). Posters from the 1920s have not received the same treatment, though the holdings in Soviet and Western libraries and archives are considerable: see, for example, the State Lenin Library, Moscow, files 2, X, X1, 1X, X11, 1X1; the State Historical Museum, Moscow, files 7, 13, 20; and the Hoover Institution Archives, Stanford University, RU/SU.

36. German, *Sertsem*, no. 64.

letarka could not by herself represent either the working class or the revolution, but she was now beginning to assume a supportive role in the drama of socialist construction. For the time being, though, it was a very minor one, and she was much more likely to figure in posters that targeted a specifically female audience and addressed topics deemed to be peculiarly the province of women. Here the female form could, and usually did, stand alone. By herself she symbolized the "emancipation of woman"—as in Adol'f Strakhov's famous poster, *8 marta*, of a serious-faced working woman against a background of factory chimneys.[37] As the Bolshevik propaganda machine consolidated and expanded its operations, so the demand for images on this theme increased. One club propagandist wrote in 1927, "We have seen carefully made posters calling on working women to attend club meetings [in which] a mighty figure of a male worker holds the text in his hand. Of course, it is male workers rather than female workers who look at it."[38] There was recognition, then, that a female audience was unlikely to pay much attention to propaganda that featured male proletarians—that women, in other words, did not always accept the male figure as the universal. The development of female icons was therefore a matter of necessity, and the Zhenotdel and a whole host of other party, government, and public organizations moved to fill this gap, producing illustrated material that addressed a female audience.[39] The red-kerchiefed *proletarka* circulated first and foremost in this new political space designated exclusively for the eyes of women.

Mothers and families had no place in the first two categories of Soviet iconography, either during the period of war communism or during NEP. The human figures featured on the coins and stamps of the new regime were there as representatives of their class, not as members of their family or kinship groups.[40] In view of the special place of the Mother of God (*bogomater'*) in the symbolic system of tsarist Russia—religious icons of the Mother and Child were carried with armies, taken on demonstrations, and used to decorate the home and the workplace as well as the church—it is hardly surprising that the Bolsheviks should have been reluctant to include mothers and families in their iconography, especially as the socialist movement provided few counterposing representations capable of linking mothers and families with revolution. The examples that did exist came almost exclusively

37. Baburina, *Sovetskii politicheskii plakat*, 49.

38. I. Blinkov, *Klubnyi i bibliotechnyi plakat* (Moscow, 1927), 98.

39. Posters targeted at a female audience were published by central and local authorities. Their artistic quality tended to be low, and many of their designers were unknown.

40. For an analysis of the instructional images of motherhood in Soviet posters, see Elizabeth Waters, "Childcare Posters and the Modernisation of Motherhood in Post-Revolutionary Russia," *Sbornik: Study Group on the Russian Revolution*, 1987, no. 13: 65–93; a more general discussion of agitational methods is in Waters, "Teaching Mothercraft in Post-Revolutionary Russia," *Australian Journal of Slavonic and East European Studies* 1, no . 2 (1987): 29–56.

from the reformist wing of the socialist movement, and their sentimental utopianism was anathema to the Bolsheviks. Further, party concern with production and class struggle, with the factory and the industrial worker, tended to relegate family and private life to the sidelines. For these same reasons mothers and families were rare characters in the poster art of the early years, appearing in only a handful of the thousands of posters produced during the civil war.

By the mid-1920s, however, the Soviet mother had followed in the foot-steps of the red-kerchiefed *proletarka* to be featured in posters that were addressed to a female audience. In this case the images were produced by organizations concerned for the health of women and children, such as the Department for the Protection of Motherhood and Infancy, and the spaces in which they circulated included clinics and maternity wards.[41] The images in these posters share certain characteristics: the mothers are drawn in a realis-tic rather than an allegorical manner, the children they carry or hold are usually infants or toddlers, and mothers and children are unaccompanied by family members, either male or female (although sometimes medical person-nel, both male and female, may be present).[42]

The realistic portrayal of the mother was prompted partly by the decline of the allegory but also, more significantly, by the didactic nature of this type of political iconography. The posters sought to convert viewers to modern methods of child care—the infant mortality rate was still extremely high in Soviet Russia—and consequently presented images with which viewers could identify. Given the absence of widespread crèche and nursery facilities and the continuing conviction on the part of government officials and the public that raising children was women's work, child care was synonymous with mothercraft. Elsewhere in the West at that time the illustrations accom-panying child care literature tended to feature the infant alone; in other words, the educational goals could be achieved without the visual repre-sentation of the mother. In coupling so insistently mother and child, the poster designers were perhaps unconsciously echoing the *bogomater'*, whose image, stripped of obvious religious symbolism, was ideologically acceptable to the authorities yet still capable of playing powerfully on the imagination of the artists and the emotions of the audience.

Why were there no husbands and fathers in these posters, no other adults apart from the occasional doctor or nurse? Was this exclusion in deference to revolutionary Marxism, which identified the family as a site of oppression,

41. The Lenin Library has a large collection of mothercraft posters (files 1–15, 16; 2. IX-1, 2, 3), as does the Hoover Institution Archives (RU/SU 904–20, 962–69, 972–75, 981–92, 1041–99, 1100–1102, 1271, 1344). A small sample of posters on motherhood protection has been published in E. M. Konius, *Puti razvitiia sovetskoi okhrany materinstva i mladenchestva (1917–1940)* (Moscow, 1954). Some of these are reproduced in Waters, "Childcare Posters."

42. Konius, *Puti razvitiia*, 168.

superstition, and religiosity and hence advocated its abolition? Such considerations were probably far from the minds of most makers and consumers of
mothercraft posters. Husbands and fathers traditionally had little to do with
child care, and their iconographical absence was rather out of respect for
social verisimilitude than out of disrespect for the "head of the family."
Although the posters were truly revolutionary in the advice they gave—the
mother should turn away from the traditional female culture of folk healing
and put herself in the hands of the doctors and their modern medicine—they
were in another sense conservative, emphasizing the continuity of the
mother-child relationship and its basis in the natural order. This reassuring
message was encoded not only in the familiar image of the mother and her
child, with its echo of the *bogomater'*, but in the composition of the poster,
which placed the mother and child outside any social context or else at a
significant distance from society and its revolutionary transformations. Two
posters produced for Motherhood and Infancy Protection Weeks in 1923, one
in Moscow, the other in Georgia, show mothers and children against a plain
background—in the Moscow poster unrelieved, in the Georgian one broken
only by stylized flowers and the branch of a tree.[43] The emblem of the Department of the Protection of Motherhood and Infancy featured in the fore-
ground a seated woman holding an infant on her lap and flanked by a toddler
and something like a palm frond (note this constant linking of women, children, and nature); she looks toward a faraway city on the horizon, which
with its factory chimneys and brightly shining sun represents the radiant
future of socialism.[44]

At the end of the 1920s socialism was declared an immediate prospect.
The ambitious industrial targets of the first five-year plan (1928–32) sparked
hopes of transforming social as well as economic life. The utopian vision of
rapid and fundamental change, suppressed since the civil war, resurfaced.
But the rhetoric of liberation masked a growing authoritarianism. With
Lenin's death in 1924 factional fighting among the Bolsheviks escalated, and
the defeat of the left and the right oppositions by the early 1930s gave Stalin
political control. Over the course of ten years the party had undergone a
change in social composition and ideological direction as the result of the
steady influx of workers and peasants for whom national development and
personal power were more important than revolutionary idealism and social-

43. Ibid., 171. This emblem was devised in 1918, when classicism and the allegory were still
in fashion; thus the woman wears long flowing robes, and the toddler at her side is cherubic and
naked.

44. For a discussion of the changes in poster production and the establishment in 1931 of a
central publishing agency, Izogiz, see E. Povolotskaia and M. Ioffe, *Tridtsat' let sovetskogo plakata*
(Moscow, 1948), 16–18; M. F. Savelov covers the same ground, remarking with approval that
in 1931–32 poster artists "emerged on the high road of socialist realism." Savelov, *Sovetskii
politicheskii plakat (1917–1932)* (Moscow, 1956), 15.

ist transformation. For the communists of this new generation, democracy was (despite the rhetoric) an expendable luxury, and they applauded the centralization of authority and the emergence of a bureaucratic elite.

Stricter party control was established over every aspect of life, including art. All professional groups and associations were disbanded and a single, government-controlled union introduced, its inauguration accompanied by the proclamation of a single, government-backed aesthetic ideal—socialist realism. As a result, priority was given to party supervision over the production of political iconography, and "petty-bourgeois" and "alien" tendencies in the past and present performance of iconographers were discovered and displayed for criticism. Persons unable or unwilling to comply with the new guidelines may have lost their jobs, but it is doubtful whether that happened often. Even under NEP the producers of political icons, for the most part unknown artists, were content to follow orders from the party and government bodies who hired them. And because political iconography had long ceased to attract the talented and experimental, the new aesthetic orthodoxy did not entail any fundamental artistic reorientation.

Certainly the iconographical representation of women did not change much during the period of the first five-year plan. The red-scarfed, youthful *proletarka*, executed in a realistic style, continued to be the central image. Indeed, she became a far more common sight. This prominence was due in part to the sharp rise in demand for political iconography, especially posters, as the government sought by every means, including the visual image, to rally support for its political and economic policies. It also shows that the red-kerchiefed *proletarka* as well as her rural sister, previously confined mainly to posters addressed to a female audience, had begun to move up from their ghetto into the wider public arena. This shift may come as a surprise, since historical studies have shown that in this period, despite the talk of female emancipation, the party gave the woman question an even lower priority than before: the Zhenotdel was closed down in 1930 (on the grounds, ostensibly, that women had become the equals of men and hence were in no further need of a special organization), and public discussion of women's rights ceased.

The greater iconographic visibility of women in an era of failing commitment to sexual equality is explained largely by economic imperatives. Government policies aimed to liberate women not for their own sakes but for the good of production.[45] The high targets set by the industrialization plan required the massive influx of women into the work force. "Wives of workers. Housewives. To the machine. To the construction site. The Urals needs 230,000 women in production," reads the text of one poster from this

45. Stites, *Women's Liberation Movement*, 386–91; Gail Warshofsky Lapidus, *Women in Soviet Society: Equality, Development and Social Change* (Berkeley and Los Angeles, 1978), 95–122.

period.[46] As far as is known, the increased frequency and new location of the female image were not the result of specific directives from above. Rather, in an era when hundreds of thousands of women were for the first time entering paid employment, political iconography was obliged to devote more attention to its female audience to achieve its agitational aims. Moreover, consumers and producers of icons were no doubt influenced, consciously and unconsciously, by the political rhetoric of the time, with its promise of socialist achievement and sexual equality.

A scarf produced by the First Textile Printing Works in Moscow in 1932 to mark the anniversary of Soviet power provides a good illustration of how women's participation in socialist construction was perceived to have changed since the revolution. The year 1917 is represented by a central group of male soldiers and by clusters of men and weapons in two of its corners; by contrast, 1932 is personified by a central group of men and women demonstrating with banners and by corner designs of women in kerchiefs and men in cloth caps.[47] Since the working woman's participation in the national economy was considered a matter of importance for society as a whole, the subject matter of posters in which she appeared was no longer limited to "women's" campaigns. Her image appeared for the first time on icons of the second category. Though coins continued to be the exclusive preserve of the male image—the only new coin minted during the first five-year plan to include a human figure featured a male worker with a shield[48]—the female form made its first philatelic appearance in 1929 with the issue of four stamps. Two, a two-kopek and a thirty-kopek stamp, bear the head and shoulders of a *proletarka*, identifiable by her kerchief; the thirty-kopek stamp places her against a background of factory chimneys. The other two, a four-kopek and a fifty-kopek stamp, show a collective-farm worker who has her scarf tied urban-style at the nape of her neck but wears a blouse and sarafan; the fifty-kopek stamp has a rural backdrop.[49] The fact that none of the dozens of stamps issued up to that time by the Soviet government (more than three hundred by the beginning of 1929) included a woman in their design had begun to draw comment. The satirical magazine *Chudak* published the humorous story of a young man who managed to jump to the head of a line of women queuing for stamps by arguing that their exclusively male images gave him precedence.[50] Was it not strange, commented the author of a book about the graphics and subject matter of Soviet stamps, that the first country in the world to give women equal rights with men should for twelve years ignore women so completely? He was pleased that finally this injustice had

46. State Historical Museum, otdel izo, file 21 11808/73071.
47. State Historical Museum, otdel tkani, 1932, 74500.
48. Spassky, *Russian Monetary System*, 246; Shchelokov, *Monety v SSSR*, 28.
49. Stanley Gibbons, *Europe 3: Stamp Catalogue* (London, 1972), 108.
50. See D. B. Valeron, *Grafika i tematika sovetskikh pochtovykh marok* (Moscow, 1929), 3.

been redressed (though he had not a good word to say for the artistic design of the stamps—the working woman was too static, the peasant woman too theatrical).[51] The Order of the Badge of Honor, instituted in November 1935 for achievements in science, the economy, and the military, also recognized the government's official commitment to sexual equality, becoming the first medal of its kind to include a female figure—a woman striding out in the company of a man beneath a red star and against a backdrop of banners.[52]

The male and female couple was a common theme in the political iconography of this period. The most famous was Vera Mukhina's statue, commissioned for the Soviet pavilion at the Paris Exhibition of 1937, consisting of two gigantic figures, shoulder to shoulder, straining forward, hands reaching toward the sky, holding high the symbols of government—one the hammer, the other the sickle.[53] The statue was subsequently reerected in Moscow at the entrance to the Exhibition of Economic Achievement and over the years became one of the most familiar of Soviet images, appearing on stamps (1938) and coins (1967) and daily flickering on countless cinema screens wherever a Mosfilm product was on display. The statue apparently affirms the equality of the sexes proclaimed by the Soviet government and enshrined in the 1936 constitution: the man may occupy the dominant left side of the statue, but the two figures are of (roughly) equal size and engaged in identical action, the only difference being that the man has his left arm raised, the woman her right. However, its real purpose, made clear by its title, *The Industrial Worker and the Collective-Farm Worker* (*Rabochii i kolkhoznitsa*), is a celebration of the alliance of the working class and the peasantry. The female image is undoubtedly a strong one, but the couple in one important sense undermines rather than affirms sexual equality because a secondary role is assigned to the woman, not by the arrangement of the figures, but by the allocation of symbols—the sickle to the woman, the hammer to the man. Though peasants still constituted the vast majority of the population, they took second place according to Soviet ideology in the struggle to build communism.[54]

The twinning of male worker and female peasant to symbolize the Soviet nation, for which precedent had been set as early as the civil war, now for a number of reasons became more common. First, there was the problem of visual differentiation: the collectivized peasant was supposed to be more modern than his predecessor in every respect including appearance and as a

51. Ibid., 3–19.

52. Werlich, *Russian Orders*, 112.

53. *Sovetskoe izobrazitel'noe iskusstvo*, no. 191. Vera Mukhina was one of the few prominent women in the Soviet art world of the 1930s. The two assistants she employed to work with her on *The Industrial Worker and the Collective Farm Worker* were also women, N. Zelenskaia and Z. Ivanova. See V. Mukhina, *A Sculptor's Thoughts* (Moscow, 1957), 15.

54. This class hierarchy ruled out the reversal of the sex roles—the representation of the proletariat by a woman and the peasantry by a man.

result became less easily distinguished from his brother worker. Second, it was easier to challenge the male peasant's monopoly on visual imagery now that his political and economic position in the countryside had been undermined. In the past his position as head of the household in all economic and political dealings with the regime had been mirrored by his iconographical visibility, even at times such as the Volga famine of 1921–22, when the modern expectation would be for women and children to be kept in sharpest focus.[55] In depriving the peasant of his former power, collectivization opened the way for the "feminization" of the peasantry.

The peasant woman did not take her place in the Soviet couple purely by default. Throughout the 1920s her iconographical range had been expanded beyond the dejected and the downtrodden. The Zhenotdel, in the course of campaigning in the countryside for literacy and welfare rights, had produced and popularized visual images that stressed woman's enthusiasm for the commonweal and her human dignity. These images, like those of the working woman and mother, had circulated largely in the female space. During the collectivization campaigns the active, politically-conscious peasant woman sprang to public visibility, perhaps because in many areas female resistance to government policies was fierce.[56] The ancient connection between the woman and the land—Mother Earth—is also likely to have provided justification for the frequent female personification of the peasantry.

The Soviet mother was slow to join the working woman and peasant woman in the public iconographical arena. Posters on child care, previously confined to the walls of the women's clinics, were now shown in public places,[57] but the higher reaches of the iconographical system still remained closed to images of mother and child. It was not until 1938 that the first stamp on this theme was issued[58] and not until the 1940s that the Order of the Glory of Motherhood—a convex medallion, oval in shape and silver in color, of a woman holding a child—was instituted.[59]

---

55. D. S. Moor's famous poster *Pomogi'* shows a single suffering figure of an elderly male peasant. See *Sovetskoe izobrazitel'noe iskusstvo*, no. 233. Of the stamps issued in aid of the famine only one depicts a family grouping with mother and children: see Gibbons, *Europe 3*, 98–99.

56. Examples of posters featuring the peasant woman as political subject include *Idi v kolkhoz* (1929–1930) and M. Cheremykh's *Krest'ianka, idi v kolkhoz* (1930), both reproduced in *Plakaty pervykh let*, 92–93. (A copy of the second poster is also held in the collection of the School of Soviet and East European Studies, London). For a discussion of women's opposition to collectivization, see Lynne Viola, "*Bab'i Bunty* and Peasant Women's Protest during Collectivization," *Russian Review* 45 (1986): 23–42.

57. W. A. Rukeyser, *Working for the Soviets: An American Engineer in Russia* (London, 1932), 83.

58. See Gibbons, *Europe 3*, 117. Earlier, in 1926 and 1927, three stamps with children (one of them the young Lenin) were issued in aid of homeless youth (*besprizornye*), *Catalogue special*, 43; in 1929 the First All-Union Pioneer meeting was commemorated, and the following year there was a series of stamps portraying *besprizornye* at work in industry and agriculture; see *Sovetskie pochtovye marki*, 14–15.

59. Werlich, *Russian Orders*, 115.

The female form, though never as visible as its male counterpart, was a staple ingredient of Soviet political iconography from the revolution to the mid-1930s. The shape it assumed and the frequency with which it was used varied over time and according to category. The periodization traditionally employed by historians in their analysis of Soviet history—war communism, NEP, the first five-year plan—is indispensable in any examination of the changing nature of iconography: female allegory fades at the beginning of the 1920s, and the *proletarka* acquires public prominence and official status at the end of the decade. At the same time a history of women in iconography does not always fit easily into the existing narrative of events. Whereas allegory changed its meaning in 1917, conventions of form had a history that stretched back to the early nineteenth century and beyond; the Soviet representations of motherhood echoed the religious icon; and the images of working women remained unaffected by the rise of the Stalinist system.

The relationship between imagery and government policy was complex. Images did not parallel official ideals and policies directly or according to any neat pattern: during the civil war the economy's need for female labor did not translate into images of women working; during the five-year plan it did. Visibility in iconography was not a necessary consequence of volubility of government support for emancipation: during the utopian era of war communism the female figure was relatively rare, whereas in the early 1930s, precisely at the time when the Zhenotdel was closed down, it became more widespread.

Nevertheless, images were never arbitrary, nor were they ever determined solely by artistic considerations. Political iconography presents a fascinating barometer of official attitudes about women. The image makers and image controllers, Bolshevik artists and party functionaries, were disappointingly unreflective about the meaning of the female form, but the unself-conscious images that were produced in this period speak volumes about their assumptions about gender difference. The party promised to transform society, to make "the last come first," and iconography accordingly replaced the tsar with representatives of the laboring classes. But the world was turned upside down only in part. Whereas images mounted a concerted assault on the class system, the challenge to the gender order was far less comprehensive. The male figure remained the universal—the symbol of the proletariat, revolution, and the victory of socialism. The female form, once allegory was abandoned, played only a supportive role, standing for women or the peasantry, subordinate social groups. Woman was the Other, or rather Others, since her personality was split: as working woman, she could aspire to political consciousness and public profile; as mother, she was the child of nature, the outsider, forever distanced from social action. Undoubtedly the catalogue of the All-Union Philatelic Exhibition was right to see political icons as a document of an epoch, but the new world they prefigured was not as brave as its authors assumed.

Women, Abortion, and the State, 1917–36

Wendy Goldman

In the spring of 1920, when abortion was still prohibited in the Soviet Union, Nikolai Semashko, the commissar of health, received a deluge of letters concerning the frightening popularity of the practice. One worker from a factory staffed largely by young women wrote, "Within the past six months, among 100 to 150 young people under age twenty-five, I have seen 15 to 20 percent of them doing abortions without a doctor's help. They simply use household products: they drink bleach and other poisonous mixtures."[1] The letters, from party members as well as workers, indicated that the prohibition against abortion was a scant deterrent to a woman who did not want to bear a child. Women readily chose to break the law rather than face the enormous consequences of an unwanted child.

That fall, in November 1920, the commissariats of Health and Justice (NKZdrav and NKIu) legalized abortion. Their decree acknowledged that repression was useless: it simply drove desperate women underground, where they were mutilated by "greedy and ignorant" abortionists. The decree permitted women free abortions in hospitals, but only if performed by doctors; *babki* (peasant midwives) or professional midwives would face criminal sanctions. Admitting that the harsh conditions of life often made pregnancy and child rearing difficult, the decree offered women a safe, legal, financially just alternative to underground abortion.[2] The Soviet Union thus became the first country in the world to give women access to legal, publicly funded termination of pregnancy.

Despite the enormous freedom the decree granted women, it never recognized abortion as a woman's right. Officials in the commissariats of Health

1. N. Semashko, "Eshche o bol'nom voprose," *Kommunistka*, 1920, no. 3–4: 19, 20.
2. *Okhrana zhenshchiny-materi v ugolovnom zakone*, ed. Ia. A. Perel' (Moscow, Leningrad, 1932), 32.

and Justice viewed abortion less as a choice than as a necessity. Labeling abortion an evil, they believed that in the future, with sufficient food, housing child care, and medical services, women would have no reason to reject motherhood.[3] The decree, strongly shaped by prevailing patriarchal notions of motherhood, showed little awareness of the limits children placed on women's ability, even under the most prosperous conditions, to enter public life. Official ideology offered maternity clinics, crèches, and day-care centers as the solution to the conflict between work and motherhood. But a woman's basic right to control fertility—the fundamental notion of choice—received little consideration as such. Even Aleksandra Kollontai, a powerful champion of women's liberation, believed that motherhood was "not a private matter." She argued that the need for abortion would disappear once child care was available and women understood "that *childbirth is a social obligation.*"[4]

Less than two decades later, in June 1936, amid a rush of propaganda, abortion was outlawed. Officials touted new advances in the standard of living and insisted that women no longer needed abortion. Stressing the temporary nature of the earlier legalization, they proclaimed that every woman could now realize her right to be a mother. Those who performed the operation were liable to a minimum of two years in prison, and even women who received abortions were subject to high fines after the first offense. The new law offered incentives for childbearing by providing stipends for new mothers, large bonuses for women with many children, and longer maternity leaves for white-collar women, and it increased the number of maternity clinics, child care institutions, and milk kitchens. In addition to its pronatalist measures, it made divorce harder to get and increased the criminal penalties for men who refused to pay alimony or child support. The prohibition against abortion was only part of a larger campaign to promote "family responsibility."[5]

Why did the state prohibit abortion? What accounted for the reversal in official ideology and the new emphasis on motherhood? Some historians point to the state's concern over the falling birthrate, and others see the reversal as part of the larger Stalinist attack on the ideals of the 1920s. Yet little research has been done to substantiate these claims. No one has systematically studied the vast amount of statistical data on abortion in that

3. Ibid.
4. Alexandra Kollontai, *Selected Writings*, ed. Alix Holt (Westport, Conn. 1977), 145, 149. Italics Kollontai's.
5. *Proekt postanovleniia TsIK i SNK SSR o zapreshchenii abortov, uvelechenii material'noi pomoshchi rozhnitsam, ustanovlenii gosudarstvennoi pomoshchi mnogosemeinym, rasshirenii seti rodil'nykh domov, detskikh iaslei, detskikh sadov, usilenii ugolovnogo nakazaniia za neplatezh alimentov, i o nekotorykh izmeneniiakh v zakonodatel'stve o razvodakh* (Moscow, 1936); G. A. Baksht, "K voprosu o zapreshchenii abortov," *Sovetskii vrachebnyi zhurnal*, 1936, no. 12: 884.

period. This will draw on this untapped material to construct a sociological profile of the women who used abortion—their geographical distribution, personal motivation, social background, marital status, family size, and previous use of abortion. It argues that abortion was one of the most popular methods for limiting fertility in the 1920s and 1930s and that it significantly depressed the birthrate. The prohibition was an attack on all Soviet women, but it had the greatest impact on young, urban, working-class and white-collar women who were already mothers of small families. For this group—the mainstay of the Soviet regime, courted and exalted by Soviet propaganda—constituted the great majority of abortion patients.

CONTRACEPTION

The role of abortion in women's lives must be understood in the context of the state's approach to reproduction, the availability of birth control devices, and women's own attitudes toward contraception. In the 1920s and 1930s the issue of contraception was markedly absent from almost all the juridical, theoretical, and programmatic discussions of women's liberation. Jurists who vigorously promoted women's emancipation through law scarcely mentioned birth control, and women party leaders such as Inessa Armand and Nadezhda Krupskaia rarely raised the issue. Kollontai had little to say about contraception in her extensive writing on women, maternity, and sexuality.[6] Moreover, basic birth control devices such as condoms and diaphragms were unavailable to most women.

Yet despite the resounding silence of the leadership, the idea and the practice of contraception were not foreign to Soviet women. Some Soviet demographers estimate that a significant share of women, peasants among them, practiced some form of contraception in the 1920s, most commonly coitus interruptus.[7] There were stirrings of interest at the local level among women's activists and doctors as well as a desperate eagerness among women themselves to find a safe, painless, and reliable means of limiting birth. Vera Lebedeva, the head of the Department for the Protection of Motherhood and Infancy (OMM), under the Commissariat of Health, made a rare appeal for reproductive freedom when she affirmed "the rationalization of sexuality, where a person wants to be a master just as in other areas."[8]

By the mid-1920s doctors constituted an organized, knowledgeable group that favored contraception. Medical journals were filled with pleas for con-

6. On contraception, see Kollontai, *Selected Writings*, 118, 212; Barbara Evans Clements, *Bolshevik Feminist: The Life of Aleksandra Kollontai* (Bloomington, Ind., 1979), 58–59; Janet Evans, "The Communist Party of the Soviet Union and the Women's Question: The Case of the 1936 Decree 'In Defense of Mother and Child,'" *Journal of Contemporary History* 16 (1981): 768.

7. A. G. Vishnevskii and A. G. Volkov, *Vosproizvodstvo naseleniia SSSR* (Moscow, 1983), 174.

8. See Lebedeva's introduction to A. B. Gens, *Abort v derevne* (Moscow, 1926), 7.

traception to reduce the widespread reliance on abortion. The Kiev Conference of Midwives and Gynecologists in 1927 declared that contraception was "a vital, moral measure at the present time" and should be incorporated into the practice of midwifery. Some doctors considered contraception an evil, but, as one writer noted, it was less evil than abortion.[9] Doctors and OMM officials became increasingly aware of the desperate need for contraception as they encountered the crippling consequences of repeated abortions. By the mid-1920s OMM had officially proclaimed that birth control information should be dispensed in all clinics and gynecological stations as an "essential means" of struggle against the increase in abortion.[10]

Women themselves—often illiterate, provincial, and "backward"—far outstripped party and state officials in their understanding of the relationship between reproductive control and liberation. Zhenotdel representatives in the rural villages reported that "women thirst for lectures on abortion and contraception."[11] The head of a Briansk hospital for railroad workers and their families noted that abortion patients begged the doctors for help: "Give us the means to prevent pregnancy, and we will stop showing up in the hospital."[12]

Women tended to rely for contraception on traditional folk practices such as coitus interruptus, douching, and barrier methods. When all else failed, they resorted to abortion, legal and otherwise. A survey of 1,087 peasant women in twenty-one villages in Smolensk Province revealed that almost half used some form of birth control: 467 practiced coitus interruptus, and 22 douched. One woman had her partner use a condom, another used a cervical cap (*kolpachok*), and four used small balls (*globuly*) to block the cervix. Despite the traditional peasant emphasis on large families, more than one out of every four of these women admitted to a legal or illegal abortion, making abortion the second most popular form of birth control after coitus interruptus.[13]

Out of two hundred women in a Saratov abortion ward, 40 percent claimed some knowledge of contraception, and 18 percent actually practiced it. Douching with water or vinegar was the most popular method, but women also injected iodine, applied alum and powdered quinine, and used balls or glycerin-soaked tampons to block the cervix. One woman even used a

9. M. F. Levi, "Itogi legalizatsii aborta v SSSR skvoz' prizmu burzhuaznoi nauki," *Ginekologiia i akusherstvo*, 1932, no. 2: 162.

10. S. S. Iakubson, "Puti okhrany materinstva i mladenchestva," *Sovetskaia vrachebnaia gazeta*, 1933, no. 21: 1016.

11. Gens, *Abort v derevne*, 45.

12. N. M. Emel'ianov, "K voprosu o roste iskusstvennogo aborta i padenii rozhdaemosti," *Ginekologiia i akusherstvo*, 1927, no. 5: 430.

13. B. Ressin, "Opyt obsledovaniia polovoi sfery zhenshchin v kolkhoze," *Ginekologiia i akusherstvo*, 1930, no. 3: 346, 344.

mushroom.[14] In a Briansk hospital most women either knew of or practiced coitus interruptus. Some used small balls (*shariki*) or water or vinegar douches. Many explained that it was frequently impossible to use any method but coitus interruptus because of living conditions (*semeinaia obstanovka*).[15] When an entire family shared a small hut, room, or curtained-off corner with no indoor plumbing, it was not easy to douche after intercourse. Only one study of 788 spinners and weavers in Moscow Province concluded that women did not use any form of contraception.[16]

Condoms and diaphragms, simple to produce and use, were almost impossible to get in the 1920s and 1930s because of the rubber shortage. Tanya Matthews, a Russian émigré in Great Britain, recalled her doctor's comments on contraception in 1933: "Things are difficult now. There are pills, but they do more harm than good. Best thing is rubber, but it is as hard to find as a pair of galoshes. We have no preventatives of any kind now."[17]

Although the data on contraception are limited, it appears that significant numbers of rural and urban women were aware of contraception, eager for information, and practicing coitus interruptus for want of a better method. Under those circumstances abortion played a critical role in enabling women to limit fertility. One Soviet demographer notes that at the end of the 1920s even in a major city like Leningrad abortion, not contraception, played the primary role in limiting births.[18]

OBTAINING A LEGAL ABORTION

The 1920 decree made the hitherto hidden needs of women visible as large numbers of women overwhelmed Soviet medical facilities with their demands for abortion. Several provincial departments of OMM tried to eliminate applicants by granting abortion for medical reasons only.[19] In January 1924 the Commissariat of Health attempted to impose some order on local officials. Each provincial OMM was instructed to establish a commission composed of a doctor and representatives from OMM and the Zhenotdel to interview women requesting abortion. The commissions were to give first priority to women with medical problems and second priority to healthy women with social insurance. The families of white-collar and blue-collar workers received insurance, but students, servants, artisans, members of the free profes-

14. L. E. Shiflinger, "Iskusstvennyi abort," *Ginekologiia i akusherstvo*, 1927, no. 1: 66.

15. Emel'ianov, "K voprosu o roste," 430.

16. G. A. Ianovitskii, "Rezul'taty ginekologicheskogo obsledovaniia rabotnits tekstil'noi fabriki im. Oktiabr'skoi Revoliutsii," *Ginekologiia i akusherstvo*, 1929, no. 3: 331.

17. Tanya Matthews, *Russian Child and Russian Wife* (London, 1949), 103–4.

18. V. V. Paevskii, *Voprosy demograficheskoi i meditsinskoi statistiki* (Moscow, 1970), 340, quoted in Vishnevskii and Volkov, *Vosproizvodstvo*, 174.

19. I. Gromov, "Pravo ne byt' mater'iu," *Sud idet!* 1924, no. 2: 108.

sions (such as writers and artists), peasants, and the unregistered unemployed did not. Among those with insurance coverage, single unemployed women registered with the Labor Exchange got first priority for abortion, followed by single working women with at least one child, married working women with three or more children, working-class housewives with three or more children, and all remaining women who were insured. Uninsured women were to be admitted after the insured, in the same order. Peasant women were considered on an equal basis with working-class housewives. The remainder of the uninsured and the unregistered unemployed were last in line for the privilege of abortion.[20]

The list was formulated according to a hierarchy based on class and social vulnerability. The unmarried and the unemployed received top priority, and workers received preference over every other social group. This list indicated which women the state considered most worthy of abortion, privileging waged labor and need. The vital labor contribution of peasant women was ignored because they did not work for wages; peasants were classified with working-class housewives. The unmarried and the unemployed, both socially needy groups, had the greatest right to abortion, followed by working-class women with large families. Married women with one or two children had a less powerful claim to make on the state's time and resources. In that sense the priority lists corresponded perfectly to the language of the 1920 decree: in the eyes of the state women needed abortion because of unemployment, social vulnerability, and poverty, and it allocated its services accordingly.

Once a woman received permission for an abortion, the operation itself was relatively safe. Women rarely died from a hospital abortion. In Moscow abortion was safer than giving birth: a woman's chances of dying from infection after childbirth were between 60 and 120 times higher than after an abortion.[21] But between 15 and 30 percent of women did experience potentially serious complications, including bleeding, inflammation, fever, and a greater risk of future miscarriage.[22] Poverty, malnutrition, and lack of medical attention left the female population in generally poor health. Unchecked venereal diseases, untreated vaginal infections, and repeated legal and illegal abortions multiplied the risks of the operation.[23]

20. Perel', *Okrana zhenshchiny-materi*, 33; Gens, *Abort v derevne*, 14; "Zakonoproekt o vzaimnom strakhovanii materinstva," *Rabochii sud*, 1926, no. 11: 765.

21. Levi, "Itogi legalizatsii aborta," 159; A. S. Madzhuginskii, "O smertnosti posle operatsii iskusstvennogo aborta," *Ginekologiia i akusherstvo*, 1933, no. 3: 60–61.

22. Ia. I . Rusin, "O pozdnem samoproizvol'nom aborte," *Ginekologiia i akusherstvo*, 1930, nos. 4–5: 565; M. Mironov, "Obzory, retsenzii i referaty," *Vrachebnoe delo*, 1927, no. 10: 773; "Vos'moi Vsesoiuznyi s"ezd akusherov i ginekologov v Kieve, 21–26 maia, 1928," *Ginekologiia i akusherstvo*, 1928, no. 4: 474, 483. Hereafter cited as "Vos'moi s"ezd."

23. On women's gynecological health, see Ressin, "Opyt issledovaniia," and Ianovitskii, "Rezul'taty." A. S. Madzhuginskii, "Dannye patronazhnogo izucheniia vliianiia iskusstvennogo vykidysha na zdorov'e zhenshchiny," *Ginekologiia i akusherstvo*, 1930, nos. 4–5: 509.

The operation itself, although safe, was excruciatingly painful. It lasted at least five to ten minutes and was performed without anesthetic. Doctors used the method of dilation and curettage, inserting an instrument through the cervix and scraping the walls of the uterus. One woman described a terrifying wait in a hospital before her abortion. She watched the doors of the operating room open every fifteen minutes as the women were wheeled out on stretchers. "Their faces looked like greenish white masks with beads of perspiration on their foreheads." After her own abortion was over, she weakly asked the doctor, "Why didn't you tell me you would do it without anesthetic?" He coolly replied, "We are saving ether for more important operations. Abortion is nothing; women stand it easily. Now that you know, it's a good lesson to you, too."[24] Some doctors, reluctant to perform abortions at all, may have seen the pain as a positive deterrent to women who "sought to escape pregnancy."[25]

DEMOGRAPHICS OF LEGAL ABORTION

Legal abortion was overwhelmingly an urban phenomenon. Women in the cities had greater access to medical care than peasant women, who often had to travel many miles to reach the nearest doctor or hospital. In the early 1920s rural medical personnel did little to inform peasant women about their right to abortion, although many performed abortions on request. The absence of legal abortion in the countryside was a result of the general scarcity of health care services. There were few hospitals before the revolution, and by 1921 many of these had ceased to function. Those that remained lacked beds, linens, medicine, and even basic instruments. Lebedeva wrote, "It seemed dangerous and simply impermissible to open the doors of the district hospitals for abortions when there were still no beds." The health authorities feared that the demand for abortion would "swamp the weak regional health care network."[26]

Most abortions were performed in Moscow and Leningrad. In 1926 doctors performed a total of 102,709 hospital abortions in all of Russia. Although Moscow and Leningrad combined held only 3.5 percent of the female

24. Matthews, *Russian Child and Russian Wife*, 104; P. I. Kolosho, "Opyt primeneniia mestnoi anestezii pri iskusstvennom aborte," *Sovetskii vrachebnyi zhurnal*, 1926, no. 8: 569.

25. This judgmental phrase appears in a number of doctors' reports. See, for example, Gens's compilation of questionnaires sent to doctors in *Abort v derevne*, 45, and "Vos'moi s"ezd," 485. Levi, "Itogi legalizatsii aborta," 154, notes that the 1920 decree was met with hostility by doctors. Two months before abortion was prohibited, one doctor suggested to his colleagues that an injection of local anesthetic would decrease women's suffering enormously. See Kolosho, "Opyt primeneniia mestnoi anestezii," 569–73. Abortion is still performed in the Soviet Union today without anesthetic.

26. Gens, *Abort v derevne*, 5.

population, they accounted for 39 percent of the abortions. The number of abortions dropped as one moved from the urban to the rural areas. Doctors performed 30 percent of all abortions in the provincial and district towns and 16 percent in the smaller towns. Only 15 percent of the nation's abortions were performed in the rural areas, although 83 percent of the nation's women lived there.[27] In other words, almost 85 percent of Russian women lived in the countryside, but 85 percent of the abortions occurred in the towns.

Women in the towns had greater access to abortion than their rural counterparts, but they also had a greater desire to limit fertility. The natality of women migrants dropped substantially after four years of city living, and the natality of long-term city residents was even lower.[28] Living outside the large, extended household so essential to economic prosperity in the countryside, urban women had less incentive to bear children. The transition to waged labor, the elimination of the family as the basic unit of production, cramped quarters, and the lack of necessary consumer goods all encouraged women to reduce family size. Thus not only was abortion more available in the cities, but also urban women were more eager to use it.

The social composition of the women who received abortions reflected the urban base of the phenomenon. Only 10 percent of the women were peasants. The majority were either married to or working as *sluzhashchie* (white-collar employees, 37 percent) or *rabochie* (blue-collar workers, 33 percent). The unemployed constituted the next-largest group (12 percent); students and members of the free professions combined accounted for less than 4 percent. An additional 4 percent comprised independent, nonagricultural *khoziaiki* (petty entrepreneurs). Fully 86 percent of the women who received abortions had made the transition to the world of waged labor and were either studying, engaged in waged work, or married to salaried workers.

The social composition of urban women receiving abortions closely mirrored the composition of the larger female population in the towns (table 1). The percentage of *sluzhashchie* in the wards was exactly the same as the share of women *sluzhashchie* in the town population. Workers were the only group whose share in the wards was somewhat greater than their share of the urban population. This fact may reflect the special preference the commissions awarded to working-class women or may suggest that workers had stronger incentives to reduce family size. Although the abortion commissions gave priority to unemployed women, and women suffered greatly from unemployment in the 1920s, it is striking that the unemployed did not figure prominently among women receiving abortions in the towns. Apparently the un-

27. The following sociological profiles of abortion patients are based on the data in *Abort v 1926 g.* (Moscow, 1929), 8, and cover all women receiving abortions in the RSFSR in 1926. *Narodnoe khoziaistvo* (Moscow and Leningrad, 1932), 2, 21.

28. Ellen Jones and Fred Grupp, *Modernization, Value Change, and Fertility in the Soviet Union* (London, 1987), 85–86.

TABLE 1.   Abortion and the Urban Female Population, 1926

	In Urban Female Pop.		Having Abortions	
Social Composition	No.	%	No.	%
Workers	511,532	28	27,605	32
Sluzhashchie	652,692	35	30,240	35
Members of free professions	7,838	0.4	349	0.4
Independent *khoziaiki*	152,665	8	3,883	4
Unemployed	234,054	13	10,635	12
Other	293,758	16	14,189	16
Total	1,852,539		86,901	

SOURCE. *Abort v 1926 g.* (Moscow, 1929), 14, 15, 32, 33, 50, 51; Valentina B. Zhiromskaia, "Sot-sial'naia struktura gorodskogo naseleniia RSFSR v vosstanovitel'nyi period (1921–1925)" (Kandidatskaia dissertatsiia istoricheskoi nauki, Institut Istorii SSSR Moscow, 1982), 216.
NOTE. All categories include women employed in a given occupation and wives of men in a given occupation.

employed had no more reason to seek abortions than did women with steady incomes. Although state officials believed that extreme need motivated women to seek abortion, the social composition of the women in the wards suggests that abortion was less a matter of desperation (as experienced by the unemployed) than of other facts of urban life.

The expectations embodied in the criteria of the abortion commissions proved a poor predictor not only of the employment status of women but of their marital status as well. Whereas the commissions gave priority to single women, the overwhelming majority of women in the abortion wards (84 percent) were not escaping the stigma of illegitimacy but were "respectably married" (table 2). The wards in Moscow and Leningrad contained the largest percentage of single women (19 percent). In the rural areas 16 percent of the women who received abortions were unmarried, although district doctors reported that fully 29 percent of the women who initially requested abortions fell into this group. Unmarried peasant women were often willing to see a doctor, but they could not make the long journey to the abortion commission or muster the required documents without their plight becoming public knowledge.[29] The need for legal abortion in the countryside by single women may have been far greater than their numbers in the wards suggest.

More than four-fifths (83 percent) of women who received abortions were already mothers (table 3). In the rural areas the percentage of childless women was even smaller than the national average, and the percentage of women with big families was larger. The abortion wards in Moscow and

29. Gens, *Abort v derevne*, 24.

TABLE 2.   Marital Status of Abortion Patients by Location

	Moscow and Leningrad		Provincial and District Towns		Other Towns		Rural Areas		Total	
	No.	%	No.	%	No.	%	No.	%	No.	%
Single	7,094	19	2,984	14	1,553	13	2,043	16	13,674	16
Married	30,996	81	18,017	86	10,844	87	10,722	84	70,579	84
Total	38,090	100	21,001	100	12,397	100	12,765	100	84,253	100

SOURCE. *Abort v 1926 g.* (Moscow, 1929), 14, 32, 50, 68.

TABLE 3. Family Size of Women Receiving Abortions, 1926

Number of Children	Moscow and Leningrad		Provincial and District Towns		Other Towns		Rural Areas		Total	
	No.	%	No.	%	No.	%	No.	%	No.	%
None	7,967	21	4,393	16	2,004	13	2,235	15	16,599	17
1	12,988	33	8,925	32	4,498	30	2,686	18	29,097	30
2	9,019	23	6,918	25	3,857	26	3,138	21	22,932	24
3	4,855	13	3,604	13	2,190	15	2,658	18	13,307	14
4	2,221	6	1,921	7	1,234	8	1,858	12	7,234	7
5 or more	1,758	4	1,996	7	1,273	8	2,457	16	7,484	8
Total	38,808	100	27,757	100	15,056	100	15,032	100	96,653	100

SOURCE. *Abort v 1926 g.* (Moscow, 1929), 18, 36, 54, 72.

Leningrad held the greatest percentage of childless women (21 percent). Women with small families (one or two children) constituted the largest group receiving abortions in the cities and towns (57 percent). In the countryside, however, women with three or more children predominated in the wards (46 percent). Thus women in urban areas opted for abortion more frequently after one child and peasant women after three children or more. Yet everywhere abortion was being used primarily by mothers. The differences in the family sizes of urban and rural abortion patients are consonant with the differences in urban and rural natality. This finding suggests that both urban and rural women were resorting to abortion to limit the size of their families; they simply differed as to what constituted the acceptable size.

The largest group of women who received abortions (60 percent) were those between the ages of twenty and twenty-nine, the next largest group (32 percent) between thirty and thirty-nine; only a tiny fraction of women were under eighteen (less than 1 percent), and only 3 percent were eighteen or nineteen (table 4). Not surprisingly, women having abortions were mainly in their twenties and thirties, a time when most had married and begun to have children. As one moved from the urban to the rural areas, the percentage of older women receiving abortions increased. The over-forty group was three times as large in the rural areas (9 percent) as in Moscow and Leningrad (3 percent), and women in their thirties constituted 30 percent of the women receiving abortions in Moscow and Leningrad but 39 percent in the countryside. Women who got abortions in the countryside tended to have larger families and thus opted for abortion later in their childbearing years. There was no difference between the countryside and the towns in regard to the younger age groups: the group under twenty constituted the same small share in every area (less than 4 percent).

Poverty was the single most important reason cited for abortion.[30] In Moscow and Leningrad more than half the women (57 percent) who got abortions cited poverty as the primary reason. This percentage was roughly the same in both towns and the countryside. Although some women may have pled poverty because they believed the commissions more likely to approve their request if they did so, rural and urban conditions make it a plausible motive. Babies required food, clothing, diapers, and living space, all of which were in short supply. Safe and healthy substitutes for breast milk did not exist, and nursing tied a woman down for at least eight or nine months. Diapers were generally unavailable, and even cloth was scarce. One woman described her "sacrifice" of a "pre-revolutionary bedsheet" to make "nappies" for her newborn.[31]

---

30. *Abort v 1926 g.*, 14, 32, 50, 68; Emel'ianov's case study of women in Briansk, "K voprosu o roste," supports these national figures.

31. Matthews, *Russian Child and Russian Wife*, 194.

TABLE 4. Age of Women Receiving Abortions, 1926

Age	Moscow and Leningrad		Provincial and District Towns		Other Towns		Rural Areas		Total	
	No.	%	No.	%	No.	%	No.	%	No.	%
17 & younger	119	<1	112	<1	73	<1	79	<1	383	<1
18–19	1,157	3	969	3	498	3	470	3	3,094	3
20–29	24,782	63	18,065	63	9,089	58	7,695	49	59,631	60
30–39	12,028	30	8,191	29	5,250	33	6,067	39	31,536	32
40 & older	1,399	3	1,219	4	811	5	1,358	9	4,787	5
Total	39,485		28,556		15,721		15,669		99,431	

SOURCE. *Abort v 1926 g.* (Moscow, 1929), 18, 36, 54, 72.

The death rate for children remained extremely high in the 1920s even as activists and medical personnel battled successfully to reduce it. A study in the mid-1920s of 541 Moscow spinners and weavers showed that fully 70 percent had lost a child, mainly to hunger and poor living conditions. The loss of a child was a common experience shared by urban and rural women. One peasant woman told a doctor, "The conditions of life are so difficult. There is no chance to bring up the children we already have."[32] The streets of the cities, the railroad stations, and the markets swarmed with abandoned children—*besprizorniki*—who were desperate for food and shelter. Child care institutions, serving only a fraction of the population, were overcrowded, understaffed, and poorly provisioned well into the 1930s.[33]

Housing conditions in the towns and cities also made it difficult to care for a child. For families crowded in tiny rooms or apartments, the presence of a wailing, fretful infant could make a scarcely bearable situation intolerable. And conditions became even worse during the first five-year plan. By 1932 only 4.6 square meters of living space were allocated to each person in the towns, scarcely enough space to lie down in. Houses lacked running water, toilets, baths, and stoves; many were cold, dank, fetid, and in a state of chronic disrepair.[34]

Peasant women contended with a different but equally trying set of circumstances.[35] In one study 2,207 rural doctors reported that poverty and material vulnerability motivated well over half (62 percent) of the women who sought abortion. In their visits to doctors women spoke of the famine of 1921–22, the poor harvest of 1924, too little land, unemployment, the difficulties in feeding a child, the loss of their huts to fire, the desire "not to propagate beggary," and even insufficient cloth to wrap the baby. About half of this group were women with large families who simply could not care for another child. One peasant woman told a doctor, with black humor, "The educated women stopped giving birth long ago. Only we silly women continue to bear children." Both doctors and women observed that more and more peasants were moving into single-family households, producing smaller families and thus increasing the woman's work. Her contribution was more

32. Ianovitskii, "Rezul'taty," 332.

33. See chapter 2, on *besprizornost'* and adoption, in Wendy Goldman, "The 'Withering-Away' and the Resurrection of the Soviet Family, 1917–1936" (Ph.D. diss., University of Pennsylvania, 1986), and the chapter entitled "From the Old Family to the New," in Elizabeth Waters, "From the Old Family to the New: Work, Marriage, and Motherhood in Urban Soviet Russia, 1917–1936" (Ph.D. diss., University of Birmingham, 1985).

34. William Chase, *Workers, Society, and the Soviet State: Labor and Life in Moscow, 1918–1929* (Urbana, Ill., 1987), 183–92; Neibakh, "Zhilishchnoe i kommunal'noe khoziaistvo vo vtoroi piatiletke," *Sovetskaia vrachebnaia gazeta*, 1932, no. 15–16: 947.

35. This information is based on Gens's questionnaires to 2,207 rural doctors. See Gens, *Abort v derevne*, 22–25, 31–36.

essential than ever in a small, poorly equipped household, and she had little time for bearing and rearing children. Many peasant women commented on how difficult it was to work while pregnant or caring for a baby.

Illness was the second reason women cited for abortion (cited by 18 percent overall), although slightly more women in the countryside cited illness (21 percent) than in Moscow and Leningrad (15 percent).[36] Rural doctors reported that peasant women suffered from a wide variety of chronic infections, complications from previous births, venereal diseases, and other illnesses exacerbated by the lack of accessible health care. Often women had to care for a sick husband or family member, leaving little time to devote to a child.[37]

The crucial difference between the motivations of rural and urban women was in their attitudes toward illegitimacy. In Moscow and Leningrad women who wanted to conceal pregnancy constituted a tiny fraction of the abortion patients (less than 1 percent), but as one moved from town to country, the share of this group expanded considerably (to 4 percent).[38] In the countryside the great shame of illegitimacy could ruin a girl's chances of marriage and provoke her father to throw her out. Unmarried, pregnant peasant women spoke of their "conscience before the people," and sought abortion due to "fear, shame, parents, and public opinion." Many of these women reflected the changes in village life wrought by the revolution and the years of war. Widows took up with soldiers temporarily billeted in their villages. Morality among young people loosened. One doctor pointed to a new sexual morality together with an unchanging traditional attitude toward illegitimacy as a primary reason for the increase in abortion.[39]

The smaller incidence of women wishing to conceal pregnancy in the towns indicates that urban women found illegitimacy less compelling than other, largely material reasons for abortion. It is not unlikely that in the transition from country to city, migrants relaxed their harsh attitudes toward illegitimacy. Urban women, freed from the constraints of the patriarchal household, may have found it easier to bear and raise children out of wedlock.

A large percentage of women (ranging from 19 percent in the cities to 14 percent in the countryside) simply told the commissions that they "did not want a child for other reasons." Numerous researchers on abortion observed that family instability, short-term unions, and a pervasive "fear of tomorrow" left many women reluctant to bear children. Although most abortion

36. *Abort v 1926 g.*, 14, 32, 50, 68.
37. Gens, *Abort v derevne*, 24.
38. *Abort v 1926 g.*, 14, 32, 50, 68.
39. Gens, *Abort v derevne*, 24–25, 35–36.

patients were married, divorce was extremely easy to obtain throughout the 1920s and early 1930s, and the divorce rate, especially in the urban areas, was exceptionally high. The prevalence of divorce and the difficulties of collecting alimony and child support must have strongly affected women's view of motherhood.[40] And there were positive as well as negative motivations for abortion. The revolution brought new opportunities for work and study. Mass literacy campaigns and the activities of the Zhenotdel expanded women's horizons and choices. One doctor noted that women who went to work or became involved in political activities showed a new "impatience with children." The "new, revolutionary life" transformed family patterns and expectations. All these changes were reflected in women's attitudes toward childbearing.[41]

Much of this information suggests that women used abortion to limit family size rather than as a stopgap solution to an accidental or out-of-wedlock pregnancy. The point is reinforced by evidence that women resorted to abortion repeatedly. Almost half of those who received abortions in Moscow and Leningrad had had at least one previous abortion. More than half had had one, one-quarter had had two, and about one-fifth had had three or more. In the provincial towns and the rural areas fewer women had had previous abortions (about one-third and one-quarter of the women, respectively), a reflection of the limited availability of abortion. Here too the repeat patients had had fewer previous abortions.[42]

In both the cities and the rural areas the more pregnancies an abortion patient had, the more likely she was to have had a previous abortion (table 5). In the abortion wards of Moscow and Leningrad 22 percent of all women with two pregnancies had had a previous abortion; yet among the women with five pregnancies fully 71 percent had had at least one abortion. The figures were somewhat smaller in the towns and rural areas.

Moreover, in Moscow and Leningrad the number of abortions a woman was likely to have had increased with the number of children she bore. The abortion rate (abortions per hundred births) among each group rose steadily with each new pregnancy from twenty-eight in the second pregnancy to thirty-seven in the third and forty in the fourth. Thus abortion, for many women, was more than a onetime solution to an accidental pregnancy. As

40. Ibid., 8; P. P. Kazanskii, "4,450 sluchaev nepol'nykh vykidyshei," *Ginekologiia i akusherstvo*, 1927, no. 6: 517; Emel'ianov, "K voprosu o roste," 430; M. Kaplun, "Brachnost' naseleniia RSFSR," *Statisticheskoe obozrenie*, 1929: 95–97.

41. Both Jones and Grupp, *Modernization*, 70–121, and Vishnevskii and Volkov, *Vosproizvodstvo*, 173–76, argue that factors such as urbanization, women's employment, and increased literacy encouraged women to reduce family size.

42. *Abort v 1926 g.*, 9; M. Gernet, "Povtornye i mnogokratnye aborty," *Statisticheskoe obozrenie*, 1928, no. 12: 111.

TABLE 5.   Number of Previous Abortions and Pregnancies among
Women Receiving Abortions, 1926

	Moscow and Leningrad		Rural Areas	
	No.	%	No.	%
Second pregnancy				
0 abortions	5,412	78	1,617	89
1 abortion	1,514	22	204	11
Total	6,926		1,821	
Third pregnancy				
0 abortions	3,729	54	1,779	83
1 abortion	2,712	39	345	16
2 abortions	501	7	27	1
Total	6,942		2,151	
Fourth pregnancy				
0 abortions	2,348	41	1,569	73
1 abortion	2,071	36	469	22
2 abortions	1,117	19	92	4
3 abortions	219	4	4	<1
Total	5,755		2,134	
Fifth pregnancy or more				
0 abortions	4,097	29	4,391	60
1 abortion	3,387	24	1,719	23
2 abortions	2,992	21	736	10
3 abortions	1,811	13	260	3
4 abortions	963	7	122	2
5 abortions	1,019	7	69	1
Total	14,269		7,297	

SOURCE. *Abort v 1926 g.* (Moscow, 1929), 10–11.

women moved through their reproductive life cycles, they relied on abortion
again and again to help limit the size of their families.

The type of woman who had an abortion in the mid-1920s confounded the
expectations of the abortion commissions and the state. Although officials
from the commissariats of Health and Justice believed that extreme need
motivated women to seek abortions and consequently structured the commissions' criteria accordingly, the typical abortion patient was not teenaged,
unmarried, or unemployed. She was not a young girl in trouble, nor was she
a woman involved in casual sex. On the contrary, she was in her twenties
or early thirties, married, and usually the mother of at least one child. She
was urban and either employed as or married to a worker or *sluzhashchii*
with medical insurance. These young, urban, married mothers came to the

abortion wards not to conceal their transgressions of the traditional rules of sexual behavior but rather to limit the size of their families.

ILLEGAL ABORTION

Even after abortion was legalized, thousands of women still turned to *babki*, midwives, hairdressers, nurses, and an assortment of self-administered home remedies to terminate their pregnancies. Their reasons varied widely: some sought to avoid the pain of the hospital procedure; others could not travel to the abortion commissions and the hospitals; some were rejected by the commissions; some wanted to keep pregnancy a secret; and many simply trusted the practices of the *babka* and midwife over those of the modern doctor.

The frequency of illegal abortion is measurable only by the number of women who ended up in the hospital. The successes and failures who never entered a hospital constituted the "dark" or unknown figure of illegal abortion. Although the women who were hospitalized represented only a small fraction of those who got illegal abortions, the numbers, in comparison to legal abortion, were still striking. In the rural areas in the early 1920s the known number of illegal abortions actually outstripped the number of legal abortions. Thus despite the legalization of abortion, illegal abortion was still widely practiced, especially in the rural areas. The percentage of illegal abortions treated had dropped by the late 1920s but remained quite significant.[43]

By 1926, 14 percent of the women in the abortion wards—20,240 out of 121,978—were being treated for the consequences of illegal abortion. The number of women treated for illegal abortion was almost the same in Moscow and Leningrad as in the rural areas. Yet because rural hospitals performed far fewer abortions, women suffering from illegal abortions occupied twice as many beds in the rural wards than in Moscow and Leningrad (table 6). The percentage treated for illegal abortions was highest in the provinces of the Central Industrial Region surrounding Moscow—Ivanovo-Vosnesensk, Riazan, Kostroma, and Nizhnii Novgorod. In Ivanovo-Vosnesensk Province, an area with a high concentration of women textile workers, fully 40 percent of the women in the abortion wards were suffering from illegal abortions. In almost half the provinces nationwide, one out of every five beds allocated for legal abortion was occupied by a woman being treated for an illegal abortion. In 1930 a study of 1,249 women in a large collective farm in the Smolensk area showed that fully half of the women had suffered an illegal abortion, either self-administered or performed by *babki*.[44]

Women continued to go underground for abortions for many reasons. In

43. Between 1922 and 1924 rural doctors performed 40,828 legal abortions and treated 41,684 women for complications resulting from illegal abortions. Gens, *Abort v derevne*, 27.

44. *Abort v 1926 g.*, 6–7; Ressin, "Opyt obsledovaniia," 344.

TABLE 6.   Legal and Illegal Abortions in the Cities and Countryside, 1926

Type of Abortion	Moscow and Leningrad	Provincial and District Towns	Other Towns	Rural Areas	Total
Legal	39,851	30,616	16,439	15,803	102,709
Illegal	5,219	3,744	3,474	4,764	17,201
% of all illegal abortions nationwide	30	22	20	28	
% of illegal abortions performed in each area	12	11	18	23	

SOURCE. *Abort v 1926 g.* (Moscow, 1929), 8.

some urbanized provinces high rates of both illegal abortion and rejection by the commissions suggest a vicious circle: women who suffered the effects of botched illegal abortions occupied beds in the abortion wards, thereby reducing the number of places available for women requesting legal abortions and in turn forcing more women to get illegal abortions. The industrialized regions around Moscow and Leningrad, and the Urals region, displayed high rates of illegal abortion together with a high percentage of rejections by the abortion commissions.

Yet other provinces showed different patterns. In Nizhnii Novgorod Province, for example, a significant 30 percent of the beds were occupied by women who had illegal abortions, but the commissions rejected only 6 percent of the applicants. Moreover, the nationwide percentage of beds occupied by women with illegal abortions (14 percent) was twice the rejection rate (7 percent).[45] Only a small percentage of women who requested abortions were turned away. Thus rejection by the commissions—or the inability of medical facilities to meet the demand—was clearly not the only reason women went underground to terminate pregnancy.

Many rural women who needed abortions never even applied to the commissions. A trip to the commission, followed by a trip to the hospital, was extremely difficult. Roads were impassable for a large part of the year. Even if a household owned a horse, it could rarely spare the animal, and a woman might have to walk thirty to forty miles to get to a hospital. Many of the hospitals in the rural areas did not even perform abortions. Moreover, the commissions required proof of pregnancy, marital status, family size, and workplace. Even if a woman could procure the necessary documents from a doctor and the local soviet, the paperwork and her subsequent absence exposed the purpose of her journey to the entire village. More than two thousand doctors reported that rural women begged them to perform abor-

45. *Abort v 1926 g.*, 8.

tions privately without permission from the commissions. In the words of one doctor, "If a hospital refuses a maid or a widow, they immediately turn to the *babki*."[46]

There were differences between the women who received legal abortions and the women who went underground, but they were not especially significant. The vast majority of women in both groups were married (about 85 percent). Peasants figured more prominently in illegal abortions (18 percent) than in legal abortions (10 percent). And the unemployed, favored by the abortion commissions, accounted for far fewer of the illegal abortion patients (5 percent) than the legal abortion patients (12 percent). But in other respects the social composition of the two groups was similar. More women who went underground were childless, perhaps because the commissions favored women with children or because the unwed sought to avoid the publicity of the commissions. Yet even among women with illegal abortions, most, like their "legal" counterparts, were already mothers, and the largest group (46 percent) had small families of one or two children.[47]

Thus women who had illegal abortions tended to be somewhat older and have fewer children than those who received legal abortions. Peasants figured more prominently in their ranks, and the rural hospitals took in a larger percentage of women suffering from illegal abortion. Yet the respective profiles of the two groups were remarkably similar. Like the women who received legal abortions, workers and *sluzhashchie* accounted for the largest group of women treated for illegal abortion, and they tended to be mothers in their twenties with small families. The similarities between the two groups suggest that illegal abortion or folk practice continued to be a popular method for urban as well as rural women to limit fertility. Women who received illegal abortions were by and large indistinguishable from the millions of married mothers whose choices about family size determined the birthrate in Russia.

ABORTION AND THE BIRTHRATE

By the late 1920s doctors and researchers had become deeply concerned about women's reliance on abortion. They made frequent references to the falling birthrate, the thousands who suffered complications after the operation, the labor time lost during recuperation, and the debilitating impact of abortion on women's health. A doctor reporting to the Scientific Association of Doctors in Simferopol in 1927 concluded that in the Crimea the large number of abortions "stands as a great antisocial factor and poses a threat to the

---

46. Gens, *Abort v derevne*, 15, 20, 38–46.
47. *Abort v 1926 g.*, 20, 38, 56, 74, and 24, 42, 60, 78.

steady growth of the population." At the First All-Ukrainian Congress of Midwives and Gynecologists, that same year, a doctor from Starobelsk announced that the abortion rate had shot up from forty abortions per hundred births in 1924 to eighty-four in 1925 and surpassed the birthrate at 107 in 1926.[48] Lebedeva felt the need to counter these dire forecasts by pointing out that abortion had not significantly affected the birthrate. Yet she noted that in Moscow there were sixty-five abortions per hundred births in 1926, and the number was growing. By 1928 a Moscow doctor at the Eighth Congress of Midwives and Gynecologists noted that the number of abortions had surpassed the number of births. He warned, "We must pay attention to the menacing predominance of abortions over births among contemporary young women and the inevitable consequences: a decrease in the birth rate and the labor capability of women. Abortion, in the final analysis, places a heavy burden on the state because it reduces women's contribution to production." One delegate from the northern Caucasus commented that there were four times as many abortions as births in his area, and another, from the Ukraine, referred to "an epidemic of abortions."[49]

By the late 1920s abortions were outnumbering births in many cities. In Briansk there were 46 legal and known illegal abortions per hundred births in 1924, 67 in 1925, 187 in 1926, and 286 in the first four months of 1927. The abortion rate by 1927 was almost three times the birthrate.[50] Not only was the number of abortions rising, but the number of births was falling as well. In Leningrad there was almost a sixfold increase in abortion between 1924 and 1928, from 5.5 to 31.5 abortions per thousand people. The ratio of abortions to births went from 21 abortions per hundred births in 1924 to 138 in 1928.[51] In Moscow in 1921 there were 19 abortions per hundred births, 21 in 1922, 19 in 1923, 19 in 1924, 31 in 1925, 55 in 1926, 87 in 1927, 130 in 1928, and 160 in 1929. By 1934 the abortion rate had jumped to 271, although it fell somewhat in 1935, to 221. By the 1930s there were twice as many abortions as births.[52] If the number of illegal abortions had been added to these figures, the effect on the birthrate would have been more striking still.

Although data on the number of abortions nationwide are not available for the late 1920s and the 1930s, the birthrate fell steadily between 1927 and 1935—from 45 births per thousand people in 1927 to 43.7 in 1928, 41.4 in 1929, 39.2 in 1930, 36.9 in 1931, 34.6 in 1932, 32.4 in 1933, 30.1 in 1934, and 30.1 in 1935. Although many factors contributed to the decline in the birth-

48. "Nauchnaia zhizn'," *Vrachebnoe delo*, 1927, no. 14–15: 1107, no. 16: 1196–97.

49. "Vos'moi s"ezd," 474–75, 478, 482, 485.

50. Emel'ianov, "K voprosu o roste," 425.

51. Vishnevskii and Volkov, *Vosproizvodstvo*, 174.

52. Frank Lorimer, *The Population of the Soviet Union: History and Prospects* (Geneva, 1946), 127; Levi, "Itogi legalizatsii aborta," 156.

rate, it coincided, beginning in 1928, with an astounding increase in abortion in many areas. By the late 1920s in Briansk, Moscow, Leningrad, parts of the Ukraine, the northern Caucasus, and other areas the number of abortions had exceeded the number of births and was continuing to rise. In the words of Soviet demographers, abortion had become "the primary means of regulating the birthrate within the family."[53]

Although we know little about the women who received abortions in the early 1930s, the figures on abortion and the birthrate suggest that the millions of peasant women who came to the cities and entered the work force in this period had powerful motivations for limiting family size. Collectivization, industrialization, and urbanization accompanied a sharp increase in legal abortions—and, most likely, illegal abortions as well. Famine in the countryside, rationing in the cities, and the forced dispossession of millions of peasants all contributed to the sharp drop in the birthrate. Legalized abortion was not the cause of this fall; it was simply one of several methods women used to keep from bearing children.

The 1936 law confused the method with the motivation. Officials assumed that the fall in the birthrate could be arrested by criminalizing abortion. This assumption was a sharp reversal of the state's earlier view, which held that criminalization could do little to change the difficult social conditions that impelled women to seek abortion. Yet by 1936 officials had abandoned the notion that repression was useless and embraced the stark thinking of the jurist who proclaimed, "It makes sense to apply more repressive measures."[54]

The sociological studies of abortion patients in the 1920s may have encouraged officials to clamp down. The profiles that emerged from these studies showed that officials had misjudged women's motivations for abortion from the very beginning. The creators of the 1920 decree believed that once poverty was eliminated, women would have no desire to refuse to bear children. The criteria of the commissions—favoring the most materially and socially vulnerable—implicitly reflected this assumption. Yet the majority of women who sought both legal and illegal abortions in the 1920s were not the unemployed, the unmarried, or teenagers but relatively secure, married mothers in the prime of their childbearing years. In short, they were not the neediest, the most vulnerable, or the most marginal. Primarily urban wage earners or the

53. Lorimer, *Population of the Soviet Union*, 134; Vishnevskii and Volkov, *Vosproizvodstvo*, 173.

54. "Obsuzhdaet zakonoproekt," *Sotsialisticheskaia iustitsiia*, 1936, no. 17: 2–4; "Rabotniki iustitsii aktivno uchastvuite obsuzhdenii zakonoproekt," *Sotsialisticheskaia iustitsiia*, 1936, no. 18: 1–4; A. Gertsenzon and A. Lapshina, "Zakon o zapreshchenii aborta," *Sotsialisticheskaia zakonnost'*, 1936, no. 10: 31; D. A. Glebov, "Zakonoproekt TsIK i SNK Soiuza SSR ot 25 maia 1936," *Sovetskii vrachebnyi zhurnal*, 1936, no. 11: 802–3; O. P. Nogina, "Zadachi okhrany materinstva i mladenchestva," *Sovetskii vrachebnyi zhurnal*, 1936, no. 5: 321–25; "V zashchitu materi i rebenka," *Sotsialisticheskaia zakonnost'*, 1936, no. 7: 17–20.

wives of wage earners, these women were responding not only to poverty and material deprivation but also to the new opportunities opened up by the revolution for education, employment, and political work in a wider world.

In 1934 Soviet statisticians undertook a study of the birthrate that found an inverse ratio between the material well-being of a family and the number of children.[55] In other words, urban families with higher incomes tended to have fewer children. This conclusion is consonant with the sociological profile of the women who received abortions in 1926. The combination of a plummeting birthrate and studies contradicting all the assumptions underlying the legalization of 1920 may have persuaded state officials that prohibition was the obvious solution.

In the public debate over the 1936 law thousands of women fired off letters to the newspapers contending that single women, mothers of large families, students, political activists, poor women, collective farmers, professional women—in short, all women—needed the right to legal abortion. Women stressed their desire to study and work; without the abortion right they would "lose their full freedom." Using the state's own language of liberation, they discussed the need for women to contribute equally to the new society and emphasized the limits maternity would place on that contribution. They spoke of their plans to study, work, and develop themselves as human beings. The campaigns to liberate women and teach them to take advantage of the new world of work had reached an enthusiastic audience.[56] The 1920 decree never construed abortion as a right, but the letters made it clear that women had appropriated it as such.

Officials lectured women loudly about their selfish failure to appreciate the larger needs of the state. Nikolai Krylenko, the people's commissar of justice, admonished, "A basic mistake is made in every case by those women who consider 'freedom of abortion' as one of their civil rights." Another official carefully explained that maternity was not only "a biological function but also a social and state one."[57] Yet ultimately the state failed to raise the birthrate substantially. The prohibition produced an immediate increase, but it lasted only a few years. By 1938 the birthrate began to drop again, and by 1940 it had returned to its level of 1935, before the prohibition on abortion.[58] Repression in the long run proved useless, for legal abortion was only one of the methods women used to limit fertility. Illegal abortion had never disappeared, even in the period of legalization, and many women un-

55. Vishnevskii and Volkov, *Vosproizvodstvo*, 173.

56. See the letters published daily in *Pravda*, May 27–June 8, 1936.

57. "Rabotniki iustitsii," 1–4.

58. On the demographic transition in Russia, see Ansley J. Coale, Barbara Anderson, and Erna Härm, *Human Fertility in Russia since the Nineteenth Century* (Princeton, 1975), 16.

doubtedly returned to the underground practices of willing doctors, midwives, and *babki*. Several scholars have speculated that the decline in the
birthrate in 1938 signaled women's success in reconstructing the networks for
illegal abortion.[59]

In mass defiance of the state women refused to return to the childbearing
practices of the partriarchal peasant family. They seized the new opportunities offered by mass education, industrialization, and urbanization. These
state-sponsored drives unwittingly created a new woman whose consciousness of her choices severely undermined the state's increasing emphasis on
the social function of reproduction. Despite Stalin's attack on reproductive
freedom, women braved back-alley abortions and dangerous home remedies
to answer Lebedeva's emancipatory call to be masters of their own sexuality.

59. See Waters, "From the Old Family to the New," 306, and her chapter "Regulating
Fertility"; Vishnevskii and Volkov, *Vosproizvodstvo*, 174.

Later Developments:
Trends in Soviet Women's History,
1930 to the Present

Barbara Evans Clements

Since 1930 Russian women, indeed all the women of the Soviet Union, have made considerable advances in educating themselves, constructing social services to alleviate their domestic burdens, and moving out of factory and field labor into more comfortable white-collar jobs. In so doing, they have continued the transformation of tradition set off by the tsars. They have accomplished all this while struggling to cope with war and domestic up-heaval in their country. It was during the Stalin years (1928–53) that the process of change became most difficult and often violent. Since Stalin's death change has come more easily, but the pattern of Soviet women's lives established under Stalin has persisted. In the postwar era economic difficul-ties and patriarchal values have blended together in the policies of the lead-ers and the choices of the followers to limit the progress of women in the public world.

THE 1930s

By 1928 Joseph Stalin had won the struggle for power among the top Bolshe-viks that followed Lenin's death. He then led his country through twenty-five years of brutal dictatorship and heroic accomplishment. Women were just as caught up in the turmoil of Stalin's time as were men. In the countryside the Communist party forced the peasants onto collective farms, with catas-trophic loss of life when the peasants resisted. In the crowded cities to which many peasants fled, all the necessities of life—food, housing, and consumer goods—were in short supply. Wages remained low. Life was a struggle, and the social programs designed to ease women's domestic burdens went under-funded. There were few day-care centers; laundries and communal dining rooms were rare.

The standard of living remained abysmally low in the 1930s in part because government leaders, almost all of them male, made a deliberate decision to invest in heavy industry at the expense of the consumer sector of the economy. Men as well as women suffered from this choice, justified in party propaganda as a temporary but necessary expedient. The party promised that once the foundations of the economy had been laid, the shortages would ease. The leadership had an additional message for women, however, one couched in far more permanent terms. In the mid- to late 1930s the Soviet media—newspapers, radio, and the arts—began to urge women to cultivate their femininity, which the government defined as women's innate capacities to nurture and serve. A succinct statement of this new ideal came in a 1936 novel, *The Village Bruski*, by F. Panforov. Here the heroine, Steka, a hardworking peasant from a collective farm, is brought to Moscow to be honored for her accomplishments. Stalin watches as Steka receives her medal. Flushed with gratitude, she makes a short speech to the audience:

> "Our feminine hearts are overflowing with emotions, and of these love is paramount. Yet, a wife should also be a happy mother and create a serene home atmosphere, without, however, abandoning work for the common welfare. She should know how to combine all these things while also matching her husband's performance on the job."
> "Right," said Stalin.[1]

This composite ideal female, the "new Soviet woman," also received endorsement from the Soviet legal system. The 1936 and 1944 marriage laws made divorce expensive and time-consuming. Abortion was outlawed in 1936. Soviet women continued to have "equal rights with men in all spheres of economic, state, cultural, social and political life," in the words of the 1936 constitution.[2] But they were also to be loving wives and devoted mothers.

The new Soviet woman was obviously useful to the government. Her unpaid labor in the home freed resources for industrialization. Her emotional services relieved some of the strains of city life, and her work outside the home built the new society. Furthermore, endorsing woman's nurturing roles may have won the government support, for this was an aspect of traditional conceptions of woman's nature dear to the hearts of ordinary Soviet citizens, women and men alike.

The government had another, more fundamental purpose in promoting the new Soviet woman. As had so often been the case in Russian history, government leaders saw woman's position in society as linked to political arrangements and objectives. Thus at the same time that government spokespeople began to enjoin women to tend to their families, they also began to teach that the nuclear family was one of the basic institutions of

---

1. Quoted in Xenia Gasiorowska, *Women in Soviet Fiction, 1917–64* (Madison, Wis., 1968), 53.
2. *Constitution (Fundamental Law) of the Union of Soviet Socialist Republics* (Moscow, 1938), 104.

Soviet society. It was to shore up the family that divorce and abortion were outlawed. These moves were a major retreat from the Marxist proposals for the abolition of the family, and they were part of a larger retreat going on since the late 1920s from all aspects of Marxist utopianism, including Marx's prediction that the state would disappear. Instead, Stalin's government proclaimed that the state would endure, that the family was the cornerstone of the state, and that women were responsible for keeping this cornerstone firmly in place.

How did women respond to the pressures and opportunities of the 1930s? I have already noted that many suffered from collectivization and industrialization. Female resistance occurred, but it was largely ineffective. The most widespread resistance came during collectivization, when peasant women banded together to defend the village from the party's assault, attacking the collectivizers in violent demonstrations called *bab'i bunty*. As they had done during the February revolution and later when angered by Zhenotdel organizers, peasant women aggressively defended their families, this time with the encouragement of men, who believed the authorities would deal leniently with rebellious women. Thousands of women took part in *bab'i bunty*, but these demonstrations were so scattered and episodic that they did little to halt collectivization.[3]

Collectivization in turn had limited effects on the patriarchalism of the peasants. The power of peasant elders over younger adult males continued to weaken, but the authority of peasant men over peasant women remained substantial. Despite a significant shortage of male labor in the countryside in the 1930s, and despite demands from the central government that women be promoted to positions of leadership, men continued to control farming, monopolizing the most lucrative and powerful jobs on the newly organized collective farms. Women did unskilled field work and tended the family's vegetable garden, tasks they had performed for centuries.[4]

Accommodation was the most successful way for women to respond to the upheaval of the 1930s, as it had been through most of Russian history. The government called on women to join the paid labor force, and millions responded by coming to the cities to find work. During the 1930s, 82 percent of

3. The best discussion of the *bab'i bunty* is Lynne Viola, "*Bab'i bunty* and Peasant Women's Protest during Collectivization," *Russian Review* 45, no. 1 (January 1986): 23–42. See also references in Robert Conquest, *The Harvest of Sorrow: Soviet Collectivization and the Terror-Famine* (New York, 1986), 157–58.

4. For a perceptive discussion of the situation of women in the countryside in the 1930s, see Roberta Manning, "Women in the Soviet Countryside on the Eve of World War II, 1935–1940" (Paper presented at the annual meeting of the American Association for the Advancement of Slavic Studies, Chicago, November 2–5, 1989). On resistance to women being promoted, or even to them being trained as tractor drivers, see 29–34 and 21–24. I would like to thank Professor Manning for making her article available to me.

those persons entering the Soviet labor force for the first time were women. By the end of the decade 71 percent of Soviet women aged sixteen to fifty-nine were gainfully employed, some of them in specialties earlier closed to women.[5] Women became engineers, university professors, and factory directors. Many had to cope with difficult working conditions, discrimination from male bosses, and harassment from male coworkers, but those who persevered despite these difficulties found the 1930s to be a decade of tremendous promise and achievement. Mariia Aleksandrovna Igleiko, a lathe operator in a Minsk steel mill, was one of many who later fondly remembered their early years in the factory. She and her female friends were doing jobs that men had said women could not do. They were working together and supporting one another, and they were contributing to the building of a new society.

> "We mastered this profession—completely new to us—with great pleasure. . . . The factory seemed big to us, although then about four hundred people worked in it. With our participation new shops were created at the factory—a foundry, mechanical assembly, and pattern shops. We began to produce drilling machines, lathes, and different equipment for the new construction. I loved my profession very much. I took great joy in the fact that I was producing a product the country needed, in turning the different details of a difficult shape [on the lathe]. I looked over the results of my friends' work with pride. We always went to work very early, got our tools, arranged them comfortably around us so as to economize on our work time. We stayed at work after our shift, helping one another when someone was late.[6]

The 1930s were a time when Soviet society offered more tangible rewards than pride to those women able to take advantage of the opportunities available to them. Many young women moved up in Soviet society, out of the peasantry and working class and into the burgeoning Soviet elite. They did so by becoming managers, professionals, or government bureaucrats and also by marrying male party leaders. In the new elite they gained a higher standard of living as well as easier working conditions. It was from the upward mobility of individual working-class and peasant women and men that the Soviet middle class was made.

In the late 1930s, however, this middle-class status brought with it considerable risk. Between 1936 and 1939 Stalin ordered the political police, the NKVD, to arrest millions of Soviet citizens in a campaign of terror designed to strengthen central control over the party and the government bureau-

    5. Michael Paul Sacks, *Women's Work in Soviet Russia: Continuity in the Midst of Change* (New York, 1976), 74; Norton Dodge, *Women in the Soviet Economy* (Baltimore, 1966), 32.
    6. Institut istorii partii pri TsK KPB, Filial Instituta Marksizma-Leninizma pri TsK KPSS, *V bor'be i trude*, 3d ed. (Minsk, 1985), 153.

cracy. Many of the victims came from the ranks of middle-echelon officials, particularly those working in economic management, the military, and the party. The consequences for women swept up in this maelstrom were disastrous. Female party members and the wives and daughters of male Communists were arrested and sent to hard-labor camps in Siberia. Those women left "free" were condemned to wait for the return of their men, often laboring under the stigma of being a wife or relative of an "enemy of the people." The human toll of Stalin's purges will not be known until the party and police archives are opened, but reliable estimates number the dead in the millions, among whom were hundreds of thousands of women.

WORLD WAR II

Soviet society had only begun to recover from the worst of the purges when a new disaster struck. On June 22, 1941, Germany attacked the Soviet Union in the largest military invasion in history. The ensuing warfare killed twenty-seven million Soviet citizens and laid waste the entire western third of the country, an area comparable in size to the United States east of the Mississippi River. Women played a crucial role in the colossal mobilization of people and resources World War II demanded. Indeed, women's contribution to the war effort was even greater than in World War I. By 1943 some eight hundred thousand female volunteers were serving in the Soviet armed forces, making up 8 percent of the military. Most worked in the medical corps, in transport, and in clerical positions, as was true in the other Allied armies, but there were also women in combat as tank drivers, snipers, sappers, and machine gunners. Three all-female air regiments flew combat missions. And women fought beside men in the underground resistance movement that bedeviled the German occupiers.[7]

Most Soviet women contributed to the victory by taking the places of men in industry and agriculture. By the end of the war women constituted 56 percent of the paid labor force, up from 39 percent in 1939. In agriculture the change was even more dramatic; the farms were virtually taken over by women, and as late as 1950 women were still 59 percent of farm workers.[8] Some Soviet women held authoritative positions as factory directors and managers on the collective farms. It was also during World War II that

7. K. Jean Cottam, "Soviet Women in Combat in World War II: The Ground Forces and the Navy," *International Journal of Women's Studies* 3 (1980): 345–57; "Soviet Women in Combat in World War II: The Rear Services, Resistance behind Enemy Lines and Military Political Workers," *International Journal of Women's Studies* 5 (1982): 363–78. For a collection of these women's memoirs see S. Alexiyevich, *War's Unwomanly Face* (Moscow, 1988).

8. Tsentral'noe statisticheskoe upravlenie pri Sovete Ministrov SSSR, *Zhenshchiny v SSSR: Statisticheskii sbornik* (Moscow, 1975), 27, 39.

women became the majority among physicians in the USSR. The labor of all the millions of Soviet women, often for twelve hours a day, seven days a week, on meager food rations, was vital to the defeat of Nazi Germany.

Women also played a real, if less concrete, part in the maintenance of Soviet morale, becoming central figures in the campaign to rally public support for the war effort. Abandoning communist internationalism for the duration, Soviet propaganda summoned the troops to drive the invaders out of "Mother Russia," portrayed in one of the best-known recruiting posters as a handsome, middle-aged woman in billowing red peasant dress and scarf, her arm raised in a summoning gesture, her expression firm and admonitory. Over her head is emblazoned, also in red, "The Motherland is calling!"[9] She appealed to two deep loyalties in Soviet men, their feeling for their land and that for their women. Both land and women were in desperate need of defenders, and both, as the war dragged on, survived the worst the Germans could inflict on them. In the iconography of the war, and undoubtedly in the minds of many Soviet soldiers, women came to stand for endurance, rebirth, and the tenderer emotions rare in the world of combat. Women as well must have drawn sustenance from this vision of themselves, for it honored their contribution to the war, justified their suffering, and legitimated their own deep feelings about their succoring role within the family and the community. It also touched ancient Russian associations of woman with motherhood and the generative land. Anna Akhmatova captured this sense of woman's connectedness to nature and renewal in a poem written in 1945 entitled "In Memory of a Friend":

> On the Day of Victory, tender and foggy,
> When the star is glowing red,
> A widow at an unmarked grave
> Is petitioned by the belated spring.
> She does not hurry to get up off her knees.
> She breathes in the bud and strokes the grass
> And helps a butterfly from her shoulder to the ground
> And gives a good scolding to the first dandelion.[10]

THE POSTWAR ERA

The first years after the war were ones of rebuilding. Women were again urged to work diligently at their jobs and to tend to their families' needs. At work women were asked to step aside so that men could reclaim the positions they had left during the war. (How many women did so is impossible to tell owing to the paucity of available statistics.) To heal the wounds, physical

9. This poster is often reproduced. See, for example, *Illiustrirovannaia istoriia SSSR* (Moscow, 1974), 348.
10. Anna Akhmatova, *Stikhotvoreniia i poemy*, 2d ed. (Leningrad, 1976), 216.

and psychological, women were encouraged to create pretty, happy homes.[11] Once again the Soviet government argued that a stable family was central to the restoration of order and that woman's nurture was central to family stability. It was a message often heard in all the combatant countries after the war; in the United States women were told to return to a hearth and home most of them had never left. (American women made up only 36 percent of the American labor force in 1945.)[12] Among the Soviet people this message had struck a responsive chord ever since the revolution, but it was probably even more welcome after the catastrophe of World War II. Women whose lives had been torn apart by the conflict had every reason to yearn for a happy family and material comforts. Female veterans later remembered their delight the first time they put on a dress after years in coarse army greatcoats. They also remembered their fear that no one would marry them because of the widespread belief among both male veterans and the men and women who had remained in the rear that the female veterans had ruined their femininity by entering the male world of combat. Once again the lines between man and woman, weakened by war, were firmly redrawn.[13]

Life was difficult for all Soviet citizens in the late 1940s. Consumer goods were scarce, patched clothes were common, and there was hunger in the Ukraine. Low wages and crowded housing remained the norm in the cities. The war had killed so many young men that many women never found husbands. There was also a resurgence of political terror in the late 1940s, although not on the scale of that of the 1930s. After Stalin's death in 1953, the new party leaders, most particularly Nikita Khrushchev, reined in the police and ushered in years of domestic tranquility and economic growth. The standard of living rose, and the migration of Soviet people into the cities continued; by 1988, 64 percent of the population lived in urban areas.[14]

For the women who stayed on in the villages, life began to improve in the 1950s, as government spending on mechanization and electrification increased. Improvements came slowly, however, and rural life remained primitive by Western standards. Many peasant women lugged water in buckets from wells, lit their huts with oil lamps, and heated and cooked with the traditional brick stoves until the late 1960s.

Patriarchal values also remained stronger in the countryside than in the cities. Those women who had been promoted to leadership positions on the collective farms during the war had to yield their place in the late 1940s,

11. Vera Dunham, *In Stalin's Time: Middleclass Values in Soviet Fiction* (Cambridge, 1976).

12. Mary P. Ryan, *Womanhood in America*, 2d ed. (New York, 1979), 189.

13. There are numerous references to the fact that the women in the military had "unsexed" themselves and therefore were not suitable for marriage after the war in Alexiyevich, *War's Unwomanly Face*. See, for example, 64–65, 89–91, 189, 244. Note also such references during World War I in Alfred Meyer's essay in this volume.

14. Minton F. Goldman, *The Soviet Union and Eastern Europe*, 2d ed. (Guilford, Conn., 1988), 2.

when returning men reclaimed control over agriculture. Most women went back to performing the lowest-paid field labor, as they had before the war; as late as 1959, 15.8 million of the 19.8 million women working in agriculture were classified as unskilled. In 1959 only 21 percent of peasant women had completed high school. Eleven years later, in 1970, that figure had risen to 48 percent, an impressive increase in one decade but still representing less than half of rural women. By contrast, 75 percent of urban women possessed high-school educations in 1970.[15] In 1978, after a decade of government efforts to recruit peasant women to better-paying jobs as machinery operators, women still constituted only 1 percent of those workers. Government spokespeople explained that peasant parents refused to allow their daughters to learn how to operate machinery because it was not "woman's work."[16] The rural woman of the 1970s was better dressed, housed, fed, and clothed than her mother had been in 1930, but she remained behind her urban counterpart in all these aspects of life.

Meanwhile, during the 1950s and 1960s the standard of living in the cities rose steadily, as did funding for social services benefiting women, particularly day care. Housing remained crowded, but vast new building projects were undertaken. The supply of consumer goods slowly improved, and by the 1970s more furniture, appliances, clothing, shoes, and even cosmetics were for sale in Soviet stores. The selection was small, shortages persisted, and the goods that were available were high in price and poor in quality; but for a nation pulling itself out of centuries of desperate poverty, these limited changes constituted genuine progress.

Women were also making progress in the paid labor force. The vast majority of women coming of age in the cities in the postwar years graduated from high school and then found jobs in manufacturing or in the clerical and service sectors of the economy. In 1980 women constituted 51 percent of the paid labor force, and most had moved out of manual labor. By the mid-1980s, 50 percent of the engineers and 80 percent of the physicians in the USSR were women. Women also made up 83 percent of all employees in retailing, 82 percent in health care and other social services, and 75 percent in education.[17] As in the West, most of these women held low-paying, low-status jobs, and even those in the professions generally worked near the bottom of the hierarchy. Female physicians, for instance, practiced mostly in primary care, earning less than skilled machinists. These differences were a consequence of pervasive assumptions in Soviet society that certain fields were appropriate for women, assumptions that derived from the definition of women as more nurturant than men, and affected the education girls re-

15. Ethel Dunn, "Russian Rural Women," in *Women in Russia*, ed. Dorothy Atkinson, Alexander Dallin, and Gail Lapidus (Stanford, 1978); 178; *Zhenshchiny v SSSR*, 57.

16. Susan Bridger, *Women in the Soviet Countryside* (Cambridge, 1987), 34, 33.

17. Novosti Press Agency, *Yearbook USSR '87* (Moscow, 1987), 163, 167.

ceived as well as employment practices. Women's opportunities were also adversely affected by their family responsibilities. However, despite their inability to achieve true equality in the paid labor force, Soviet women could take comfort from the fact that their work was physically easier and more lucrative than women's work had been in the past.

With these economic improvements came a relaxation of social controls that eased the most restrictive of the Stalinist family policies. In 1955 abortion was legalized once again. In 1968 a revision of the marriage law made divorce much simpler to obtain. Revisions of the criminal code incorporated a progressive definition of rape that included forcible sexual intercourse between spouses. Party leaders during the administration of Leonid Brezhnev (1964–82) cautiously permitted the continuation of Khrushchev's efforts to open the Soviet Union to Western influences. Goods from Europe, North America, and Japan flooded into the black market that flourished in the big cities, travelers from the West came in increasing numbers, and Soviet awareness of the world beyond the nation's borders grew throughout the 1960s and 1970s.

Despite these improvements most Soviet women in the cities still had to put up with serious difficulties created by the economy and the persistence of patriarchal values. A small number of women—professionals, managers, party officials, or, more commonly, the wives of party officials—lived lives of privilege, with access to the high-quality consumer goods, medical care, education, and housing set aside for the elite. But the great majority of Soviet urban women worked the infamous "double shift," putting in an eight-hour day at their jobs and then coming home to deal with children and housework, tasks made enormously time-consuming by the still-backward economy. Women stood in line to buy consumer goods; they shopped for food every day; they spent hours commuting to and from work as well as taking children to school or day-care centers; they cooked in kitchens shared with several other families; they washed clothes in the bathroom sink. Medical care was available without charge, but it was often of poor quality; contraceptives were unreliable, forcing women to continue to rely on abortion to control family size. By the 1960s many Soviet women were undergoing several abortions during their childbearing years.

There were many single women in the USSR after the war because of the wartime losses of men and the high divorce rate. Some of these women managed to move up into important positions in the professions, industrial management, and the arts but most worked in the same low-paying jobs as married women. This situation made their lives difficult before retirement and even more difficult after, when their pensions provided a bare subsistence income. Parenthood also limited the options of many single and divorced women, and they suffered, as did married women, from discrimination against mothers in the workplace. For instance, it was common for employers to penalize women who took time off to care for sick children.[18] The unenviable situation of unmarried women may have intensified the value Soviet women in general attached to marriage. Leningrader Ekaterina Aleksandrova wrote in the late 1970s, "The stamp 'married' in a passport confers innumerable social benefits, and, perhaps more important, Soviet women need this stamp for their own psychological sense of well-being, for their own self-affirmation."[19]

By the 1970s it had become clear that domestic responsibilities were limiting women's participation in the public world, just as Marx, Engels, and Lenin had predicted. Soviet commentators, many of them women, noted in the press that women's double shift was preventing them from getting promotions and, in too many cases, a full night's sleep. The remedy proposed was usually the same as that advocated since the revolution—greater funding for public services. But with the economy slowing throughout the 1970s, Soviet leaders did not provide that funding. As they had done since the 1930s, they chose to spend their country's meager resources on heavy industry and defense and to allow women's unpaid labor to support daily life. Commentators also discussed discrimination against, and harassment of, women by male bosses, urging that such men be punished.[20] The Brezhnev regime responded by permitting the criticisms to be published, but it launched no campaigns to reeducate abusive managers. The government's official position remained that Soviet women were the freest and most privileged women in the world.

Ordinary Soviet women also seemed reluctant to move beyond the standard proposals for greater funding for public services to examine the continuing existence of patriarchal values. Private citizens who talked to foreigners expressed pride in their considerable accomplishments since the revolution and complained that women were often prevented (presumably by men) from achieving political and economic equality. But such women also seemed to accept the proposition that women's lives properly centered around their families. Anna, a young Muscovite mother and wife, told Swedish interviewers in the late 1970s, "From time immemorial, women's instincts have been rooted in taking care of their families, tending to their husbands, sewing, washing—all the household chores. Men are supposed to

18. For complaints about the difficulties of single parenthood, see Carola Hansson and Karen Liden, *Moscow Women* (New York, 1983), 3–25; Natasha Maltseva, "The Other Side of the Coin," in *Women and Russia*, ed. Tatiana Mamonova (Boston, 1984), 111–16.

19. Ekaterina Aleksandrovna, "Why Soviet Women Want to Get Married," in *Women and Russia*, 31–32.

20. *Women, Work, and Family in the Soviet Union*, ed. Gail Warshofsky Lapidus (Armonk, N.Y., 1982). For the classic short story on the double shift, see Natalya Baranskaya, "A Week Like Any Other Week," trans. Emily Lehrman, *Massachusetts Review* 15 (Autumn 1974): 657–703. The story, "Nedelia kak nedelia," was originally published in *Novy mir*, 1969, no. 11.

provide for the family; women should keep the home fires burning. This is so deeply ingrained in women that there's no way of changing it."[21]

Of course it should be noted that Soviet women were not in any way encouraged to develop a critical analysis of the new Soviet woman. In the 1950s American women, also constrained by a social ethos that stressed the virtues of conformity, demonstrated similar tendencies to complain about the injustices of a male-run society while accepting definitions of gender that justified women's inequality. The rebirth of feminism in the United States in the 1960s enabled American women to see that their personal difficulties were a consequence of the patriarchal values that undergirded all the institutions of their society. But the political freedom that permitted feminism to flourish in the West simply did not exist in Brezhnev's Soviet Union. Instead, the government persecuted all critics relentlessly. Feminism was condemned as a bourgeois evil, and the feminist writings of earlier generations of Russian women were consigned to the closed stacks of a few libraries. "We see . . . a lot," said Liuba, another Muscovite interviewed in the late 1970s. "But since we feel powerless, we try not to think about it."[22]

There was one small attempt in the late 1970s to resist the authorities' ban on feminist discourse. A group of women in Leningrad launched an underground, avowedly feminist magazine, *Woman and Russia: An Almanac* (*Zhenshchina i Rossiia: Al'manakh*). Like the feminists of the past, they were educated, middle-class women, sensitive, like their predecessors, to the problems of all women, including the urban poor, peasants, and ethnic minorities. They designed the almanac as a forum for women from these groups. The government's response was as immediate as it was predictable. After the first issue of *Woman and Russia* began to circulate in *samizdat*, the KGB called the editors to police headquarters and ordered them to stop publication. The women refused. When two more issues appeared, four leaders of the group, including the chief editor, Tat'iana Mamonova, were stripped of their Soviet citizenship and deported.[23]

The Brezhnev era ended in the early 1980s, in an atmosphere of rising discontent over economic and political stagnation that the regime seemed incapable of reversing. Pressures for reform grew until in 1985 they brought to power a new generation of leaders, headed by Mikhail Gorbachev. After 1985 criticism became the order of the day throughout Soviet society, and

21. Hansson and Liden, *Moscow Women*, 50. See also *Soviet Sisterhood*, ed. Barbara Holland (Bloomington, Ind., 1985). For more recent expressions of such attitudes, see "Heroines of Soviet Labor," *Time*, June 6, 1988, 28–37.

22. Hansson and Liden, *Moscow Women*, 152.

23. For a collection of articles published in *samizdat* by these feminists, see Mamonova, *Women and Russia*. Mamonova has continued to develop her feminism in emigration; see *Russian Women's Studies: Essays on Sexism in Soviet Culture* (Oxford, 1989).

from the beginning it included discussion of women's situation. Whether these discussions will lead to concrete improvements in the social services available to women, and to a thorough analysis of the sources of women's problems, remains to be seen.

Soviet women will participate in the ongoing transformation of their society, as Russian women have for centuries. Perhaps they will be able to place women's needs high on the list of reforms. Perhaps they will be able to call into question the values that still buttress female subordination. Having accomplished major change since the revolution, Soviet women are in a better position than any of their foremothers to make their voices heard. They are also heirs to a reform tradition that always considered women's needs to be important. It will be ironic if the very achievements of the Soviet period prove to be a liability, enabling opponents to argue that no more change is necessary. The rethinking of relations between women and men is so radical, touching the organization of the family as well as of the political structure, that it may be avoided in the Soviet Union, just as it has been elsewhere. If so, Soviet women will continue to accommodate themselves to a world governed by men. It is a task for which they have accumulated centuries of experience.

GLOSSARY

Artel	A group of workers engaged in a trade together and pooling their labor and income as well as sharing living expenses and living quarters.
Baba	A pejorative noun denoting a married woman or a woman in general; also can mean wet nurse or midwife.
Babka	Old woman; midwife.
Barshchina	Labor dues paid by serfs to their landlord; corvée.
Birchbark documents	Correspondence or civil contracts from medieval Novgorod engraved on birchbark.
Bogomater'	Mary, the Mother of God.
Boyarina	Muscovite term for a woman of the elite; mistress.
Bol'shukha	Wife of the head-of-household.
Bride-price	Payment by the groom's household in exchange for rights to the bride and indirect dowry.
Burmistr	Estate manager.
Byliny	Epic poems from the Kievan and Muscovite periods.
Central Industrial Region	The area where Russian industry was concentrated. It included the provinces of Moscow, Tver, Vladimir, Iaroslavl, Nizhnii-Novgorod, Kostroma, and parts of Riazan, Tula, and Kaluga.
Church Statutes of Vladimir and Iaroslavl	Law codes compiled in the fourteenth and fifteenth centuries.
Desiatina (pl. *desiatiny*)	Unit of area equivalent to 2.7 acres.

Dvoeverie	Lit. "dual faith," a combination of pagan and Christian practices.
Grivna	A monetary unit measured in gold, fur, or, usually, silver.
Guberniia (pl. *gubernii*)	A province in prerevolutionary Russia.
Head tax	A tax on peasant males instituted in 1718 and abolished in 1886.
Intelligentsia	A term loosely applied to all university-educated people; commonly used to describe those university-educated people critical of the Russian (or Soviet) status quo.
Izba	A peasant room or hut.
KGB	*Komitet Gosudarstvennoi Bespechnosti*, the Soviet police agency in charge of espionage and the control of political dissent; formerly named Cheka, NKVD, and MVD.
Kopek	Unit of Russian currency: 100 kopeks to a ruble.
Krest'ianka	A peasant woman.
Kulak	Lit. "fist," a pejorative term for prosperous peasants.
Kustar'	Domestic production of handmade items for sale.
Male soul	Basis for assessment of taxes (*see* Head tax).
Meshchanstvo	The petty bourgeoisie; also coarseness and acquisitiveness associated with those who engage in trade.
Mestnichestvo	A system of precedence ranking for the Muscovite elite; abolished in 1681.
Mir	The peasant commune; also means universe and peace.
Narkompros	People's Commissariat of Enlightenment, in charge of education under the Soviets.
NEP	New Economic Policy, the set of economic policies initiated in 1921 that legalized a limited private market in grain and other foodstuffs; more loosely, the name given to the 1920s, a decade marked by social experimentation and a more relaxed political atmosphere than the subsequent Stalinist period.
NKVD	*Narodnyi Komissariat Vnutrennikh Del* (*see* KGB).
Nihilists	Radicals of the 1860s who took their name from their belief that all established truths must be denied as a first step to social reform.

Oblast' (pl. *oblasti*)	After 1929 the chief administrative subdivision of a republic within the USSR.
Obrok	Rent in cash or kind that a serf owed the master; quitrent.
Okrug (pl. *okruga*)	After 1929 the administrative subdivision of an *oblast'*; equivalent to the prerevolutionary *uezd*.
Otkhodnichestvo	Peasant practice of leaving the home village to work elsewhere.
Redemption payments	Annual assessments required of the peasants to compensate the government for the land allocated to them in the emancipation of 1861; abolished in 1905.
Revizii	National censuses compiled periodically between 1718 and 1858 to determine assessments for military conscription and the head (soul) tax.
Rod	A pre-Christian fertility god; also patron of a family's ancestors.
Rozhanitsy	Rod's consorts; also protectors of ancestors, fertility, and clan, as well as guarantors of the harvest.
Russkaia Pravda	Civil law code of the Kievan period.
Samizdat	Lit. "self-publishing," the underground press begun during the Brezhnev years (1964–82).
Skhod	The village assembly.
Sluzhashchie	Lower-ranking, white-collar workers, predominantly clerical.
Socialist realism	The Stalinist cultural credo that required all arts to promote positive attitudes toward Soviet society. It produced rigorous censorship and artistic mediocrity yet remained dominant in the Soviet Union until replaced by *glasnost'* (the call for honesty and openness) in the mid-1980s.
Soldatka	A soldier's wife.
Soul tax	*See* Head tax.
Soviet of People's Commissars	An executive body established in November 1917, composed of the heads of commissariats, the major administrative departments of the Soviet government.
Stariki	Village elders.
Terem	Women's quarters within the houses of the elite during the Muscovite period.
Tiaglo (pl. *tiagla*)	An agricultural labor unit normally composed of a husband and wife.

Uezd (pl. *uezdy*)	Administrative subdivision of a *guberniia*; district.
Ulozhenie of 1649	Conciliar law code in which the Muscovite government defined the prerogatives and obligations of the various strata of Russian society and in so doing legalized serfdom.
Usad'ba	A peasant farmstead, including residential and farm buildings as well as a garden.
Volost' (pl. *volosty*)	Administrative subdivision of an *uezd*.
Votchina	Patrimonial land; land owned by the elite in the appanage and early Muscovite periods that carried no service obligation to the crown.
White Army	The forces opposing the Bolsheviks during the civil war, 1918–21.
Yellow ticket	The document registered prostitutes received in return for their passports, which they had to surrender to the police.
Zemstvo (pl. *zemstva*)	An elected organ of local self-government charged with promoting public health, education, and general welfare. Established in 1864, it ceased to exist during the revolution.
Zhenotdel	The department of the Communist party created in 1919 to organize and propagandize women; abolished 1930.

RECOMMENDATIONS
FOR FURTHER READING

TRADITION

Alexander, John. *Catherine the Great: Life and Legend*. New York, 1989.

Black, J. L. *Citizens for the Fatherland: Education, Educators, and Pedagogical Ideals in Eighteenth Century Russia*. New York, 1979.

———."Educating Women in Eighteenth-Century Russia: Myths and Realities." *Canadian Slavonic Papers* 20 (1978): 23–43.

Challis, Natalia. "Glorification of Saints in the Orthodox Church." *Russian History* 7, pts. 1–2 (1980): 239–46.

Claus, Claire. *Die Stellung der russichen Frau von der Einführung des Christentums bei den Russen bis zu den Reformen Peter des Grossen*. Munich, 1959.

Curtiss, M. A. *Forgotten Empress: Anna Ivanovna and Her Era, 1730–40*. New York, 1974.

de Madariaga, Isabel. *Russia in the Age of Catherine the Great*. New Haven, 1981.

Dewey, H. W., and A. M. Kleimola. "Muted Eulogy: Women Who Inspired Men in Medieval Rus'." *Russian History* 10, pt. 2 (1983): 188–200.

Dukes, Paul. *Russia under Catherine the Great*. 2 vols. Newtonville, Mass., 1977.

Eck, Alexandre. "La situation juridique de la femme russe au moyen âge." *Recueils de la société Jean Bodin pour l'histoire comparative des institutions* 12, pt. 2 (1962): 405–20.

Goehrke, Carsten. "Die Witwe im alten Russland." *Forschungen zur osteuropaischen Geschichte* 38 (1986): 64–96.

Griffiths, D. "Catherine II: The Republican Empress." *Jahrbücher für Geschichte Osteuropas* 21 (1973): 323–44.

Grossman, Joan Delaney. "Feminine Images in Old Russian Literature and Art." *California Slavic Studies* 11 (1980): 33–70.

Hellie, Richard. "Women and Slavery in Moscow." *Russian History* 10, pt. 2 (1983): 213–29.

Hubbs, Joanna. *Mother Russia: The Feminine Myth in Russian Culture*. Bloomington, Ind., 1988.

Hughes, Lindsay. "Sofia, 'Autocrat of All the Russias': Titles, Ritual and Eulogy in the Regency of Sofia Alekseevna (1682–89)." *Canadian Slavonic Papers* 28 (1986): 266–86.

———. "Sofiya Alekseyevna and the Moscow Rebellion of 1682." *Slavonic and East European Review* 63 (1985): 518–39.

Kollmann, Nancy Shields. "The Seclusion of Elite Muscovite Women." *Russian History* 10, pt. 2 (1983): 170–87.

Levin, Eve. "Infanticide in Pre-Petrine Russia." *Jahrbücher für Geschichte Osteuropas* 34 (1986): 215–22.

———. "The Role and Status of Women in Medieval Novgorod." Ph.D. diss., Indiana University, 1983.

———. *Sex and Society in the World of the Orthodox Slavs, 900–1700.* Ithaca, 1989.

———. "Women and Property in Medieval Novgorod: Dependence and Independence." *Russian History* 10, pt. 2 (1983): 154–69.

Levy, Sandra. "Women and the Control of Property in Sixteenth-Century Muscovy." *Russian History* 10, pt. 2 (1983): 201–12.

Lewitter, L. R. "Women, Sainthood, and Marriage in Muscovy." *Journal of Russian Studies* 37 (1979): 3–11.

McNally, Suzanne J. "From Public Person to Private Prisoner: The Changing Place of Women in Medieval Russia." Ph.D. diss., State University of New York at Binghamton, 1976.

Meehan-Waters, Brenda. "Catherine the Great and the Problem of Female Rule." *Russian Review* 34 (1975): 293–307.

———. "Popular Piety, Local Initiative, and the Founding of Women's Religious Communities in Russia, 1764–1917." *St. Vladimir's Theological Quarterly* 30, no. 2 (1986): 117–41.

———. "Russian Convents and the Secularization of Monastic Property." In *Russia and the World of the Eighteenth Century*, ed. R. P. Bartlett, A. G. Cross, and Karen Rasmussen, 112–24. Columbus, Ohio, 1988.

Nash, Carol S. "Educating New Mothers: Women and the Enlightenment in Russia." *History of Education Quarterly* 21 (1981): 301–16.

———. "The Education of Women in Russia, 1762–1796." Ph.D. diss., New York University, 1978.

———. "Students and Rubles: The Society for the Education of Noble Girls (Smol'nyi) as a Charitable Institution." In *Russia and the World of the Eighteenth Century*, ed. R. P. Bartlett, A. G. Cross, and Karen Rasmussen, Columbus, Ohio, 1988.

Oldenbourg, Zoé. *Catherine the Great.* New York, 1965.

Pushkareva, N. L., and Eve Levin. "Women in Medieval Novgorod from the Eleventh to the Fifteenth Centuries." *Soviet Studies in History* 23, no. 4 (Spring 1985): 71–90.

Raeff, Marc. *Catherine the Great: A Profile.* New York, 1972.

Ransel, David L. *Mothers of Misery: Child Abandonment in Russia.* Princeton, 1988.

Rasmussen, Karen. "Catherine II and the Image of Peter I." *Slavic Review* 37 (1978): 51–69.

Roman, Stanislaw. "Le statut de la femme dans l'Europe orientale (Pologne et Russie) au moyen âge et aux temps modernes." *Recueils de la société Jean Bodin pour l'histoire comparative des institutions* 12, pt. 2 (1962): 389–403.

Thomas, Marie A. "Managerial Roles in the Suzdal'ski-Pokrovskii Convent during the Seventeenth Century." *Russian History* 7, pts. 1–2 (1980): 92–112.

———. "Muscovite Convents in the Seventeenth Century." *Russian History* 10, pt. 2 (1983): 230–42.

Troyat, Henri. *Catherine the Great*. New York, 1980.

Vernadsky, George. "Studies in the History of the Muscovian Private Law of the Sixteenth and Seventeenth Centuries. Inheritance: The Case of the Childless Wife." In *Studi in Memoria di Aldo Albertoni*, 3:433–54. Padua, 1935–38.

Zguta, Russell. "The Ordeal by Water (Swimming of Witches) in the East Slavic World." *Slavic Review* 36 (1977): 220–30.

———. "Was There a Witch Craze in Muscovite Russia?" *Southern Folklore Quarterly* 41 (1977): 119–28.

———. "Witchcraft and Medicine in Pre-Petrine Russia." *Russian Review* 37 (1978): 438–48.

———. "Witchcraft Trials in Seventeenth-Century Russia." *American Historical Review* 82 (1977): 1187–1207.

TRADITION VERSUS TRANSFORMATION TO 1917

Atkinson, Dorothy, Alexander Dallin, and Gail Warshofsky Lapidus, eds. *Women in Russia*. Stanford, 1977.

Bergman, Jay. *Vera Zasulich*. Stanford, 1983.

Bernstein, Laurie. "Sonia's Daughters: Prostitution and Society in Russia." Ph.D. diss., University of California, Berkeley, 1985.

Bobroff, Anne. "The Bolsheviks and Working Women, 1905–1920." *Soviet Studies* 26 (1974): 540–67.

———. "Russian Working Women: Sexuality in Bonding Patterns and the Politics of Daily Life." In *Power of Desire: The Politics of Sexuality*, ed. Ann Snitow, Christine Stansell, and Sharon Thompson, 207–27. New York, 1983.

———. "Working Women, Bonding Patterns, and the Politics of Daily Life: Russia at the End of the Old Regime." 2 vols . Ph.D. diss., University of Michigan, 1982.

Breshkovskaia, Catherine. *Hidden Springs of the Russian Revolution*. Stanford, 1931.

———. *Little Grandmother of the Revolution*. Boston, 1930.

Broido, Vera. *Apostles into Terrorists*. New York, 1977.

Confino, Michael, ed. *Daughter of a Revolutionary: Natalie Herzen*. La Salle, Ill., 1974.

Curtiss, John S. "Russian Sisters of Mercy in the Crimea, 1854–1855." *Slavic Review* 25 (1966): 84–100.

Donald, Moira. "Bolshevik Activity amongst the Working Women of Petrograd in 1917." *International Journal of Social History* 27, pt. 2 (1982): 131–60.

Dudgeon, Ruth. "The Forgotten Minority: Women Students in Imperial Russia, 1872–1917." *Russian History* 9 (1982): 1–26.

Durova, Nadezhda. *The Cavalry Maiden: Journals of a Russian Officer in the Napoleonic Wars*. Edited and translated by Mary Fleming Zirin. Bloomington, Ind., 1988.

Edmondson, Linda H. *The Feminist Movement in Russia, 1900–1917*. Stanford, 1984.

———. "Russian Feminists and the First All-Russian Congress of Women." *Russian History* 3, pt. 2 (1976): 123–49.

Engel, Barbara. *Mothers and Daughters: Women of the Intelligentsia in Nineteenth-Century Russia*. New York, 1983.

———. "St. Petersburg Prostitutes in the Late Nineteenth Century: A Personal and Social Profile." *Russian Review* 48 (1989): 21–44.

———. "The Woman's Side: Male Outmigration and the Family Economy in Kostroma Province." *Slavic Review* 45 (1986): 257–71.

———. "Women in Russia and the Soviet Union." *Signs* 12 (1987): 781–96.

Engel, Barbara, and Clifford Rosenthal, eds. *Five Sisters: Women against the Tsar*. New York, 1975.

Engelstein, Laura. "Gender and the Juridical Subject: Prostitution and Rape in Nineteenth-Century Criminal Codes." *Journal of Modern History* 60 (1988): 458–95.

———. "Morality and the Wooden Spoon: Russian Doctors View Syphilis, Social Class, and Sexual Behavior, 1890–1905." *Representations* 14 (1986): 169–208.

Farnsworth, Beatrice. "The Litigious Daughter-in-Law: Family Relations in Rural Russia in the Second Half of the Nineteenth Century." *Slavic Review* 45 (1986): 49–64.

———. "The Soldatka: Folklore and the Court Record." *Slavic Review* 49 (1990): 58–73.

Glickman, Rose L. *Russian Factory Women: Workplace and Society, 1880–1914*. Berkeley and Los Angeles, 1984.

———. "Women and the Peasant Commune." In *Land, Commune, and Peasant Community in Russia: Communal Forms in Imperial and Early Soviet Society*, ed. Roger Bartlett, 321–38. London, 1990.

Goldberg, Rochelle. "The Russian Women's Movement." Ph.D. diss., University of Rochester, 1976.

Griesse, Ann, and Richard Stites. "Russia: Revolution and War." In *Female Soldiers*, ed. N. Goldman, 61–84. Westport, Conn., 1982.

Heldt, Barbara. *Terrible Perfection: Women and Russian Literature*. Bloomington, Ind., 1987.

Johanson, Christine. *Women's Struggle for Higher Education in Russia, 1855–1900*. Montreal, 1987.

Kaplan, Temma. "Women in Communal Strikes in the Crisis of 1917–1922." In *Becoming Visible: Women in European History*, ed. Renate Bridenthal, Claudia Koonz, and Susan Stuard, 2d ed., 429–51. Boston, 1987.

Knight, Amy. "Female Terrorists in the Russian Socialist Revolutionary Party." *Russian Review* 38 (1979): 139–60.

———. "The Fritschi: A Study in Female Radicals in the Russian Populist Movement." *Canadian-American Slavic Studies* 9 (1975): 1–17.

Koblitz, Ann H. *A Convergence of Lives: Sofia Kovalevskaia: Scientist, Writer, Revolutionary*. Boston, 1983.

McNeal, Robert. "Women in the Russian Radical Movement." *Journal of Social History* 2 (1971–72): 143–63.

Mazour, Anatole. *Women in Exile*. Tallahassee, Fla., 1975.

Ransel, David. *Mothers of Misery: Child Abandonment in Russia*. Princeton, 1988.

———. "The Problem of Measuring Illegitimacy in Prerevolutionary Russia." *Journal of Social History* 16 (1982): 111–27.

————, ed. *The Family in Imperial Russia: New Lines of Historical Research.* Urbana, Ill., 1978.

Stites, Richard. "Prostitute and Society in Pre-Revolutionary Russia." *Jahrbücher für Geschichte Osteuropas* 31 (1983): 348–65.

————. "Women and the Revolutionary Process in Russia." In *Becoming Visible: Women in European History,* ed. Renate Bridenthal, Claudia Koonz, and Susan Stuard, 2d ed., 451–71. Boston, 1987.

————. *The Women's Liberation Movement in Russia: Feminism, Nihilism, and Bolshevism, 1860–1930.* Princeton, 1978.

Tishkin, G. A. *Zhenskii vopros v Rossii v 50–60 gg. XIX v.* Leningrad, 1984.

Wagner, William. "The Trojan Mare: Women's Rights and Civil Rights in Late Imperial Russia." In *Civil Rights in Imperial Russia,* ed. Olga Crisp and Linda Edmondson, 65–84. Oxford, 1989.

Worobec, Christine D. "Customary Law and Property Devolution among Russian Peasants in the 1870s." *Canadian Slavonic Papers* 26 (1984): 220–34.

————. *Peasant Russia: Family and Community in the Post-Emancipation Period.* Princeton, 1991.

————. "Temptress or Virgin? The Precarious Sexual Position of Women in Post-emancipation Ukrainian Society." *Slavic Review* 49, no. 2 (1990): 227–38.

————. "Victims or Actors? Russian Peasant Women and Patriarchy." In *Peasant Economy, Culture, and Politics of European Russia, 1800–1921,* ed. Esther Kingston-Mann and Timothy Mixter, 177–206. Princeton, 1991.

TRADITION VERSUS TRANSFORMATION, 1917–80

Alexiyevich, S. *War's Unwomanly Face.* Moscow, 1988.

Atkinson, Dorothy, Alexander Dallin, and Gail Warshofsky Lapidus, eds. *Women in Russia.* Stanford, 1977.

Baranskaya, Natalya. "A Week Like Any Other Week." Translated by Emily Lehrman. *Massachusetts Review* 15 (Autumn 1974): 657–703.

Blekher, Feiga. *The Soviet Woman in the Family and in Society.* New York, 1980.

Bridger, Susan. *Women in the Soviet Countryside.* Cambridge, 1987.

Brown, Donald R. *The Role and Status of Women in the Soviet Union.* New York, 1968.

Browning, Genia K. *Women and Politics in the U.S.S.R.: Consciousness Raising and Soviet Women's Groups.* New York, 1987.

Buckley, Mary. "The 'Woman Question' in the Contemporary Soviet Union." In *Promissory Notes: Women in the Transition to Socialism,* ed. Sonia Kruks, Rayna Rapp, and Marilyn B. Young, 251–81. New York, 1989.

————, ed. *Soviet Scientists Talking: An Official Debate about Women.* London, 1986.

Celmina, Helene. *Women in Soviet Prisons.* New York, 1985.

Clements, Barbara Evans. "The Birth of the New Soviet Woman." In *Bolshevik Culture: Experiment and Order in the Russian Revolution,* ed. Abbott Gleason, Peter Kenez, and Richard Stites, 220–37. Bloomington, Ind., 1985.

————. *Bolshevik Feminist: The Life of Aleksandra Kollontai.* Bloomington, Ind., 1979.

————. "Emancipation through Communism: The Ideology of A. M. Kollontai." *Slavic Review* 30 (1973): 323–38.

———. "The Enduring Kinship of the *Baba* and the Bolshevik Woman." *Soviet Union* 12 (1985): 161–84.

———. "The Impact of the Civil War on Women and Family Relations." In *Party, State and Society in the Russian Civil War*, ed. Diane Koenker, Willlam Rosenberg, and Ron Gregor Suny, 105–22. Bloomington, Ind., 1989.

———. "Working-Class and Peasant Women in the Russian Revolution, 1917–23." *Signs* 8 (1982): 215–35.

Cottam, K. Jean. "Soviet Women in Combat in World War II: The Ground Forces and the Navy." *International Journal of Women's Studies* 3 (1980): 345–57.

———. "Soviet Women in Combat in World War II: The Rear Services, Resistance behind Enemy Lines and Military Political Workers." *International Journal of Women's Studies* 5 (1982): 363–78.

Danilova, Ekaterina Zakharovna. *Soviet Women.* Moscow, 1975.

Dodge, Norton. *Women in the Soviet Economy.* Baltimore, 1966.

Dunham, Vera. *In Stalin's Time: Middleclass Values in Soviet Fiction.* Cambridge, 1976.

Evans, Janet. "The Communist Party of the Soviet Union and the Women's Question: The Case of the 1936 Decree 'In Defence of Mother and Child.'" *Journal of Contemporary History* 16 (1981): 757–75.

Farnsworth, Beatrice. *Alexandra Kollontai: Socialism, Feminism and the Bolshevik Revolution.* Stanford, 1980.

———. "Communist Feminism: Its Synthesis and Demise." In *Women, War, and Revolution*, ed. Carol R. Berkin and Clara M. Lovett, 145–64. New York, 1980.

———. "Village Women Experience the Revolution." In *Bolshevik Culture: Experiment and Order in the Russian Revolution*, ed. Abbott Gleason, Peter Kenez, and Richard Stites, 238–60. Bloomington, Ind., 1985.

Gasiorowska, Xenia. *Women in Soviet Fiction, 1917–64.* Madison, Wis., 1968.

Geiger, H. Kent. *The Family in Soviet Russia.* Cambridge, 1967.

Ginzburg, Evgeniia. *Journey into the Whirlwind.* Translated by Paul Stevenson and Max Hayward. New York, 1967.

———. *Within the Whirlwind.* Translated by Ian Boland. New York, 1981.

Goldman, Emma. *Living My Life.* 2 vols. New York, 1931.

———. *My Further Disillusionment in Russia.* Garden City, N.Y, 1924.

Goldman, Wendy Z. "Freedom and Its Consequences: The Debate on the Soviet Family Code of 1926." *Russian History* 11 (1984): 362–88.

———. "The 'Withering-Away' and the Resurrection of the Soviet Family, 1917–1936." Ph.D. diss., University of Pennsylvania, 1986.

———. "Women, the Family, and the New Revolutionary Order in the Soviet Union." In *Promissory Notes: Women in the Transition to Socialism*, ed. Sonia Kruks, Rayna Rapp, and Marilyn B. Young, 59–81. New York, 1989.

Goscilo, Helena, ed. *Balancing Acts: Contemporary Stories by Russian Women.* Bloomington, Ind., 1989.

———. *Russian and Polish Women's Fiction.* Knoxville, Tenn., 1985.

Halle, Fannina W. *Women in the Soviet East.* Translated by Margaret M. Green. New York, 1938.

Hansson, Carola, and Karin Liden. *Moscow Women.* New York, 1983.

Hayden, Carol. "Feminism and Bolshevism: The Zhenotdel and the Politics of

Women's Emancipation in Russia, 1917–1930." Ph.D. diss., University of California, Berkeley, 1979.

———. "The Zhenotdel and the Bolshevik Party." *Russian History* 3, pt. 2 (1976): 150–73.

Heitlinger, Alena. *Women and State Socialism: Sex Inequality in the Soviet Union and Czechoslovakia.* Montreal, 1979.

Holland, Barbara. "'A Woman's Right to Choose' in the Soviet Union." In *Home, School, and Leisure in the Soviet Union,* ed. Jenny Brine, Maureen Perrie, and Andrew Sutton, 55–69. London, 1980.

———, ed. *Soviet Sisterhood.* Bloomington, Ind., 1985.

Ispa, Jean. "Soviet and American Childbearing Experiences and Attitudes: A Comparison." *Slavic Review* 42 (1983): 1–13.

Jancar, Barbara. *Women under Communism.* Baltimore, 1978.

Kingsbury, Susan M., and Mildred Fairchild. *Factory, Family, and Woman in the Soviet Union.* New York, 1935.

Kollontai, Alexandra. *Selected Writings.* Translated and with an introduction by Alix Holt. Westport, Conn., 1978.

Lapidus, Gail Warshofsky. *Women in Soviet Society: Equality, Development, and Social Change.* Berkeley and Los Angeles, 1978.

———. *Women, Work, and Family in the Soviet Union.* Armonk, N.Y., 1982.

Lenin, V. I. *On the Emancipation of Women.* Moscow, 1965.

McAuley, Martin. *Women's Work and Wages in the U.S.S.R.* London, 1981.

McNeal, Robert. *Bride of the Revolution: Krupskaya and Lenin.* Ann Arbor, 1972.

Mamonova, Tatiana. *Russian Women's Studies: Essays on Sexism in Soviet Culture.* Oxford, 1989.

———. *Women and Russia.* Boston, 1984.

Mandel, William. *Soviet Women.* Garden City, N.Y., 1975.

Mandel'shtam, Nadezhda. *Hope Abandoned.* Translated by Max Hayward. New York, 1974.

———. *Hope against Hope: A Memoir.* Translated by Max Hayward. New York, 1970.

Massell, Gregory. *The Surrogate Proletariat: Moslem Women and Revolutionary Strategies in Soviet Central Asia, 1919–1929.* Princeton, 1974.

Ruthchild, Rochelle Goldberg. "Sisterhood and Socialism: The Feminist Movement in the Soviet Union." *Frontiers* 7, no. 2 (1983): 4–12.

Sacks, Michael Paul. *Women's Work in Soviet Russia: Continuity in the Midst of Change.* New York, 1976.

St. George, George. *Our Soviet Sister.* Washington, D.C., 1973.

Schlesinger, Rudolph, ed. *The Family in the U.S.S.R.: Documents and Readings.* London, 1949.

Shlapentokh, Vladimir. *Love, Marriage, and Friendship in the Soviet Union: Ideals and Practices.* New York, 1984.

Stites, Richard. "*Zhenotdel*: Bolshevism and Russian Women, 1917–1930." *Russian History* 3, pt. 2 (1976): 174–93.

Tolkunova, Vera. *Women in the U.S.S.R.* Moscow, 1985.

Trotsky, Leon. *Women and the Family.* 2d ed. New York, 1973.

Waters, Elizabeth. "From the Old Family to the New: Work, Marriage and Motherhood in Urban Soviet Russia, 1917–1931." Ph.D. diss., University of Birmingham, 1985.

———. "In the Shadow of the Comintern: The Communist Women's Movement, 1920–43." In *Promissory Notes: Women in the Transition to Socialism*, ed. Sonia Kruks, Rayna Rapp, and Marilyn B. Young, 29–56. New York, 1989.

———. "The Soviet Approach to Sexual Inequality." In *Three Worlds of Inequality*, ed. C. Jennett and R. G. Stewart, 318–39. London, 1987.

———. "Teaching Mothercraft in Post-Revolutionary Russia." *Australian Slavonic and East European Studies* 1, no. 2 (July 1987): 29–56.

Viola, Lynne. "*Bab'i Bunty* and Peasant Women's Protest during Collectivization." *Russian Review* 45 (1986): 23–42.

Yedlin, Tova, ed. *Women in Eastern Europe and the Soviet Union*. New York, 1980.

CONTRIBUTORS

RODNEY D. BOHAC is Associate Professor of History at Brigham Young University. He has published articles in the *Journal of Interdisciplinary History* and *Slavic Review*.

BARBARA EVANS CLEMENTS is Professor of History at the University of Akron. She is the author of *Bolshevik Feminist: The Life of Aleksandra Kollontai* and of articles in *Russian History, Signs, Slavic Review,* and *Soviet Studies*.

BARBARA ALPERN ENGEL is Associate Professor of History at the University of Colorado. She is coeditor and translator of *Five Sisters: Women against the Tsar* and author of *Mothers and Daughters: Women of the Intelligentsia in Nineteenth-Century Russia*. She has published articles in *Journal of Social History, Russian History, Russian Review, Signs,* and *Slavic Review*.

LAURA ENGELSTEIN is Professor of History at Princeton University. She is the author of *Moscow, 1905: Working-Class Organization and Political Conflict* and has published articles in *Journal of Modern History, Representations,* and *Review in Infectious Diseases*.

ROSE L. GLICKMAN is Adjunct Associate Professor of History at the State University of New York at Buffalo. She is the author of *Russian Factory Women: Workplace and Society, 1880–1914* and has published articles in *Canadian Slavic Studies* and *Slavic Review*.

WENDY GOLDMAN is Assistant Professor of History at Carnegie-Mellon University. She is the author of an article in *Russian History* and of the forthcoming *Revolution in the Family: Soviet Law and Social Change, 1917–1936*.

VALERIE A. KIVELSON is Assistant Professor of History at the University of Michigan.

NANCY SHIELDS KOLLMANN is Associate Professor of History at Stanford University. She is the author of *Kinship and Politics: The Making of the Muscovite Political System, 1345–1547* and of articles in *Jahrbücher für Geschichte Osteuropas, Russian History, Russian Review,* and *Slavic Review.*

EVE LEVIN is Associate Professor of History at Ohio State University. She is the author of *Sex and Society in the World of the Orthodox Slavs, 900–1700* and of articles in *Jahrbücher für Geschichte Osteuropas, Russian History, Soviet Studies in History,* and *Vestnik Moskovskogo universiteta.*

ALFRED G. MEYER is Professor of Political Science at the University of Michigan. He is the author of *Marxism: The Unity of Theory and Practice, Leninism, The Soviet Political System,* and *The Feminism and Socialism of Lily Braun* and coeditor of *Women, State and Party in Eastern Europe.*

JUDITH PALLOT is University Lecturer and College Tutor at Christ Church, Oxford University. She is the author of articles in *Slavic Review* and *Soviet Studies.* She coauthored *Planning in the Soviet Union* and *Landscape and Settlement in Romanov Russia, 1613–1917.*

N. L. PUSHKAREVA is Candidate in the Historical Sciences at the Institute of Ethnography of the Academy of Sciences of the USSR. She is the author of *Zhenshchiny drevnei Rusi* and has published articles in *Istoricheskie zapiski, Sem'ia i shkola, Sovetskoe gosudarstvo i pravo, Soviet Studies, Vestnik Moskovskogo universiteta,* and *Voprosy istorii.*

DAVID L. RANSEL is Professor of History at Indiana University. He is the author of *The Politics of Catherinian Russia: The Panin Party, Mothers of Misery: Child Abandonment in Russia,* and numerous articles. He edited *The Family in Imperial Russia: New Lines of Historical Research.*

ELIZABETH WATERS is Lecturer in History at the Australian National University in Canberra. She has published an article in *Australian Slavonic and East European Studies.* Her book, *Women in a Bolshevik World,* is forthcoming.

CHRISTINE D. WOROBEC is Assistant Professor of History at Kent State University. She is the author of *Peasant Russia: Family and Community in the Post-Emancipation Period* and has published articles in *Canadian Slavonic Papers, Journal of Social History, Russian Review,* and *Slavic Review.*

INDEX

Abbesses, 26, 69

Abortion

—pre-Petrine, 39

—imperial Russian, 185–86; criminologists and, 187, 200; feminists and, 194, 198; jurists and, 12, 143, 186, 193, 199–206; the law and, 12, 188–89, 192–93, 200, 203; peasant women and, 131, 196, 199, 205; penalties against, 188n, 190, 199–200; physicians and, 12, 143, 186–87, 189–99, 201, 206; prostitutes and, 196; radicals and, 202–3; rate of, 192, 195, 198; reformers and, 202, 203–5; Russian Orthodox church and, 195; single women and, 197; urban women and, 197, 205; women's autonomy and, 205–7; women's rights and, 192, 193, 194, 195, 200; working-class women and, 195–97, 205

—post-1917, 10; access to, 247–50; age of recipients of, 254; birthrate and, 245, 262–65; as contraception, 147, 245–46, 254, 258, 262, 264–65, 275; illegal, 260–62, 265–66; jurists and, 264; law and, 11, 147, 243, 244, 251, 264–66, 268–69, 275; methods of, 249; mothers and, 245, 248, 251, 258–60, 262, 264; officials and, 243–44, 264–65; peasant women and, 147, 246, 248–54, 256–57, 261–64; penalties against, 244; physicians and, 249–50, 262–63; rate of, 243, 258, 260, 262–64, 275; reasons for, 147, 254–57, 261, 264–65; right to, 11, 243–44; risks of, 248; single women and, 248, 251, 257, 262; urban women and, 249–54, 257, 259, 262,

264–65; views of, 243–44; women's autonomy and, 265; women's rights and, 265; working-class women and, 243, 250, 260, 264

—in England, 187, 190

—in the United States, 187, 190, 196

—in Western Europe, 187, 192, 196

Adams, Henry, 12–13

Adultery, 41, 42, 62, 72

Akhmatova, Anna, 272

Aleksandrova, Ekaterina, 276

Alexis, Tsar, 80

Alexander I, 8, 137, 219

Alexander II, 8, 9, 138

Alexander III, 8

Alt'man, Natan, 226

Aristocratic women. *See* Elite women

Armand, Inessa, 145, 245

Artels, 140

Aspit, A., 227

Avvakum, Archpriest, 28

Baba, 50, 52, 136. *See also* Midwives; Wet nurses

Bab'i bunty, 241, 269

Balov, A. V., 121n

Baptism, 45, 46, 49–50, 54, 57, 117

Bashkirs, 125, 127, 129–30. *See also* Muslim women

Berberova, Nina, 123

Betrothal, 31, 32

Bezpalova-Letova, Nadezhda, 192

Bezprizornye, 216, 241n, 256

Text: 10/12 Baskerville
Display: Baskerville
Compositor: Asco Trade Typesetting Ltd.
Printer: Edwards Brothers, Inc.
Binder: Edwards Brothers, Inc.